If They Don't Win It's a Shame

• • •

The Year the Marlins Bought the World Series

by
Dave Rosenbaum

McGregor
PUBLISHING
TAMPA, FLORIDA

Publisher's Cataloging in Publication
(Prepared by Quality Books Inc.)

Rosenbaum, Dave.
    If they don't win it's a shame : the year the Marlins bought the World Series / by Dave Rosenbaum
    p. cm.
    Includes index
    Preassigned LCCN: 97-75702
    ISBN 0-9653846-8-3

    1. Florida Marlins (Baseball team) 2. Baseball teams—Florida—Miami   I. Title.

GV875.F5R67 1998   796.357'64
                               QBI97-41496

PHOTO CREDITS

Front cover:
Gary Sheffield: Zoran Milich/Allsport
Darren Daulton, Bobby Bonilla, Jim Leyland: Stephen Dunn/Allsport
Moises Alou: Elsa Hadoh/Allsport
Robb Nen: Jed Jacobsohn/Allsport

Back cover and interior:
Denis Bancroft/Florida Marlins

Interior design and typesetting: Sue Knopf/Graffolio

Published by McGregor Publishing, Inc., Tampa, Florida

Printed in the United States of America

For my grandfather, Louis Peskin
For my brother Alan
With Love

Contents

1

Field of Cows

Maybe in a child's wildest, most innocent, dreams it happened this way. There would be a warm October night in a baseball stadium packed with more than 60,000 fans. The tension would be excruciating, the air filled with a nervous buzz. There would be real green grass, a perfect night sky filled with stars, and millions of people watching on TV, because this was Game Seven of the World Series, the culmination of every child's wildest dreams.

There would be a manager sitting in the corner of the dugout, a thin, gray-haired man who had spent thirty-one years in baseball waiting for the ultimate victory that had eluded him so many times and he would be so close, right now. There would be a big, burly third baseman, with a face that always lit up with a gleaming smile, limping back to the dugout. He would be hurting because he had given everything he could give, just not enough, and he would be praying that the kid at the plate, the 22-year-old shortstop who had come through in the clutch all season, could come through one more time.

And there would be a runner on third base, a 27-year-old midwestern man with the face of a Boy Scout, who until this season had played three games in the major leagues, and now was staring down the baseline, waiting ninety feet away from home plate, to score the run that would win the World Series for a team that, five years ago on this day, did not exist.

The bases would be loaded in the bottom of the eleventh inning, and the score would be tied, and then there would be a pitch, then silence during the seconds it took for the ball to travel from the pitcher's hand to home plate. And then there would be a swing, the crack of the bat, contact! A line drive lofting slowly toward centerfield, motion on the bases, fielders desperately lunging, the crowd rising from its seats, the manager inching up the dugout steps, the third baseman ready to scream, a moment away from exultation, a moment away from agony, and then . . .

◆ ◆ ◆

Wake up! Snap back to reality! And, for goodness sakes, stop dreaming, already. Because maybe that's the way it happens in a child's dream, or even in the movies, but it certainly wouldn't happen like that in real life. No way.

The burly third baseman? He has a reputation for attacking reporters.

1

The gray-haired manager? He once vowed loyalty to the Pittsburgh Pirates, then two weeks after that vowed loyalty to himself.

Somewhere in that dream, there's a leftfielder who chose playing for money over playing for his father, a rightfielder who called his boss a liar and played hard when he felt like it, and a pitcher who was considered one of the biggest jerks in baseball.

As for the fans . . . well, where'd they come from? For the past few years, the stadium in which the team played had been mostly empty on game nights.

Really, that must've been a dream. It couldn't have happened like that.

It happened like this.

◆ ◆ ◆

On February 21, 1997, opening day of training camp for Major League Baseball teams, Don Smiley pushed hard on the accelerator of his shiny Jaguar and roared up Florida's Turnpike from Miami to Melbourne.

Smiley, the 42-year-old president of the Florida Marlins, could hardly wait to reach his destination, because he was filled with optimism, and dreaming too, imagining what the upcoming season might bring, and allowing himself to think there might be an October night with a packed stadium and his team playing for the World Series.

But he was keeping those dreams to himself. A few hours later, having completed his journey up the Turnpike, he stood on a baseball field, talking with the news media about expectations, and trying not to get too carried away, because anything he said could be used against him in October.

Cows grazed a few hundred yards south of where Smiley was standing. They grazed for as far as the eye could see, over the fence of the Carl Barger Baseball Complex and beyond, over the flat landscape to the horizon. But Smiley's gaze was pointed in the opposite direction, toward a group of very expensive baseball players, dressed in teal and white, who were walking slowly to a practice field for the first workouts of spring.

"It's a very big year for us," Smiley said. "The idea was to put together the best team we could, get the best manager we could get, win as many games as we can, and see if we can get the fans involved. And at the end of the year, we'll add it up and evaluate."

So here's what they did. The Marlins spent $89 million on free agent players, more than any team had ever spent, for the purpose of creating a winning baseball team and finding out if the fans in South Florida would support a winner.

The team had all kinds of problems. Player salaries had increased beyond its original projections when Florida was granted a National League franchise in 1991. Home attendance had decreased precipitously, from a high of more than three million in 1993, the Marlins' first season, to 1.7 million in 1996, even though their record had improved every year. In 1996, the Marlins claimed losses of $20.1 million. Only once, in their first season, had the Marlins claimed a profit.

Most pressingly, the Marlins felt they needed a new stadium, and Wayne Huizenga, the team's billionaire owner, of Blockbuster Video fame, had no intention of paying for it. Maybe, he figured, if the team won and fans started coming out again, some generous politician would stand up and say, "We'll build you one, Wayne."

The gamble: No baseball team had ever spent so much on free agents. Some teams that had spent nearly as much weren't rewarded with success. And even if the Marlins won, would they win enough to bring back the fans?

"Wayne was not going to come up with $300 million to buy a retractable domed stadium, so there were two ways to go," Smiley said. "Spend more and get into the playoffs, or spend less, get the business stabilized, and make a run for a ballpark. Wayne's opinion was if you win, you have a better chance to get the ballpark."

In reality, it wasn't much of a gamble. Huizenga planned on finding out in one season whether South Floridians had any interest in Major League Baseball and whether they would support a competitive team. He was testing the value of his investment by investing more. He was buying a competitive baseball team for South Florida and threatening South Florida at the same time.

If the fans didn't come out, Huizenga would take away their team.

If they did come out, then maybe he would get a new stadium, free of charge. In the baseball movie *Field of Dreams*, the catch phrase was, "If you build it, he will come." For the 1997 Florida Marlins, it was, "If they come, maybe they'll build it."

◆ ◆ ◆

The Marlins decided which high-priced players they wanted during their organizational meetings in October 1996. These were complex brainstorming sessions. They were run by Dave Dombrowski, the Marlins' 40-year-old general manager with the dimpled chin and blue eyes, and he was surrounded for days by the manager, the coaches, and all of his scouts. They were some of the brightest people in the business and spread out before them were reams of paperwork.

The Marlins decided their main needs were a third baseman, a leftfielder, and a starting pitcher.

Their first choice at third base was Robin Ventura. They wouldn't get him. Their first choice in leftfield was Barry Bonds. They wouldn't get him. Their first choice for a starting pitcher was John Smoltz. They wouldn't get him.

They were 0-for-3

Their second choice at third base was Matt Williams. They wouldn't get him. Their second choice in leftfield was Albert Belle. They wouldn't get them.

Now they were 0-for-5.

Their second choice for a starting pitcher was Alex Fernandez. They got him.

When the Marlins finished spending in December, they had signed their third choice at third base, Bobby Bonilla, their third choice in leftfield, Moises Alou, their second choice at pitcher, plus two bench players—Jim Eisenreich and John Cangelosi—and a left-handed relief pitcher, Dennis Cook, for a total of $89 million.

They considered their off-season to be a grand success.

◆ ◆ ◆

They also got a manager, Jim Leyland, who on the first day of spring training, sat behind his desk in his office at Space Coast Stadium, talking with the media.

He was a slight man, at 6', 180 pounds, with salt-and-pepper hair and mustache, a receding hairline, short sideburns, and hollow cheeks that creased down the middle when he smiled. His cheeks looked like he had taken a deep drag out of a cigarette and never exhaled.

The manager was leaning back in his chair and patiently answering questions. He had his shirt off, chest exposed, his pants off, long johns exposed, his shoes off, toes exposed, and his feet propped up on the desk. A plate of chicken wings was in front of him, but he didn't seem too hungry. He would pick up a chicken wing, take one bite, then throw it back onto his plate. He would pick up another chicken wing, take a bite, then throw it back onto his plate. He did this with a dozen chicken wings, taking a bite out of each one. By the time he was done, he had a plateful of barely eaten chicken wings. Chickens could fly with what was left of those wings.

After he finished eating, he picked up a pack of cigarettes from his desk, removed one cigarette, lit it with a disposable lighter, and smoked the cigarette. He smoked the cigarette like he ate chicken wings, taking a quick drag, then blowing out the smoke, a quick drag, then blowing out the smoke. He clearly had no patience for eating and no patience for smoking, but he clearly liked smoking more, because a few minutes after he finished one cigarette, he would light up another.

The man who sat here was considered a baseball genius with a special talent for communicating with people. His price tag was $1.2 million a year for five years. That was how much it took for the Marlins to sign Leyland after he decided to leave the Pittsburgh Pirates, a team he had managed for eleven years. Leyland loved Pittsburgh, where he won three division titles, and wanted to live there forever. In fact, as recently as five weeks before he left, he announced publicly he would honor the remaining four years of his contract.

Two weeks after that, Leyland decided he didn't have the patience to stick around for two or three or four, or whatever it took, years, while the Pirates slashed their payroll and tried to win with young prospects. Leyland, who at 51 seemed to be hurrying to an early grave by smoking too many cigarettes and drinking too much coffee, told the Pirates he wanted to leave. They reluctantly agreed.

After a tearful farewell with the fans, Leyland ended his Pirates career on September 29, 1996, then sat back with his wife in their suburban Pittsburgh home and waited for the offers to pour in, which they did, from the Marlins, the Chicago White Sox, the Boston Red Sox, and the California Angels. Four days later, after considerable monetary flattery from all four teams, Leyland and his wife, Katie, picked apart the pros and cons of each offer.

They preferred the Marlins because Leyland had been best friends with the team's first president, Carl Barger, who died in 1992. Through Barger, Leyland had become friends with Huizenga and Smiley. He knew Dombrowski from the early 1980s, when both were with the White Sox. When the Marlins were born in 1991, Leyland could have been their first manager, but he decided to stay in Pittsburgh out of loyalty.

4

This time, like in '91, money wasn't the primary factor. Chicago and Boston had both offered Leyland more. Still, money was part of the decision. The Marlins appealed to Leyland because they had promised to spend a lot of it to buy the players that would instantly transform them from a mediocre 80-82 team into pennant contenders.

The Marlins, along with the rest of the baseball world, had thought from the start they would be Leyland's first and only choice. Dombrowski was sure of it when the bidding started on Monday, September 30. But by Wednesday, with the White Sox and Red Sox throwing mega bucks at Leyland, Dombrowski was so uncertain that he and Smiley flew to Pittsburgh and met with Leyland face-to-face. They weren't the only ones there. Just as Smiley and Dombrowski were leaving Pittsburgh, Leyland was driving to the airport to pick up the people from Boston for a dinner meeting.

Leyland finally made his decision on Thursday night, while sitting in bed with his wife. He had been agonizing over the decision for days, but just out of the blue, he turned to her and said, "Let's go to Florida, Momma."

"Let's go," agreed Katie Leyland, who is not his mother.

The next day, Leyland was introduced to the South Florida media. For this meeting, he was fully dressed in a gray business suit, a white pressed shirt that hung loosely around his thin neck, and a black tie dotted with red, blue, yellow, and green balloons. He offered his view on what it would take to transform the Marlins into winners.

"There can only be one heartbeat," Leyland said. "We can all have our different personalities, we can all second guess the manager, we can get on all the players, we can do all the things that are part of this business that we have to accept, but there can only be one heartbeat. That's the only way we can get this done."

That was October 4, 1996. A little more than two months later, the Marlins finished their spending spree. And now Leyland was sitting in his new office, picking at chicken wings and smoking cigarettes, talking about baseball, and looking like a man who needed nothing more than a shirt.

"I don't know a thing about hitting," he said.

Uh-oh.

"I like people to be on time."

Uh-oh.

◆ ◆ ◆

Bobby Bonilla wasn't taking any chances. When he arrived at training camp a week earlier, the first thing the 34-year-old Bonilla did was place an alarm clock on the top shelf of his locker.

The next thing he did was conduct a short interview. Bonilla was a prime candidate for an interview because not many players were around. Position players weren't due to report for another week.

"Why are you here so early?" a reporter inquired.

"I wanted to jerk off in private," Bonilla joked.

He was smiling when he said this. Bonilla smiles when he says just about every-

5

thing. He is a huge man, at 6'4", 240 pounds, with huge arms, huge thighs, a slightly larger than regulation athletic size gut, and a huge, bright smile.

He was smiling four years ago in New York, when he said to an offending reporter, "I'll show you the fucking Bronx." Bonilla knew the Bronx well, because that's where he came from, but he wasn't offering a guided tour. He was threatening to beat the crap out of the man.

During his time in New York, he had also punched a cameraman, called the press box to complain about an error, and worn earplugs to block out the booing New York fans.

The past year and a half, which Bonilla spent in Baltimore, was marginally less controversial. Bonilla was a productive hitter, as long as manager Davey Johnson didn't ask him to be the designated hitter. Unfortunately, that's exactly what Johnson asked him to do, and they took their feud public.

"I don't even think I remember the first half of last year," Bonilla said. "I don't care to remember it. I kind of blocked it out."

The Marlins weren't overly concerned about Bonilla's behavior because they had the great mitigating factor: Jim Leyland. Leyland had been Bonilla's manager in Pittsburgh for the first six and most productive seasons of his career, and they got along great. Leyland had pushed hard for the Marlins to pursue Bonilla.

"He's always been a father figure to me," Bonilla said on the day the Marlins signed him to a free agent contract worth $23.3 million over four years.

But Dad wasn't in the clubhouse during the first week of training camp when Bonilla interrupted catcher Charles Johnson's interview with reporters, warned Johnson that the media would betray him, and bellowed, "There's a new sheriff in town!"

Later, the new sheriff enforced the "No Parking" regulation in the clubhouse when he deposited an unattended TV camera in a trash bin. Some cameraman had made the mistake of leaving his stuff in front of Bonilla's locker. Four times Bonilla asked who the camera belonged to, and rather than push it aside, he threw it away.

Of course, he did it with a smile.

Then the cameraman showed up and Bonilla told him to, "Get your ass on out to the truck."

He did that with a smile, too.

A few days later, he was still smiling as he carried his 3-year-old son through the clubhouse while singing out curses.

Talk about your father figures.

◆ ◆ ◆

Another father figure in the Marlins' clubhouse was Gary Sheffield, who had fathered three children with three different women and hadn't married any of them. But that was Sheffield's past. Now, standing in the Marlins' clubhouse at Space Coast Stadium, surrounded by boxes of brand new sneakers and a representative from a sneaker company, was Sheffield's present.

Sheffield's past also included arriving late for games and calling general manager Dave Dombrowski a liar because Dombrowski promised not to trade him, but appeared to be reneging on his promise. Sheffield also accused Dombrowski of not doing enough to improve the team and threatened to retire because he wasn't having any fun playing baseball. Of course, he was also making over $6 million a year.

His past was dotted with several off-the-field incidents. In 1995, St. Petersburg, Florida, police received an anonymous tip that four men had been hired to kill Sheffield's mother. There was never an attempt on her life. Later in the season, sheriff deputies pulled Sheffield off a team flight and checked his luggage for drugs. No drugs were found. Sheffield insists he has never done drugs, but was under suspicion by association: His uncle, pitcher Doc Gooden, had twice been suspended from baseball for drug use.

"Doc's my big brother and I've helped him through a lot of his problems," Sheffield said. "But people speculate that I had the same problems because we were so close."

Sheffield claimed he was tested for drugs several times in the late 1980s and early '90s, when he played for the Milwaukee Brewers, but never tested positive. Controversy, however, kept following him. During the 1995 season, a bizarre rumor circulated that Sheffield had AIDS. And in October 1995, Sheffield was driving in Tampa, four blocks from his house, when he was shot in the shoulder. It was a walk-by shooting. The shooter walked right up to the car while Sheffield waited at a red light and fired through the window. With his shoulder bleeding, Sheffield floored the accelerator and got away, but after about a block, he turned back to confront the shooter. That's when he realized he wasn't carrying his gun.

"The only thing that saved that man that night was I didn't have mine," Sheffield told *The Sporting News*. "That was it. Bottom line, I just slipped that night. But I won't ever slip again."

He was not the kind of man you wanted around.

Not the kind of man you wanted around, that is, unless he was coming off of a season in which he hit .314 with forty-two home runs and one hundred twenty RBIs. In that case, you wanted him around for as long as possible, which was why the Marlins and Sheffield's agent were negotiating a contract that would keep him in a Marlins uniform for at least six more years.

But talking in this clubhouse, still dressed in his uniform after practice and wearing two Reebok wristbands, a black Marlins jacket, and diamond studs in both ears, Sheffield insisted he had changed. He had undergone a life-altering experience.

That experience was a phone conversation during the winter with heavyweight boxer Evander Holyfield. Holyfield, who had met Sheffield at an NBA All-Star game, called one morning to talk about religion.

"We talked and then the conversation just ended all of a sudden," Sheffield said. "He said, 'Got to go train,' and that was it." Sheffield hung up the phone, shook his head, and thought: *God sent me a message.*

There was a calmness about Sheffield as he stood in front of his locker and talked about finding God. He spoke in an even voice, looked reporters in the eyes when he answered their questions, and sounded like he meant what he said. He had given up going out late to nightclubs and hanging out with the wrong crowd. He told reporters about his newfound faith, and also talked about the new house he was building in St. Petersburg: 12,000 square feet on a man-made island with a pond in front— filled with turtles, because "I just like turtles"—and surrounded by a six-foot high concrete wall with infrared laser beams to discourage intruders.

"I'm just trying to do the right things now," Sheffield said. "A lot of guys don't feel comfortable with being a role model, but now I'm putting in an effort to be a role model. I don't want people to be disappointed when I make a mistake."

◆ ◆ ◆

On the Marlins' first day of full-squad workouts, Leyland gathered his team around him, pulled out a sheet of yellow legal paper on which he had written some notes, and delivered the remarks he had been preparing for months.

He told the players that this short speech was the most important one he would make all year. He also told them, "If you like something I say, put it in your pocket. If you don't like something, just throw it away." Then he repeated his one heartbeat line. And mindful of the writers who were predicting the Marlins to challenge the Atlanta Braves for the National League East title, he said, "Let's remember one thing, fellas. This group hasn't done shit yet."

Indeed, the Braves had won five consecutive division titles and were the outstanding team of the '90s. The best the Marlins had done was go 80-82 in 1996.

"This isn't my show," Leyland said. "This is your show. I'm here to shoulder the responsibility if we don't do well and give out the credit if we do. The people don't come to see me or the umpires. They come to see you."

There were fifty-five players listening to Leyland's speech, and although they all listened intently, or at least appeared to, only about thirty-two would have any use for what he was saying. They were the only thirty-two with any chance of making the team. This figured to be one of the least contentious training camps in baseball history, so one of its most interesting moments was Leyland's speech.

About three hours later, when the workout ended, several players talked about how much they enjoyed their first day under Leyland. Sheffield said, "I always wondered what it would be like to play for the guy." Now he was finding out: not so difficult. In fact, playing for Leyland was not only easier than playing for other managers, it was less time-consuming. Some managers held two workouts a day during the first week of spring training. With Leyland, there was a morning workout that ended at around 12:30. The players had the rest of the day to play golf or do whatever they pleased.

"You'd better work hard, because he'll jar your ass if you don't," Bonilla said. "You do your drills, it's over, you're done."

◆ ◆ ◆

About those drills: The average major league workout is only slightly more exhausting than morning calisthenics at your local summer camp and far less exhausting than a half-hour aerobics class. Basketball, football, and hockey players would laugh if they saw what baseball players considered "working out."

8

In basketball, players run up and down the court for hours. In football, players bang into each other at full force in ninety degree heat. In hockey, players literally fight for jobs. They drop the gloves and beat up their teammates.

On the morning of the Marlins' first workout, Moises Alou was distracting Bonilla during batting practice, so Bonilla turned to him and said, "C'mon, Mo, I have to concentrate. They're paying me the big bucks."

Bonilla returned to what he was doing, which was hitting against a 50-year-old coach who was throwing the ball, at most, seventy miles per hour.

◆ ◆ ◆

The typical day began with stretching and running. Stretching consisted of the players walking about a hundred feet forward and a hundred feet in the opposite direction, lifting their legs as high as possible, as if they were walking through a field of snake-infested grass. Running consisted of jogging fast for about fifty feet, then walking another fifty feet.

By that time, the players were sweating because of the hot and humid Florida weather. Then they headed off in groups to four fields. Pitchers would throw batting practice on two fields. Coaches would throw batting practice on the other two fields.

During the first week of training camp, Alex Fernandez was having a difficult time throwing a pitch past Moises Alou. This wasn't alarming to the Marlins, because at this point in spring training, hitters were generally ahead of pitchers.

Or were pitchers ahead of hitters?

Nobody could quite figure that out.

This much was certain: Fernandez had signed with the Marlins because general manager Dave Dombrowski was ahead of his competition. Dombrowski had been on a shopping trip in Miami with his wife in December when, at 2 o'clock in the afternoon, he pulled into the parking lot of a Christmas store. At that very moment, the bidding had opened on free agent Alex Fernandez.

"I'll meet you inside," Dombrowski told his wife. "I need to make a phone call."

While Karie picked out Christmas ornaments, Dombrowski sat in a crowded parking lot, talked on his cellular phone with Fernandez's agent, Scott Boras, and began the Marlins' bidding on the centerpiece of their off-season spending spree: A Cuban-American pitcher from Miami who in 1996 had won 16 games for the Chicago White Sox.

Fernandez, 27, was a perfect fit for the Marlins. Born in Miami of Cuban parents, Fernandez and his wife, Lourdes, lived in Miami during the off-season. He had been a standout at Pace High in nearby Opa-Locka, and the fans who had packed the stands to watch him there followed him to the University of Miami and Miami-Dade South Community College. After spending seven years with the White Sox, Fernandez wanted to pitch at home, in front of his family and friends.

The Marlins wanted him, too. Nearly sixty percent of the 1.36 million Hispanics who live in Dade County, where Miami is located, are Cuban. More Cubans live in Miami than anywhere in the world except Cuba. For the first four years, the Marlins had been criticized for not having enough Hispanic players. Fernandez would be the star of their new Hispanic marketing program.

By the time Karie Dombrowski finished shopping, her husband had already made his first offer for Fernandez, $28 million over five years. That night, the Dombrowskis attended a hockey game and got home at about 11. Fernandez was at a party in Miami with his wife when Boras sent along word that the Cleveland Indians had offered $40 million over five years.

"Scott Boras called me that night and said Alex said that if we pay seven million a year for five years, he will pitch for the Florida Marlins," Dombrowski said. "And I said, 'Yes.' All things being equal, if Alex doesn't say, 'I'm going to stay in Florida for seven million dollars,' Scott Boras would have taken him to Cleveland for eight million. This was one of the fastest negotiations I've ever had."

Fernandez wasn't being magnanimous. Although the difference in salary was $1 million a year, Fernandez would retain more of his salary with the Marlins because Ohio had a state income tax and Florida didn't. In Cleveland, Fernandez would have had to buy a new house. In Miami, he was already building a new house. By the time he returned home from the party that night, he had decided to play for the Marlins.

Fernandez, penned-in by Leyland as the Marlins' third starter, had been one of the most reliable and durable starting pitchers in baseball the previous four seasons. But on this day at Marlins training camp, Fernandez looked neither reliable nor durable.

He looked fat. According to Fernandez, he weighed fifteen pounds over his ideal pitching weight of 215, even though he had been arriving at the ballpark at 6:30 every morning and working out diligently in the weight room. The extra fifteen pounds looked like much more on his stout 6'1" body. Fernandez insisted he liked pitching with extra weight, but his first pitch to Alou sailed ten feet over the catcher's glove and hit the backstop. A few pitches later, Alou hit the ball four hundred feet over the leftfield fence.

This wasn't necessarily a bad thing. The Marlins had paid $25 million for Alou, the last of the six free agents they signed, and here he was putting on a batting practice show against one of the best pitchers in the majors. Alou, 30, was smiling when he finished taking his cuts and made his way to another field. He was happy.

"I feel wanted here," he said. "Montreal never made me feel wanted."

Alou felt wanted with the Marlins because they were paying him $5 million a year. He didn't feel wanted in Montreal, even though his father, Felipe, was the manager, because there was no way they were going to pay him $5 million a year. They didn't have that kind of money.

For Alou, a career .292 hitter who had homes in West Palm Beach—about seventy miles north of Miami—and the Dominican Republic—two hours by plane from Miami—want was expressed by the size of his paycheck.

In Alou, the Marlins knew they had a dependable player with one of the most famous surnames in baseball history.

They also knew they had a guy who could hit home runs off of Alex Fernandez.

◆ ◆ ◆

Over on Field 1, the daily workout continued with Leyland's lesson in defending the double steal. As he taught and watched, he paced up and down along the baselines with his right hand tucked inside the back of his pants and his left hand holding a baseball bat. He looked like Abner Doubleday's version of Napoleon.

Leyland was teaching because he didn't have much else to do. While in other training camps around Florida and Arizona players were battling for positions, not much was up for grabs in Marlins camp.

The regulars had been established. The catcher was Charles Johnson, who had won the Gold Glove in his first two major league seasons. Jeff Conine, a two-time All-Star and an original Marlin, would move from leftfield to first base. The middle of the infield would consist of two of the best young fielders in the majors: second baseman Luis Castillo, a 21-year-old Dominican, and shortstop Edgar Renteria, a 21-year-old Colombian who was the runner-up for National League Rookie of the Year in 1996. The third baseman was Bonilla. The outfield consisted of Alou in left, Sheffield in right, and Devon White, 34, an outstanding fielder with great speed, in center.

Leyland had decided on most of his bench players, too. The backup catcher would probably be Gregg Zaun, a talkative, tattooed, switch-hitting 25-year-old. The backup infielders were Alex Arias, an original Marlin, and Kurt Abbott.

The three reserve outfielders would be Joe Orsulak, Jim Eisenreich, and John Cangelosi. This was virtually certain because the Marlins had spent a lot of money on all three of them, especially Eisenreich and Cangelosi.

The starting pitchers were Kevin Brown, Al Leiter, Alex Fernandez, and Pat Rapp, another original Marlin. One spot was open for Tony Saunders, Rick Helling, and Mark Hutton, to fight over. The bullpen consisted of closer Robb Nen, free-agent Dennis Cook, hard throwing Dominican lefty Felix Heredia, and Helling, Hutton or both. Two spots were open.

This would not be a spring of knock-down, drag-out battles for jobs. Most of the competition had ended when the Marlins signed players in December.

◆ ◆ ◆

So the team was virtually set and the exhibition games would be exhibitions in the purest sense. They were exhibitions for the fans, who the Marlins were trying to win back after a four-year labor dispute that resulted in a 232-day players strike, canceled the 1994 World Series, and alienated fans. Especially fans in South Florida.

"If you asked, 'Who got hurt the most by the strike?' you'd have to say the Florida Marlins," Don Smiley said. "Everything hit a wall in August of 1994. It threw out all of our plans and projections."

The Marlins already knew their off-season spending spree was having a positive effect at the box office. The day Leyland signed, the ticket office was swamped by requests for season ticket information. Interest was high. By early February, the Marlins had surpassed their 1996 season ticket total of 12,500. When single game tickets went on sale, the Marlins sold 44,000 over two days. In 1996, they had sold only 17,000. In 1996, the Marlins sold out only two games. Already, they had sold out three for 1997: Opening day, plus two games against the New York Yankees.

"You don't have to be a rocket scientist to figure out that even though it's a spring training game, people are excited," Leyland said. "I want to hang around .500 if we can. It's cosmetic, but it might help sell some tickets."

◆ ◆ ◆

While the Marlins rehabilitated their relationship with the fans, Bobby Bonilla spent the first two weeks of spring rehabilitating his image. As he dressed in the cramped visitor's clubhouse at Fort Lauderdale Stadium after the Marlins won their spring opener on February 28, he turned to the waiting reporters and said, "I'm putting it on as fast as I can for you guys. You know I'm trying to change my image."

There had been no Bobby Bo incidents since the camera-in-the-garbage and "new sheriff" episodes, and Bonilla was charming in his first official meeting with the South Florida press a week earlier.

"Just talk to me," he told them. "Don't worry. I'm going to get to know each and every one of you. I'm actually a very nice guy."

There was one subject Bonilla couldn't be a very nice guy about, former manager Davey Johnson. The Marlins playing the Orioles in the first exhibition game gave Bonilla several opportunities to respond to Johnson's reported comment that the Marlins' leftfielder had better be prepared to back up Bonilla at third because a lot of balls would be getting through.

Bonilla responded by calling Johnson a "hot air balloon" who is "in his own fantasy world."

So Bonilla's image was a work-in-progress.

◆ ◆ ◆

Learning fundamentals: Leyland taught backup catcher Gregg Zaun the steal sign.

"If I jump up and don't ever come down," Leyland told him, "you steal."

◆ ◆ ◆

A sellout crowd of 8,188 packed Space Coast Stadium the next afternoon for the Marlins' spring home opener and watched Brown, the Marlins' ace, pitch two shutout innings in an 8-7 win over the Orioles. Brown, who had won seventeen games with a sparkling 1.89 ERA in 1996, reported that he had a busy off-season.

"Well, let's see," he said. "I moved forks back and forth to my mouth a lot. I worked my thumb real hard on flying airplanes."

Brown somehow stayed in shape with this grueling off-season training regimen. At 6'4", 200 pounds, he has a basketball player's physique with long legs and muscular, well-defined arms that he dressed in tank tops while lounging around the clubhouse.

Brown had also sharpened the tongue that had helped earn him the honor "one of the ten biggest jerks in baseball" by *Sports Illustrated* magazine.

Brown is a perfectionist who had been known to curse loudly in the dugout after a four-pitch inning. That was one pitch too many, in Brown's book. Obviously intelligent, Brown, who lived in Macon, Georgia, and majored in chemical engineering at Georgia Tech, had been described as a "nerd" by those who knew him best. In fact, it never took long to realize that Brown thought of himself as smarter than anyone else.

"What are the one or two traits Kevin Brown has that have helped him become successful?" a radio reporter asked.

Brown looked up and stared at the questioner. Then he smirked. Then he said, "Probably the best trait I have is that I don't answer questions like that because they get you in trouble."

He laughed at that, but nobody else did. Then another radio reporter asked this question: "Kevin, one useable soundbite. Coming off a career year, what are you looking for in 1997?"

"One useable sound bite, huh?" Brown answered. "Does it have to entail the world bite? It would probably be bite me."

He chuckled at his wit and answered the question.

◆ ◆ ◆

Jeff Conine is a sensible man who realized complaining about his manager wasn't a good idea. Early in training camp, Conine learned he would bat seventh in the Marlins' lineup. He learned this not from the manager, but from the reporters who rushed to his locker after Leyland announced the opening day lineup: Castillo batting first, followed by Renteria, Sheffield, Bonilla, Alou, White, Conine, and Johnson.

This was news because Conine had batted .293 with ninety-five RBIs in 1996 while usually batting cleanup.

Leyland: "To me, it's a luxury when you have a guy in the seven hole who can score a guy from first."

Conine: "You don't normally think of the seven spot as being much of a run production spot."

But he stopped short of second-guessing Leyland.

With his All-American looks, Conine, 30, could pass for Clark Kent in a baseball uniform. He was the most popular player with the fans and the media and had been with the Marlins from the start, when they selected him in the 1992 expansion draft. He was called Mr. Marlin.

Conine could recall the Marlins' first spring, when they played their games a few miles up the road in a dilapidated old park called Cocoa Expo. In 1995, he became a hero in South Florida when he hit the game-winning home run in the All-Star game and was named Most Valuable Player. The Marlins didn't win much the first four years, but Conine was their most dependable hitter.

"I've seen it all," Conine said. "I've been here from the start and this is the best club we've had since I've been here. But we can't look at this season like we have to win back the fans and save the franchise. We have to worry about winning on the field. Everything else is out of our control."

Including the starting lineup. That was in only one man's control.

◆ ◆ ◆

Leyland on talking baseball: "I don't want to talk about strategy in the paper, because I don't want to sound like I'm smart."

Of course. How could anyone expect a baseball manager to talk about strategy?

◆ ◆ ◆

Gregg Doyel, a reporter from *The Miami Herald,* had a Bobby Bonilla experience. He had written a story that detailed Bonilla's crimes against the media during the first week of spring training and explained that Bonilla wasn't being mean, he was just being playful, a bit overly outgoing.

Wrote Doyel: "That's Bonilla. That's not him talking trash. That's him talking. He walks through the clubhouse sing-songing four-letter words—while carrying his 3-year-old son. This doesn't exactly make him a guy you want speaking Sunday at your local church, but it doesn't make him an ogre, either."

Bonilla didn't appreciate the tone of the article or people knowing the details of his parenting methods. The next day, he was talking to Jody Jackson of WQAM radio when he pointed across the clubhouse and asked, "Who's that?"

"That's Greg Doyel from the *Herald,*" Jackson answered, having unwittingly become Bonilla's stool pigeon.

Bonilla was shrewd enough to confront Doyel when no TV cameras could record his actions. A day later, he was standing alone behind the batting cage at Chain O' Lakes Park in Winter Haven, windmilling his bat, when Doyel walked over.

"I wouldn't come over here if I were you," Bonilla warned, smiling and looking straight ahead as he spoke.

Doyel was stunned. He had no idea why Bonilla was so angry.

"If you write about my family again," Bonilla advised, "I will fucking hurt you."

"Is this about the story in Sunday's paper?" Doyel asked.

Bonilla nodded. Doyel walked away. No punches were thrown and Bonilla didn't offer Doyel a tour of Winter Haven.

◆ ◆ ◆

Here's how much the results of spring games mean to the players. Al Leiter was sitting in a conference room at Space Coast Stadium, talking to the media shortly after his first outing of the spring against the Braves on March 5. Outside, the game was still going on in front of a packed house, and Leiter, his work day finished after pitching two innings, was icing down his arm.

As it had so many times this spring, the conversation came around to the Braves, and somebody asked Leiter whether the Marlins and Braves were "measuring" each

14

other. But before Leiter could answer the question, a clubhouse attendant walked in from the field, followed by a few players.

"Game's over?" Leiter said matter-of-factly.

"Yeah."

"No shit. Did we win? What was the final?"

"6-5."

"Who won?"

"We did."

Leiter nodded his head and went on to answer another reporter's question.

◆ ◆ ◆

Leiter, along with Kevin Brown and Devon White, belonged to the Marlins' first free agent class of winter 1995 and, like Brown, had the best season of his career: 16-12 with a 2.93 ERA. He also pitched the first no-hitter in Marlins history, on May 11, 1996, against the Rockies. But other than that both had their best seasons in 1996, there are no other similarities between Brown and Leiter.

Leiter is congenial, quick with a smile, willing to poke fun at himself, and always patient when answering questions. He makes people feel welcome and is by no means thin-skinned. He'll joke about the long home runs he sometimes allows, saying you have to throw them hard for batters to hit them that far, and plays along when people tease about his propensity for getting behind in the count. One day during the spring, a reporter asked Leiter if he had been trying something new when he walked the opposing pitcher.

"Yeah," Leiter said. "I was trying to see if I could walk him on four pitches and I did."

Likely Kevin Brown response to the same question: "Bite me."

Other differences between Brown and Leiter: Brown is a righty. Leiter is a lefty. Brown is from the deep south. Leiter is from the northeast, Toms River, New Jersey. Brown is tall and lanky. Leiter is an inch shorter at 6'3" and a little heavier at 220 pounds. He has brown eyes, light brown hair, and wears a thick, gold rope chain around his neck.

Brown is a control pitcher who throws his fastball, sinker, and slider, at three speeds: hard, harder, and hardest. He invites opponents to make contact and hit the ball on the ground. Leiter relies on a fastball and a slider and goes for strike-outs. As a result, he frequently falls behind in the count and allows too many walks.

Told that Leyland planned on giving up cigarettes once the season started, but would keep a pack handy on the days Leiter pitched, Leiter laughed and said, "Well, I don't want to be responsible for anybody's bad habits."

Likely Kevin Brown response to the same statement: "Bite me."

Leiter doesn't take his job any less seriously than Brown. Far from it. He is painfully self-analytical and can fill a reporter's notebook with quotes about what he's doing right or wrong. Brown prefers keeping his analysis to himself. Leiter will share it with the world.

◆ ◆ ◆

The Marlins won their first six games, had beaten the Braves twice, and everybody wanted to know what it meant. Surely it had to mean something, didn't it?

Well, not quite, as Leyland pointed out all the time, although every day, after every Marlins win, and without fail, a reporter would stick a microphone or tape recorder in Leyland's face and start a question by saying, "Jim, I know it's only spring training but . . . "

Leyland's answer usually went along these lines: "I'm going to say it for the twentieth time, and I'm going to say it for the last time. We are in the same division with the Braves, but in no way, shape, or form, yet, are we in the same class with the Atlanta Braves. Believe me when I tell you that. Not yet. Hopefully in the near future, I don't know. But right now? No. Ain't no way."

Maybe Leyland was saying it for the twentieth time, but he certainly wasn't saying it for the last time. He would have to say it over and over before March ended.

◆ ◆ ◆

The Marlins won twice on March 7, improving their record to 9-0, and Don Smiley said, "There's no question the enthusiasm and excitement are growing day by day. It's translating into ticket sales and that's exactly what we're looking for."

Told that Smiley was pleased with the Marlins' record, the usually reticent Devon White said, "I'm sure he is. His job is probably on the line."

Smiley and White joked about it later on, but White's analysis of the situation was not far off. Smiley knew it. Back in September, when he, Dombrowski, and assistant general manager Frank Wren calculated that building the team they wanted would take a $45 million payroll, Smiley passed along the information to Huizenga.

"What's it going to cost us to win and what's it going to cost us to have a legitimate shot at the playoffs?" Huizenga asked.

Smiley told him.

"How many tickets can we sell?" Huizenga asked.

"We'll average about 29,500 a game," Smiley said.

"What does that translate to in losses?"

"It's about a $30 million loss, or thereabouts," Smiley said.

"OK," Huizenga agreed. "But we need to get into the playoffs."

As it turned out, the Marlins had to spend more money than they had planned. The 1997 payroll turned out to be $49 million, nearly $17 million over the 1996 payroll. Now they really needed to make the playoffs.

◆ ◆ ◆

Leyland walked over to the batting cage, leaned against the railing, and watched Kurt Abbott take his swings.

"I want two hits, Abby," Leyland demanded.

Abbott popped up the first pitch.

"Oh for one," Leyland growled.

Abbott popped up the second pitch.

"Oh for two."

Abbott hit a line drive to rightfield on the third pitch, but on the fourth popped up again.

"That was horseshit," Leyland grumbled.

And Abbott responded, "I'm a game hitter."

Abbott was already one of Leyland's favorites, and not just because, like Leyland, he came from a small town in Ohio. At first glance, Abbott seems unapproachable, because he often has a pained look, but it doesn't take long to discover that he's a personable man—a good ol' boy, really—who enjoys his job, whatever his job might be. For the first time in four years, the 27-year-old Abbott arrived in camp without a spot in the everyday lineup. Nonetheless, he worked hard to keep whatever job he had left.

The manager noticed his diligence. During the spring, Leyland mentioned Abbott as often as he mentioned any other player, and he never used the word "horseshit" to describe him.

What he did say was, "Abbott showed me how to bait a hook the other day."

Maybe that's why he kept him around.

◆ ◆ ◆

The conversation came around to Gary Sheffield, so Leyland put in a plug for his rightfielder.

"I'm going to tell you something," Leyland told the writers as they eagerly pulled out their notepads. "I'm going to give you something pretty good.

"All I know is, I saw Gary Sheffield come out in West Palm Beach the other day. After he played, he ran his ass off in the outfield, sweating like hell, and on his way in signs autographs for a half an hour, but nobody mentions a thing about it. Gary Sheffield's got a heart of gold, I know that already. He probably does a lot of stuff that nobody knows about and nobody talks about because he probably doesn't really care if it's known or not. But I've seen a lot of those guys do stuff like that and I've been totally impressed with the way he's gone about his business. Gary Sheffield's a good guy, I can tell you that right now. He's a good person. Gary Sheffield comes in, he works hard, he's ready to play. He's nice to people. What the hell? What more do you want? I like him."

Dave O'Brien of the Fort Lauderdale *Sun-Sentinel* was taking all this in while sitting on the couch next to Leyland's desk and never once did he stop nodding or stop smirking.

"I like him, too," O'Brien agreed.

"I'm sure you do," Leyland said. "I don't know why you wouldn't. I really like him."

O'Brien refused to be one-upped.

"I *really* like him, too," he said.

"I do, too," Leyland replied.

"Damn it, I like him more. I always have," O'Brien said, chuckling.

"I really like him," Leyland said. "That's all I can tell you. I'm really impressed with him. He's a professional, in my opinion."

"The Sheff," O'Brien agreed.

Another time, the discussion centered around Dustin Hermanson's self-proclaimed "bulldog" approach to pitching: Get on the mound, be aggressive, and challenge the hitters. Leyland didn't quite agree with that philosophy.

"All that kind of stuff is fine if you're in control of yourself," he said. "It's OK, but if Barry Bonds steps in, you can't say, 'I'm going to throw as hard as I can.' That ain't worth shit. You have to have a plan. You have to keep things under control. You can't run out there like a maniac and say, 'I'm going to throw it as hard as I can.' That doesn't work. There's a difference between working hard and working smart."

He turned to the reporters. "You guys can go up there and write your ass off for hours and hours, but if you don't know what you're writing about, you worked eight hours, but you got shit. You go up there, you got a plan. Boom! You sit down, you get it done, you're done."

"I don't know what that's like," O'Brien said.

"Well, then," Leyland said. "Maybe you guys had better hang around with Dustin Hermanson."

◆ ◆ ◆

Soundtrack of spring: Leyland singing. He could carry a tune and was often heard singing in the dugout or in his office. When Leyland sang, his cigarette-ravaged voice became deep and mellow. One of his favorite songs was *You Are My Special Angel* and during the off-season he sang it on stage with *The Vogues*. "One of the biggest thrills of my life," he said.

Anyway, Leyland was talking about how Elton John once signed an album for him, and how he was friends with Clint Black and Hank Williams, when he leaned across his desk and said, "Did you know it took Elton John only an hour to write *Candle In The Wind?* That's unbelievable."

The conversation quickly moved on to another subject, but then he said it again. "It took Elton John only an hour to write *Candle In The Wind.*" He sounded like it was the most incredible thing he had ever heard.

◆ ◆ ◆

March Madness had taken over the clubhouse. The start of the NCAA men's basketball tournament was a day away, and Bobby Bonilla had taken it upon himself to organize the team's tournament pool. For a hundred dollar buy-in, you drew a number from 1 to 64. If you drew No. 1, you got the first choice of teams. If you drew No. 64, you got the last choice. Whoever chose the tournament champion won the pot.

Not enough of his teammates wanted to play, so Bonilla opened the pool to the media. By some miraculous coincidence, most of the players drew low numbers, while most of the media members drew high numbers. And each time he collected $100, Bonilla would smile broadly and say, "Thanks for the donation."

A day later, the Marlins held a closed-door players-only meeting. The purpose of the meeting was for the players involved in the pool to pick their teams.

◆ ◆ ◆

One day, Leyland was sitting in his office with reporters, talking about the house near Melbourne he had rented for the spring. The house was huge, he said, and had cost him $5,000 for the month, but he wasn't using it much because his wife and children were down in Parkland, a suburb of Fort Lauderdale. The house, he said, was "kind of spooky." It was too big, didn't have enough furniture, and when he spoke, his voice echoed off the walls. And that wasn't the only problem.

"The other day, I woke up at two in the morning, looked up, and saw my reflection in this big mirror on the wall in the bedroom," Leyland said. "It scared the shit out of me."

He paused.

"You know, I ain't no oil painting."

Sheffield on his manager: "You can open up to a person like that."

Leyland had two goals in spring training: getting his team ready for the season and going to the dog track as frequently as possible. After a game in Winter Haven, Leyland rushed out of the clubhouse, cradling a bunch of notebooks in one arm and a greasy box of fried chicken in the other. A fan leaned over the fence and begged him to sign a baseball bat.

"One more, Jim!" the fan screamed.

"I'll try," Leyland said. "But I'm in a hurry. I have to get to the dog track."

Leyland wasn't happy about spending $5,000 on a house he rarely used when he could have saved his money, stayed with third base coach Rich Donnelly, and spent it on something else.

"Shit," he said. "I could've spent it on the dogs."

◆ ◆ ◆

Milt May, the batting coach Leyland brought along from Pittsburgh, spent the spring working with Charles Johnson on shortening his swing. Johnson, 25, and entering his third season, had a long, loping swing that didn't move fast enough through the strike zone. In 1996, he had more strikeouts, ninety-one, than he did hits, eighty-four.

Leyland, dubiously, on May's work with Johnson: "If he hits, he helped him a lot. If he doesn't hit, he didn't help him worth shit."

◆ ◆ ◆

Pat Rapp, who was enjoying one of the best springs of any Marlins pitcher, revealed on March 25 in Fort Lauderdale that the secret to success was "staying within himself."

Presumably, what Rapp meant was that in 1995, when his record was 14-7, he also stayed within himself, but in 1996, when his record was 8-16, he stayed within somebody else's self. Whoever it was, wasn't very good. Rapp had to hope he didn't show up again.

◆ ◆ ◆

A reporter asked what the relief pitchers' "roles" would be—such as setup man, long reliever, middle reliever—and Leyland responded with his one outburst of the spring. The theme: Role My Ass. The message: Leyland doesn't believe in things such as setup men and long relievers.

"I don't give a shit!" Leyland started. "Role my ass. Guy pitches two years in the big leagues and wants to know his role? Your role is to come to the park and be prepared to help this fucking team win and do whatever the manager asks. Rolls are something you put butter on. Role my ass. It gets to be an excuse. Guy isn't doing well and he says it's because he doesn't know his role. I can't stand it. Role my ass."

Obviously, Dennis Cook and the others would have to play it by ear.

◆ ◆ ◆

Although they never established roles, the Marlins had a remarkable spring. They won their first eleven games and finished with a record of 26-5, believed to be the best in Grapefruit League history. None of their regulars suffered serious injuries. The hitting was almost too good to be true. Not only did the Marlins hit for average and power—Bonilla broke Leyland's car window with a home run over the rightfield fence at Space Coast Stadium—but they hit smartly and to the opposite field. One trade was made: Joe Orsulak and Dustin Hermanson were sent to the Expos in exchange for 24-year-old outfielder Cliff Floyd, a player Dombrowski had long coveted.

The Marlins' confidence grew by the day. Leyland was at ease. Some mornings he would sit on the outfield grass with a bunch of prospects, just shooting the breeze, even though they had no chance of making the team. He'd spend games walking up and down the dugout, talking to all his players. He went to the dog track. He sang. One afternoon in Kissimmee, he bonded with a midget. A dancing midget.

The midget was the Houston Astros' batboy and Leyland bumped into him in the dugout before the game on March 24. They were just exchanging small talk—Leyland was asking questions and the midget was telling him about his job, which of course was dancing, collecting bats, and being a midget.

"I work hard," the midget complained.

"Don't let them work you too hard," Leyland said compassionately.

The midget showed up again later, during the seventh inning stretch. He was behind home plate, doing the chicken dance, when Leyland strolled over, shook the midget's hand, and spoke to him for a few more minutes. Then Leyland walked back to the dugout, as if shaking a dancing midget's hand during a baseball game was the most natural thing in the world. To Leyland, maybe it was.

Rookie Tony Saunders had the best spring of any player. Mark Hutton, Rick Helling, and Matt Whisenant had the worst springs. Hutton, 27, and Helling, 26, both had experience as major league starting pitchers and thought they were the leading candidates for the fifth spot in the starting rotation. Saunders, who pitched the previous season at Double-A, didn't think he had much of a shot.

But although Hutton and Helling both pitched well and did nothing to hurt their causes, Saunders impressed Leyland the most. At 22, he had the most potential. He also had some guts. Leyland liked the way Saunders worked his way out of trouble in a difficult start against the Mets when he didn't have command of his pitches. Six days later, Leyland said Saunders was his fifth starter. Helling and Hutton didn't take it very well.

"Nothing against Tony, but I don't think he has proven himself," Helling said.

That sounded like something against Tony.

Hutton's response, in his strong Australian accent: "I'm shocked. Disappointed. Pissed off."

The good news for Helling and Hutton was that they both had jobs in the bullpen. As consolation prizes went, they were of no consolation.

◆ ◆ ◆

Whisenant's was the saddest story of all. He had spent seven years in the minors, slowly working his way up from rookie ball to Triple-A. Last spring, he came as close as he ever had to winning a spot on a major league roster, and missed by one. The Marlins made him their final cut. He went back to the minors and had a miserable season.

Whisenant's problem was control. He had a ninety-five-mile-per-hour fastball, but couldn't get it over the plate. In 1996, he walked more batters than he struck out. But hard-throwing left-handers are always in demand in the major leagues, and this spring, Whisenant had been given another long look by the Marlins. He made the team.

Whisenant was elated. He called his wife to break the good news. She was elated. Less than six hours later, Whisenant strained a muscle in his right side while pitching against the Mets. He was shattered and tried putting a positive spin on his situation.

"I can live with being on the DL in the big leagues," Whisenant said. "For twenty-five years and so many days, I've been waiting for this moment, and now I have to be a spectator for ten more days."

That's what he was hoping for. Jay Powell, who had already been sent to the minors, received a last-minute reprieve. The same thing had happened to Powell last year: He was sent to Charlotte, then got called back to Florida a few games into the season when Terry Mathews landed on the disabled list with a strained rib cage. Whisenant knew what happened next: Powell remained with the Marlins for the rest of the season and Mathews was traded.

◆ ◆ ◆

21

Bolstered by the team's performance, the Marlins' front office had a good spring, too. A three-game series against the Yankees in June was sold out and sales were brisk for games against the Braves and Orioles. Season tickets were selling at the rate of about a hundred per day.

"Last year, if we sold twenty-five tickets in a day, we would be out celebrating," said Mark Geddis, the Marlins' director of communications.

A few hours before the Marlins' final spring game in Melbourne, owner Wayne Huizenga visited the clubhouse, shook hands with the players and wished them luck, and told reporters that the phones were "ringing off the wall" back at the Marlins' office. He had the excited look of a salesman who was about to make a big transaction. His blue eyes gleamed. He smiled.

"I don't know if experiment is the right word for what we're doing, but we were hoping that what we did would generate fan interest," Huizenga said. "So far, it seems like it worked. Now let's see how many games we win."

Huizenga spoke for five more minutes about the problems the Marlins had attracting fans to Pro Player Stadium because of the constant threat of rain in South Florida. Then he turned to his father, Harry, who had been standing beside him the whole time, just listening.

"C'mon Dad," he said, taking him by the arm and leading him out of the clubhouse. "I'll buy you a hotdog."

It was like a scene out of a movie. Or a dream.

2

Bring Me the Head
of Billy the Marlin

April 1, 2, 3 vs. Chicago
April 4, 5, 6 vs. Cincinnati

Jim Leyland had a look of serenity as he rocked slowly in the wooden chair given to him eleven years ago by his clubhouse man in Pittsburgh. The start of the regular season was a day away, and Leyland was discussing the personal changes he would undergo: fewer casual bull sessions with the media, no lounging on the outfield grass with the younger players, and switching to a regular daily routine. That meant getting up a little later, hanging out with his son a little longer, reading the paper, having breakfast, and trying to resist temptation.

"Starting tomorrow," he vowed while puffing on a cigarette in the cramped manager's office at Pro Player Stadium. "No cigarettes and no caffeine."

The vow sounded as heartfelt and long-lasting as a New Year's resolution and about as reasonable as telling a living thing not to breathe. Leyland hadn't even weaned himself off his bad habits and here he was vowing to stop at the stroke of midnight. If this wouldn't drive his wife Katie crazy, nothing would.

"She's not too happy about it," Leyland admitted. "She knows how I get when I don't smoke."

"Grumpy?" someone asked.

"Very grumpy."

Leyland felt he had no choice but to quit. As concerned as he was about suffering from the effects of caffeine and nicotine withdrawal, he knew if he didn't quit smoking, he'd light up in the dugout by force of habit and in violation of Major League rules. He had quit once before, six years ago in Pittsburgh after making the same pre-season vow, and he was confident about doing it again.

"Hopefully I'll sleep in longer, maybe a half hour or so," Leyland said, figuring out a way to make his days shorter. "In the spring I'm up at 5:30 or so. Today, I was out of bed at seven. But I'm an early riser during the season. Maybe this year not as much. I love getting up, having a pot of coffee, reading the paper, and smoking a cigarette. I won't be doing that."

He looked up and cracked a sly smile. "Maybe I'll give up reading the paper, too."

Leyland mused about the good things in life—a steak with a baked potato, accompanied by a vodka martini, then a cigarette and a cup of coffee—and insisted he was up to the challenge of dropping two of those luxuries cold turkey. And, he promised, "I'm not gonna sneak it. I don't want to get caught."

Leyland's resolution immediately became the main subject in the clubhouse, and none of the players had much faith in their manager making it through the season, let alone opening day. Some joked about setting an over-under betting line on how many days it would take before Leyland fell off the wagon. Two months? A month? A week? A day?

Wednesday sounded like the best guess. Second game of the season, Al Leiter pitching. The first time Leiter went to a full count on the opposing pitcher, Leyland would be reaching for the smokes. But with Kevin Brown on the mound tomorrow, Leyland figured to last through opening day.

◆ ◆ ◆

Bobby Bonilla was standing by his locker on Monday, March 31, flashing the smile that makes people wonder whether he's all an act. For the moment, he was only half-serious. He had been looking around, checking out the surroundings, figuring out the nooks and crannies of the Marlins' clubhouse, and he wasn't sure he liked what he had seen.

"There really aren't any good places to hide from the media," he told the reporters standing around him. "I've scoped. You guys have too much access here."

Meanwhile, Jeff Conine was standing halfway across the room in an entrance-way under a sign that read, "Authorized Personnel Only." He wore nothing but a towel around his waist, and as he stepped back and forth over the imaginary forbidden line, he good-naturedly taunted another group of reporters.

"Na-na-na na-na!" Conine sang. "You can't come here!"

Conine, who had spent the past four seasons in this clubhouse, knew the truth: There were plenty of places to hide. Bonilla just hadn't found them yet.

◆ ◆ ◆

In fact, there were so many places for the Marlins to hide in their clubhouse that not only was it possible, but it was entirely likely, that at any time, all twenty-five players could be somewhere in the clubhouse without any of them being in the central locker area. A visitor could walk in and think, *Nobody's home,* when in fact, everyone was within fifty feet, behind one wall or another.

The home clubhouse at Pro Player Stadium is laid out like a pool table with one side pocket instead of two. The main area, where the players have their stalls, is at the center. There are portals at all four corners and another at the midsection of a long wall, where Conine was standing. If Conine had continued through the portal and down the hall, he could have made a left turn into a shower area, complete with steamroom and sauna, or a right turn into a lavishly equipped trainer's room, where players can sit in a whirlpool, get a massage, or undergo treatment on aching muscles.

Back in the main area, then through another portal in the southwest corner, there's a mirrored workout room that can make any Gold's Gym seem underequipped. Across the hall is a small clubhouse dining room, where players can get a meal, a snack, or a drink whenever they wish.

Back again into the main area, through another portal and down a short hallway, is a dimly lit, high-tech video room with monitors and tape machines. In this room, players can watch tapes of opposing pitchers or run back from the dugout during games to see what they did right or wrong in their last at-bat. Further down the hall, then to the left, is the coaches' locker room. And between the coaches' area and the video room is the manager's office, which has its own shower, couch, TV, and an oval conference table. The smell of smoke means the manager is in.

The central clubhouse area is where the players get dressed and spend most of their time. There's room for about forty, including batboys, bullpen catchers, clubhouse men, and first base coach Tommy Sandt, who preferred being with the players, rather than the other coaches. Bonilla, Sheffield, and White had the northern wall to themselves. Conine could be found across the room, between Charles Johnson and Jim Eisenreich. Most of the Latin players occupied the west wall: Moises Alou, Edgar Renteria, Alex Arias, Felix Heredia, and Luis Castillo. Most of the pitchers occupied the opposite wall: Kevin Brown, Pat Rapp, Dennis Cook, Al Leiter, Mark Hutton, Robb Nen, and Alex Fernandez. Fernandez, who had twice as many T-shirts as anyone else, was the only player with two stalls.

The middle of the room is dominated by a long, stationary table with roomy cabinets underneath. The side of the table has slots for outgoing mail and trays from which players may grab handfuls of their favorite gum. There's more Bazooka and Wrigley's Spearmint than they could ever chew in a lifetime. The tabletop is covered with newspapers, sheets on which players can enter their ticket requests for family and friends, and media game notes. Four color TVs hang from the ceiling. Couches and chairs are at either end of the table.

Players could live here if they wanted because all of the necessities of life are at their disposal: food, showers, clothing, and television. And three clubhouse attendants to wait on their every need. All they have to do is ask. Sometimes, they don't even have to do that.

◆ ◆ ◆

None of the players were hiding from the media on Monday, because they were too busy moving in. Seven of them—Alou, Bonilla, Cangelosi, Cook, Eisenreich, Fernandez, and Saunders—were in this clubhouse for the first time, and many of them, including Bonilla, had their stuff laid out all over the floor. The place was a mess.

Then Cheryl Rosenberg from the *Palm Beach Post* walked over to Bonilla's locker, pointed to the hockey sticks and in-line skates lying on the floor, and asked, "What are those?"

"They're hockey sticks," Bonilla answered.

"I know that," Rosenberg said.

"Oh," Bonilla shot back, nodding and grinning. "I thought it was a trivia question or something."

"You skate?" she tried again.

Bonilla was amused. "Yeah, I skate," he said, shattering the stereotype of black men. "And I swim, too."

◆ ◆ ◆

The Marlins are the only major league team that wears T-shirts and long, baggy black shorts for batting practice, rather than their regular game uniforms. It looks strange, but makes sense in an area where the daytime summer temperatures rarely drop below ninety and the humidity rarely drops below eighty percent.

Actually, it made sense to everybody but Bonilla, who wasn't sure he wanted to sacrifice fashion for comfort. So while everyone else, even Leyland with his bony white legs, wore shorts and T-shirts, Bonilla came out for BP wearing long, hot uniform pants and a teal Marlins jersey. No shorts for him.

"I just couldn't get myself to put them on," Bonilla explained. "Not yet."

Bonilla stood out again when he stepped into the batter's box to take his first swings as a member of the home team at Pro Player Stadium. For the past half hour, most of his teammates had been airing popups into the perfect sky and ruining the new turf with ground balls, but Bonilla struck towering shots into the right-field seats three hundred sixty feet away and hammered a line drive three hundred eighty-five feet against the teal leftfield scoreboard. He was feeling right at home.

"I'm fired up," Bonilla said. "I'm really looking forward to it." Then he pointed to Sheffield and said, "They're going to be expecting that big man right next to me to be jacking 'em, and I'll be right behind him." Tomorrow, he would open a season with his third team in as many years. He was looking forward to it more than ever.

◆ ◆ ◆

Leyland slept well the night before the first game, even though he had a house full of friends and relatives, including third base coach Rich Donnelly and his wife. At around 10 o'clock, two hours before his no smoking, no coffee vow kicked in, he curled up with his 5-year-old son Patrick, then later in the night went to sleep in his own bedroom. He awoke at dawn, decided to sleep in a little longer, then got up and played with Patrick.

The morning crawled. Leyland picked at his bacon and eggs, and Donnelly realized they wouldn't be sitting around much longer. Without cigarettes and coffee, and with the added pressure of opening day, Leyland was getting antsy. So he and Donnelly left for the ballpark at around 8 o'clock, stopped for a haircut along the way, and walked into an empty clubhouse at 9:30, seven hours before game time. Then Leyland went about his pre-game business: reviewing the batting and pitching charts, meeting with the coaches, and going over scouting reports. And, to some degree, working out.

Donnelly on Leyland's workout routine: "If Jim ever got on a treadmill, he'd break out in a rash."

But he still hadn't smoked a cigarette, or had a cup of coffee.

◆ ◆ ◆

You'd never convince an outsider there's anything special about opening day in South Florida. The mercury rose from dawn, then relaxed in the high 70s to low 80s with relatively little humidity, at least for Florida. But the weather had been perfect for months, so what did it matter? Winter is the good time of year in this part of the country, and the arrival of baseball season means increasingly hot, humid, and oppressive days. Forget about romantic visions of opening day as a time of renewal, a sign that spring is here. It means nothing to the South Florida baseball fan. The sun is shining, the sky is blue, just as it is for three hundred out of three hundred sixty-five days a year.

In their dreamiest states, baseball purists talk about how the foul lines stretch to infinity, starting at home plate and diverging forever into never-never land. At Pro Player Stadium, the foul lines bump right into bright, yellow foul poles that are shaped like giant pencils and have Office Depot written on the side. And if those lines did go on, through the fence and the stadium walls, they'd eventually bump into an angry alligator in the Everglades, just about ten miles to the west.

The purists enjoy waxing poetic about the cool of the grass and the reddish dirt. Well, the grass is never cool in South Florida, and although that reddish stuff in the infield is dirt, the reddish stuff on the warning tracks isn't: It's synthetic dirt, designed for better drainage.

More bad news for the baseball purists: Pro Player Stadium isn't even a base-ball stadium. It's a football stadium with three decks of seating areas on all four sides and scoreboards at two ends. For baseball, the outfield seats between the foul poles are covered with blue tarps, because blue tarps look better than empty orange seats.

And if, after seeing all of this, a baseball purist still insists on hanging onto his poetic vision, there's Billy the Marlin, the team's teal, big-finned mascot, to break his reverie. Or the GAP clothing store advertisements on the walls in the outfield gaps. Or this comment from billionaire Wayne Huizenga, on why he bought a base-ball team: "Bringing in the Marlins was a business deal because it brought more activity to Pro Player Stadium," which he owns.

But there was something special about this opening day. At Pro Player Stadium, the mood was unlike any other opener since 1993, when the franchise was new and the promise of a baseball game was all it took to fill the park. Charlie Hough threw out the first ball, which made sense because Hough threw the first pitch in Marlins history back in 1993. Now the Marlins were about to start a new stage of their history: Huizenga spent $115 million for a Major League franchise; then he had to spend another $89 million for one that could compete.

He would find out quickly whether his money was well-spent. In 1996, the Marlins lost Game One and opened with a record of 11-21. In 1995, the Marlins broke from the gate at 9-27. And in their second season, they were 7½ games out of first and five under .500 by April 26. All three times, they were out of the play-off race by May.

If the Marlins didn't get off to a fast start, there'd likely be grumbling in the clubhouse among Huizenga's millionaires. More importantly, the Marlins' attendance, which had been dwindling for the past three seasons, would continue dwindling, but this time it would be happening with one of the highest payrolls in baseball. High expenses. Low return. It's not a good formula for doing business.

"I don't believe it's early," Alex Fernandez said. "We have to play well at the beginning."

◆ ◆ ◆

The gates opened at 2 o'clock. Bonilla, realizing it's awfully hot in South Florida, opted for comfort over fashion and wore shorts and a T-shirt for batting practice. Fans, wearing Marlins T-shirts and the old style teal Marlins caps—the players now wore black caps—scooped up "limited edition" souvenirs, then rushed down to the field level seats and watched the two teams hit. A reporter from a local newspaper, opting for style over objectivity, wore a Marlins cap.

At around 4:20, radio and TV play-by-play man Joe Angel introduced the players. The loudest ovation was for Leyland, who clapped his hands in embarrassment when the fans wouldn't quiet down. Bonilla received a mixed reaction, mostly boos but some cheers. Conine, the most popular player for the first four seasons, received a warm reception, apparently having remained most popular despite the new arrivals. The crowd of 41,412, a sellout but the Marlins' lowest attendance of their five home openers because of the increased placement of blue tarps—the back five rows in the upper deck were covered—settled into their seats.

And high over Pro Player Stadium, part of the pre-game ceremony went astray. The part in question was Billy the Marlin's head, which was being worn by a Navy SEAL skydiver as he jumped out of a plane from seven thousand feet up. His scheduled mission was to deliver the game ball. He failed.

"The head is off! The head is off!" the Navy team leader shouted into his walkie-talkie, while somewhere in South Florida, Billy's head fell to the ground. *Bring Me The Head of Billy The Marlin.* As general manager Dave Dombrowski walked through the press box, the symbolism couldn't have been clearer: If the Marlins didn't have a winning season, it would be his head.

◆ ◆ ◆

Other than Billy losing his head, the day went almost perfectly. Brown pitched seven innings and allowed one hit, a high-hop single, and afterward he said, "Pitching with a lead is what it's all about. You can't win if you're not ahead."

No wonder Brown is considered one of the smartest players in baseball.

Alou, who struggled all spring with a variety of ailments, hit a solo homer in his first at-bat, and Brown left after seven, leading 4-0.

According to Brown's reasoning, that gave him a very good chance to win the game.

But at that point, Leyland might have been the only person in the ballpark who wasn't so sure. He sat in a corner of the dugout with his arms folded, paced in front of his players, and walked up and down the steps while furiously chewing on a piece of gum that would have to substitute for one of his beloved cigarettes.

He could have used an entire pack. Closer Robb Nen, who a day earlier had proclaimed himself mentally and physically ready for the season, discovered that pitching with a *big* lead is not what it's all about. Nen came in to pitch the ninth, and when Kevin Orie doubled home the Cubs' second run, the Marlins' lead was two and Chicago had the tying run on second. Finally, with the game on the line, Nen struck out Scott Servais for the third out, and Leyland relaxed for the first time in twenty-four hours.

"I got a little nervous at the end," he said while rocking back and forth in his office chair. "But I was nervous the whole game, so it didn't make any difference."

The air was clear of cigarette smoke and Leyland's desk was clear of coffee cups. A clubhouse attendant delivered Leyland's post game meal—no steak, no vodka martini, no baked potato, certainly no cigarettes or java. The manager paused, then considered his tangible reward for victory.

"I'll sleep good tonight," he said assuredly.

Maybe so, but only because he hadn't heard this conversation between Leiter and Dave O'Brien of the *Sun-Sentinel*.

O'BRIEN: Hey, Al. See if you can get us out of here in under three hours tomorrow.

LEITER: For that, I'm going to walk twelve.

◆ ◆ ◆

Leiter didn't walk twelve. He walked three, three too many. The Marlins won, 4-3, but with each pitch by Leiter, Leyland moved closer to breaking his no-smoking, no-coffee vow. Finally, in the third inning, Leyland snapped.

The next afternoon, Leyland's coffee mug was back on his desk, as was the ashtray and a pack of cigarettes.

"Leiter got me," Leyland grumbled. "I looked like Smokey the Bear by the third inning. I had fire coming out of both ears."

Vintage Leiter—falling behind hitters, running counts to three and two, then working his way out of trouble—was far too much for Leyland's frail nerves to stand. Leiter walked the leadoff hitter in the first inning, but escaped without any damage. He walked the leadoff hitter again in the fifth, but didn't allow a run. Finally, in the sixth inning, with the Marlins leading 4-0, Leiter and Leyland both had their personal comings-apart. Without any idea why he was doing what he was doing, Leiter started aiming his pitches and lost what was left of his control.

As did Leyland. He waved in Rick Helling from the bullpen, then went back to a corner of the dugout and lit up another cigarette. Then another. And another. Leyland's lungs seemed to be in serious danger when he called on Nen to pitch the ninth, but this time, in a real save situation, Nen retired the side in order.

Leyland celebrated with another smoke.

29

◆ ◆ ◆

On Tuesday, Alex Fernandez had let everybody know that family is more important than baseball. "I'm a husband and a father first, then I'm a baseball player,"
Fernández said. "I have my priorities straight."

He was standing in front of his locker with his shorts pulled halfway down his
buttocks when he said it, and the whole scene was altogether touching. It was also
the most insightful thing any reporter would hear him say until after he pitched
Thursday night. Not only did Fernandez not plan on speaking to the media on his
pitching days, but he didn't plan on speaking the day before he pitched. He had
established the routine as a rookie for the White Sox in 1990 and he didn't plan
on changing it now.

"You won't want to talk to me again until October 30," Fernandez promised.

"October 30?"

"Yeah," he said. "When the World Series is over."

◆ ◆ ◆

Sheffield finally signed his six year, $61 million contract extension a few hours
before Wednesday's game, so Bonilla said, "I know who's paying every time I go
out to dinner. I'll have no problem sliding that check over to his side."

Sheffield would make $6.1 million in 1997, and then $10 million-plus per year
for the remainder of his contract. Bonilla was making $23.3 million over four years,
or about $6 million per. Which meant that the next time they went out for dinner,
Sheffield and Bonilla could pick up the checks for every diner in the room, and
still not worry about paying the next month's mortgage.

Sheffield already appeared to have spent a large portion of his winnings on ostentatious jewelry. He sat at the press conference wearing a diamond watch on one
wrist, a diamond bracelet on the other, and big diamond studs in both ears. He looked
like a rich man and he smiled like a rich man. And if he invested his money wisely,
the 3-year-old boy sitting in his lap would someday be a rich man, too. That was
his son, Gary Jr.

The deal made Sheffield the wealthiest player in baseball history and contributed
to the grave-spin that Branch Rickey—former cheap Major League Baseball team
owner—and Mickey Mantle—former grossly underpaid superstar—must have been
experiencing six feet under. Including the Marlins' $11 million option for the 2004
season, the total value of Sheffield's contract was $72 million.

Put into perspective, if that's possible, $72 million is about a quarter of what
it would cost to build a new domed stadium in South Florida. It is two-thirds the
entire cost of Pro Player Stadium.

With $72 million, Gary Sheffield could take his buddy Bobby Bonilla out for
lavish $100 dinners and pick up the check every day for the next 1,972 years.

Before taxes, that's 21,884,498 Big Mac Extra Value Meals at McDonald's. Over
$80,000 for each RBI in a one hundred twenty-RBI season. It's . . . ah, forget about
it. There is no such thing as perspective when you're talking about that kind of money.

"I'm spaced out, basically," Sheffield said. "Am I worth it? All I can say is, I think the Marlins think so. I can just do my job and be rewarded for it."

Did he say rewarded? There are words to describe what it means to play baseball for a living and get paid that kind of money. Rewarded doesn't go nearly far enough.

As for general manager Dave Dombrowski, here was the ultimate proof he was willing to let bygones be bygones. The previous summer, Sheffield had called him a liar and questioned his moves as general manager. And this was how Dombrowski responded—by paying him more than any baseball player had ever been paid.

◆ ◆ ◆

On Thursday, Leyland declared that not only didn't he know anything about hitting, but he didn't know anything about pitching, either. A reporter asked whether he planned on saying anything to Alex Fernandez about his start that night and Leyland said, "What am I going to say to him? I don't know anything about pitching. I'm not going to say anything about hitting or pitching. No way."

In 1966, his best minor league season, Leyland batted .243 with sixteen RBIs.

Another thing Leyland liked telling reporters was that he didn't know more about executing hit-and-runs, sacrifices, and double steals than any other manager. Huizenga would have been comforted to know his money was buying a man of special talents.

◆ ◆ ◆

Apparently, Leyland did know something about an area of the Marlins' operation called "in-game entertainment." Now, to the uninitiated, in-game entertainment might mean strikeouts, home runs, great fielding plays, and maybe an occasional dirt-kicking argument between the umpire and a manager. Well, not quite. In the 1990s, in-game entertainment refers to everything but the game. For the Marlins, it's Billy the Marlin doing the hokey-pokey on top of the dugout, a screaming P.A. announcer, ultra-loud music videos, and a band of backpack-wearing glee-teamers called The Bleacher Brigade sling-shotting T-shirts into the crowd.

In-game entertainment is Leyland's idea of "silly stuff."

In-game entertainment is a lot of people's idea of "silly stuff."

But it wasn't silly stuff to the Marlins' front office workers. In-game entertainment, they had long ago decided, was a necessary way of attracting fans who were relatively new to Major League Baseball.

Leyland disagreed. The problem was, instead of expressing his opinion to the front office staff, he expressed it to a national publication.

An article in *The Sporting News,* which painted Leyland as an old-school baseball man, discussed his desire to "shout down the louts who pump up the marketing volume in the ballpark." The article quoted him as saying: "I personally think baseball makes a mistake by trying to create too many sideshows through marketing, instead of focusing on what the real product is. I think we're trying to be too creative and have too much gingerbread surrounding the game. I'm sure Mr. Huizenga isn't going to like this, but I think we're trying to force extra entertainment on the fans, instead of bringing the people out there for what they supposedly came to see . . . I mean, you don't need any tricks."

These comments weren't taken well by the fifty or so Marlins front office staffers whose jobs, directly or indirectly, were involved with silly stuff. What Leyland had done in *The Sporting News* was belittle the entire front office.

That would have been OK if Leyland had criticized them privately. Many of them agreed with his opinions and had voiced their concerns at staff meetings. The Marlins had already toned down their silly stuff by getting rid of the Macarena—MACARENA. SILLY DANCE CRAZE. R.I.P. was written on a mock grave in the publicity office—and between-innings games such as You Rate The Record.

What the Marlins' front office staffers didn't understand was why Leyland had to criticize them through a national publication. The article was a sore subject with just about everyone in the front office and Don Smiley let Leyland know that he shouldn't have opened his mouth. Leyland, who was so reluctant to criticize his baseball peers and show off his baseball knowledge, saw nothing wrong with badmouthing people who were, in reality, his co-workers.

Co-workers, meaning that they all had their checks signed by the same man.

It made them wonder whether Leyland was really the salt-of-the-earth, midwestern gentleman he had made himself out to be.

◆ ◆ ◆

Every game this season, the Marlins' home attendance would be looked upon with nearly as much interest as the outcome itself. As Fernandez walked to the mound Thursday night for the third game of the Cubs series, sections of the upper level were empty and only a smattering of fans sat in the outfield seats downstairs. But by the time Conine hit a grand slam in the bottom of the first, the lower level was nearly full, and only the last four sections on each side of the upper deck had large patches of empty seats.

"I told you, Cubans run late all the time," Fernandez said later. "I know I'm just like that, too. They're late, always."

The announced attendance of 32,592, though far below the sellout the Marlins had hoped for when they signed Fernandez, was about ten thousand more than what the Marlins feared might turn out. Just a week earlier, Don Smiley had sat in the dugout at Space Coast Stadium and worried aloud that Alex Fernandez Night would attract the smallest crowd of the homestand. That day, Smiley was grasping onto the hope that the entire Cuban population of Miami could be pigeonholed as procrastinators, while Fernandez put a blunter slant on the matter.

REPORTER: "Maybe going to a baseball game isn't high on their list of priorities."

FERNANDEZ: "Exactly. Maybe they're cheap down there."

Fernandez was joking then, but he was dead serious when he used the opportunity to remind the Marlins' marketing department that they could no longer depend upon his smiling face and personal appearances to help sell tickets. The way Fernandez saw it, he had done his job during the off-season.

"I'm here to win some games for them and pitch two hundred-plus innings," he said. "That's all I'm concerned about. I'm not worried about putting people in the seats. I don't worry about that. And if they expect me to, they're in for a long year."

The lesson of Fernandez's first start was that he wouldn't have a Fernando Valenzuela-like effect on the Marlins' attendance. When the Mexican-born Valenzuela came to the Dodgers in the early 1980s, nearly every game he pitched at Dodger Stadium was sold out. Recently, Japanese pitcher Hideo Nomo had been having a similar effect on the Dodgers' attendance.

Fernandez was no Valenzuela, no Nomo.

◆ ◆ ◆

Fernandez walked from the dugout to the mound for the first inning and felt different from any of the other one hundred ninety-nine times he had made that trip in his major league career. It was the feeling that when you're a Cuban American in South Florida, you're pitching for every other Cuban American in South Florida. Angel and Nelly Fernandez, Alex's parents, knew it, too. On their way to the ballpark, they stopped at a church and prayed for their son.

As the crowd filed in, Fernandez threw his first pitch as a Marlin, a low, outside fastball. Later in the inning, he made a nice grab on a sharp grounder up the middle. His night ended in the seventh inning after hitting Scott Servais with a pitch, but by that time the Marlins had a comfortable lead. Leyland removed him from the game and Fernandez walked off to a standing ovation, having allowed only one run in 6⅔ innings. Fernandez tipped his cap. Later, after an 8-2 Marlins win, he revealed the gesture was meant for his teammates, not the crowd.

But he also said, "I felt that standing ovation behind me, and it was meaningful for me. It's something you have to be able to go through to be able to explain it, to experience it. You can't say it felt great. It was bigger than great, and I'm thankful for that."

There's an aspect of Fernandez's personality that's difficult to figure. Perhaps it's because he had established a limit to how much of himself he'll reveal to the public. Once in a while he'd stray over that line, but not for long.

Fernandez on what the game meant to him: "It wasn't Alex Fernandez Night. It was a Marlins night."

But then: "I've pitched in the playoffs before, which were great feelings, and pitched very well, but it was something different. It was just because of my background, my friends here, the people that really know me. There were a lot of people out there that know me, a lot of people I've been associated with."

In other words, it was Alex Fernandez Night.

◆ ◆ ◆

Bonilla, whose fielding had been spotty during the spring, made his first error of the season in the Fernandez game. An easy grounder skipped under his glove, but he refused to blame the error on a bad hop.

"I can fuck up some shit!" Bonilla said, grinning and nodding. "I can create some bad hops."

Bonilla also pointed out that bad hops didn't seem to bother Castillo or Renteria. That's why the Marlins' infield fielding gameplan went like this: Renteria, at short-stop, would go after everything. Bonilla would go after anything that Renteria couldn't get to as long as it was hit right at him.

◆ ◆ ◆

Leyland winced whenever he heard the Marlins described as having the perfect lineup, because he realized perfection depended upon Charles Johnson hitting better than .218, his 1996 average, and Castillo figuring out how to get the ball out of the infield.

As for the starting rotation, he rightly felt comfortable—or as close as Leyland gets to comfortable—with his top three of Brown-Leiter-Fernandez. But the effectiveness of Pat Rapp and Tony Saunders, his fourth and fifth starters, could decide how the season played out. The formula is simple: Win every two of three games with your first three, split with your next two, and you have a .600 club, ninety-seven wins, and a pennant contender.

Rapp, who had pitched well all spring, proved his ability to create nervous energy by going out on the mound Friday night against the Reds and pitching like he did in 1996. Which is to say, badly. He was fine until the fifth inning, but fell apart after diving for a bunt with two outs. He couldn't finish the inning and walked back to the dugout having allowed three runs and five walks.

Then, with the Marlins leading, 6-3, Mark Hutton relieved Felix Heredia in the seventh and proved that maybe Leyland was wrong. Maybe Hutton should have been the No. 5 starter. Hutton had been saying all along he didn't belong in the bullpen, and he proved this by pitching a poor one-third of an inning in relief, allowing a homer, three walks, and five runs. The Marlins lost for the first time, 9-7.

The first test for the No. 4 starter was ugly. An early test for Johnson turned out better: He homered in the fifth.

◆ ◆ ◆

A major league clubhouse is full of rich men, but there isn't a workplace in the world where the economic gap between wealthiest and least wealthy is so wide. Take the Marlins' clubhouse. On one side, Gary Sheffield, Bobby Bonilla, and Devon White, would cash more than $15 million in before-taxes paychecks in 1997. And on the opposite side of the clubhouse were Charles Johnson and rookie pitcher Tony Saunders. Combined 1997 salaries: $440,000.

So while Sheffield was wondering about where to buy his next diamond, Saunders, who was earning the major league minimum of $150,000, was thinking about where it was prudent to live.

"Are you renting or buying?" a reporter asked.

"Oh, I think I'll always rent in Miami," Saunders said. "I don't make enough money to buy a house."

Well, there you have it. Surrounded by such wealth, Saunders might have thought he wasn't well off. Compared to most of the people standing around him, he wasn't. But he was compared to the rest of the world. With an annual salary of $150,000, Tony and his wife, Joyce, could have bought a very nice house. He just didn't realize it.

Saunders did know that he had come a long way in five years, from the day Marlins scout Ty Brown signed him as an undrafted free agent for $1,000 to this Saturday afternoon, three hours prior to his major league debut. Yet, he showed no outward signs of nervousness as he sat in the dugout with his older brother Billy, as if this was a normal day. In a way, it had been: He got up early, picked up his brother at the airport, went home, ate lunch, sat around, and then left for the ballpark in the middle of the afternoon.

And at night, he would pitch against the Cincinnati Reds with 38,598 fans watching.

"I'm probably more nervous than he is," said Billy, who taught his brother the changeup he used seventy-five percent of the time. "You'd never know he's about to pitch in a major league game. It's hard to believe he's only 22, but that probably comes from hanging out with older kids. He's used to playing with older kids."

"I guess the Cincinnati Reds qualify as older kids," Billy was told.

He laughed at that. "I guess so."

◆ ◆ ◆

The older kids—Deion Sanders, Barry Larkin, Reggie Sanders, and Hal Morris—didn't fare well against the rookie. Saunders pitched 6⅔ innings, allowed three runs on four hits, and at one point retired seventeen in a row. He was supported by solid fielding. Alou, Renteria, Sheffield, and Bonilla all made fine plays. Most importantly for the Marlins, they received a strong performance from their fifth starter, one day after getting a bad one from their fourth starter. Leyland called Saunders "outstanding."

The Marlins won, 4-3, in eleven innings on an inside-the-park home run and an RBI single by Renteria, who was applauded by his teammates when he walked into the clubhouse after conducting a TV interview. But the story of the night was Saunders, who pitched like a phenom, not like a bargain-basement amateur free agent.

"The special thing about this is that this isn't a kid who signed for $10.5 million and his agent is looking for the last $35,000," said Ty Brown, who the Marlins had flown in for the game. "This is an old-time baseball story about a kid who didn't get a million dollars and still made it. We could have signed him for a can of Skoal. This is a kid who would have given me $1,000 to sign. I feel like a stepdad to him, like Uncle Ty."

Brown spoke to reporters for a few minutes, then walked over to Saunders' stall. The pitcher was dressed modestly in blue jeans, new sneakers, and a blue print polo shirt. Across the room, Sheffield was carefully buttoning one of his new designer suits. Both of them had been lauded by the crowd on this night—Sheffield with chants of "Gah-ree!" when he came to bat in the seventh, and Saunders with a standing ovation when he left the game—but for only one of them was the game memorable.

"That's a feeling I'll never forget, no matter how many times it happens, walking off that field tonight," Saunders said. "It's overwhelming. This is what I've been playing baseball for all my life."

◆ ◆ ◆

Sheffield said, "I could go out and do what Tony Gwynn does, but I chose to have the whole package. It's going to affect the batting average sometimes."

Gwynn, a singles and doubles hitter, had led the National League in batting seven times. He had also never had a contract worth anything near the value of Sheffield's new one. Power hitters get the big bucks.

Gwynn, however, gets pitches to hit. In 1996, Sheffield walked one hundred forty-two times, far more than Gwynn's total for the past three seasons combined. The way opposing managers saw it, getting hurt by Sheffield was worse than getting hurt by Gwynn, because Sheffield's bruises were home runs, while Gwynn's were singles.

Key lesson of opening week: Teams had no intention of pitching to Sheffield. They'd rather walk him and take their chances with Bonilla. Cubs manager Jim Riggleman said his team wouldn't pitch to Sheffield until the summer. Confessed Reds pitching coach Don Gullett: "If you see us give Gary Sheffield a pitch to hit, it's because we made a mistake."

Sheffield was walked or hit by a pitch in ten of fifteen plate appearances against the Cubs and didn't get many more pitches to hit against the Reds.

"He has the fastest bat speed I've seen," Leyland said. "Unfortunately, I haven't seen it this week. They walk him every damn time."

Sheffield tried hiding his frustration, but he was obviously flustered. The Reds took the strategy a little too far in the seventh inning on Sunday when, with the game tied, they pitched around Sheffield and ended up putting the potential winning run on base. Sheffield came around to score when Alou, John Cangelosi, and Conine also walked.

Leyland said teams were trying to mess with Sheffield's mind and praised his star for not letting it affect him. But after the Chicago series, Sheffield had no trouble recalling exactly how many hittable pitches he saw in his fifteen plate appearances.

"Two, and I was actually taking the two that I saw," Sheffield said. "Hopefully, this isn't going to last for a long time. But it doesn't make the game fun and it's tough for me."

Besides, the Marlins weren't paying $61 million for a guy who walked a lot.

◆ ◆ ◆

Opening week had been full of good signs for the Marlins. They had four crowds of more than thirty thousand and drew 198,929 for the homestand, just short of the two hundred thousand they had hoped for. On Sunday, they won for the fifth time in six games, 3-2, behind another seven strong innings by Brown. They were off to their best start ever and in first place, a game ahead of the Braves.

"The confidence level is up," Conine said. "Confidence is a big part of baseball and we've got it right now."

Everything was going well for the Marlins.

Almost everything. Billy the Marlin's head was still missing. And Leyland's menu needed fixing. He was sitting in his office after the final game against the Reds, having just finishing answering one question after another about the Marlins' fast start.

"I never talk about fast starts because you set yourself up," Leyland said. "What happens if you don't get off to a fast start? Do you cancel the schedule May 1 or May 15? The record, I can't worry about that."

Besides, Leyland had other things to worry about, like eating. A clubhouse attendant had placed a hotplate on his desk, and Leyland fumbled with the lid, then picked up a fork and brought a hunk of food to his mouth.

"Ahhh, shit," Leyland moaned as he dropped his fork onto the plate. "Meat loaf. Goddamnit."

It was a temporary problem. There were no sure things for the rest of the season, but there was this: No way would the manager ever be fed meatloaf again. As for Billy's head, the search continued.

3

If a One Hundred-Pound Chimpanzee Can Throw a Three Hundred-Pound Object with One Arm, Then How Far Can It Hit a Baseball?

April 8, 10 at Chicago
April 11, 12, 13 at Cincinnati
April 15, 16, 17 vs. St. Louis
April 18, 19, 20 at San Francisco
April 22, 23 at Colorado

Chicago was frozen, so most of the Marlins stayed inside on Monday, an off day. A few bundled up, hopped into cabs, and attended the Chicago Bulls basketball game, but for the rest, Chicago during the second week of April was no time for walks along Lake Michigan and bar-hopping downtown. Even the famous ivy that covers the outfield fence at Wrigley Field hadn't yet bloomed.

In 1997, Major League Baseball had come up with the brilliant idea of scheduling as many games as possible during the first week of the season in warm cities. That it took so many years to recognize the obvious didn't speak well for the schedule makers at Major League Baseball, but they failed to take this idea a step further. The *second* week of April in Chicago is as cold as the first. The wind chill made the air feel like one degree on Tuesday, April 8, opening day at Wrigley, and the Marlins were bundled up and shivering in their tropical teal and white parkas and ski masks.

"It was miserable," Leyland said. "As cold as I've ever been. I can usually sit for a game, but I was walking around. I could not sit still. I was freezing my ass off, and I know the players were, too."

The Marlins won anyway, 5-3, on a two-run double in the seventh by Charles Johnson that preserved another strong outing by Leiter. The big news: The Cubs pitched to Sheffield, who made them pay with a homer and a double. Oh, and there

38

was nearly a bench-clearing brawl when Cubs pitcher Frank Castillo tagged Devon White a little too hard, and White shoved him back.

"He's lucky I didn't knock him out," White said.

◆ ◆ ◆

Gregg Zaun figured something was wrong when Charles Johnson wasn't in his regular batting practice group Thursday morning. So later, when he was shagging flyballs in the outfield and saw Leyland trudging in his direction, he had an idea his day would be more eventful than expected.

Zaun nudged Kevin Brown. "Watch this," he said. "I'm catching."

Leyland walked up to him and stopped.

"You're catching," he said.

The temperature was thirty-seven degrees, the wind chill made it feel like thirteen, and Zaun had planned on spending the afternoon bundled up and sitting as near a heater as possible. Instead, he would spend it in a squat, his right hand bare to the elements, trying to fend off the cold with only a long, cotton undershirt and a baseball jersey to protect him. Johnson had a twinge in his shoulder and Leyland didn't want to risk making it worse on such a cold day. Better, he thought, to throw Zaun to the elements.

But from the first pitch Alex Fernandez threw in the bottom of the first inning, it wouldn't have mattered who was behind the plate. Usually when a pitcher is unhittable, he moves his pitches around, challenging inside with a fastball to back the hitter off, then going outside with a nasty breaking pitch. Up, down. Inside, outside. Not Fernandez. He kept placing his pitches in the same spot—low and on the outside corner. As the game continued and his dominance increased, Zaun kept setting up further and further outside and the umpire gave them the strike calls.

"When Alex has control like he had today, it makes a catcher's job easy," Leyland said. "When he put the glove there, most of the pitches were there, or real close."

Between innings, Fernandez sat on a chair in the tunnel leading back to the clubhouse, trying to stay warm. Zaun stayed out of the way. If Fernandez didn't want to talk to him, he didn't try to talk to Fernandez. For six innings, Zaun's only concern was winning the game, but when Fernandez went three-up, three-down in the seventh, his focus changed. He wanted the no-hitter badly.

"What surprised me was that nobody in the stands was saying anything," Zaun said. "I thought the drunken idiots in Chicago would be yelling, 'No-hitter! No-hitter!' but nobody in the stands said anything. I guess they figured the Cubs are 0-7, and if they're going to go 0-8, they might as well see a no-hitter."

Fernandez retired the Cubs on nine pitches in the eighth. He was still throwing everything outside and low, and although the Cubs knew what was coming, they couldn't hit it. Sitting in the dugout, three outs away from his first career no-hitter, Fernandez received some advice from pitching coach Larry Rothschild. It was the obvious stuff: Concentrate on the hitter. Don't think more than one pitch ahead. Zaun, who had quit chewing tobacco during the off-season and sometimes had trouble sitting still, surprised himself by staying calm. Then the Marlins went

39

down in the ninth, and Zaun's excitement built as he walked out for the bottom of the inning.

Fernandez started off pinch hitter Dave Clark with a slider on the outside corner. Clark looked at the next pitch for a ball, fouled off strike two, and didn't even take the bat off his shoulders as Fernandez got the strike call on another low, outside slider. Fernandez was two outs away.

Dave Hansen, another pinch hitter who hit .221 in 1996, came up next in what looked like a mismatch. The count was two and two when Hansen reached to foul off two low, outside breaking pitches.

"I had a feeling after breaking ball, breaking ball, breaking ball, and with Hansen pulling off the ball, that if we got a good, low fastball on the outside corner, we'd get him," Zaun said. "Usually the book on him is pitch him in, but the way he was pulling off, I didn't think pitching in would be a good idea. He was pulling off, almost cheating to get to a ball inside."

Zaun silently urged on Fernandez. Hansen guessed wrong again on Fernandez's seventh pitch of the at-bat, a fastball on the outer corner of the plate. But it wasn't low enough. Three or four inches higher, maybe, and Fernandez would have had his man, but the pitch ended up belt high. Hansen swung awkwardly and sent a hard ground ball toward the mound.

Fernandez was finishing his follow-through as the ball bounced toward him. Castillo and Renteria raced toward second base in case the ball got past the mound. Fernandez stuck out his glove, but the ball caromed off of his right thigh and toward shortstop. Castillo and Renteria tried to reverse direction, but they were too late. Hansen was safe at first with the Cubs' first hit of the game.

"You know as soon as the ball is hit whether there's a chance for it to be a hit," Zaun said. "He hit it pretty good and it hit Alex in the thigh and got away from him in an awkward manner. I thought that was peculiar, because normally the ball bounces in front of him, and then he's out."

Fernandez, although disappointed with himself for not making the play, now had to worry about protecting a 1-0 lead. And when he struck out Ryne Sandberg for the fourth time, he had his imperfect game: A one-hit shutout that was not only the pitcher's best game ever, but the best game Zaun had ever caught, too.

◆ ◆ ◆

The cold weather and good pitching followed the Marlins to Cincinnati, where they extended their winning streak to five with a 10-0 win over the Reds on Friday. Rapp, in his second start of the season, bounced back from his previous poor outing and pitched a complete game, but the Marlins' bats went cold for the final two games and they lost both.

◆ ◆ ◆

Monday, April 14, was an off-day and the manager used his time well. He took his son, Patrick, and his daughter, Kellie, to Lion Country Safari, a zoo in which visitors drive through a natural habitat. The kids took pictures from behind the car window—nobody would dare roll it down when wild lions were roaming around— and Leyland listened intently to the taped cassette guide. He couldn't believe what he was hearing.

"It's pretty interesting," Leyland recounted the next day. "They said they had a chimpanzee there, and it said a one hundred-pound chimpanzee can throw a three hundred-pound object with one arm. A three hundred-pound object, one arm."

Leyland couldn't get over this. Twice he repeated the information about the one hundred-pound chimpanzee and its million dollar arm, as if it was the most amazing thing he had ever heard. It wasn't hard to read Leyland's mind: *If a one hundred-pound chimpanzee can throw a three hundred-pound object with one arm, then how far can it hit a baseball?*

◆ ◆ ◆

Rain canceled batting practice for the Marlins and Cardinals on Tuesday, so Tony La Russa sat in the visiting manager's office at Pro Player Stadium telling stories about his friend Jim Leyland. La Russa and Leyland go way back, to 1982 when La Russa was managing the White Sox and hired Leyland as his third base coach. To this day, Leyland speaks of La Russa as the man who "made me a major league manager. No doubt about it."

La Russa told about the time in 1985, when he got suspended for two games, and Leyland managed in his place.

"I was watching from the press box in Milwaukee and they were difficult games, but he was on time with every move," La Russa recalled. "He wanted to know if I should be at a phone to communicate with him, and I said, 'For what?' The one difference between me and him was that smoke kept coming from the dugout. He had six cigarettes lit at one time.

"When he came to Chicago, he had been a manager for eleven years and I for only three and a half, and we had these conversations about who was a better manager. If you put his hand on a Bible, he'd have said it was him. Tommy Lasorda once told me, 'He's a great manager. The best manager in baseball.' His personality's the best I've ever seen for keeping a club going all year long. I think I have a good understanding of players, but I've never seen anyone that can't play for Jim."

The relationship between La Russa and Leyland had changed over the past two years in a way that saddened both of them. When La Russa was managing in the American League, they talked by phone a few times a week. Then La Russa broke their understanding to never manage in the same league and took the job with the Cardinals in 1996. Although they spoke to each other less frequently, their friendship remained strong.

"I don't think we're real different," La Russa said. "We have much more in common. He can sing. I can't sing. He tells better jokes than I do."

◆ ◆ ◆

The Marlins lost their third straight, 9-3, to the Cardinals in the series opener, and after the game Leyland snapped at a reporter who asked about moving up Conine in the order. Conine was hitting .410 with nine RBIs, while Bonilla hadn't had an RBI since opening week.

"I will not talk about changing lineups," Leyland insisted. "I'm not going to panic. I like talking about baseball, but that's silly stuff."

He proceeded to talk about his lineup for the next five minutes.

"One thing I can assure you is that nobody down here is going to panic," Leyland said. "That sends a real bad message. This is not a damn college football game on a weekend, a rah-rah game. We play one hundred sixty-two games. This is my team and I like my team. Luis Castillo is my leadoff man and I like Luis Castillo as my leadoff man. And Edgar Renteria hits second and Sheffield hits third. I like our team. We're not going to win every game. The best teams lose sixty something. Maybe seventy. The best."

"Do you have to keep reminding yourself of that?" a reporter asked.

Leyland looked up. "No," he said. "I have to keep reminding you guys of that."

He should have reminded his team, too. The clubhouse emptied quickly after the loss, leaving publicity director Ron Colangelo searching hard to find a guest for WQAM's morning show. Sheffield spoke briefly to reporters and went home. Bonilla was nowhere to be found. And Fernandez, who had allowed four runs in six innings, said, "I'm too strong a guy to let this bother me."

The next night, Sheffield flipped his bat in anger after taking a four-pitch walk in the first inning, and made the Cardinals pay for pitching to him in the third by hitting a hanging changeup into the second level behind the leftfield fence. *Wow, I finally hit one!* Sheffield said to himself as the ball left his bat. The Marlins won, 2-1, and just like that, the team was in a jovial mood.

The lineup hadn't changed, either.

◆ ◆ ◆

The talk in the manager's office came around to the Cardinals' next stop, Honolulu, Hawaii, for a weekend series against the San Diego Padres. Leyland was asked whether he would mind playing in Hawaii and answered, "I go wherever the bus takes me."

And Joe Angel, the Marlins' play-by-play man, reminded him, "The bus isn't going to take you to Hawaii."

◆ ◆ ◆

Leyland on South Florida rain, which canceled batting practice Tuesday and Wednesday and forced the Marlins to hit indoors: "That's all part of it."

According to Leyland, other things that are "all part of it" include injuries, slumps, bad breaks, tough losses, and making cuts in spring training. Apparently, "It" is very big. "It" is huge.

◆ ◆ ◆

The final day of the three-game stopover at Pro Player Stadium started with Fernandez mooning one of the trainers, sunny skies and outdoor batting practice for the first time all week, and Leyland reflecting the weather with a sunny disposition in the clubhouse. The Marlins had ended their three-game losing streak the night before and nobody was asking Leyland about his lineup.

The day ended with the rap group Freak Nasty blasting on the clubhouse stereo, Mark Hutton putting on an Ozzy Osborne T-shirt, and Kevin Brown frowning as if he'd rather bite the head off of one of Ozzy's live rats than talk to the media. Julio Sarmiento, the Marlins' assistant director of publicity, uncomfortably excused Brown by saying he was in a hurry to make the plane, but the rest of the players were going on the same flight, and they were in no great hurry. They appeared to be pretty happy.

As well they should have been. Jeff Conine stood a few feet in front of the blaring speakers, stiffly wiggling his hips and looking more like The All American Boy than a ghetto hip-hopper. That morning, he had woken up with a virus. Then, after sitting on the bench for eight and a half innings, he homered with one out in the ninth for a 2-1 Marlins win.

"I wish I could end every day the same way," Conine said.

Halfway across the room, Zaun was patiently explaining a tough day behind the plate. Meanwhile, Brown was grabbing his clothing and heading off to a quiet place to change. Any place would do, as long as it was off-limits to the media. After walking five and getting pulled after the seventh inning, Brown was in no mood to talk about himself.

◆ ◆ ◆

Sheffield had resisted the urge to beat the life out of pitcher Todd Stottlemyre after getting hit under the armpit by a pitch in the first inning. Then he explained himself by saying, "I'm not a violent person in that manner on the field."

Brown, however, was a violent person in this manner on the field: He retaliated by waiting for Stottlemyre to bat, then threw at him three times. This was unusual because pitchers usually don't take out their anger on other pitchers. They usually take out their anger on the other pitcher's teammates. But Brown, who is about as ornery and mean as pitchers come, passed up the opportunity to throw at five different Cardinals batters before Stottlemyre came up in the top of the third.

The revenge backfired. Zaun fumbled a pitchout, allowing a run to score, then Brown walked Stottlemyre.

Leyland had been furious in the dugout when Sheffield got hit and he didn't disguise his anger after the game. He came as close as he ever would to criticizing his friend La Russa when he said, "A lot of guys are being pitched inside, but it's strange that only Sheffield is getting hit." It was a carefully worded, yet blatant, accusation: Teams were throwing at Sheffield.

Sheffield, who had already been hit by four pitches, was angry yet controlled. "It's been like that all year," he said. "It's funny that I didn't get hit much in the

43

spring and now the season starts, they're pitching around me and hitting me with the ball. It's frustrating."

And Brown said . . . well, Brown said nothing.

◆ ◆ ◆

Conine's game-winning homer did wonders for the Marlins' spirits on the six-hour flight from Miami to San Francisco, but it did nothing for his health. He spent the entire time rushing back and forth from his seat to the lavatory and he wasn't feeling any better when the plane landed or the next day. Neither were the Marlins.

A rainy, miserable night at 3Com Park, the former Candlestick Park, ended with Robb Nen pitching the ninth inning in a downpour. He couldn't protect a 4-2 lead and the Marlins lost, 5-4.

The worst was yet to come. Bizarro Baseball. The sun came out just in time Saturday afternoon for Sheffield to lose an inning-ending fly ball in the sun, allowing two runs to score, and the Giants to win, 3-2. The Marlins' hitting slump continued Sunday afternoon. White missed his fourth straight game because of an aching knee. Bonilla received two cortisone shots in the left wrist he had injured lifting weights in spring training. Fernandez pitched well, but the Marlins lost, 2-0.

Hmmm . . . If a one hundred-pound chimpanzee can throw a three hundred-pound object with one arm . . .

A trip to Colorado and the thin air of Coors Field didn't cure their woes. The Rockies hit, the Marlins didn't, losing 13-4 and 7-3, to drop four games behind the Braves. Rapp's pitching line in the first game was memorable: 2⅔ innings, thirteen hits, ten runs, all earned.

After their 8-1 start, the Marlins were an average team at 10-9, and their seven straight road losses were an unwelcome reminder of 1996, when they were nearly unbeatable at home and inept on the road. Leyland had looked forward to the chance to show off his team on the road. Instead, they were getting shown up, and he wasn't taking lightly their bad baserunning, poor fielding, and untimely hitting.

"This team's not playing as aggressive or confident as I think it should," Leyland said. "In San Francisco, I heard a couple of people saying this was a tough place for us to play, and that's bullshit. If you play well, you can win in a phone booth. This team can win anywhere it plays. If we have to come out here at 2 o'clock every day, that's what we'll do. We haven't played very well and I'm not very happy."

The season was twenty-three days old, but Bonilla had no RBIs in thirteen games and no homers for the season. The managers who feared Sheffield for two weeks were finally letting their pitchers take their chances, and Sheffield wasn't making them pay. Castillo wasn't getting on base in the leadoff spot. Moises Alou was the sole source of offense. Leyland's daring baserunning gambits were mostly turning into outs.

That one hundred-pound chimpanzee was sounding better every day.

The attendance picture wasn't any brighter. Fierce late afternoon rains had kept the crowds down for the first two games of the St. Louis series, and only 18,416 showed up for Fernandez's second home start, just a week after he had nearly pitched a no-hitter. Sellouts were expected for the first two games of an upcoming week-end series against the Dodgers, but competition for the local sports fan's attention was intensifying. The Panthers were in the NHL playoffs and the Heat was in the NBA playoffs. If the Marlins didn't start winning, home and away, they would soon get lost in the South Florida shuffle.

NATIONAL LEAGUE EAST STANDINGS

	W	L	Pct.	GB
Atlanta	14	5	.737	—
Marlins	**10**	**9**	**.526**	**4**
Montreal	9	9	.500	4.5
New York	8	12	.400	6.5
Philadelphia	6	13	.316	8

4

Split Personalities

April 25, 26, 27 vs. Los Angeles
April 28, 29 vs. San Diego
April 30, May 1 at St. Louis
May 2, 3, 4 at Houston
May 5, 6 vs. Pittsburgh

The Marlins have a security guard stationed outside their clubhouse entrance, but a psychologist would be more appropriate. The good doctor could hold up color-coded cards indicating approximately what mood the manager and the players were in on any given day. Most of the time, it would have a lot to do with whether the team was winning or losing, but sometimes, it wouldn't have to do with anything.

Maybe they'd be better off with a psychic.

So you take the plunge. You take the walk. Through the press gate at the ball-park, past the friendly white-haired guard, and then down a long, carpeted hall-way. Hang a right, then continue through the dimly lit tunnel that circles the stadium. Networks of exposed wires and giant water pipes hang from the ceiling, but when you walk through the clubhouse door, a gush of cool air sweeps over you and with your next steps you're journeying into a lush, private world.

The activities are limited for the ballplayers who work here. They might be loung-ing on the new black leather couches and recliners that greeted them upon their return from the road trip—"That must be our reward for losing five straight," one player joked—or watching a baseball game or the *Fitness America Pageant* on ESPN2 and commenting lasciviously on the shapely, toned bodies that fill the screen.

Jeff Conine might be sneaking up on a reporter and barking loudly in his ear. Because most adults don't expect grown men to sneak up on them and bark loudly in their ears, the surprise usually works. Alex Fernandez might be bending over, spreading his butt cheeks, and mooning a teammate or clubhouse man.

Others are small talking, working out in the weight room, trying out a new bat or a new pair of spikes, or answering a reporter's questions. There is not a great deal to do here, but these players do it for a long time. For a night game, the play-ers' days start when they arrive at the ballpark at around 3 o'clock and often don't end until nearly midnight.

On Friday, April 25, the clubhouse was nearly empty when the doors opened to the media at 3:30, because most of the players had been out taking extra batting practice since 2. Devon White wasn't among them. The day before, he had been diagnosed as having torn cartilage in his left knee.

The Marlins had been carefully watching White's knee since March, and became concerned when it swelled considerably after playing on the artificial turf in Cincinnati. But White had been playing so well the Marlins were content to let him monitor the situation on his own. Prior to the final game of the Colorado series, Leyland told him, "Instead of you saying if you can play every day, just let me know if it's not OK."

"I didn't think anything of it," Leyland said.

But White did and wasn't surprised, just disappointed, when Leyland told him the bad news Thursday afternoon: He would undergo arthroscopic surgery and get placed on the fifteen-day disabled list. Early projections had the Marlins' starting centerfielder out for at least a month, so he would return home to Mesa, Arizona, for a few weeks of rest and rehab. No sense hanging around.

"It's not a very bright day," Leyland said.

◆ ◆ ◆

Dan Graziano of the *Palm Beach Post* wasn't having any luck getting Fernandez to talk for a story he was researching about Fernandez's high school coach. "You know I don't talk to the media the day before I pitch," Fernandez scolded Graziano. "This has been my routine for seven years. How can you not respect that?"

Fernandez, who speaks to everyone else the day before he pitches—and doesn't even change his home routine, right down to changing the baby's diapers and answering phone calls—actually had one thing to say. As Graziano turned and walked away, he heard Fernandez calling out behind him.

"Mother fucker!"

Graziano kept walking, out the clubhouse doors and to the dugout bench, where he sat shaking his head in bewilderment. Minutes later Fernandez summoned Ron Colangelo to complain about Graziano's intrusion.

The Marlins were in a snippy mood.

◆ ◆ ◆

That afternoon Bonilla and Warren Cromartie sat around the dugout talking about real estate. Pro Player Stadium real estate. Cromartie, a former major leaguer who had been helping Bonilla with his swing since February, pointed to the teal scoreboard in left-centerfield, three hundred eighty-five feet away, and said, "There's a lot of money out there. You gotta start aiming for that clock."

Bonilla nodded his head in agreement. The next night, he was still in a slump and sitting glumly in front of his locker—eyes staring straight ahead in a menacing glance, lips pursed—looking unapproachable after one of his worst games of the season: His only hit in five at-bats came on a popup the shortstop lost in the lights. He left four men on base, was thrown out at the plate trying to score from second on a single, and committed a throwing error that could have been costly.

The fans booed him after he popped meekly to first in the sixth inning, and nobody, even Bonilla, could blame them.

All around the clubhouse, teammates were celebrating their second straight win over the Dodgers in front of the second consecutive crowd of more than forty thousand. Charles Johnson, whose three-run homer in the seventh inning put the Marlins ahead for good, was surrounded by reporters. Bonilla sat by himself, proof that winning doesn't always make an entire team happy, or even content.

◆ ◆ ◆

At the same time, Jeff Conine was standing on the opposite side of the room and patiently trying to avoid sounding like he had a problem with the manager. Conine was hitting .361 and batting seventh. To radio talk show callers, that meant he should be moved up in the order. So Conine stood steely eyed, arms crossed hard across his chest, brow wrinkled, smiling slightly, eyes staring down at the reporter as he deflected one question after another.

REPORTER: Do you enjoy batting seventh?

CONINE: There's nothing I can do about it. It's his decision to put me in the seventh spot.

REPORTER: Did he ever talk to you about it?

CONINE: No.

REPORTER: Has it been an adjustment?

CONINE: It didn't change my mental outlook on the game. I've gone about it the same as I always have.

REPORTER: Do you think you should be batting higher?

CONINE: I'm not going to get myself in trouble by answering that question.

Which, of course, was his answer right there.

◆ ◆ ◆

Then there's Rick Helling, who comes to the ballpark every day and has no idea whether or not he's going to play. So he grabs his glove a few minutes before game time, trudges down to the Marlins bullpen, takes a seat in one of the director's chairs, and watches. Then he spends five or six innings waiting for the call from the manager that might not come for a week or two weeks. When it does come, he has to warm up as quickly as possible, then pitch an inning or two. Sometimes his innings matter, sometimes they don't.

"I'm not happy, but I'm willing to accept it," Helling said.

Helling didn't have any choice but to accept his situation. Besides, the complaint department was officially closed. Two straight wins had done nothing to lift Leyland's mood. When the beat reporters arrived at 4:30 Sunday afternoon—three and a half hours early for the 8:05 game—Leyland refused to talk, claiming they were supposed to be there at 3:30. He finally consented to answering a few questions in the dugout, but when Jeff Miller of the *Sun-Sentinel* asked about the Dodgers, Leyland snapped, "I don't want to talk about the other team," and walked away.

The reporters settled for a half hour audience with effusive ESPN basketball analyst Dick Vitale.

Nobody asked him questions about the lineup.

◆ ◆ ◆

The White Man's Tribute To Jackie Robinson came to Pro Player Stadium for the Friday night game against the Dodgers. It was fifty years ago, in 1947, that white baseball owners graciously allowed the black man to play Major League Baseball, so to celebrate the event, every team in the league was having Jackie Robinson Nights and the players were wearing special patches on their uniform shoulders.

Gary Sheffield on the patches: "It's a joke. Fifty years and we get a patch."

Sheffield was forgetting about something: They also got a commemorative plastic garbage bag. The Marlins unveiled their tribute to Robinson, a giant rendering of the patch on the tarp covering the upper deck seats.

◆ ◆ ◆

Speaking of tolerance, Sheffield got thrown out of Friday's game for arguing a called third strike with umpire Terry Tata, and afterward he said, "Nobody has any tolerance these days."

Sheffield was getting frustrated and decided the best remedy was ignoring the umpires. Actually, it didn't sound like a bad idea.

"If they call it my way or not, I have to go about my business," he said. "I depend on them a lot, since I don't get many strikes, but I'm not saying anything else to them."

◆ ◆ ◆

Bonilla picked up his first RBI in three weeks on a sacrifice fly to leftfield in the fifth inning of a 4-3 victory over the Dodgers on Sunday, and afterward he said, "I don't remember the last time I had an RBI. I'll have to search the Internet for the last time I had one."

His search for answers had taken him everywhere else: to Warren Cromartie, without his manager's blessing.

"If you're having a problem with your hitting, you talk to Milt May," Leyland grumbled.

To May, the batting coach, and finally to the team doctor, who gave him a cortisone shot in his ailing left wrist. Bonilla didn't like that at all. The shot hurt. It burned. He preferred good old common sense to modern medicine: *Hmmm, three hundred thirty feet to leftfield, three hundred forty-five feet to right. Better go to left.*

"I have to try to take advantage of Pro Player, the shorter porch to leftfield," Bonilla said. "Rightfield is kind of big here and it's kind of useless to waste some good drives on the warning track. That's not going to be useful."

He hoped the search was over. He didn't want another shot. And Leyland certainly didn't want Bonilla getting batting tips from Cromartie. He would have rather Bonilla went to a voodoo doctor.

◆ ◆ ◆

When the TV camera beyond the leftfield fence zooms in on the Marlins dugout, it sees Leyland sitting at the end of the bench, arms folded, his expression never changing. He looks so calm, but the camera tells big-time lies. Leyland's heart is racing a mile a minute. He has smoked more than a pack of cigarettes in a four-hour game. When he isn't smoking, he nervously nibbles on sunflower seeds. Scooping up a handful, shoving them into his mouth, chewing on the shells, spitting them back out. The camera is an intrusion, but Leyland had given up on trying to hide his bad habits. He was more concerned with what the camera gave away.

"I don't like that," Leyland said. "The visiting team can sit in the clubhouse and take my signs."

So Leyland, who had already given the marketing department advice on selling baseball, got involved in TV production and asked for the camera to be moved. These are the things Leyland worried about, because he worried about everything. Even without evidence that the other team was stealing signs, Leyland could never be too careful.

Besides, in 1984 he was third base coach for the White Sox. Twenty-third inning, tie game. Man on first, two outs, three-two count. Runner is going on the pitch. Single up the middle. He rounds second and races to third. Leyland raises his arms to stop him right there, and as the runner pulls up, he and Leyland inadvertently brush hands. Suddenly, the opposing team's players come pouring out of the dugout. They had been watching the game on TV in the clubhouse and saw the play. Batter called out for coach's interference.

"It was the most embarrassing thing that ever happened to me in baseball," Leyland said.

And it was all because of a well-positioned camera.

◆ ◆ ◆

On the subject of cameras, Leyland was discussing why he started Charles Johnson in the Sunday night game against Los Angeles. The game was being televised nationally on ESPN, and Leyland wanted the large audience to see the two-time Gold Glove catcher.

Now, that sounds perfectly reasonable, until you realize that Leyland was the manager who set his lineup at the start of the season and didn't plan on changing it for anything. He said he didn't care about anyone's opinion but his own after a game started, so what did he do? He started Johnson instead of Zaun because the game was on ESPN.

Store that one in the file of Leyland doing the unexpected.

◆ ◆ ◆

On Monday, April 28, Tony Saunders allowed six runs in four innings, but the Marlins won anyway, 12-9, over San Diego in a game that ended at 12:30 a.m. It was a hideous evening of baseball: damp, long, miserable. Terribly pitched. A rain delay at 11:05 p.m. By the time the game ended, only about a thousand fans remained, and Saunders was still berating himself.

"You can't be happy with what I did out there," he said. "It was an ass whipping, plain and simple."

The following afternoon, Leyland was in complete agreement with Saunders' assessment. As Leyland knelt under his desk to tie a shoelace, a reporter asked, "What did you think of Saunders last night?"

"He stunk," Leyland barked.

Then his head popped up.

"No," he said. "I'm just kidding."

Nobody would have known. Leyland hadn't kidded since spring training, but there was reason for his good humor: Bonilla had four hits to continue his breakout; Sheffield and Alou both hit grand slams. The Marlins had a chance to set the National League record of three grand slams in one game, but Zaun walked with the bases loaded in the eighth.

Leyland on Zaun's at-bat: "He was trying to hit one, but where he hits, they don't have any foul lines. He would've hit a peanut vendor."

He was kidding again.

There was no way of knowing which Leyland would show up on any day. The unhappy Leyland, who gave one-word answers. Refused to discuss his lineup. Walked around with his black fungo bat as if he was ready to swing it at someone. Or the happy Leyland, who took good-natured shots at his own players. Chided the *Sun-Sentinel's* O'Brien about his haircut and WQAM radio's Jody Jackson about her shoes. Teased a visiting reporter because he could tell she had never before been around a ballfield. Told publicity director Ron Colangelo that Colangelo's "got this thing running like a finely tuned machine." Reminded everyone that it's a long season and he can't get too happy or upset about winning or losing a game or two. Can't get too up or too down.

The camera isn't the only thing that lies.

◆ ◆ ◆

Dennis Cook's favorite T-shirt says, "Man, Fuck" on the front. Read it with exasperation and you'll get the idea.

◆ ◆ ◆

Brown got no run support again in the final game of the homestand, a 2-1 victory over the Padres in which both Marlins runs scored on a triple by Bonilla. For the second time in less than two weeks, the Marlins embarked on a five-game road trip coming off an emotional, last at-bat win that pushed them six games over .500.

Brown's lack of run support had been a story since the start of his Marlins career, so the story had become the story.

"Are you tired of being asked about a lack of run support?" a reporter asked.

Brown looked up and smirked. "I'm tired of being asked if I'm tired of being asked about it," he shot back. "Is that sufficient?"

Man, fuck, it'll have to be.

◆ ◆ ◆

Leyland figured that maybe the Marlins had so much trouble winning on the road because the hot, humid South Florida weather wore them down for road trips. He was reaching for answers. Leyland actually had no idea why the Marlins couldn't win on the road.

The trip opened with a 6-2 loss to St. Louis on Wednesday, April 30, that was notable for this reason: Bonilla did not hit a home run and finished the month with no homers in eighty-eight at-bats, a poor statistic for any cleanup hitter. The good news: He had doubled his RBI output to eight over the past four games. The bad news: He had fewer home runs than Edgar Renteria, Reds pitcher Pete Schourek, or Jenny McCarthy, whose only plate appearances were on MTV's *Celebrity Softball*.

And more bad news: Leiter's right knee, which had started bothering him in San Francisco, gave out. He allowed five runs in the fifth inning of Wednesday night's loss, and the next morning returned to Miami to have his knee examined by doctors. The diagnosis was a deep bone bruise and Leiter was placed on the fifteen-day disabled list.

That afternoon, the Marlins were no-hit by a rookie for 5⅔ innings, and Conine finished off a 3-2 loss to St. Louis in the role previously played by Bonilla: flying out meekly to center field with the bases loaded and two out in the ninth inning. The loss was their ninth straight on the road, tying the club record.

"I'm not going to concede that we can't win on the road yet," Leyland insisted.

Yet?

They lost in Houston Friday night, 2-1, to set a club record of ten road losses in a row. Pretty awful for a team with a $49 million payroll. Pretty awful for a team with a $20 million payroll. They had to play the longest game in club history, four hours and fifty-four minutes, and use twenty-two players to end the streak Saturday night, 9-8, in thirteen innings. But on Sunday, Darryl Kile of the Astros pitched a four-hit shutout.

Leyland did say, "Yet," didn't he?

◆ ◆ ◆

Leyland had planned to use the same lineup all season, but with Sheffield and Bonilla both struggling, that eventually had to change. It did for the Saturday night game in Houston.

Leyland dropped Bonilla from fourth to sixth in the batting order and moved Sheffield from third to cleanup. With White hurt, Alou had already moved from left-field to center, and whoever played left would bat third. The moves were necessary.

Although Bonilla had insisted all month he wasn't bothered by opposing pitchers avoiding Sheffield to face him, Leyland suspected otherwise. The way Leyland saw it, teams were doing a psych job on both Sheffield and Bonilla, although the one on Sheffield was more obvious. The psych job on Bonilla passed through Sheffield. Bonilla blamed his troubles on a bad wrist, but that wasn't his only problem, Leyland suspected. Too many bad thoughts were going through his head. *Opposing teams don't respect me. It's my job to protect Sheffield. I have to hit.*

"I think very few guys in baseball can protect Gary Sheffield and Gary Sheffield's one of them," Leyland insisted. "I don't think in any way, shape, or form, it's disrespect for Bobby. I think it's the maximum respect for Sheffield."

By the way, Bonilla said being dropped to sixth didn't bother him. Of course not. He was probably relieved.

◆ ◆ ◆

Copies of the duPont Registry of fine homes were scattered on the table in the middle of the clubhouse when the Marlins returned to Pro Player Stadium on Monday, May 5. This month's featured home: five thousand square feet on an acre with a winding circular drive, grand foyer, chef's kitchen, and "imagination room." Pool and lanai. The price: $787,500. Less than a year's salary for most of these guys.

Brown, the day after his 1-0 loss to the Astros, dozed on a leather recliner. Players watched a video of *Jerry Maguire,* which wouldn't be available to the rest of the world until May 29. "Show me the money!" Cuba Gooding's character belted out early in the movie. Brown opened one eye, then went back to sleep.

Shortly before batting practice, John Cangelosi, who had batted only twenty times this season, was lounging around in the dugout with Abbott, Bonilla, and Sheffield.

"Let's blow out someone today," he said. "So I don't have to warm up and stretch eighty fucking times."

◆ ◆ ◆

Leyland's former team, the Pirates, were in town for the first time this season, so Leyland and third base coach Rich Donnelly spent batting practice chatting behind the cage with manager Gene Lamont and the Pirates' coaches. The next morning, Leyland and Lamont would have breakfast together, and whoever won Monday night's game would pick up the check.

Lamont and Leyland roomed together in 1966 at Rocky Mount in the Carolina League and became fast friends, then best friends, and for seven seasons Lamont was Leyland's third base coach in Pittsburgh. This year, for the first time since 1978, when Leyland was coaching Lakeland and Lamont was coaching Fort Myers in the Florida State League, they would be on opposite sides of the diamond.

"It's good to see friendly faces and old friends, but other than that, it's just another game, and I think that's the way you've got to keep it," Leyland said while sitting in the dugout talking to the Florida and Pittsburgh media. "I miss Pittsburgh. I had a relationship in Pittsburgh like I'll never have again. I hope it happens for Gene. I love Pittsburgh, but it'll never be the same."

Then he yelled down the dugout to Paul Meyer, the beat reporter for the *Pittsburgh Post-Gazette* who is one of his closest friends.

"You got a cigarette, Paul?" Leyland asked. Meyer reached into his pocket and grinned, because some things will always be the same.

◆ ◆ ◆

First base coach Tommy Sandt was walking toward the dugout after batting practice, carrying a bat and wearing black socks with TOMMY written down the side in white.

"Nice socks," yelled out Gene Lamont.

"I just got 'em today," Sandt shouted over his shoulder.

"You wear them on the field?"

"I'm gonna wear 'em tonight," Sandt answered, as he kept walking, past a young security guard who had overheard the conversation.

"What's that?" the guard asked, pointing to the socks. "Tommy Hilfiger?"

"No," Sandt replied. "Tommy Sandt."

◆ ◆ ◆

Helling, who replaced Leiter in the starting rotation, allowed two hits in six innings of a 3-0 victory over the Pirates Monday night, but Leyland was in a bad mood the next day anyway. This time, he was angry because people were asking whether Helling had a chance to win Saunders' spot in the rotation.

"If Helling keeps throwing like that . . . " a reporter said.

Leyland cut him off. "Don't even start," he snapped, holding up his hands.

Saunders hadn't gone past the third inning in his last two starts. Helling had allowed only three runs in twenty-three innings.

Leyland sounded like he was about to go off on a tirade, but Kurt Abbott came bouncing into the dugout and, not realizing the manager was sitting there, called out to Boog Sciambi, a sports talk host for a local radio station.

"Hey, Boog!" Abbott shouted. "Nice answer to Mike in New York . . . Oops!"

Abbott, embarrassed because he hadn't known he was interrupting anything, covered his mouth. Leyland smiled.

"Hey, Abby," Leyland asked. "Cum laude or magna cum laude?"

Abbott walked away, but returned a few minutes later sucking on a blueberry Popsicle. Leyland shook his head.

"You feel real good going into war," he said, "when your player is eating a little Popsicle like that."

Abbott left the dugout again, then returned a few minutes later with a red Popsicle.

"Hey, Abby," Leyland yelled. "You have any more of those?"

◆ ◆ ◆

Then Leyland walked over to the batting cage and watched Leiter practice bunting. Leiter wasn't doing well. He bunted three pitches foul before Leyland lost patience, grabbed the bat out of his hand, and grumbled, "Jesus. You've been playing baseball your entire life. Hasn't anybody ever showed you how to bunt?"

And then Leyland, who supposedly didn't know anything about hitting, laid down three perfect bunts.

◆ ◆ ◆

The Pirates won the series finale, 4-0, Tuesday night, and afterward a reporter asked losing pitcher Alex Fernandez, "Does this make you feel like you need to pitch a perfect game every time out there?"

Fernandez, without missing a beat, replied, "What kind of fucking question is that?"

The response was played on the radio the next day—with the obscenity bleeped out—and a stupid question had been turned into Fernandez making himself sound vulgar for the South Florida listening audience. So much for hometown heroes.

The forecast for a positive mood change wasn't bright with the Atlanta Braves coming to town for a two-game series. Pitching for the Braves: four-time Cy Young Award winner Greg Maddux and one-time winner Tom Glavine. Pitching for the Marlins: Rapp and Saunders.

The pitching matchups weren't the Marlins' only problems. Conine was slumping, and the questions about moving him up in the order had suddenly stopped. Bonilla didn't have a home run. Sheffield was batting .214 and getting so frustrated by the walks that every little setback bothered him. He had promised to give umpires the silent treatment, but that didn't mean he couldn't react with body language. Every time Sheffield disagreed with a strike call, his mind would be messed up for the rest of the at-bat.

Alou was hitting, which was remarkable considering he was the only Marlin who hadn't hit well during the spring. He had carried the Marlins through the first thirty-one games and was tied for third in the National League with thirty-one RBIs. But no one else was hitting well consistently.

"Just average pitching has stopped us. That's what's surprising," Leyland complained. "I don't know what's wrong with the hitting. We're not even lukewarm."

Nonetheless, the Marlins were surviving with a 17-14 record, all because of their pitching staff. Brown was in 1996 form—although he wasn't getting the extra runs he had expected—and Fernandez was solid, workmanlike, pitching plenty of innings and keeping games close.

The bullpen had been outstanding, one of the best in the National League. Cook had allowed only one run in fifteen innings and rookie Felix Heredia was impressive with his fastball and ability to stay calm in difficult situations. Heredia, 20, from the Dominican Republic, spoke little English and looked less like an athlete than anyone on the team, maybe any athlete in the world. He strolled into the clubhouse every day wearing a T-shirt and baggy, denim shorts, on his thin, 6', 175-pound frame, and you might have sworn he was the kid you just saw on line at the local convenience store. Then he went out onto the mound, threw 95-mile-per-hour fastballs, and made you wonder, *How can that be?*

And bad news for Matt Whisenant: Jay Powell was pitching so well, throwing in the high nineties and not allowing a run in eight consecutive appearances, that Whisenant's prospects of returning to the majors were getting slimmer by the day.

"If Jay Powell continues to pitch the way he has, he's not going anywhere," Dave Dombrowski said.

But the pitchers' efforts were merely enough to keep the Marlins competitive, and if the small crowd at Tuesday's game against the Pirates was any indication, South Florida's sports fans had started suspecting that the Marlins were $49 million fakes. Although the Panthers were out of the NHL playoffs and the Heat was off, only 18,063 fans showed up. Only 16,616 had attended Monday's game. The weather was beautiful—blue skies without a hint of rain in the forecast—but the attendance for both games was lower than it had been for the same dates in 1996.

Maybe the fans were passing judgment on the Marlins. What's the use of winning at home when you can't win on the road?

"When this club gets on a roll, and I believe it will, and turns around the trend of losing on the road, we'll experience attendance commensurate with our performance on the field," Don Smiley said. "But it's our job to prove that."

The Marlins would get their chance against the Braves. Four of their next eight games were against Atlanta, the team they were supposed to battle for the National League East title. If they won three out of four, their situation would change dramatically for the better. If they lost three out of four, they'd be in danger of falling out of the pennant race by mid-May. And that wouldn't help attendance or anyone's mood.

NATIONAL LEAGUE EAST STANDINGS

	W	L	Pct.	GB
Atlanta	22	9	.700	—
Marlins	**17**	**14**	**.548**	**5**
Montreal	16	14	.533	5.5
New York	15	17	.469	7.5
Philadelphia	10	20	.333	11.5

5

La Primera Gran Batalla

May 7, 8 vs. Atlanta
May 9, 10, 11, 12 vs. Houston
May 13, 14 at Atlanta
May 16, 17, 18 at Pittsburgh

The Braves arrived in Miami for the first opportunity to compare what the Marlins had bought with their $49 million payroll to what the Braves had with their $53 million payroll. Of course, the Braves already had four trips to the World Series in the 1990s and one world championship. They also had three Cy Young Award winners—Greg Maddux, Tom Glavine, and John Smoltz—and Denny Neagle, who pitched for Leyland in Pittsburgh and was having the best season of his life.

The Marlins had no Cy Young Award winners, a slumping $61 million right-fielder, a catcher who couldn't hit, a leadoff man who couldn't get on base, and the minor comfort of knowing they had beaten the Braves seven out of thirteen times in 1996. According to a recent newspaper survey of forty-six baseball executives, the Marlins also had the best manager in baseball.

Advantage Atlanta. On top of everything else, the Braves had great uniforms and abundant confidence. It showed in the quiet way they went about their business in the visitor's clubhouse before the first game, without any music blaring or much fooling around. They even dressed with the air of a winner, as if they knew they were good.

And they were. With a record of 22-9, the Braves were off to their best start ever and were scoring plenty of runs for their Cy Young pitchers. They had no problems.

"There's nothing like pitching for the Braves, is there?" a reporter asked.

Smoltz nodded his head. "You got that right," he said.

◆ ◆ ◆

The schedule-maker was guilty of unfortunate timing. On the same night the Marlins played their first game of the season against the Braves, the Heat opened their second-round NBA playoff series against the New York Knicks fifteen miles down the road at Miami Arena. Sports fans in South Florida had their choice between Greg Maddux vs. Pat Rapp, or Patrick Ewing vs. Alonzo Mourning.

57

They chose Ewing vs. Mourning.

The paid crowd for Marlins-Braves was 26,838, about fifteen thousand short of a sellout. Very few tickets were sold during the week leading up to the game. About 20,000 fans bothered showing up and many of them watched the basketball game on the TVs throughout the stadium.

La Primera Gran Batalla!—The First Big Battle—screamed the Marlins' ads in the Spanish papers.

South Florida responded to *La Primera Gran Batalla* by watching the NBA's *Primera Gran Batalla*.

◆ ◆ ◆

The schedule-maker was guilty of having no flair for the dramatic.

Thanks to Major League Baseball's balanced schedule, the Marlins and Braves would play each other only twelve times this season and would meet for the final time on August 3. Pennant race or not, the Marlins and Braves would never go head-to-head in September.

Baseball's schedule had changed for the worst. Up until the early '90s, division rivals played each other sixteen times a season and could count on a head-to-head series or two in September. Not anymore.

"It's unfortunate," Smoltz said. "Too bad we don't play each other twenty times. If this series was in September, it would mean a lot more."

Maybe not a whole lot more. Under the new system, a team no longer had to win its division to make the playoffs. The winner of each of the three divisions qualified, along with the second place team with the best record. Even the runner-up in this *Gran Batalla* between the Marlins and Braves had a good shot at making the playoffs.

◆ ◆ ◆

The teams were guilty of failing to promote the product.

Braves manager Bobby Cox: "It's not do-or-die. If one team wins both, it doesn't mean anything."

Thanks for pushing the series, Bobby.

Leyland: "We've got to win baseball games. It doesn't matter who we're playing."

Way to drum up the rivalry, Jim.

Jeff Conine: "It's just another series. It's not a big deal. If it were in September, then it's a big deal."

The problem was, the Marlins and Braves wouldn't play in September.

Of course these games were meaningful. Wayne Huizenga hadn't spent $89 million so the Marlins could keep pace with the Mets and the Expos. He did it to challenge the Braves.

When the Marlins' clubhouse opened Wednesday night after Atlanta's 3-2 victory in extra innings, John Cangelosi was sitting in front of his locker with his head buried in his hands. Pat Rapp, dressed in street clothes, predicted that he wouldn't fall asleep until 5 o'clock in the morning, and only after hours of channel flipping. Bobby Bonilla strolled in fifteen minutes later, still dressed in his uniform pants and a black T-shirt. He had been lying on the dugout steps the whole time and now he was glassy-eyed and facing the media.

Rapp had a good night. He went pitch-for-pitch with Greg Maddux for seven innings, allowed two runs, and left the game with the Marlins trailing, 2-1.

Bonilla had a tough night. He couldn't get the ball out of his glove in the fifth inning, allowing the Braves to score their first run. The crowd booed. He singled in the seventh, driving in the Marlins' first run. The crowd cheered. In the tenth, with runners on first and second, he let Michael Tucker's ground ball hop between his legs, scoring the winning run. Loud boos.

No excuses, Bonilla said.

"I missed the ball. That's all. That's it."

◆ ◆ ◆

A tall, thin, blonde woman walked past several Marlins sitting in the dugout prior to the second game of the series and one of them asked, "Why is it so hard to find a tall woman with a small ass?"

A few of the players nodded their heads in agreement, but none of them came up with an answer. Life went on.

◆ ◆ ◆

A little later, backup catcher Gregg Zaun walked through the dugout.

"Hey, Zaunie," Leyland called out.

"Yeah."

"C. J. tonight." That meant Charles Johnson was catching.

"I can hit Glavine," Zaun insisted.

"Yeah? How many hits you got against him?"

"I never faced him."

"No shit."

"You gonna put me in?"

"No."

◆ ◆ ◆

Poor Tony Saunders. He had gone to bed Wednesday night thinking, *I'm going to pitch against Tom Glavine tomorrow,* and he was excited because Glavine was his idol. A lot of young left-handers idolized Glavine, baseball's most successful lefty of the '90s, and Saunders had been watching him for ten years.

This is how Saunders treated his idol: In the third he hit the first homer of his career, starting a five-run inning. In the fifth, he hit Glavine on the left hand with a pitch. Glavine went down, gripping his pitching hand in pain, and Saunders, horrified by what he had done, took a few steps off the mound toward home plate.

"I didn't get scared," Saunders said later. "I just got really concerned for him, because the first thing that came to my mind was, 'Oh, man, his finger's broken.' You never think the positives in a situation like that and I was thinking the worst. *He's down for the year.* I felt like crawling underneath a rock and just hiding. I wanted to run up to him and say, 'I'm sorry.'"

The apology came later. Glavine got up after a few minutes and left the game. Saunders, after a little counseling from pitching coach Larry Rothschild, stayed in and pitched six shutout innings to earn his first major league win. Fortunately for both Glavine and Saunders, who might have been mentally wrecked for the rest of the season, the X-rays were negative. And the Marlins got a split of the series by beating the Braves, 5-1, in front of 32,088.

◆ ◆ ◆

The Marlins knew what they were getting in late March when they acquired Cliff Floyd from the Expos. Dave Dombrowski was general manager of the Expos when they drafted Floyd in 1991, and had since coveted the big, fast, power-hitting outfielder/first baseman who seemingly had so much potential. Floyd's problem was that he was always getting hurt. In 1995, he broke six bones in his left wrist.

That's why it wasn't surprising when Floyd pulled a hamstring while running out a double in Thursday's game. He was placed on the fifteen-day disabled list. Todd Dunwoody was called up from the minors. And the Marlins' list of wounded read White, Leiter, Castillo, and Floyd.

◆ ◆ ◆

The Marlins won three out of four from the Astros to complete a 5-3 homestand and improve their record at Pro Player Stadium to 17-5. The discrepancy between their performance on the road and at home was getting larger by the day. Their home record over the past two seasons was 69-34, the best in baseball. Their road record over the past two seasons was 33-64, one of the worst in baseball. They had no idea what was wrong.

"It can't be home cooking, because I don't have anyone at home cooking," Zaun said. "Maybe we should bring the wives on the road trip."

Easy for Zaun to say. He didn't have a wife.

◆ ◆ ◆

Pitcher Felix Heredia got his first major league hit in the final game against Houston and Leyland said, "Let's get one thing straight right now. He can't hit shit. I don't think he has a clue what he's doing up there."

So congratulations, Felix.

◆ ◆ ◆

On to Atlanta for two more games against the Braves. What they say about the rich getting richer is true. Not only did the Braves have the best team in baseball, but they also had one of the best stadiums in baseball. Turner Field, located across the street from old Atlanta-Fulton County Stadium, was built for the 1996 Summer Olympics and then handed over to the Braves, who had helped with the financing.

Walk south across Ralph David Abernathy Drive, away from the old stadium, and the site is overwhelming. Turner Field is an intimate, baseball-only, open-air ballpark with a red brick facade, exposed trusses, and three levels of dark blue seats that make it look a little like Yankee Stadium and a little like Coors Field in Denver. The view from the upper deck seats in leftfield is of downtown Atlanta. On all levels, every seat is pointed toward the infield. The new trend in baseball is designing ballparks reminiscent of the cozy ones built around the turn of the century, without the obstructive girders but with plenty of sky boxes, restaurants, shops, and wide concourses.

The Marlins wished they had one.

◆ ◆ ◆

Leyland sat in the visitor's dugout at Turner Field on Tuesday, May 13, and told the reporters that Charles Johnson, who didn't play in the final game against Houston, would play in the opener against the Braves. He also said that Zaun would be getting more playing time because of his superior hitting ability.

So Gregg Doyel from *The Miami Herald* asked, "Are you getting close to a platoon situation with Zaun and Johnson?"

The question sounded familiar to Leyland. It sounded like the question a Spanish TV reporter asked him a few weeks earlier, when Tony Saunders was struggling and Rick Helling pitched well in his first start.

He didn't like either question.

"Now there you go again," Leyland snapped. "I'm going to play whoever gives me the best chance to win. That's just the way it is. It's just like that horseshit from the fucking Spanish station, asking about Helling. If I answered that question and said, 'Yes, Helling has a shot at getting into the rotation,' you'd be at Helling's locker right away asking him about it."

"What if we didn't ask and you did it?" Doyel asked.

"Hey, you can lie to me, but you can't bullshit me," Leyland shot back, sounding angry but looking like he was trying to control his laughter. "I know why you write that shit: To sell papers."

"We're not a tabloid," Doyel protested.

"Bullshit," Leyland barked back, his voice getting louder as he stared Doyel right in the eyes. "You're not held fucking accountable! I'm the one who's held accountable and has to answer for that shit! You wrote that shit about Helling getting into the rotation, but you're the same guy that was kissing Saunders' ass the week before!"

"You're telling me that if Saunders pitched like he did the last two starts and Helling pitched like he's been pitching, there was no chance of him getting into the rotation?" Doyel asked.

"No chance," Leyland said, now standing up and leaning on his fungo bat. "Just like that question with Zaun and C. J. I don't care what the fuck you write, but you're not held accountable. But I know what you're doing. I'm no fool. You just want to stir up shit."

With that, Leyland climbed the dugout steps and walked away with publicity director Ron Colangelo after completing the first media blowout of his Marlins career.

"See?" Leyland said to Colangelo. "I told him."

◆ ◆ ◆

There must have been something in the Atlanta air, because the next day Leyland was back on his soapbox. Having already discoursed this season on the role of a team's marketing department, proper angles for TV coverage, and investigative journalism, Leyland expressed his opinion on two weightier subjects: The women's liberation movement and political correctness.

He had his body curled up on the undersized couch in the visiting manager's office when the press walked in and he seemed a little sleepy and a lot grumpy. Perhaps the "NO SMOKING" signs scattered through the ballpark had gotten to him, or maybe it was the driver who the day before had told him he couldn't smoke on the team bus. Gutsy driver.

"I can't smoke, they've got these big no smoking signs up, but a guy can go to a game, get drunk off his ass, and drive home," Leyland said. "You know what that is? It's money. I'm 52 years old and people are telling me what I can and can't do. I can't smoke on the bus. We pay for the goddamn charter and I can't smoke on the bus.

The conversation moved on to New York Mets pitcher Jason Isringhausen, who had recently caused an uproar over his speaker-phoned comments to publicity director Jay Horwitz. "Jew boy," Isringhausen had called him at the end of a conference call, ostensibly—according to both Horwitz and Isringhausen—as a term of endearment.

"Why is everybody so sensitive all of a sudden?" Leyland continued, still curled up on the couch. "This country used to be great. Now you can't fool around with anybody. You can't say anything these days without people being offended. I think people oughta loosen up. If you wanna know the truth of the matter, it's just like me. I feel like I'm being discriminated against . . . by her."

With that, he pointed to *Palm Beach Post* reporter Cheryl Rosenberg, who was sitting in a chair next to the couch, just listening.

"I feel embarrassed to have to walk around naked," Leyland went on. "I walk out in the middle of the goddamn floor in my clubhouse and I have to worry about female reporters being there. But I don't do it. I show her respect. I put on a towel. But I feel like that's an invasion of my privacy, if you wanna know the truth."

Leyland sat up. He was just getting started.

"The ruination of this country was the women's liberation movement," he said. "We've lost the family tradition in this country, and that's the problem with this country. There's no more family tradition. None. When I was a kid, my mother was always home, but then women had to start going off to work. I like it when a man takes a woman out to dinner, holds the door for her, and pays. I don't like when she's smoking a cigar and paying half."

Rosenberg was speechless, but Dave O'Brien of the Fort Lauderdale *Sun-Sentinel* asked, "So why do you clean up your language in front of female reporters?"

"Because I'm not ignorant," Leyland replied.

But for Rosenberg, as for any female reporter in a male clubhouse, this would be another episode to store away, another reminder that despite Major League Baseball policy and Supreme Court rulings, she was still an oddity to the players, managers, and coaches. Only a week earlier Kurt Abbott had asked her out of curiosity, "Have you ever dated a player?"

"Of course not," Rosenberg replied.

"Why not?" Abbott said.

"First of all, I'd get fired," Rosenberg explained. "And second of all, I know how baseball players are."

"Don't put us all in the same heap," Abbott said.

◆ ◆ ◆

Wednesday's *USA Today* would contain baseball writer Rod Beaton's list of the ten booms and busts of the off-season free-agent market and Bonilla was listed among the busts. So Beaton, standing outside the visitor's clubhouse after the first game of the series Tuesday, asked Gregg Doyel, "Do you think he'll be angry about it?"

"Don't worry," Doyel responded, remembering his run-in with Bonilla during the spring. "He only gets mad when you talk about his family or his personal life."

Bonilla had refused to speak to Doyel in anything but group situations for the next two months, but started speaking to him again in early May. What brought about the change of heart was impossible to say. Who knows how to explain Bonilla, other than that he is a complex, emotional person who can't be pigeonholed as either a good guy (Leyland's version) or a bad guy (the New York and Baltimore media's version)?

The good Bonilla had just come off his best game of the season: three hits, including his first homer of the season, a grand slam in the fourth inning of an 11-5 win for the Marlins. When Bonilla emerged from the shower room, he was greeted at his locker by a group of reporters, and asked them to wait while he got dressed. But then Moises Alou walked by and told him the bus was leaving in two minutes.

Now, Bonilla could have told the reporters, "Sorry, guys, I have to make the bus," and walked away without answering their questions. Instead, he told Alou that he would take a taxi back to the hotel.

But Bonilla's confrontational side surfaced a few minutes later when a reporter asked a strategy question.

"You'll have to ask the manager about that," he responded curtly.

The reporter rephrased the question. Bonilla looked at him hard and said, "The manager's office is right in there. You can go ask him."

"I already did," the reporter said.

"Well, what did he tell you?" Bonilla said, glaring angrily. "That's not a question for me."

The reporter walked away, no doubt thinking, *Bonilla's an asshole* and having confirmed the general perception of the man. If he had stuck around, he would have heard Bonilla patiently answering questions for the next fifteen minutes and reflecting upon his season.

For example, the three-hit day lifted his batting average to .304 with twenty RBIs, hardly the numbers of a free agent bust.

"How do you keep from getting irritated when you hear people saying, 'Bobby's gone this many games without hitting a home run?'" a reporter asked.

"You gotta remember," Bonilla said, smiling the megawatt smile. "I had good practice in New York, so stuff like that doesn't affect me at all."

Bonilla had done nothing to help himself in New York. His relationship with the media went from bad to unbearable. Bonilla was viewed as the symbol of all that was wrong with the overpaid, underachieving Mets of the early 1990s.

"I got bitten in New York and sometimes I bit back," Bonilla said. "But don't give me what front office people or media people say. Poll every player, every teammate I've had and then you'd be telling me something."

Bonilla had already established himself as a clubhouse leader with the Marlins, meaning he wasn't afraid to stand up and say something that needed to be said. His relationship with the media had come a long way since the spring training incidents with the cameraman and Doyel. Even when things were going badly for him on the field, like they were during April, Bonilla rarely hid in the trainer's room. There were no more confrontations.

Perhaps Leyland's presence had soothed Bonilla. Or maybe Bonilla realized that, at age 34, he had a final chance to change his image.

"I've done the full circle of things," he said. "I've driven in runs, hit thirty home runs, hit over forty doubles. I've gone to post-season. My only focus is to get to the World Series. But I guess it's all how you look at it. First they weren't worried about my hitting, they were worried about my defense. Now I don't get any questions about defense, and all I hear about is the home runs. So, either way, I'm not going to win."

◆ ◆ ◆

On Tuesday, Leyland was asked for his assessment of John Cangelosi, who was batting .167 with two RBIs.

"Off the record?" Leyland asked.

"OK."

"He's been horseshit."

"On the record?"

"On the record? He's struggling."

◆ ◆ ◆

The ball went up and Gary Sheffield raced forward. The ball came down and Sheffield tumbled down, just short of making the catch. When he landed, his glove struck backwards against the turf, then against his fallen body, and Sheffield immediately knew something was wrong with his left thumb, the same one he had broken two years ago. *I'm out for the season,* he thought.

Sheffield is the least graceful rightfielder you'll ever see, and this injury, which occurred in the sixth inning of the series opener against Atlanta, was the result of his poor fielding: He misjudged the ball, got a late start, and ended up diving awkwardly.

Sheffield was taken by ambulance to a nearby hospital and recalled during the trip what many of his teammates had told him. "Don't dive!" He was almost certain, because of the lack of swelling, that the finger wasn't broken, but as he stood outside the examining room, negative thoughts rushed through his mind.

Inside, the doctors were looking at his X-rays. Sheffield paced up and down the hallways and tested his left thumb, moving it back and forth, and comparing its movement to that of his uninjured right hand. Finally, after what seemed to Sheffield like hours, but was only minutes, the doctors came out with their prognosis: Sheffield had a mild sprain and could probably return to the lineup in a few days.

The next afternoon, Sheffield walked around the clubhouse wearing an electronic blood stimulator—it looked like a Walkman for the thumb—and talked like a man who had just been granted a reprieve. His teammates felt the same way.

"I don't mean to sound selfish, but when somebody like that goes down, you feel for the team, then you feel for him," Moises Alou said before the second game of the series. "Hopefully, he'll be back in a few days. Maybe he'll play tomorrow."

He wouldn't. Further X-rays revealed the sprain was worse than the doctors originally thought. Sheffield joined White, Leiter, Floyd, and Castillo on the Marlins' growing disabled list.

◆ ◆ ◆

The $49 million Marlins took the field Wednesday night with a bargain basement lineup and beat the Braves again, 4-3. Dunwoody, the 22-year-old leftfielder, hit his first career home run in the sixth off Denny Neagle, and Robb Nen barely held on to a one-run lead in the bottom of the ninth. After Nen allowed two singles, Leyland ordered him to intentionally walk Chipper Jones, bringing up power hitter Fred McGriff.

"We were in deep trouble, believe me," Leyland said. "I knew it. They knew it. Robby knew it. The fans knew it. The umpires knew it. Heck, my mom back home knew it. You don't feel real comfortable walking somebody to get to Fred McGriff."

The crowd of 38,902, far less than a sellout, was up and doing the tomahawk chop. Leyland nervously nibbled on sunflower seeds. Nen threw a ninety-five miles per hour fastball and if McGriff got all of it, the Braves would have won. Instead, he sent a sharp grounder to Conine, who scooped it up and ran to the bag for the final out.

There was no celebration, not for winning three out of four from the Braves in mid-May, even though the Marlins had reduced Atlanta's lead to three games. Almost to a man, the Marlins refused to say it was a big deal. Only Dunwoody said what must have been on everyone's mind.

"I don't like those guys," he said. "They win too much."

◆ ◆ ◆

Tony La Russa once said there had never been a relationship between the fans and a manager like the one between Pittsburgh Pirates fans and Jim Leyland. The Marlins arrived in Pittsburgh on May 16 to play a three-game series against the Pirates and find out whether the relationship could pass the test of time and distance. Leyland wasn't optimistic.

"I'm sure I'll get some boos," Leyland said. "They just booed the shit out of Neagle."

The blue-collar, working class fans in Pittsburgh had adored the no-nonsense, blue-collar manager from Perrysburg, Ohio, who never played at a higher level than Double-A and spent eleven years managing in the minors before getting his big league break. Leyland had received five long standing ovations from the crowd during his final game in Pittsburgh last September, reducing him to tears.

"They're real common folk," Leyland said. "I consider myself the same thing."

On the day of his return to Pittsburgh, Leyland took a cab to Three Rivers Stadium at noon, visited with Gene Lamont and Pirates general manager Cam Bonifay, and then remembered to turn left to the visitor's clubhouse, not right to the Pirates' clubhouse.

"No matter what the reception is, good or bad, nobody can ever take from me what I had in Pittsburgh," Leyland said. "I know who I am. I gave my heart and soul to this organization for eleven years, and in return I got the heart and soul of the fans. I couldn't ask for anything more than that."

The oddest aspect of Leyland's return was the fans' reaction when he walked from the dugout to home plate and delivered the lineup card prior to the first game. Some fans booed, others cheered politely, but for the most part, the reaction was one of indifference. Leyland's return would attract nearly seventy-eight thousand fans for the three games, double the Pirates' season average. If they didn't come to boo and they didn't come to cheer, they must have come to watch Leyland sit in the dugout nibbling on sunflower seeds and smoking cigarettes. Who in the world goes to a game to watch a manager manage?

But if that's what the fans came for, they saw Leyland in prime form. The Marlins won all three games to complete a 5-0 road trip, their best ever, and stretch their winning streak to eight. All of a sudden, their road woes were behind them.

They did it without the wives coming along, but with women in the clubhouse. Leyland noticed that the Marlins had gone undefeated with Cheryl Rosenberg of the *Palm Beach Post* making her first road trip of the season and was disappointed to hear that she wasn't making the next trip.

"We'll buy you a ticket," he offered.

And if he had to wear a towel in the clubhouse, he'd wear a towel. Some sacrifices were worth making.

NATIONAL LEAGUE EAST STANDINGS

	W	L	Pct.	GB
Atlanta	30	13	.698	—
Marlins	**26**	**16**	**.619**	**3.5**
Montreal	24	17	.585	5
New York	23	20	.535	7
Philadelphia	16	26	.381	13.5

6

"Education?
I'm All For It."

May 20, 21 vs. Mets
May 23, 24, 25 at San Diego
May 26, 27 at Los Angeles
May 29, 30, 31, June 1 vs. Colorado
June 2, 3, vs. San Francisco
June 4, 5 at Mets
June 6, 7, 8 at Colorado
June 9, 10, 11 at San Francisco

Jim Ross once had a job many men would envy. One month each year for two years, he escorted supermodel Elle MacPherson around the world on promotional gigs for the *Sports Illustrated* swimsuit issue. In one of the greatest teases since Marilyn Monroe stood over a subway grating, Ross went to sleep every night in a hotel room right next to Elle's.

When the beautiful Elle made her first appearance on *The Late Show* with David Letterman in 1985, Ross was, literally, right in the background. Paul Schaefer introduced the band members, and after Letterman asked, "Who is that guy over there in the red tie?" the camera switched to a shot of Ross standing in the dark near the bandstand.

"That's my accountant," Paul joked.

"Who are you?" Dave asked pleadingly. "What are you doing here? What is your name?"

"My name?" Ross deadpanned. "My name's Jim."

"Jim, what do you do for a living?" Dave demanded.

"I work for a living."

"Who do you work for? Why are you standing over there?"

"Where would you like me to stand?" Ross asked.

"I think he may be in the business," Paul suggested.

"No, just tell me," Dave insisted. "What do you do?"

"For a living?"

"Yeah!" Dave said, sounding exasperated. "For a living!"

"I work," Jim said. "I work for a magazine."

"For which magazine?"

"For *Sports Illustrated.*"

That ended Ross's speaking role in this little mystery. Letterman had heard enough, so he got up from behind his desk, grabbed Ross by the arm, and escorted him out of the studio, down the hall, and into a waiting elevator.

"What the hell is the deal?" Letterman asked as he walked back to the studio. "You try to put on a little show and a guy shows up here in a suit."

But as soon as Letterman got back to his desk, Ross stepped off of the elevator, walked back down the hall, and made a right turn into Elle's dressing room. As Dave and the audience watched in shock on the studio monitors, Elle greeted Jim from *Sports Illustrated* with a big hug.

"Oh, now, wait a minute," Letterman said. "Maybe I was too hasty. He didn't explain it like that, you see."

Two years later, Ross left *Sports Illustrated* and took a job with the New York Mets as director of marketing. That meant he had given up one month a year with Elle MacPherson for eight months a year with a bunch of guys named Lenny, Mookie, and Wally. He should have had his head examined.

◆ ◆ ◆

In 1997, as he sat in his parking lot-view office at Pro Player Stadium, Jim from *Sports Illustrated* had graduated to being Billy the Marlin's direct superior. He also was in charge of the Bleacher Brigade, the screaming P.A. announcer, the scoreboard that begged the fans to make more noise, and anything that had to do with the marketing and promotion of the Florida Marlins.

At age 35, Ross had one of the toughest jobs in baseball: Convincing reluctant South Floridians that coming out to Pro Player Stadium for a Marlins game was a good way to spend the evening, even though that evening might include a one hour rain delay and could result in severe neck cramps.

His official title was vice president of sales and marketing.

That meant he was directly responsible for how many tickets the Marlins sold. Depending upon your viewpoint, that could be either a good responsibility or a bad one.

The first guy who had this job, Don Smiley, sold over three million tickets the first season. He became president of the team.

The second guy who had this job oversaw a two year decline in attendance. He was moved into another position.

If Ross didn't do his job properly, there was an outside chance there would no longer be a Florida Marlins Baseball Club Inc., and a better chance he would be out on the streets looking for work and wishing he had never left his job with Elle MacPherson.

"There is a real sense of urgency around here," he said. "I've been told that it's a make or break year."

Making Ross's job more difficult were the two biggest problems with selling baseball in South Florida: the weather and Pro Player Stadium. They were related problems. For example, in the finicky South Florida market, the Marlins could hold Diamond Ring Night—one free to every paying fan over the age of 18—but if it rained within two hours of game time, hardly anyone would show up. But if Pro Player Stadium had a roof, the Marlins wouldn't have to hold Diamond Ring Night because fans wouldn't have to be coerced into showing up.

But the Marlins couldn't do anything about the rain, not without God on their staff, or at least a person who was willing to spend about $300 million on building a retractable-roof domed stadium. Even owner Wayne Huizenga wasn't that person, which was a little unsettling because he was one of the richest men in Florida.

In 1990, when Huizenga made his first pitch for the franchise, he pulled out his check book and offered in jest to write a check to the National League for the $95 million expansion fee. Later, he promised in writing that if weather was a problem in South Florida, as the existing owners feared, he'd consider putting a roof on Pro Player Stadium or building a new domed stadium.

Key word: *Consider.*

He didn't consider it for long.

◆ ◆ ◆

At first glance, Pro Player Stadium seems perfectly adequate for baseball, until you come back from visiting a real ballpark, like Turner Field, and realize what's wrong with the place. It's just . . . nothing. Solid banks of orange and blue seats. No history. No view of anything but the South Florida sky. Outfield seats that face the outfield, where most of the action isn't, rather than the infield, where most of the action is, and cause strained necks for anyone foolish enough to pay good money for a ticket out there.

Pro Player Stadium is not a baseball stadium. It's a football stadium that was opened in 1987 by Joe Robbie, who at that time owned the Miami Dolphins of the National Football League. Robbie later sold the Dolphins and the stadium to Huizenga, along with its key financial problem: The baseball and football teams don't get a dime from the sale of luxury boxes and executive suites because Robbie pledged it all to pay off the stadium debt.

So you might wander around Pro Player Stadium with a sense of longing after visiting Turner Field, knowing there never used to be a ballpark right here and still isn't. No Cracker Jacks (just something called Crunch 'n' Munch, as if the words to the song were *Buy me some peanuts and Crunch 'n' Munch*). A dugout that's really a canopy over a hollowed-out bench area. A rightfield fence that's much further away from home plate than the leftfield fence because football fields are longer than they are wide, as are football stadiums.

That left the Marlins' marketing and promotions department with a daunting task: Marketing a team without being able to market the stadium in which the team plays. Coors Field in Denver sells out constantly not only because people in Colorado like watching the Rockies hit hundreds of home runs, but because Coors Field is a pleasant place in which to spend an evening. The same is true for Orioles Park at Camden Yards, Wrigley Field, and Fenway Park. The same is not true for Pro Player Stadium, which has all the atmosphere of an outlet shopping mall.

Worst of all, it doesn't have a roof to keep out the rain, or render the threat of rain unimportant. Pro Player Stadium could be the worst dump in the world—which it isn't—but with a roof, or a retractable roof, it would be adequate.

And that's where the Catch-22 comes in. Even if Huizenga paid for a roof over the Marlins' heads, they'd still have the problem of all that missing luxury box revenue. Pro Player Stadium was one of the rare places where you could build a roof and still not fix the leak.

◆ ◆ ◆

For the first four years of the Marlins' existence, the sales and marketing staff tried everything to render the stadium's shortcomings and the unpredictable weather insignificant. As one staff member said, "We were just throwing everything against a wall and hoping something stuck."

Very little stuck. Attendance sank. Giveaways became meaningless because there were so many of them fans expected to get something every time they went to the ballpark. Not enough of Dade County's 1.36 million Hispanics attended Marlins games. When Huizenga bought the franchise, he had been told by local community leaders that Cubans loved baseball and would support the team. They didn't.

"Everybody had an opinion why," Ross said. "'You didn't sign the right players.' 'You didn't call the team the Miami Marlins.' 'Your advertising isn't effective.'"

The solution: Less is more in some cases. More is more in others.

Less is more: They ended the Growth Chart and pogs giveaways and started giving away stuff that might attract fans. Every Sunday home game in 1997 was designated a Head-to-Toe day, in which children would receive one part of a baseball uniform. By the time the season was over, they would have a full uniform: Jersey, shorts, socks, wristbands, bat, and glove. The Marlins had beach towel night, cooler night, several pin nights, and car flag night. They had fishing rod night.

Fishing rod night?

"They're great rods," Ross enthused. "They might be our best giveaway of the season."

OK. Maybe great was a strong word, but cut Ross some slack. His predecessors were Ringling Brothers, Barnum, and Bailey. Great is a strong word for anything that's given free at a ballpark.

Key word: *Free.*

More is more: They intensified their marketing efforts on attracting Hispanics and opened an office in the Little Havana section of Miami. They reduced ticket prices in most sections of the stadium and devised special season ticket packages.

"If our planning had any worth, to the slightest degree, every Friday, Saturday, and Sunday we'd have real good crowds, maybe thirty-five plus," Ross said. "Weekdays would go as the club goes. We were looking to draw twenty-nine and change per game."

71

Early indications were that their efforts worked. Through their first twenty-two home games, the Marlins' average attendance was 28,237, slightly below projections. By April 25, the Marlins had already sold as many tickets as they had sold in all of 1996. Their Hispanic season ticket base had tripled. Season ticket sales had increased from twelve thousand in 1996 to sixteen thousand six hundred in 1997.

They had tried to control everything they could and make sure everyone in South Florida knew Wayne Huizenga had spent a lot of money on a competitive team. What they couldn't control was the team's performance, those bad outfield seats, and the weather.

That's why figuring out who did what at Pro Player Stadium was never difficult. The players were the ones wearing the baseball uniforms. The security guards were the ones wearing the striped polo shirts. And the people in the marketing department were the ones whispering into their walkie-talkies and looking up at the sky, praying it didn't rain.

◆ ◆ ◆

"Education? I'm all for it," Robb Nen proclaimed to a room full of eighth graders.

"What are your plans for when you're finished with baseball?" a 13-year-old boy shyly asked.

Nen considered the question for a few seconds, then answered.

"I haven't really thought about it," he said. "I'm planning on pitching for at least another four years, so maybe I'll think about it then."

Like he really had to. Nen was making $3 million a year and wouldn't have to work a day in his life after baseball if he didn't want to.

Nen was in the classroom as part of World of Baseball Week, part of the Marlins' World of Baseball program. It's an ingenious concept. Kind of like the Big Bad Wolf convincing the Three Little Pigs to let him in by offering to show his recipe for pork chops.

In World of Baseball, the school curriculum is taught around baseball. Children learn math by computing batting averages and fielding percentages. They learn about computers by devising programs related to baseball.

Broken down to its bare essentials, World of Baseball is a training ground for future season ticket holders. If these children learned their lessons well, then one day they'd graduate from high school and go on to college. Someday, they'd even buy their own Marlins tickets.

◆ ◆ ◆

The Marlins' marketing machinery is enormous, sometimes intrusive, and always visible. One Saturday afternoon, Leyland paused in the dugout to smoke a cigarette, only to find himself surrounded by twenty children. He caught the attention of one of the front office staffers and panned his eyes as if to say, "What the hell is going on here?"

Players returning to the dugout after taking their swings in the batting cage could count on being greeted by a Bat Kid or two or three asking for autographs. The

Marlins had Ballpark Buddies and Diamond Dashes, in which children got to run the bases after games, and Sunday autograph sessions, and let four hundred season ticket holders take batting practice on the field.

Sometimes the weather hindered their efforts. One day, a Marlins staffer was at wits' end because an all-day rain had canceled batting practice, leaving her to entertain a disappointed Bat Kid. She tried everything.

"That's where the players get ready to hit," she said, pointing to the on-deck circle.

The little girl nodded.

"That's where the manager sits," she said, pointing to the corner seat in the dugout.

The little girl nodded.

"And that," she said, pointing to a drain on the floor, "is where the players spit their sunflower seeds."

The little girl nodded.

◆ ◆ ◆

On Wednesday, May 28, the Marlins returned from a five-game west coast trip, went home for some sleep, and had the rest of the day free. The only significant event occurred two thousand miles away in Chicago, where the Heat's long playoff run ended with a loss to the Bulls. With the Heat and Panthers gone from the playoffs, the South Florida sports scene belonged to the Marlins for the next three months, until the Dolphins began their season. Then they'd be at football's mercy. The Dolphins dominated the South Florida market so thoroughly that even in March and April, a person could tune in the local sports talk radio station and hear nothing but football being discussed for hours.

After splitting two games against the Mets at Pro Player Stadium a week earlier, the Marlins had continued playing well on the road and won three of five in San Diego and Los Angeles. Tony Saunders had landed on the disabled list with an injured right knee, but Leiter and Floyd were healthy again, and White and Sheffield were on the verge of returning to the lineup.

The Marlins had a record of 30-20 and were 4½ games out of first place when the Rockies came to town for four games. The weekend series invited the inevitable comparisons between the two expansion teams, which entered the league in 1993 but matured at different rates. The Marlins matured slowly. The Rockies matured fast. They had already been to the playoffs and played their home games in Coors Field, a beautiful, downtown, taxpayer-financed baseball stadium in which 3.8 million fans watched them in 1996.

For the first four years, fans in South Florida couldn't help but compare the two expansion teams. *If they could win right away, why couldn't we?* they'd ask. The answer was that the Marlins had chosen to go the slow, patient route and build through their farm system, while the Rockies—knowing they had a new stadium in their immediate future—went for veteran talent with higher salaries.

Now that the Marlins had discarded the slow, patient plan in favor of the spend-lots, get-good-fast plan, the fans had no reason to be envious. But Don Smiley did. When he looked at the Rockies, all he saw was Coors Field.

"If people want to compare us to the Rockies, then fine, let that be the measure by which we're compared," he said. "I'd still like to have that ballpark."

◆ ◆ ◆

Alex Fernandez allowed three gargantuan home runs in a 6-5 loss to the Rockies in the series opener Thursday night, and Leyland declared that allowing three gargantuan home runs is "all part of it." Fernandez agreed that allowing three home runs is all part of it, but he disputed whether it was all of it.

"I made bad pitches and after that I didn't make a mistake," an impatient Fernandez said to reporters. "There were a lot of better things that happened in this game than what I did. We played great defense. We scored some runs, so why don't you write about that stuff?"

Nen allowing three runs in the ninth inning and blowing his third save in five chances was also part of it. After completing his handiwork, Nen was booed so loudly and heartily that it was as if every fan in the ballpark was thinking, *Here's this guy who's paid $3 million a year to pitch an inning once in a while, and he can't even do that.* Nen felt so bad—about the boos, not his performance—that he said, "I've got nothing to say to these fans. What do they want me to do, apologize? They've already got their opinion of me."

Nen had his opinion of them, too. On Friday, Dave O'Brien from the Fort Lauderdale *Sun-Sentinel* and Dan Graziano from the *Palm Beach Post* walked up to Nen, but before they could ask a question, he held up his hands.

"I'm not talking," Nen said. "The newspaper is for the fans and they have their own opinion of me. Fuck 'em. That's how they get their information and I'm not going to do anything for them anymore. They've got their own opinion of me, so fuck 'em. I'm not doing anything for them. Not signing, nothing. They don't know what I'm going through and they don't care. Until I change my mind, that's the way I feel about it. If you guys want to put that in the paper, that's fine."

Of course, Graziano and O'Brien did just that and reported Nen's comments, *sans* fuck 'ems.

The next morning, Jim Ross and his staff awoke to the unpleasant sight of Nen's comments in the newspapers and realized they had a public relations problem on their hands. NEN BOOS BACK: HE WON'T TALK TO FANS read one of the headlines over a subhead that described Nen's silent treatment as "punishment to the fans."

Key word: *Punishment.*

There's nothing like a $3-million-a-year relief pitcher punishing the fans after blowing his third save in two weeks. It's the kind of behavior that can wipe out all of the positive things some players do to erase the perception of athletes as overpaid, selfish louts. Several Marlins players, including Nen, were active in community service. Jim Eisenreich, who has Tourette's Syndrome, spoke to children with Tourette's. Al Leiter spoke to troubled youths. Kevin Brown donated money to a children's cancer care center.

But a player saying he's "not doing anything for them," when "them" are the people paying his salary, is a public relations disaster.

"If that article is accurate, Robbie made a mistake," Leyland said. "The fans have a right to do that. They're paying the freight. Some of these fans, they're broken-hearted when we lose. As long as they're fair, I expect my players to face the consequences. They weren't booing Robbie Nen for a lack of effort. They were booing the results of a pitching performance."

"Are you sure he knows that?" a reporter asked.

"Well, shit," Leyland said. "If he don't, he'd better figure it out."

Nen figured it out quickly, with the help of several Marlins PR staffers. At first, Nen insisted his comments were spoken off the record, a remarkable claim considering two reporters from competing papers both heard him say, "If you guys want to put that in the paper, that's fine."

Nen never claimed he had been misquoted, although that would have been a more believable claim, considering the content of his quote. It showed too much emotion for Nen, whose post-game quotes usually ran the gamut from "I just try to go pitch-by-pitch" to "Every batter you face is dangerous." Fascinating stuff. Nen, 27, always entered games at Pro Player Stadium to the AC/DC hard rock song *Thunderstruck.* Thunderstruck also described the mental condition of reporters after speaking to Nen for five minutes and ending up with a notebook full of clichés.

But Nen never backed off his disingenuous claim that the comments were spoken off-the-record and instead displayed remarkable ability at passing the blame.

"Now I know who I can talk to and who I can't," Nen told O'Brien and Graziano.

Nen's only way out of this mess was by rescinding his punishment and doing the opposite of what he said he was going to do. Before Saturday's game, he signed autographs. Then, after pitching a scoreless ninth in an 8-4 Marlins loss, he took a deep breath, faced the media, and apologized to the fans.

"The fans have all the right to boo, to do what they want," the new Nen declared. "They pay the money to come to games. If I came to a game and somebody wasn't doing what they needed to do, I'd give them a hard time, too. That's their right. My thing is, I didn't want to make excuses about the way I pitched. I suck right now. I made bad pitches and they hit 'em."

Two nights later when the Marlins played the Giants, the fans were back on Nen's side when he ran in from the bullpen to pitch the ninth inning. Then they turned against him when he put the tying runs on base. Then they were back on his side when he retired Barry Bonds to end the game. By that time, Nen should have detected a pattern. *Boo me when I do bad. Cheer me when I do good.*

The fan's heart is an awfully resilient little muscle.

◆ ◆ ◆

Leyland summed up the Colorado series by saying, "We got outmanaged, outplayed, outpitched, and outhustled the whole series. Basically, we stunk. I was horseshit and consequently the ball club was horseshit."

They were also outbrawled and shown up in their own ballpark. The Marlins lost three out of four games in a series that had no shortage of excitement.

On Saturday afternoon, a crowd of 35,032 and a national TV audience watched Kevin Brown allow a spectacular grand slam to Andres Galarraga in the fourth inning. The ball thundered off of Galarraga's bat and kept rising before landing five hundred twenty-nine feet away, next to the Jackie Robinson sign halfway up the upper deck in leftfield. It was the longest home run ever hit in Pro Player Stadium and one of the longest in baseball history.

The crowd cheered Galarraga as he rounded the bases. Bonilla, standing at third base, was amazed. He just stared at Galarraga and shook his head.

"That's a dream home run," Bonilla said.

Brown was not pleased. He circled the mound and never looked at Galarraga.

Four innings later, Dennis Cook congratulated Galarraga by patting him on the arm with an 88-mile-per-hour fastball thrown from a distance of sixty feet, six inches. Now Galarraga was not pleased. Instead of circling the mound, he charged it, and the 6'3", 190-pound Cook had to deal with the horrifying sight of a 6'3", 245-pound angry body hurtling right at him.

Galarraga's nickname: The Big Cat.

Key word: *Big.*

I hope he doesn't kill me, Cook thought.

Bonilla, who at 6'4", 240 pounds, could fight in the same weight class as Galarraga, rushed to Cook's rescue and grabbed Galarraga as both benches emptied.

"I was just making sure I got hold of the Big Cat and make sure he wasn't doing any damage," Bonilla said. "That's a big boy. Then everything just pretty much calmed down."

The Rockies were sure Cook had purposely thrown at Galarraga. Manager Don Baylor claimed one of his players overheard one of the Marlins say, "When somebody hits one nine miles, what do they expect?"

Cook's response: "I didn't say that. And besides, I would never hit a guy for hitting a ball nine miles, so that's crazy."

Maybe so, but even if Cook was being dishonest, he had nothing to gain by honesty. Admitting to throwing at Galarraga would have resulted in a long suspension. As it was, when Cook arrived at the ballpark on Tuesday, a fax from National League president Leonard Coleman was waiting on his chair. It said something to the effect of, "Dear Mr. Cook. You have been suspended for three games and fined $1,000."

But Cook, who planned on appealing the suspension, stuck to his story, although the evidence was overwhelmingly against him. Even his teammates thought he had purposely hit Galarraga. They praised him for sticking up for Sheffield, who had been hit by a pitch in the previous inning.

Cook didn't want their praise.

"It just got away from me," he said.

He would tell it to the judge.

◆ ◆ ◆

"Attention media," Ron Colangelo announced in the press box. "Billy the Marlin's head is at Gate G."

Found: The five-pound head of the Marlins' mascot. Two months to the day after Billy's head fell to earth, it was spotted by a passing motorist on Florida's Turnpike, a few miles from Pro Player Stadium.

"We saw him, we skidded to a halt," said the driver. "Smoke was coming from the tires. My head hit the windshield."

Strange fact No. 1: Billy's head was found on a retaining wall on the side of the Turnpike. The driver had passed the same spot an hour earlier, but Billy's head wasn't there.

Strange fact No. 2: Billy's head was intact. Other than a few scratches here and there, he had survived the seven thousand-foot fall quite nicely.

A suspicious person might have thought the Marlins planted Billy's head as a publicity stunt.

"I wish we had thought of it," Jim Ross insisted. "But we're not that smart."

◆ ◆ ◆

Don Smiley sat in the Marlins' dugout a few hours before the opener of a two-game series against San Francisco and looked forlorn. He had his right leg crossed over his left leg and a cigarette in his hand as he watched the head groundskeeper standing near the tarp.

"Look at the poor guy," Smiley said. "He doesn't know whether to take the tarp off or keep it on. He doesn't know what to do."

Nor did Smiley. The previous Thursday, the Marlins drew only 19,145, their lowest Thursday night crowd of the season, for the opening game of the Colorado series. It was the first time all season Smiley and Jim Ross were surprised and disappointed by the size of a crowd. The Marlins had the third best record in baseball and the Rockies were the Marlins' expansion rivals, but a year earlier more people had turned out for a Thursday night game against the Cubs. The final three games of the Colorado series attracted over one hundred ten thousand fans, but that didn't impress Smiley.

"Everybody draws relatively high on weekends," he said.

Smiley spoke about the new retractable-roof domed stadium that was going up in Phoenix for the expansion Arizona Diamondbacks and how great it would be to have something like that in South Florida. From open to shut in ten minutes, then open again in another ten. The answer to the Marlins' attendance woes.

But there was no roof, retractable or otherwise, attached to Pro Player Stadium, and from where he sat, Smiley could gaze up and see dark clouds in all directions. Within a span of three minutes, the rain stopped and started three times before it finally came down in torrents. Disgusted, Smiley stood up and walked away.

"I can't even watch," he said.

◆ ◆ ◆

Bobby Bo roared into New York with a long memory, his gleaming smile, and a booming laugh. He was looking forward to sleeping in his own bed in Greenwich, Connecticut, for a few nights and getting reacquainted with his wife and children, but he also knew there'd be plenty of time to get reacquainted with the Shea Stadium fans and the reporters covering the Mets. His script was prepared.

"It'll be beautiful," Bonilla had said a few days earlier.

"They have the Welcome Back Bobby Bo banners all ready," a reporter cracked.

"Oh, I'm sure," Bonilla said, leaning against the wall of his locker and laughing at the thought. "It'll be fun. It usually is."

"Are you looking forward to it?"

"I'm just thinking about going home and seeing my kids," Bonilla insisted. "It's the only thing I'm thinking about. The Mets are secondary as far as I'm concerned. That's something I'll deal with after I talk with my kids and my wife. Going home, to sleep in my bed. That's all I'm thinking about."

"You know the reporters will want to talk to you."

"They won't have a chance. Why do they need to talk to me? They'll talk to you!" Bonilla said, before changing his voice to a whisper. "They'll say, *How's he acting? Is he all right? Has he been cool?* And you know what my answer is gonna be? Fuck 'em all! I'm pretty good at that! What else are they gonna say? Fuck. *How's Bobby. How's this? How's he been?* What the fuck, get a life!" he roared. "But that's just the way it is in New York. Ain't nothing you can do about it. You gotta be a prick. It's good practice there."

Then he switched to a deeper, more serious tone as he anticipated another exchange with his New York buddies.

"'No, I don't want to talk to you,' I'll say. Then they'll say, 'Why, you're not talking to the media?' And I'll tell them, 'No,'" Bonilla said. "Then they'll say, 'Same old Bonilla.' That's what they'll say. You guys'll get a kick out of it, 'cause you know I'm gonna do it! I'm letting you know right now!"

Publicity director Ron Colangelo walked over. "By the way, Bobby . . ."

"Yes sir," Bonilla responded.

"The *Daily News* and *The New York Times* requested an interview with you."

Bonilla let out a hearty laugh.

"You just watch," he promised. "Just watch me for a couple of days over there. I'll give you a show!"

But Bobby Bo disappointed and the show never materialized. Only five reporters surrounded him on the steps of the visitor's dugout at Shea Stadium prior to the first game of the series on June 4 and only one TV guy tested his patience.

TV GUY: What do you think went wrong here?

BONILLA: I don't know. I know for a fact I played as hard as I could.

TV GUY: How do you think the fans feel about you here?

BONILLA: I don't know. You'd have to go in the stands and ask them.

TV GUY: How do you think the fans will welcome you?

BONILLA: I figure they will throw roses at me.

TV GUY: Will you throw them back?

BONILLA: There's a good chance I might.

TV GUY: Can you explain your fabulous start with the Marlins?

BONILLA: Ahhhh. So now I'm off to a fabulous start.

TV GUY: What are your memories of playing here?

BONILLA: Memories? You don't want to know.

TV GUY: How about the good memories?

BONILLA: You don't want to know.

TV GUY: Just another chapter in your book, huh?

BONILLA: An interesting chapter. It could be a long chapter.

Bonilla smiled through the whole exchange. He also smiled when he walked to the plate in the second inning—batting .343, fifth in the National League, the scoreboard noted—and the crowd booed. They chanted "Bobby Sucks!" after he struck out swinging, kept booing when he singled and scored the winning run in the sixth, and booed louder with each at-bat in the two-game series. Bonilla's production for the two games was two hits in six at-bats and no run-ins with the media. The people in New York must have hardly recognized him.

◆ ◆ ◆

Bonilla had a better time in New York than Jeff Conine and Kevin Brown. Conine, whose average had dropped from .361 on April 25 to .223, got benched. Brown got hit hard for the second straight start, allowing six runs on twelve hits in seven innings, including a long home run by Bernard Gilkey, in a 6-0 win for the Mets in the series finale.

Whatever was troubling Brown, he refused to discuss it after the game. He left without answering questions, so reflection and analysis was saved for pitching coach Larry Rothschild. Leyland had suggested that National League hitters had adjusted to Brown, but Rothschild disagreed. He thought Brown was throwing too many hittable pitches down the middle of the plate.

Brown's next start, in five days against the Giants in San Francisco, would be telling. He had dominated the Giants more than any other team in 1996, allowing only two runs in twenty-six innings. If Leyland's theory was right and Rothschild's theory was wrong, they'd find out in San Francisco.

◆ ◆ ◆

If they ever got to San Francisco. First they had to get through a three-game series with the Rockies in Denver.

And about that beautiful taxpayer-financed stadium the Rockies play in: It doesn't have a retractable roof. On June 6, 7, and 8, it needed one.

Fifty-three hours passed between the time the Marlins arrived at Coors Field Friday afternoon until they left Sunday night. Devon White spent some of his time on the trainer's table after reinjuring his calf muscle. His return to the disabled list was imminent. The Marlins won two out of three games after waiting through one rainout, numerous rain delays, thunderstorms, a tornado warning, and an 11:05 start Sunday morning. By the time the weekend ended, they knew every inch of the visitor's clubhouse at Coors Field and had done everything possible to keep themselves occupied. Everything.

Al Leiter had allowed seven runs in five innings in the first game of Sunday's doubleheader and, with the second game not scheduled to start for three hours, fig-

79

ured he'd try to kill some time. Dressed in stirrups, flip-flops, mesh shorts, and a Florida Marlins T-shirt, with his hair a mess and without having showered, Leiter went walking through the streets outside Coors Field. He hardly blended in with the crowd, but nobody seemed to recognize or notice the pitcher who a year earlier tossed a no-hitter against the Rockies.

But there he was, standing on a street corner, looking a bit out of sorts, when one of the Marlins' broadcasters walked over.

"How're you doing?" the broadcaster asked.

"Hey," Leiter said matter-of-factly. "You know any place around here that I can play pool?"

◆ ◆ ◆

On June 10 in San Francisco, Kevin Brown said these words: "I'm happy with the way I threw the ball." Record them for prosperity. None of the reporters covering the Marlins had ever heard Brown say those words over the past year and a half, even in 1996, when the games in which he allowed more than three runs could have been counted on one hand. A notorious perfectionist—a surly, self-critical perfectionist—Brown finally found happiness at 3Com Park.

The second no-hitter in Marlins history was as close as possible to being a perfect game. Pitchers traditionally credit their fielders after no-hitters. In most cases, it's impossible to pitch a no-hitter without the help of a few great fielding plays, but that wasn't the case this time. The Giants didn't come close to getting a hit off Brown and spent the afternoon flailing at sinkers and fastballs. They hit only three balls out of the infield. When the game ended, the official scorer walked up to Brown and said, "Thanks for making my job easier." He could have slept through the Giants' at-bats.

"You feel helpless," said Giants manager Dusty Baker. "He wasn't perfect, but he was damn near perfect. He'd struggled in his last two starts, so I figured he would be good today. But not that good."

Brown, who had spent the past four days working hard on the sidelines with Larry Rothschild, retired the first nine batters he faced on strikeouts and groundouts. Darryl Hamilton flied out to left in the fourth, then Brown retired eight more in a row on strikeouts and groundouts.

"After the first pitch, I knew it was going to be a long day," Hamilton said.

The Marlins weren't doing much either against Giants starter William VanLandingham. They scored their first run in the fifth on a walk, followed by a balk, but didn't have a hit until the seventh. Brown and VanLandingham were pitching a double no-hitter. Then the Marlins scored seven runs on two errors and six hits, including a two-run homer by Charles Johnson, and the only remaining suspense was whether Brown would allow a hit.

There wasn't much suspense.

"I've never pitched a game like this, not even in Little League," Brown said.

The Giants went down like Little Leaguers.

"I've seen some no-hitters when a guy really doesn't dominate, but that was dominant," Leyland said.

Brown's toughest inning was the seventh. Hamilton led off with a deep drive to center that Moises Alou caught on the run. With two outs, J. T. Snow hit a grounder up the middle, but Castillo ran it down and threw to first to get the slow runner. Brown's sinker was sinking improbably and the Giants couldn't adjust. Neither could catcher Charles Johnson.

"It's tough to catch," Johnson said. "Playing here with all that wind, it sinks even more."

Brown's perfect game ended with two outs in the eighth, when pinch-hitter Marvin Benard got hit on the left leg with an inside fastball. Benard, who was wearing a kneepad, didn't bother avoiding the pitch, but was awarded first base.

"It was disappointing," Brown said. "But I didn't want to lose my focus."

Brown had the small crowd at 3Com on his side by the ninth inning. Meanwhile, Leiter, the only other Marlin who had pitched a major league no-hitter, sat on the bench and watched nervously, remembering all the times Brown had said to him, "I'll never pitch a no-hitter."

Bill Mueller opened the ninth with a routine groundout to Conine at first. Pinch hitter Stan Javier hit a hard one-hopper to short, and Edgar Renteria made an easy play. Only Hamilton stood between Brown and a no-hitter, and as he walked to the plate, the crowd stood and cheered.

"I didn't know if I was in Florida or San Francisco," Hamilton said.

They were cheering for Brown. Hamilton looked at the first two pitches for strikes. He fouled off the third pitch. The fourth pitch was a fastball on the inside corner. Umpire Greg Bonin called strike three and the no-hitter was complete.

At first, Brown didn't know how to react. He walked off the mound toward first base as if he was in a daze. Then he punched his fists, threw his arms in the air, and let out a scream. He turned toward home and saw Charles Johnson coming toward him, then the entire team came running out of the dugout, and suddenly, Brown was at the center of happiness. It was a strange place for him to be.

"I was just trying to figure out how to act," Brown said. "It was kind of disbelief. Part of me wanted to run."

Brown, who twice this season had run when reporters wanted him to speak, allowed himself to enjoy the rest of the day. His teammates soaked him with champagne and Brown stood against a wall and answered reporters' questions for a half hour. For a change, he couldn't find fault in his performance. He couldn't even find fault in their questions. It was the rarest of days.

NATIONAL LEAGUE EAST STANDINGS

	W	L	Pct.	GB
Atlanta	42	22	.656	—
Marlins	**37**	**26**	**.587**	**4.5**
Montreal	35	28	.556	6.5
New York	35	28	.556	6.5
Philadelphia	21	41	.339	20

7

"We Just Changed Our Minds"

June 13, 14, 15 vs. Yankees
June 16, 17, 18 at Detroit
June 20, 21, 22 at Montreal
June 23, 24, 25 at Philadelphia

Back in February, Dennis Cook had dropped by Pro Player Stadium the day tickets went on sale and saw hundreds of New York Yankees fans, wearing navy blue and white jerseys, T-shirts, and caps, waiting on a long, snaking line. They outnumbered the people wearing teal by a large margin, and right then Cook knew Major League Baseball's first inter-league experiment would be a success in South Florida.

The Yankees' box office appeal in South Florida, an area populated by tens of thousands of transplanted New Yorkers, came as no surprise to Don Smiley. The Marlins had always been ardent supporters of inter-league play between American and National League teams. When the major league owners finally decided to forego tradition and cash in, Smiley made certain the Yankees were on the Marlins' home schedule.

The series on June 13, 14, and 15 was the most eagerly anticipated of the season. All three games had sold out well before opening day and the marketing department treated the Yankees' arrival as a chance to put on its best show. The stadium would be packed and, if all went well, the fans would come back for more baseball later in the season.

"There'll be a lot of people rooting for the Yankees tonight," Leyland said prior to the first game. "Who cares? What's wrong with that? As long as they're here and rooting for baseball. But I can't get caught up in inter-league play. They're the world champions. I hope that someday I look back at this day and talk about it, but right now, we have to win some ball games."

Leyland would remember this weekend, all right. So would every baseball fan in South Florida, and not entirely in a positive light.

◆ ◆ ◆

Joe DiMaggio, the famed Yankee Clipper, threw out the first ball prior to the series opener. He threw it not to an actual catcher, but to Billy the Marlin, which the reporters covering the Yankees decided was appalling. They would have been even more appalled if they had known that earlier in the season Gregg Zaun volunteered to catch when Miss Universe threw out the first ball. Nobody stepped up for DiMaggio, so Billy the Marlin it was.

◆ ◆ ◆

The atmosphere was unlike anything South Florida had ever experienced for baseball. The stadium started filling hours before the game, and fans lined four deep behind the Yankees' dugout for autographs. Chants of "Let's Go Yankees" drowned out the opposing cheers of "Let's Go Marlins." It sounded like "Let's Go Marlkees."

In the first game Friday night, the Marlins trailed, 1-0, in the bottom of the ninth, when Moises Alou tied it with a single to left. Felix Heredia retired the Yankees in the tenth, and the Marlins came up in the bottom of the inning looking forward to facing a pitcher other than Yankees starter David Cone.

Then it started raining.

◆ ◆ ◆

The grounds crew covered the field at 9:57, which was exactly when the weekend started going downhill. Any hopes the Marlins' marketing department harbored of using this weekend as an advertisement for baseball in South Florida would soon be washed away. There was rain and there was wind and most of all, there were a lot of people running around not knowing what to do next.

Well, about thirty-two thousand people knew what to do next. They went home. Another ten thousand stayed through a rain delay of nearly one hour to watch the Marlins win, 2-1, in the bottom of the twelfth. About a third of the remaining crowd cheered. The rest were Yankees fans.

Another sellout crowd was filing into the ballpark Saturday night at the same time a string of dark clouds filed into the area around Pro Player Stadium. Several thousand fans made the mistake of sitting down. They were the optimists. Most of the fans stayed under cover in the concourses. They were the realists. On this weekend, the realists had it over the optimists by a wide margin, both in numbers and in powers of prognostication.

The game started an hour and ten minutes late. Gary Sheffield hit a grand slam in the bottom of the first. Only he and the optimists among the Marlins fans dared get excited. The pessimists knew what would happen next.

Many of those pessimists were sitting in the press box. They were the Yankees beat reporters and they had no doubt those rain clouds in the distance would, in no time at all, settle right over Pro Player Stadium and never move. Ever. At least not this weekend. They were sitting in front of their computers, praying a rain delay wouldn't make them miss their deadlines, but they knew it was hopeless. At 9:42, the rain came down in sheets, and the grounds crew covered the field.

"It is raining harder than I have ever seen it rain in my entire life," Suzyn Waldman reported to WFAN radio in New York.

"This place is hell," said one of the New York reporters.

Torrential showers flooded the field and rain poured off the upper deck, as if Niagara Falls had opened a tributary at Pro Player Stadium. A few fans sitting behind home plate refused to budge. They just sat under a clear plastic sheet while the rain splattered around them. These people could have been called brave. They could have been called optimistic. But despite the plastic, they could definitely be called wet.

South Florida was wet. The fans were wet. The grounds crew was wet. The only people who weren't wet were the people complaining most about the weather: They were the New York reporters, cozy and warm in the press box, who were dining on free hot fudge sundaes, popcorn, and soda. They acted as if they had never seen rain before.

"This place is hell," the out-of-town reporter said again.

And this was a man who spent his summers in the Bronx.

"I think Miami needs a dome, to tell you the truth," said Wade Boggs of the Yankees.

By 11:30, the game still hadn't been called and only a few thousand people were still in the stadium. The rain slowed and the grounds crew used squeegees to remove water from the infield. They might as well have used pails to drain the Atlantic Ocean. Under normal circumstances, the game would have been postponed, but these weren't normal circumstances. This was the only series between the Yankees and Marlins and, unless the teams played a doubleheader on Sunday, there was no other time during the season to reschedule the game.

But at 12:10 a.m., as a man in the lower level danced crazily to the '70s disco song *Stayin' Alive* and a group of fans formed a conga line, the game was called off.

Too bad nobody told the fans.

They weren't told because Dave Dombrowski and Don Smiley were down in the Yankees' clubhouse, meeting behind closed doors with David Cone, the Yankees player representative, and trying to decide whether the teams would play a day-night doubleheader on Sunday, or a regular doubleheader, with one game played immediately after the other.

The difference was economic. If a regular doubleheader was played, the Marlins would have to offer refunds or rainchecks to the 42,845 people holding tickets for Saturday's game. That was the last thing they wanted to do. But the Yankees didn't want to play a day-night doubleheader with a three-hour break between games. They wanted to play a regular doubleheader.

Smiley and Dombrowski rushed from the trainer's room to the visiting manager's office to the visiting clubhouse manager's office. They called the National League office, then the American League office, then both offices, and nobody knew whose rules to follow, because Major League Baseball hadn't accounted for the possibility of a rainout when it devised the inter-league schedule.

The two sides could have haggled all night. Instead, they compromised. The teams would play a split doubleheader on Sunday with an hour and a half between games.

By then it was after 1 o'clock in the morning, and the few thousand fans remaining in the stadium had been totally forgotten. Most of the Yankees had returned to their hotel. Most of the Marlins were showered and dressed. But the fans were just milling around the stands, dancing in the rain, splashing in the puddles, ignoring the scoreboard operator's pleas to form another conga line, when Smiley walked into the press box and glanced through the window out into the stadium. He was like the party host who wakes up in the morning to a house full of company that unexpectedly decided to stay over.

"They're still here?" he said in shock.

Of course they were still there. Nobody had told them to go home.

"I think we need to make a P.A. announcement," Smiley proclaimed.

Not a bad idea.

◆ ◆ ◆

Around that time, Leyland announced his pitchers for the doubleheader: Pat Rapp in the first game and rookie "Yvon Hernandez" in the second game.

"You mean Livan Hernandez?" asked a reporter.

"Yvon, Livan," Leyland snapped. "What the fuck."

◆ ◆ ◆

Seven hundred thirty miles to the north, Livan Hernandez was lounging around his apartment in Charlotte, North Carolina, when he received an unexpected phone call from Carlos Tosca, the manager of the Marlins' Triple-A team.

"Livan," Tosca told him. "You're pitching tomorrow for the Marlins."

Hernandez reacted calmly. He phoned his agent, Joe Cubas, and asked him to meet him at the airport the next morning, but didn't call anyone else because there was nobody else to call. His entire family lived in Cuba. So he packed his bags, got three hours sleep, and caught an early flight from Charlotte to Miami. Later in the morning, he walked into the Marlins' clubhouse, a place nobody had expected him to be for at least a few years, if ever.

"I was a little surprised," Hernandez said through an interpreter. "I didn't expect it."

Making a quick exit was nothing new to the 22-year-old pitcher. He had done it once before, on September 27, 1995, when the Cuban national team was training in Monterrey, Mexico. After sneaking past the team's chaperones, he ran out the hotel door, sprinted across the street, narrowly avoided getting run over, and jumped into a waiting car. He had just defected from Cuba, and all he could think about was the family he had left behind.

Lots of money awaited him. Hernandez spent the winter playing ball in the Dominican Republic in what amounted to an audition for major league scouts. There were plenty of suitors, including the Yankees, who wanted to pay Hernandez a half million dollars more than any other team was offering. But the Marlins were proactive. Huizenga sent a helicopter to pick up Hernandez and fly him to Miami.

Hernandez toured the Little Havana district with its large Cuban population. It felt like home. Hernandez declined the Yankees' offer and signed with the Marlins for $4.5 million, including a $2.5 million signing bonus.

Money didn't buy him happiness. Hernandez, who had known only poverty in Cuba, suffered through a long period of culture shock. He was lonely, missed his family, and worried about his mother.

"When people arrive in this country, they arrive blind," Hernandez said. "They do not know what they are getting themselves into."

Lost in a new country, he did the only thing he could to ease his anxiety: He ate and spent money. The day he received his signing bonus, he sent $50,000 to his family in Cuba. He bought three cars. He used those cars to go out to eat. He couldn't drive past a McDonald's or a Burger King without taking a detour through the drive-through. Already a big man at 6'2", 220 pounds, Hernandez had ballooned to 250 pounds when he reported to training camp in February 1996. The Marlins' $2.5 million bonus baby had become a fat bonus baby and general manager Dave Dombrowski knew it was time to place Hernandez on a strict diet and training regimen. Otherwise, the Marlins' money would end up in a fast food restaurant's coffers.

Hernandez adjusted his eating habits. By spring training 1997, he had made the transition from overweight, overpaid bust to slimmed-down prospect by following a simple formula. "Last year, when I passed by a Burger King, I had to stop," he said. He rediscovered Cuban food, soup, and salads, and took off most of the weight.

But the slimmed-down Hernandez had no chance of making the improved Marlins and was in Leyland's first group of cuts. He returned to Triple-A, struggled again—five wins, three losses, with a 3.98 earned run average—and displayed minor, but encouraging, improvement. The Marlins thought he was a year away from the majors.

Hernandez wouldn't have made his first major league start in the second game of the doubleheader if Leyland and Dombrowski had another choice. But Tony Saunders was on the disabled list. Alex Fernandez had pitched three innings in the postponed second game. It would have to be Livan, Yvon What The Fuck against the world champions. Not the Marlins' most promising matchup of the season.

◆ ◆ ◆

Not the most promising weather, either. Of course, there was more rain in the forecast, and by the time the first game started at about 1:05, the New York beat reporter's opinion of baseball in South Florida had gone from "This place is hell" to "Why did they put a team down here?"

The afternoon went like this:

1:30: Dark clouds overhead. What else is new?

1:33: Rain. Between innings, Jim Ross is interviewed on the field by Sports-Channel and raindrops are falling on his head. He is smiling when he starts the interview, but that smile is gone by the time he's finished. His weekend is on the verge of ruination.

1:34: Armageddon. Gale force winds blow a panel of padding off the left field fence. Fortunately, the panel is captured by the grounds crew before it causes any damage.

1:38: Serious, torrential rain.

1:39: Home plate umpire Greg Bonin decides it might be a good time to cover the field. The other option is playing baseball in a hurricane.

1:55: After sixteen minutes of heavy rain, the sun comes out, but more clouds are rolling in from the east. By this time, the New York reporters are convinced they will never get out of South Florida alive. But they don't care, as long as they can get out of South Florida.

2:13: More rain.

2:30: The grounds crew removes the tarp.

2:32: Publicity director Ron Colangelo announces the game will resume at 2:56. Nobody believes him.

2:51: Colangelo was wrong. The game resumes five minutes early—if early is the word to describe anything that happened this weekend—after a rain delay of one hour, twelve minutes.

3:30: Fans start arriving for the second game. Some of them, unaware of the rainout the night before because they didn't bother turning on their radios, think it's only game. When they walk up to the gate, they are informed they can't come in until the first game is over. None of them try to storm the building. Most of them just walk over to the party tents and have a beer.

4:30: The gates are opened while the first game is still being played. The fans for the second game are invited to find an empty seat, which won't be difficult because there are plenty. Only thirty-five thousand fans would end up watching two games that eighty-five thousand had paid to see.

There was baseball, too. Robb Nen blew another save, Kurt Abbott caught a ball he shouldn't have tried to catch, and the Marlins lost, 8-5.

By the time the second game started, the skies had cleared and no more rain was in the forecast. Hernandez got off to a bad start and allowed three runs in the first two innings. But on a weekend when early leads meant nothing, the Marlins rallied to win, 6-5, on a two-run error in the bottom of the ninth.

"There's no adversity after a game like that," insisted Leyland.

But while the series featured three last at-bat victories, the overwhelming message of the weekend was clear: Come out to Pro Player Stadium and you'll see some good baseball. You'll also get wet.

"To me, the series could have been the great momentum builder for the rest of the season," Jim Ross said. "And it was good but it could have been better."

Count the ways. If only it hadn't rained. If only a few thousand fans weren't left sitting in the stadium one hour after a game had been postponed. If only the one hundred twenty-seven thousand fans who had paid to see baseball actually got to see baseball.

And if only Wayne Huizenga had picked a better time to speak his mind.

◆ ◆ ◆

87

"HUIZENGA UNHAPPY, SAYS SELLING AN OPTION," read the headline in Sunday's *Miami Herald*. The story quoted the owner of the Marlins as saying, "I don't want to sell, but we are going to lose more than $30 million this season and that cannot continue. When you have clubs like Colorado averaging forty-eight thousand and we're at twenty-eight thousand, that's disappointing. We have a contending team and more people should be coming."

"It's devastating," said a front office staffer, predicting the effect of Huizenga's comments on employee morale.

"He's bluffing," said another member of the staff.

Nobody knew quite what to make of this announcement, or why Huizenga had chosen the biggest weekend of the season to make it.

"Selling is an option," Huizenga had said. Nobody outside of Huizenga's inner circle could have known at the time, but there was reason to believe the decision to sell had already been made.

◆ ◆ ◆

This wasn't the first time Huizenga had threatened to sell the Marlins. He had said back in August 1996 that the 1997 season was a test. "If attendance is up marginally, then forget it. If it goes up quite a bit, we may say, 'Well, let's give it a shot again next year.'"

Then, a few days before the Yankees series, Huizenga appeared on the paid TV talk show *Miami Tonight* and discussed the Marlins' burgeoning losses. The host didn't ask many questions, but Huizenga had a lot of answers. It was the most informative and revealing infomercial in television history, beating out Psychic Friends Network and Vegamatic by a huge margin.

"If I had to do it all over again," Huizenga said, "I wouldn't have bought the Marlins, Panthers, or Dolphins."

Maybe Huizenga could have used some psychic friends to tell his future.

The oddest aspect of Huizenga's statement in *The Herald* was how he spoke of losing $30 million and averaging twenty-eight thousand fans per game as if it was an unexpected development.

September flashback, conversation between Huizenga and Smiley when Smiley asked permission to increase the Marlins' payroll to over $45 million.

"How many tickets can we sell?" Huizenga asked.

"We'll average about twenty-nine thousand five hundred a game," Smiley said.

"What does that translate to in losses?"

"It's about a $30 million loss, or thereabouts."

"OK," Huizenga agreed. *"But we need to get into the playoffs."*

With the three sellouts against the Yankees, the Marlins were averaging 29,525, an increase of thirty-five percent over 1996. The money Huizenga paid for free agents appeared to be well spent. The Marlins were only two and a half games behind the Braves. The combination of a pennant race, summer, and visits by the Braves and Orioles figured to boost attendance.

But eleven days after the Yankees series, Huizenga would stand behind a podium on the second floor of Pro Player Stadium and announce he was selling the team.

"We wanted out," Huizenga said, his ice-blue eyes sparkling, the smile that he wore into the press conference barely gone, his hands up—palms out—in a show of surrender. "We just changed our minds about being willing to accept higher losses. Six or seven months ago when I gave Dave Dombrowski the authority to spend the money, I had the mental attitude that I'd take the losses. Today, I don't have the same mental attitude. I just said we can't go on with this anymore."

"We just changed our minds."

The losses were as projected.

The attendance was as projected.

The team was winning.

On the surface, Huizenga's change of heart had occurred for no reason at all.

◆ ◆ ◆

The man was accustomed to getting his way. Huizenga, a 59-year-old billionaire with a ruddy complexion, round physique, and eyes you'd notice first even if he dropped a million or two in cold cash on the floor, had built his fortune on collecting piles of garbage and renting stacks of videos. By the mid-1990s, he had taken to buying hotels and car dealerships all over the United States and was known in Wall Street circles for having a Midas touch. Almost any company he touched turned to gold.

His wish was everybody else's command. The state legislature handed him a $60 million tax rebate for Pro Player Stadium in 1991 and a special tax district for his proposed sports and entertainment theme park in 1994. The idea fell through when Huizenga sold Blockbuster Entertainment. In 1995, he threatened several times to move the Panthers hockey team out of South Florida if someone didn't build him a new hockey arena. His threats were ignored for months, until the team began winning. By February 1996, cities in South Florida were lining up to build the Panthers their $185 million home.

When it came to the Marlins, however, Huizenga's Midas touch had deserted him.

Baseball's contentious four-year labor dispute hadn't gone according to plan for Huizenga. He, along with several hard-line owners, had demanded a salary cap to control payroll increases and prevent the richest teams from outspending the less-wealthy teams. Their demands fell apart in November 1996 when some of the hard-liners, including Huizenga, started bidding extravagantly on free agents.

But the worst setback for Huizenga was his failure to receive a second $60 million tax rebate for renovations on Pro Player Stadium. As recently as early April, it had looked like the legislature would approve the bill, but then the public caught on to what the politicians and Huizenga were doing.

"I've received angry phone calls," said one member of the Florida House. "They said things like,'That greedy billionaire doesn't need any money.'"

The bill had turned into a referendum on tax breaks for the wealthy, particularly Huizenga. On April 28, the bill was defeated.

The rebate request had nothing to do with the Marlins. The request was on behalf of the Dolphins. But its defeat had everything to do with Huizenga, who realized public sentiment was squarely against him.

"I think the light went on when that happened," said Smiley, who was familiar with Huizenga's thoughts because they spoke every day. "He was thinking, 'If I can't get that done, how am I going to get a baseball park built?' And I think that may have made him come to the conclusion he had to remove myself from this process to have a baseball park built."

Nothing else had changed. Not the Marlins' payroll, not their projected losses, not their projected home attendance.

Only two things changed: Huizenga didn't get his salary cap and the tax-break defeat made it clear he would never get his stadium. And he needed the stadium, not only because of the weather problems in South Florida, but because he wanted the luxury suite money that at Pro Player Stadium was going directly into a bank's pockets instead of his own.

Now he had to find a way out.

◆ ◆ ◆

Only two types of sports owners criticize their team's attendance: owners who are planning on selling their teams and owners who are planning on moving their teams. Otherwise, owners exaggerate their attendance, knowing the general public follows what's hot.

Huizenga flashback, March 29, talking about ticket sales: "The phones are ringing off the wall."

Less than six weeks later, after the tax-break defeat, here's what he said to the Fort Lauderdale *Sun-Sentinel:* "What's very disappointing is attendance. The other night we had Alex Fernandez pitching and there were twelve thousand people there. Here's a local player that we are paying a lot of money to and all we got were twelve thousand people to go out."

Huizenga was referring to a May 6 game against the Pirates, when 18,063 paid for tickets, but only twelve thousand attended the game.

Right after the Yankees series, Huizenga met with his upper echelon employees to make a final decision about selling or keeping the team. His decision wasn't difficult. Smiley added up the team's losses and came up with $229 million, including the franchise fee and startup costs. Those losses didn't, however, include the money that circled right back to Huizenga through Pro Player Stadium and SportsChannel, both of which he owned. Before the week ended, Huizenga had reconfirmed his conviction that he wouldn't, because he couldn't, ask the public to finance a stadium. He had to sell the team.

"Cutting back payroll was one option," Huizenga said. "But we knew we could make the playoffs and we wanted to give it a shot."

The next step was announcing the sale. Huizenga knew if he had any hope of selling the team by spring training 1998, he had to put up the "For Sale" sign as soon as possible. He decided to wait until the team returned from its road trip in a week. Until then, his plans would be kept secret.

Which wasn't easy. The news media was asking questions. Huizenga and his employees had to indulge in creative answering.

"We're going to have a meeting for my people to try to advise me as to what they think we should be doing," Huizenga said on June 20, speaking from the New York Stock Exchange.

"A decision has not been made," said Rick Rochon, president of Huizenga Holdings, on June 25.

"HUIZENGA WEIGHING POSSIBLE MARLINS SALE" read a newspaper headline on June 26.

"I couldn't say which way he's leaning," said Stan Smith, the spokesman for Huizenga Holdings.

"I couldn't say . . ." was the closest any of them had come to the truth in over a week. The decision had already been made.

◆ ◆ ◆

Meanwhile, the Marlins were far away from South Florida on a nine-game road trip. In Detroit, they continued inter-league play by winning two out of three games from the Tigers. Bobby Bonilla hit a four hundred fifty-nine-foot home run that sailed between the light stanchions atop ancient Tiger Stadium and onto the adjoining street. A fan, claiming to have retrieved the home run, showed up at the Marlins' clubhouse door the next day wanting to trade the ball for some of Bonilla's bats. But Javy Castro, one of the Marlins' clubhouse attendants, picked up immediately on the ruse. The man was holding a National League ball. The game had been played with American League balls.

Perrysburg, Ohio, where Leyland grew up, is only about seventy miles south of Detroit, so instead of staying in the team hotel, Leyland brought along third base coach Rich Donnelly and video coordinator Mike Carr to stay with his mother. Leyland took them on a tour of Jim Leyland Field, where the Perrysburg High team plays. Donnelly was impressed.

"They had the infield marked with all of his longest hits," he cracked.

The Marlins won two out of three games in Montreal. Gary Sheffield accused Expos pitcher Jeff Juden of throwing at his head. Fragile Cliff Floyd pulled his hamstring running to first and again ended up on the disabled list. A reporter asked Kevin Brown for his thoughts on the possible sale of the Marlins.

"I'm ignoring the issue, just like I'm ignoring you," he responded.

In Philadelphia, the Marlins won two out of three again. In the final game of the road trip, Leyland used his "bomb squad" lineup—Jim Eisenreich in left, Todd Dunwoody in center, John Cangelosi in right, John Wehner at third, Kurt Abbott at short, and Zaun behind the plate—on an afternoon when the on-the-field thermometer read one hundred sixty degrees. The Marlins won, 7-5.

Then it was time to come home. Anybody but a fool would have said, "We'll stay right where we are."

◆ ◆ ◆

Back in October, when Leyland was deciding whether to work for the Marlins, the White Sox, or the Red Sox, he had asked general manager Dave Dombrowski a prophetic question: "Do you think Wayne's selling the team?"

"No," Dombrowski answered. "But I think it's better that you ask him that question."

That's what Leyland did. He spoke to Huizenga, who told him that he didn't plan on selling.

So Wednesday afternoon, June 25, while his employees were still insisting a decision hadn't been made, Huizenga called Katie Leyland to apologize for selling the team. That night, while the denials were still coming forth, Huizenga rushed to Fort Lauderdale Airport and met the Marlins' arriving flight. He pulled aside Leyland, told him the team was for sale, apologized for his decision, and asked him to stay with the team.

"But I'll let you do whatever you want to do," Huizenga said. "I know it looks like I misled you, but I didn't mean to."

"I understand," Leyland said. "The only problem is, I have a house for sale in Pittsburgh, and I paid $650,000 for my house here."

"Jim, I'll write you a check for your house tomorrow," Huizenga said. "If you and Katie decide you want to make Pittsburgh your home, I will take responsibility for the house and I will write you a check."

They conducted two other business transactions that night. When Leyland signed with the Marlins in October, he had been given a choice of two contracts—$1.5 million a year, or $1.2 million with various perks, including use of the company plane, a membership in Huizenga's golf course, and other options that would make him "one of the boys" in the Huizenga hierarchy. Leyland had taken the $1.2 with perks. Now, with the realization Huizenga wouldn't own the team much longer, he asked for the $1.5 million contract. Huizenga agreed to the switch.

Huizenga also agreed to add an escape clause that would allow Leyland to leave the team if it was sold.

When the meeting ended after an hour, Leyland was approached by reporters and asked whether he knew anything about an impending sale.

"I don't want to talk about that," he said. "We just had a great road trip."

But by then, he knew the homestand would not be business as usual.

NATIONAL LEAGUE EAST STANDINGS

	W	L	Pct.	GB
Atlanta	48	28	.632	—
Marlins	**45**	**30**	**.600**	**2.5**
New York	43	33	.566	5
Montreal	42	33	.560	5.5
Philadelphia	23	51	.311	24

8

"Cross My Heart and Hope to Die"

June 26, 27, 28, 29 vs. Montreal
June 30, July 1, 2 at Boston
July 3, 4, 5, 6 at Mets

One day earlier, the Marlins were a baseball team. A team constructed of multi-million-dollar free agents, of course, but at least free agents with long-term contracts. The players figured to be around for a while.

"We had said, 'Let's not just do it for one year, and if it doesn't work, cut back,'" general manager Dave Dombrowski recalled of his meetings with Don Smiley in September. "We said, 'If we do it, and we're relatively successful, let's stay at that number so we can be competitive year after year.' The $89 million was spent over a five-year period."

Maybe so, but it wasn't going to be spent by Wayne Huizenga. When Huizenga, wearing a blue business suit and a silver and red tie, stepped behind a podium at Pro Player Stadium and announced the Marlins were for sale, they had been turned into his $89 Million Mistake.

"We made the same mistake a lot of others have made," he confessed. "We've spent too much."

So Moises Alou was a mistake, just as Bobby Bonilla, Alex Fernandez, Kevin Brown, and Al Leiter were mistakes. And Gary Sheffield—talk about mistakes! Less than three months earlier, Huizenga had approved a new six-year contract for Sheffield worth $61 million. Not only had Huizenga made mistakes in October, November, and December, but he had made them as recently as April 2. Now it was June 26.

It kind of made you wonder: How in the world did this guy ever become a billionaire?

◆ ◆ ◆

Who would suffer for Huizenga's mistakes? Well, Don Smiley for one. It was Smiley who back in September received permission from Huizenga to spend the money on free agents. Huizenga knew the deal. Smiley had told him exactly how many

93

fans they were going to draw and much money they were going to lose. Then Smiley warned his sales and marketing staff that this was a make or break season. If the Marlins won but attendance projections weren't met, Huizenga would dump the team. The staff thought it had been entrusted with saving the franchise and had the entire season to carry out the job. They thought they were doing their jobs well.

But, here it was, late June, with over three months remaining in the season, and time had run out on them. *Sorry, guys. Did I say twenty-nine thousand five hundred per game? I meant twenty-nine thousand five hundred per game and a $60 million tax rebate. Plus a salary cap. Oh, yes, and a new baseball stadium.*

Smiley hadn't slept well the night before the press conference, or the night before that, and woke up before sunrise. All sorts of ideas were rolling around his mind, such as what he would tell the staff, how the fans and players might react, and even what his future might hold. He had considered piecing together a syndicate of area businessmen that would buy the team, maybe thirty or so at $5 million a pop, but temporarily pushed the idea to the back of his mind.

Twenty minutes before the press conference, the front office staff gathered around Smiley. He cried and they cried. He cried because he had been with the team from Day One—had even helped fill out the original franchise application—and was sad for many of these people. They cried because they had put their hearts into selling the Marlins to the public, and also because they feared for their jobs.

After all, if Huizenga was spending more money on the Marlins than he was bringing in, he might want to start chopping here and there. Who knew where here and there started and ended?

Smiley tried to reassure them that wouldn't happen. They'd keep their jobs. At least until the end of the season. They could keep on working hard. At least until the end of the season. They had nothing to worry about. At least until the end of the season.

But the staff would suffer. Selling baseball to the South Florida sports fans, already difficult, would get tougher with a team that was on the auction block and might not be around for long.

Marlins salesperson: "Your season ticket purchase entitles you to the same great seat year after year . . . if there is another year."

Who knew?

After all, Huizenga had just admitted to a gigantic mistake. A whopping mistake. The mistake to end all mistakes.

He had followed his heart, is what he said.

He also said there should have been a compromise in the players-owners dispute.

He also said, "We would love to have a new ballpark, but that isn't going to happen under my watch."

So what he had done was follow his heart for a while, then make a sharp detour back onto the money trail. He knew the trail well.

◆ ◆ ◆

And poor Jim Ross. He stood off to the side during Huizenga's press conference and looked stricken. His face was ashen. Ross was not liking what he was hearing.

"Anything I have that's losing money is always for sale," Huizenga replied when asked whether SportsChannel Florida, which he owned, was also on the market. Clearly, a major league team was no more precious to Huizenga than a video or a car dealership or a trash compactor. Actually, it was far less valuable, because videos, car dealerships, and trash compactors had made him rich. The baseball team was leaking money by the millions. At the current rate, his entire fortune would be gone in, say, two hundred years.

Ross also had the pleasure of standing there, along with the rest of his staff, and listening as Huizenga basically belittled their efforts.

"We have trouble getting twenty-five thousand fans some nights," Huizenga said. "Yes, we sold out for the Yankees series. That was nice, but we had more Yankees fans in the stadium than we did Marlins fans."

How could the front office staff have known? Not only did they have to attract fans, but they had to attract the right kind of fans. What they should have done all along was add information to their nightly attendance reports: Paid attendance, 35,000. Marlins fans: 32,000. Rooting for the other team: 2,000. Didn't care who won: 750. Came for the soggy hot dogs: 250.

But Huizenga's announcement wasn't about attracting the wrong kind of fans. It was about one thing: the $60 million tax rebate that wasn't. Huizenga would deny his decision to sell had anything to do with the rebate, but nothing else made sense.

"I heard through the grapevine," Leyland said, "that Huizenga was pissed off about not getting the $60 million tax break, and that was it."

Of course that was it. And it happened.

◆ ◆ ◆

Huizenga's suffering would be minimal. He had bought the Marlins because Pro Player Stadium, which he owned, needed a tenant. Between the Miami Dolphins, concerts, and college football games, the stadium wasn't used more than twenty times a year until the Marlins were born. When the Marlins' losses exceeded the additional revenue gained by the stadium, Huizenga had hoped the public would build him a new one someday. But that day wasn't going to come, so this day came instead.

As Huizenga talked about regret and "personal failure," his face betrayed the steely, unemotional eyes of a businessman. "We just changed our minds," he said. He looked like a businessman, but didn't sound like one, which was why it was so hard to believe him.

Here was a man who had prided himself on success, submitting to failure in front of a roomful of reporters. He was admitting to grievous losses while hoping some other rich man or woman would step forward and buy the team.

Was this a ploy by Huizenga to induce the public into building him a new baseball stadium? The formula sounded simple: If nobody in South Florida bought the team, then Huizenga would either have to keep it or sell it to an out-of-town buyer.

Then Huizenga would be back in the bargaining position he enjoyed with the Panthers: Build me a stadium or your team is gone.

"Wayne, why should we believe that you're not just bluffing?" a reporter asked. "Is this for real?"

"This is for real," Huizenga responded.

"Cross your heart and hope to die?"

"Cross my heart and hope to die."

◆ ◆ ◆

Meanwhile, downstairs in the home clubhouse, The $89 Million Mistakes had arrived at the ballpark and were going about their business as usual.

"Hey, Sheff," Moises Alou yelled out. "You gonna buy the team?"

Sheffield shook his head. Then he greeted the first wave of reporters, who couldn't wait to hear the Marlins' reactions to the news.

"Is this unsettling for you?" a reporter asked.

"As a player, you do what's best for the organization," Sheffield said. "I'd hate to see the franchise move, for Florida and Florida baseball fans."

"How did you feel when you heard the news?"

"I was disappointed. I came to spring with a lot of high hopes for this franchise. I love it here in Florida. Basically, I want to set my roots here and not have to worry about ever moving again."

"When you were negotiating your contract, did the possibility of Wayne selling ever come up?"

"No. We never thought this situation would ever occur. Anything Huizenga touches always turns to gold. We thought the team would always be here and the fans would support the team. That's the only disappointment."

Not quite the only disappointment. The way Sheffield viewed the situation, Huizenga's sale announcement was the latest in a series of setbacks . . . for him. There was the grand slam against the Yankees that got nullified by a rainout. He had hurt his finger diving for a ball in Atlanta. He couldn't get a pitch to hit. Umpires weren't giving him a fair break.

Now this: Huizenga was selling the team. Poor Sheff.

He didn't mention the one thing that had gone right in his season: signing a $61 million contract.

Nor did any of The $89 Million Mistakes mention that even if the Marlins were sold, or if they were traded to dump payroll, their contracts were valid wherever they went.

On the list of people to feel sorry for on June 26, 1997, The $89 Million Mistakes didn't make the cut.

◆ ◆ ◆

Then, just as Sheffield was talking about the distractions the announcement would create, Leyland roared through the clubhouse shouting, "All media, out! Please.

Immediately!" He said it a few more times, and although he didn't look angry, he sounded like a man who had identified the enemy of the day. Five minutes later Huizenga entered the clubhouse and spoke to the players.

"You could read the disappointment in his face," Charles Johnson said.

Which made sense. Huizenga was, literally, staring his failures right in the face.

While Huizenga spoke inside the clubhouse, publicity director Ron Colangelo stood outside and informed the media that Leyland had no intention of answering questions about the day's events. Leyland, however, couldn't prevent questions from being asked, which they were after the clubhouse reopened.

"Jim," a reporter tried. "We know what the rules are. We were told that you don't really want to talk about . . ."

"Well, then don't even bring it up," Leyland snapped. "Don't ask me anything about it. I'll tell you that right now. If you want to talk about the series with Montreal, I'll talk about it. If you want to talk about anything else, you might as well leave. That's none of my business. I'm a field manager, period. I'm not going to discuss it."

"But, Jim, one thing Wayne did say in his news conference is that . . ."

"You guys were at the press conference," Leyland interrupted. "You heard everything at the press conference, so don't ask me about the press conference. If you heard it, then you don't have to ask me questions about it. If you want to talk about the game tonight, let's talk. If you don't, I'd appreciate it if you'd move out."

"Well, he said he apologized to you for his decision to sell the team."

"I'm going to tell you this," Leyland said. "Wayne Huizenga has been more than fair to me. He has been honest with me. He's a friend, he will always be a friend, and I came here to win a World Series. Period."

Fair wasn't a strong enough word to describe Huizenga's treatment of Leyland, considering their conversation and quick negotiations at the airport the night before. But Leyland, who looked shaken and sounded scared, had reason to be upset. He had left the instability and long-term building plan of Pittsburgh for the stability and short-term guarantees of Florida and chose the Marlins for less money than the White Sox and Red Sox offered. He was prepared to settle down in South Florida with his wife and two children, but seventy-five games into his first year with the Marlins, he was already in danger of being uprooted.

"This is serious," Leyland would say a few days later, after Huizenga not only offered to buy his house, but let him live in it, rent free. "It'll affect a lot of people. It's already affected me. We're in limbo. We're packing already. My wife will move back to Pittsburgh with Patrick and Kellie and I'll stay here, maybe rent an apartment or sleep in the office, then move back to Pittsburgh for the off-season. But I want my kids to stay in one school system. Patrick loves it here. He doesn't want to move. But it's unstable here. I don't know what's going to happen. I've already been through this three times. I've seen what happens."

In Pittsburgh, Leyland knew, the Pirates were sold to an owner who minimized his losses by cutting payroll to the point where the team had almost no chance of being competitive. That's why he left.

If the same thing happened in Florida, the 1997 Marlins would not only be Wayne Huizenga's $89 Million Mistakes. They'd be a bunch of hired guns. A one-shot, one-season deal, bought to win the World Series.

◆ ◆ ◆

Then again, maybe this sale announcement wasn't so bad. Conine and Sheffield sat in the dugout before batting practice, discussing the day's events and how it might affect them on the field. They decided it couldn't hurt.

"What's it gonna do, make us go in a slump?" cracked Conine, who had been hitting .188 over the past fifty-six games.

"Shit," said Sheffield, who was hitting .224 with only twenty-nine RBIs. "It might help."

◆ ◆ ◆

Not quite. Sheffield homered, but the Marlins completed a miserable day by losing to the Expos, 5-2. After the game, Mike Phillips from *The Miami Herald* strayed back onto dangerous ground when he asked Leyland how the sale announcement affected the team's play.

"I really don't have any comment on that," Leyland grumbled between bites of food. "I ain't gonna respond to those questions. I've told you guys twenty times today that I'm not gonna talk about that, and you guys keep searching. You're not gonna get anything, so you might as well not even waste your time. That has nothing to do with anything. I mean, we didn't hit the ball good, their pitcher pitched good, period. And Rapp was inconsistent. It's as simple as that."

There would be no more questions. Leyland slammed down his fork and stormed into the bathroom, muttering under his breath loud enough for the exiting reporters to hear.

"Fucking media," Leyland growled. "Fucking questions. I told them twenty fucking times I'm not talking about this."

He was in bad spirits for a man who needed less than an hour to sell his house, receive a $300,000 raise, and get *carte blanche* from his boss to walk out of his contract whenever he pleased.

On the list of people to feel sorry for on June 26, 1997, Leyland didn't make the cut, either.

◆ ◆ ◆

The next few days were not a happy time at Mistake Ground Zero. Only 26,169 fans, the smallest Friday night crowd since opening weekend, showed up for the second game of the Expos series. The third game Saturday drew 39,348, rather than the sellout Marlins officials expected before the sale announcement. Although the crowd stood and cheered for Robb Nen's one-two-three ninth inning, the atmosphere in the Stadium felt like it had the previous two years, when the fans sat and watched without any emotion or energy. "LOUDER!" the message board begged.

There was no response. Something was missing, as if a growing relationship between the fans and the team, and even the team's employees and their bosses, had been disturbed.

A middle-aged woman who sat in the club level behind home plate had affectionately been dubbed "The Knitting Lady" by press box staffers because she knitted through every home game. On Thursday, The Knitting Lady wore a black veil and a black shawl, as if she was attending a funeral, or mourning a soon-to-be-departed loved one.

The effect on the team wasn't quite as apparent. Kevin Brown was outstanding in a 2-0 loss Friday, and Livan Hernandez, up from Charlotte once again, won his first major league game in a 4-2 victory on Saturday. But the Marlins, who had been winning without hitting, couldn't break out of their season-long slump. Even in the victory, they counted on fielders' choices, sacrifice flies, and errors for most of their offense.

The fans finally came out of mourning for the final game of the series Sunday, and the Marlins responded with their most energetic effort of the weekend. A crowd of 38,443 included an above-average number of fans who bought their tickets on the day of the game, indicating that some of them had decided to move on and enjoy the season. The Marlins won, 5-3.

Leyland's miserable mood brightened, too. He had been thrown out of the game in the eighth inning for arguing a call with the first base umpire, but didn't mind because Jerry Manuel, his bench coach, took over. A few days earlier he had jokingly told Manuel, "I'm gonna say to the umpire, 'Kick me out. Kick me out.' And then I'm gonna say to you, 'Bring 'em home, Shooter!'"

Leyland was alluding to a scene in *Hoosiers,* his favorite movie, in which the lead character, a high school basketball coach, has the referee throw him out of the game—"Kick me out. Kick me out!"—so the assistant coach, a barely reformed drunk named Shooter, can take over. "Bring 'em home, Shooter," the coach urges.

When the Marlins returned to the clubhouse after the win, Leyland was standing in the doorway, wearing nothing but his long johns, smiling and laughing.

"Way to bring 'em home, Shooter!" Leyland barked out to Manuel. He had just lived out his Hollywood fantasy.

◆ ◆ ◆

Fascinating aspect about the sale decision: It was made during a period in which the Marlins played twenty-four of thirty-one games on the road and didn't have much chance to improve their home attendance. When the Montreal series ended, they went back onto the road for their final seven games prior to the All-Star break.

The players were exhausted from this long stretch. Bonilla had been playing every day and was batting .313 despite a bad Achilles and a sore wrist, but he shook his head when asked if he hoped for a spot on the National League All-Star team.

"It would be an honor," Bonilla said wearily, "but I need three days off."

Leyland wasn't about to let the Marlins coast into the All-Star break, not when they were only 4½ games behind the Braves. Bonilla would get a breather against

99

the Red Sox in Boston by being the designated hitter for a few games. Otherwise, Leyland expected his team to play hard.

"You have to be a fucking man to play this game and survive it," Leyland said. "I'll be on them this week to bust their asses and then come back and start out fresh."

For the Marlins, going back on the road allowed them a break from the turmoil and questions in South Florida. Unfortunately for Leyland, a new city with new reporters meant another round of questions about the sale. He didn't answer the Boston reporters, either.

◆ ◆ ◆

Fenway Park is a baseball cathedral, a beautiful old ballpark tucked into an old neighborhood, with nearly perfect sightlines—unless you're sitting behind a pole—and a big, green, thirty-seven-foot-high fence in leftfield known as The Green Monster. It's a great place, unless you're a left-handed pitcher, a member of the visiting bullpen, or a visiting first base coach. The place is a little too cozy for any of them.

Tommy Sandt, the Marlins' first base coach, spent the first game of a three-game series getting taunted by a leather-lunged fan who knew his lifetime major league statistics by heart.

"Hey, Sandt!" the fan yelled out. "Two-oh-nine batting average!"

"Hey, Sandt! Three RBIs!"

"Hey, Sandt! How many stolen bases did you have? None!"

Said Sandt the next day, laughing at the recollection: "That guy did his homework."

◆ ◆ ◆

Alex Fernandez rediscovered why Fenway is so tough on pitchers, even right-handers, in an 8-5 victory for the Marlins in the series opener. Fernandez picked up his team-high ninth win, but not before he allowed two home runs that looked long, but probably would have stayed in any other ballpark.

Earlier in the day, Gregg Doyel of *The Miami Herald* had asked Leyland about the difficulty of playing The Green Monster, and Leyland said, "You come out here tomorrow and we'll see how you play it."

Doyel, who had some high school baseball experience, took him up on the offer. Before the second game of the series, he squeezed into Leyland's uniform pants and a Marlins' practice T-shirt, and tried his luck at playing the wall. Leyland fun-goed. Doyel tried to catch. One of the balls hit him in the face. Doyel broke his glasses. When they were done, Leyland complemented his effort and offered some advice: "Don't throw away your pen."

◆ ◆ ◆

Gary Sheffield's stunning ability to say everything on his mind cost him again. A week earlier in Philadelphia, he had complained vehemently about the umpires, claiming he never got the benefit of the doubt and was batting with a larger strike zone than other superstars. He had also related a conversation with Gene Ozra, the executive counsel of the players' association. Ozra had suggested Sheffield tone down his behavior because umpires feared for their well-being after he struck out.

"I don't know what they're thinking," Sheffield said. "I've never argued with an umpire so viciously that it was the big headline of the day. I've been ejected, that's it. But it becomes sometimes like your hands are tied. They say I play the game with too much emotion, so I try to control that and it takes away from the other things you need to do."

Sheffield's comments were reported in the newspapers. The umpires, who prided themselves on being unbiased arbiters of the sport, were not pleased.

On the other hand, throughout baseball history they had been accused of being blind, inconsistent, dead wrong, and generally incompetent.

Apparently, accusations of bias were too much for them to stand. They urged National League president Leonard Coleman to take disciplinary action against Sheffield.

Dombrowski and Leyland agreed with the content of Sheffield's remarks, but not the tact. They, too, thought umpires occasionally broadened his strike zone. Prior to taking the Marlins job, Leyland had been warned that some umpires had a vendetta against Sheffield. But neither Leyland nor Dombrowski could win anything by fighting this fight for Sheffield. Some arguments simply weren't worth the trouble.

Dombrowski knew that. In 1996, when Sheffield called him a liar, Dombrowski could have responded publicly. He didn't. He knew nothing was to be gained by getting into a public shouting match with one of his best players.

In this situation, nothing was to be gained by getting into a public shouting match with the men who called balls and strikes.

Dombrowski, along with Leyland, met with Sheffield and strongly urged him to offer a written apology and contribute $7,500 to charity. Sheffield, made aware he could be suspended or fined, possibly even sued for libel, if he didn't go along, grudgingly complied.

"It has become apparent to me that some comments I made have been interpreted as derogatory towards the umpires," the statement read. "That was never my intent. I apologize for my comments and any negative implications."

But he wasn't happy about having to apologize. Nor was he happy that the Marlins didn't take his side in the matter. Sheffield thought the team should have supported him and viewed this slight as another example of the organization's lack of appreciation toward him.

Like when they gave him a $61 million contract?

"I don't like the feeling of having people walk on me," he said. "I can't do that. I can't let that happen. I don't know that I should have to apologize for it."

Sheffield also said, "I have to watch what I say. I'm under a microscope."

But for a man who realized he was "under a microscope," Sheffield never refrained from speaking his mind. His locker had become a favored spot for the beat reporters because they knew if they waited around long enough, Sheffield would say something controversial or newsworthy. Occasionally he'd respond to a question by saying, "I don't want to talk about that," then answer the question, anyway, often at length, while detouring onto other juicy topics.

In this case, Sheffield was aware he had said something that would cause controversy and possibly get him into trouble.

"You knew we were standing there with our notebooks and pens," a reporter asked. "Why did you say it?"

Responded Sheffield, "Because I was asked."

That was all it ever took.

◆ ◆ ◆

A sad Pat Rapp is one of the sorriest sights in baseball. He has a square face that droops like a child's after a bad performance, and a strong Bayou twang that makes him sound like Andy Griffith when he's happy and Jim Nabors when he's unhappy. It's a nasal whine that starts out low and gets higher. The urge is to pat him softly on the back and tell him everything's going to be all right.

That would have taken some convincing after Rapp lasted only three innings against the Red Sox in the second game of the series and suffered his fourth straight loss. Rapp walked six in a dismal performance that had nothing to do with the short fences at Fenway—the Red Sox didn't hit a home run.

"I don't have much luck right now, and when you walk six guys, you're not gonna have much luck," Rapp pouted. "I was lucky to get out of the next two innings."

Bad news for Rapp: In his past five outings, he had an ERA of 7.04.

Worse news for Rapp: His bosses noticed.

"Right now, he's not doing the job," Dombrowski said.

And Larry Rothschild added, "No ultimatum. He's just got to go out and pitch like he's capable."

After a strong spring, Rapp hadn't justified Leyland's vote of confidence in making him the fourth starter. He tried to ignore the obvious—that his spot in the rotation was not as secure as it had been back in March—and a day earlier denied his start against the Red Sox was more meaningful than any other. The look on his face said otherwise. Rapp was troubled and did nothing to help his cause.

On a night when the Marlins managed only two runs off the unheralded Vaughn Eshelman, Rapp's bad performance looked even worse.

◆ ◆ ◆

More from the Sheffield Will Say Anything front. This time, he suggested the Marlins hadn't spent enough money on players. They needed to spend more.

"We might as well go for it now because we've proven we have a chance to win this year," he told the Fort Lauderdale *Sun-Sentinel.* "They've spent so much money already, what's a little more? When you have a chance to win, you have to go all out. Offense is just like pitching, you can never have enough of it. Another hitter would look great around here. We could use a spark."

He should have looked in the mirror. The extra hitter the Marlins needed was named Gary Sheffield, and he was batting .233 and on pace to get only sixteen homers and sixty-four RBIs. Sheffield didn't say anything about that.

◆ ◆ ◆

Moises Alou had a good news/bad news day on Wednesday, July 2. He was waiting for a flight in Atlanta when he found out that he had been named to the National League All-Star team for the second time in his career. The bad news had to do with why he was in Atlanta while his teammates were in Boston: He was flying home to Florida to be with his wife, Austria, who was having complications with her pregnancy.

Alou had been the Marlins' best player during the first half with a batting average of .297 and sixty-four RBIs, but the All-Star selection hardly soothed his troubled mind.

"It didn't mean shit," Alou said. "I had other things to take care of."

But it played out as a good news/good news situation. The unborn baby and Austria turned out to be fine, and Alou could play in the All-Star game.

Brown, the Marlins' other All-Star, won his eighth game and the Marlins beat the Red Sox, 3-2, in the series finale.

◆ ◆ ◆

Dennis Cook went to New York and had his three-game suspension for hitting Andres Galarraga in May reduced to two games. That was all right with Cook, who would serve his suspension during the Marlins' four-game series against the Mets. His day in court had gone well.

"He's a fair man," Cook said of National League President Leonard Coleman, sounding like it was the highest compliment he could offer anyone. He nodded after he said it and pursed his lips.

Cook could also be described as a fair man, although he doesn't convey that on first impression. He comes off as a stoic Texan who's suspicious of the media and doesn't say much. His descriptive phrases are not very descriptive.

Cook's description of the room in which the hearing took place: "It was little."

His account of the meeting: "I just went in and I was honest."

But his reticence is really modesty. Cook is low-key and doesn't ask for any credit or attention, although that's exactly why he and fellow relief pitcher Jay Powell stand out in the clubhouse. Both of them wear off-the-rack jeans and pullover shirts, even on travel days when most of their teammates are putting on a fashion show. None of the Marlins had ever seen them in a suit.

Cook, 34, is a Texan through and through, raised in Dickinson, south of Houston, and a resident of Austin. He liked to joke—or was he joking?—that he wore a tuxedo T-shirt, black Wranglers, and cowboy boots on his wedding day. Although he insisted he hired a limousine for the occasion, Powell suspected it must have been a four-wheel drive limo.

"You got that right," Cook said proudly in his sharp twang. "You got that right" is one of Cook's favorite phrases. He also says, "Yessir," and "Thank you, ma'am," which sets him apart from a lot of athletes. He is respectful and never came close to second-guessing the manager.

Typical Cook quote about how Leyland used him out of the bullpen: "If he tells me to get up and pitch, I'll pitch. If he tells me to sit down, I'll sit down."

Cook loved hunting and used to bring his dog, Stonewall, onto the field when he played for the Texas Rangers. Stonewall was less of a presence around the Marlins, but whenever the team returned from a road trip, Cook's wife, Tammi, was at the airport with the dog in tow.

"If my dog went to the airport, he'd probably wind up out on the runway," third base coach Rich Donnelly said. "Cookie's dog is trained."

In other words, if you told him to get up, he'd get up. If you told him to sit down, he'd sit down.

The Marlins' bullpen of Cook, Powell, Felix Heredia, Robb Nen, Rick Helling, and Mark Hutton had been their strength all season. Cook allowed only one run in April. Powell had a 0.90 ERA in May. Heredia didn't allow a run in June. They weren't to blame when, after the final game in Boston, Leyland's post-game spread consisted of four packs of cigarettes, a can of Bud Light, and a glass of milk. Outside, the rest of the team dined on lobster, tortellini, and turkey. They owed their appetites to the bullpen.

◆ ◆ ◆

Leyland recorded his nine hundredth career victory in a 10-4 win over the Mets in the first of a four-game series at Shea Stadium, and the next day claimed he had no inkling of the milestone.

"I didn't know about it until I was watching *SportsCenter* and they flashed my picture," he said. "I thought, *Damn, that guy must have robbed a bank today.*"

Leyland was feeling good. A day earlier, he had snapped at a reporter who asked him repeatedly about the sale announcement, but then the Marlins scored eight runs in the first two innings.

Sheffield had two hits, Conine hit a two-run homer, and the Marlins appeared to be breaking out of their hitting slump. On Friday before the second game, Matt Whisenant finally came off the disabled list and made it to the major leagues for the first time. He sat in the bullpen. Moises Alou returned after missing two games to be with his wife. The Marlins had won five of their last six games—including two straight without Alou—and were heading into the break on a high.

But in the second game of the series, Al Leiter continued his pattern of pitching poorly on the road by losing, 6-2. In the third game, Sheffield showed how much he had learned from his mistakes by arguing a called third strike, getting thrown out of the game, and tossing his helmet into the Marlins' dugout. His teammates were angry . . . at him. They couldn't understand how their most important player, who already had two hits, could act so childishly and get ejected from a game they trailed by only one run. The Marlins lost, 5-3.

The symbolic first half of the season—symbolic because the Marlins had played their 81st game on July 1 in Boston—ended on Sunday, July 6. That morning, Charles Johnson learned he had been selected to replace injured Mets catcher Todd Hundley on the National League All-Star team. Johnson was hitting only .226, but hadn't committed an error or had a passed ball all season, and was so effective at throwing out runners that opposing teams were hesitant to steal against him.

And that afternoon, the Marlins crashed.

◆ ◆ ◆

First, Gary Sheffield lost the ball in the sun. He twisted and turned his body, trying to make the sun go away, but it wouldn't, and Alex Ochoa's popup struck the heel of his glove and fell to the ground. Ochoa ended up at second. The next batter grounded a single into rightfield. Sheffield approached the ball with slightly more speed than he had recently mustered in jogging out infield grounders, which wasn't much. His one concession to expediency was bending over to pick up the ball bare-handed, but that didn't work, either. The ball dropped out of his right hand, and by the time he bent over to pick it up again, Ochoa was only thirty feet from home plate and closing fast with the winning run.

Sheffield knew there was no use throwing. He completed a day in which he had gone hitless in five at-bats by dropping his shoulders and trudging off the field. The Marlins had lost, 3-2, in twelve innings, their third straight defeat by the Mets, and no player was more at fault than Sheffield.

◆ ◆ ◆

A few years ago, Leyland launched a tirade in the Pittsburgh Pirates clubhouse, during which he started fully dressed and ended up stark naked as he roared around the room, tipped over a table of food, and berated his players. They could barely control their laughter.

This time, he was sitting in the cramped visiting manager's office at Shea Stadium, behind an old metal schoolteacher's desk, wearing only a T-shirt and a pair of long johns as he answered questions from reporters. The question that set him off: "Do you need to trade for another bat?"

Leyland didn't look or sound like a schoolteacher when he answered the question. He started out calmly, but quickly built up steam, and his selection of words . . . well, they didn't belong in any classroom.

"People are always saying, 'We have to go get somebody, we have to go get somebody,'" Leyland said. "Well, Dave Dombrowski went and got six guys. He did his fucking job! Everyone says, 'Do something. Do something.' These guys should start worrying about what they're doing instead of worrying about what we should be doing. You can't put anything on the general manager or the owner. They fucking did their job. It's up to us to start doing our jobs. I'm talking about from the manager on down."

He sounded like he was talking about Gary Sheffield. After all, Sheffield was the only player who suggested the Marlins should go out and get somebody. With each word, Leyland's voice grew louder and angrier, and when he stood up from behind the desk, he began pulling off his underwear. He paused between thoughts as he walked around the room. His face turned red.

"It's time for the coaches, the players, myself, everyone, to do our jobs," Leyland continued, yanking off his shirt. "Right now I'm horseshit, they're horseshit, we're all horseshit. We had some holes, but we filled those fucking holes. We added on to what was supposed to be a good fucking team. Guys are supposed to fucking do something. I get tired of hearing that bullshit."

He kept pacing and getting angrier and angrier. He threw his shirt onto the floor, then started pulling off his long johns. He was raging.

"We can't keep having the same guys having ten horseshit at-bats every day, day after day after day," Leyland growled. "I'm tired of guys breaking out in poison ivy every time there's a man in scoring position. Maybe it's time for everyone to look in the fucking mirror. Dave Dombrowski did his job. He more than fucking did his job! I can get some guys and sit their fucking ass on the bench. Why don't you go out there and ask them who's not good enough so we know who's got to go and who has to sit on the bench? Montreal, Atlanta, and New York, haven't gotten anybody. We signed more than anybody. Where are the benefits? Our organization did every fucking thing under the sun. Now it's time for me, the coaches, and the players, to do something. Dave Dombrowski did every fucking thing under the sun. Go out and get somebody? That's weak."

Leyland went on for nearly ten minutes, repeating themes and changing a profanity every once in a while. When he was finished, he was standing in the middle of the room without a stitch of clothing on his body.

And that's how the first half ended.

NATIONAL LEAGUE EAST STANDINGS

	W	L	Pct.	GB
Atlanta	57	30	.655	—
Marlins	**50**	**36**	**.581**	**6.5**
New York	48	38	.558	8.5
Montreal	47	39	.547	9.5
Philadelphia	24	61	.282	32

9

One Irregular Heartbeat

July 10, 11, 12, 13 vs. Philadelphia
July 14, 15 vs. Montreal
July 16, 17 vs. Los Angeles
July 18, 19, 20, 21 vs. San Diego

Calmer heads still hadn't prevailed four days later when the Marlins returned to Pro Player Stadium on Thursday, July 10. Leyland gathered his troops in the clubhouse at 3 p.m. for a team meeting that lasted, according to Jeff Conine, "between five minutes and an hour and a half." Conine was being evasive. The meeting actually lasted fifteen minutes and featured only one speaker: Leyland. It was the manager's feel-good session, and he had no intention of listening to second opinions.

For Leyland, the All-Star break meant three days away from baseball for his body, not his mind. He had dinner with his wife, went ice skating with his children, and had a good time, but never stopped thinking about baseball. Mostly, he composed a little speech he delivered to the players when they came back on Thursday. He was not lacking confidence in his communication skills.

"It was short and to the point, and most important, it was true," Leyland said.

He told them they had played well, but could play better. He asked the players to make the contributions expected of them, but to not try to carry the team.

"I have responsibility, Conine has responsibility, Charles Johnson has responsibility, Sheff has responsibility, Bobby Bo, all the coaches, we all have responsibility," Leyland said. "We all have responsibility here, and we've done OK so far, but we can do better. We're better than we've played. We're a better defensive club. We're better running the bases. We're better offensively for sure than we've showed.

"If we need to add something, we're not afraid to try something. Dave Dombrowski is the last guy who somebody can say is afraid to do something. But let's look at what we got here. Why are we looking elsewhere? Just look at what we got inside this clubhouse. When I came here, I wanted Alex Fernandez. I got him. I wanted Moises Alou. I got him. I wanted Bobby Bonilla. I got him. I wanted Eisenreich and Cangelosi. I got them. I wanted to extend Gary Sheffield. I got it. We have to be careful as a team that the perception to the fans and everybody else isn't that we always need more—take, take, take. It's time for us to step up and do the job. That's all. And I know we can do it."

The players listened. Leyland said what was on his mind. He promised no more meetings for the rest of the season.

In some ways, the message had already gotten through. The team had been quiet on the plane ride home from New York before the break. Everybody felt exhausted and angry.

"He didn't really have to say anything," Bonilla said. "It's show time now. We play baseball now. No excuses."

◆ ◆ ◆

Near panic had set in. There was trade talk in the newspapers and criticism on sports radio. Should the Marlins get power hitter Mark McGwire from the A's, second baseman Mickey Morandini from the Phillies, or pitchers Tom Gordon or Curt Schilling? The Marlins had spoken with the Phillies about Morandini, but hadn't made an offer. As for Schilling, he had a no-trade clause in his contract. McGwire said he didn't want to play in the National League. Dombrowski had spoken with the A's, as had two other GMs, but a deal didn't look likely.

The odd thing was, the Marlins had a strong first half despite their hitting woes, and were fourteen games over .500. Until their visit to New York, they had won six straight series and split one. What if they had won that final game against the Mets, or won three out of four? Then their first half would have been praised. Indeed, the concerns and second-guessing seemed to be the knee-jerk reaction of all time.

The reason was simple: The Marlins had decided they wanted to win now. Not next year or the year after.

But problems scratched at the surface, and everybody knew it. Luis Castillo was a serious problem. He had been overmatched by big league pitchers and should have spent the season in Triple-A. Right around May, Leyland realized his every-day second baseman couldn't hit a fly ball or drive in a run. Six RBIs in two hundred twenty-five at-bats for a leadoff man. Pretty pathetic, but no accident. Castillo hammered at the ball as if he was trying to drive it into the ground. The most dangerous places in the stadium when Castillo batted were the seats to the left and right of the backstop screen. He sliced foul balls back there all the time, sending the fans ducking for cover.

The Marlins' 18-11 record in one-run games was the best in the majors, but good teams usually don't play in so many one-run games. They win big. The bullpen had been outstanding, but could that continue? While it's true a team can't win without a setup man and a closer—look at the Yankees in 1996 with Mariano Rivera and John Wetteland—not many World Series winners have pointed to their bullpen as the main reason for their success. And for how much longer would a team want to rest its hopes on Dennis Cook, Felix Heredia, Jay Powell, Rick Helling, Mark Hutton, and even Robb Nen?

Then, as if to prove the point, Tony Saunders, pitching for the first time since going on the disabled list in mid-May, allowed only two runs in six innings and left with a 7-2 lead against the Phillies, but the bullpen allowed them back into the game. Facing a team that would lose ninety-four games, Heredia was hit hard for the first time all season. Nen came on in the ninth inning to protect a 7-5 lead and proceeded to throw seven straight balls. Then three straight strikes. Then four straight balls. By the time the inning was over, the Phillies had tied the game, and if not for a strong throw from leftfield by Moises Alou, a great reaching tag by Charles Johnson at home plate, and Darren Daulton's lack of speed, the Marlins would have been behind by a run. Arias finally won the game in the bottom of the ninth when he singled over shortstop and drove home Bonilla.

Leyland on Arias: "That fucker can hit."

It was an ugly way to start the second half, and although the Marlins scored eight runs, it wasn't as if they had torn the cover off the ball. Philadelphia's pitchers combined to walk twelve.

But Leyland's speech—or maybe the three days off, or maybe both—apparently had its intended effect on Gary Sheffield. He struck out three times and popped up with a runner on third in the sixth inning, but mustered rare hustle chasing down a foul popup in the top of the eighth. Sheffield couldn't reach the ball and slammed left-hand first into the bullpen wall. He went down in a heap, grabbing his injured left thumb, while a very worried Leyland raced out to see if he was OK. But what was left of the crowd had forgotten all about that by the time Sheffield struck out in the bottom of the inning, and obviously didn't notice he had to shake off the pain in his thumb after whiffing at the second strike. They booed him for the fourth time of the night.

Sheffield offered a minor complaint about the booing, but stopped well short of criticizing the fans. Besides, they weren't all against him. When he showed up for work that afternoon, a red carnation in a vase had been placed in front of his stall, along with several party balloons. "Thinking of you" and "You're special," two of them read, as if the recipient was a teenage crush. Another balloon had one of those yellow smiling faces from the 1970s. A good-humored gift from a teammate? Perhaps a practical joke to lift Sheffield's spirits? Nope. Sheffield opened the accompanying card. It was a gift from a fan.

"I'm surprised I still have one," Sheffield said.

◆ ◆ ◆

The first sign the Marlins were ready for the big time arrived by FedEx during the All-Star break: A copy of Major League Baseball's post-season manual, containing guidelines for ticket sales, hotel accommodations, and media relations. It was sent to all contending teams, which means at this point of the season, only a handful of teams didn't get one.

◆ ◆ ◆

The beat reporters weren't happy with Leyland because of a column by Harvey Araton in the previous Sunday's *New York Times*. In it, Leyland was quoted as saying he was selling his house in Florida and moving his family back to Pittsburgh. No problem, except that a week earlier, he had told the same thing to a small group of Florida reporters and insisted the entire conversation was off the record. Now here was a New York reporter scooping the Florida reporters on something they already knew.

"You know, they sell the *New York Times* down here," Dave O'Brien of the Fort Lauderdale *Sun-Sentinel* said to Leyland in a matter-of-fact, wise guy way. The comment came out of nowhere during the manager's meeting with reporters before the first game of the Philadelphia series, and Leyland made like he had no idea what O'Brien was talking about.

"So? Who gives a shit?" he said, also matter-of-factly.

"You talked to us about moving up to Pittsburgh, told us not to write that, then you tell the guy from the *New York Times.*"

"So what? I don't give a shit."

"Well, we honored your embargo . . ."

"Well, I don't give a shit. Write it. Put it in the fucking headlines for all I care."

"Well, you asked us not to, so we didn't."

"Well, I don't give a shit," Leyland barked again. "My point is, to be honest with you, maybe down here that's a story. In New York, that's no story."

"Yeah, but if they write it there, it's going to be here in an hour."

"Well, put it in the fucking paper. I don't give a shit."

"I'm just telling ya," O'Brien said, laughing.

"I don't give a shit how it ended up in your papers, and I don't give a shit when it ended up in your papers. We're moving back to Pittsburgh," Leyland said, seeming a little embarrassed. "You can put it in the fucking headlines if you want."

Leyland didn't have a clue. In fact, this was a classic example of Leyland not understanding or respecting the reporters' jobs. Here they were looking bad because they chose to respect Leyland's wishes, and here he was showing total indifference and disrespect. Then Leyland made a bad situation worse by trying to go off the record again on the same subject.

"Sell the house yet?" O'Brien asked.

"The house is sold," Leyland replied.

"Really. You don't have trouble selling 'em here like in Pittsburgh, huh?"

"Well, not when the owner buys it," Leyland said. "Wayne bought my house. But that's not for the papers."

"At least not until the *New York Times* reports it," O'Brien shot back.

All of the reporters laughed at that. Leyland didn't.

But with the season only halfway through, the regular reporters had long passed the point where they trusted Leyland or enjoyed his sense of humor. They had heard enough of his talking about another reporter behind the reporter's back and always had in mind a comment he made to a visiting reporter: "The Florida media knows nothing about baseball."

One day Leyland would refuse to answer a question, the next he'd answer the same question from a different reporter. A perfect example came during the Yankees series. Leyland had used his entire bullpen in the series opener and would have had to use one of his starters if the Marlins hadn't won the game in the bottom of the twelfth inning.

"Who would you have used in the thirteenth inning?" asked Gregg Doyel from *The Herald.*

"You'll never know," Leyland replied.

"Did you have a plan?" Doyel persisted.

"I had a plan," Leyland said. "But you'll never know what it was."

The next afternoon, another reporter asked the same question and this time Leyland answered: The pitcher would have been Rapp.

To most of the men and women on the beat, Leyland was a curiosity. They often joked about his constant mood changes—sometimes from one sentence to the next—and a few had taken to calling him Multiple Personality Manager. A typical conversation between two reporters about Leyland:

REPORTER 1: He has quite a personality.

REPORTER 2: Which one?

Another point of contention was Leyland's definition of "silly stuff." To Leyland, "silly stuff" included questions about bench-clearing brawls, pitchers throwing at hitters, potential trades, lineup changes, and five hundred-foot home runs hit by the opposition. Basically, anything that he didn't feel like talking about. Apparently, Leyland considered the sale of the team to be "silly stuff," too, at least when talking on the record to reporters. Although branding such off-limits subjects as "silly stuff" served Leyland's purpose of not answering questions, it made him sound as if he had a skewed sense of reality, which obviously he did.

Ever since Huizenga announced he would sell the team, the public and media had been questioning whether he really intended to do it, or if it was just a threat to gain leverage in asking local officials to build him a new stadium. But when the manager of the team decides to move his family back to Pittsburgh, and the owner of the team offers to buy the manager's house for $650,000, that's a pretty good indication that either the owner means business, or the manager—who is friendly with the owner and trusts him—thinks he means business.

Not exactly silly stuff.

◆ ◆ ◆

The Marlins had a nightly promotion in which two fans said why they should be the team's Fan of the Game. The bit was shown on the video boards and the crowd cheered for the fan it liked best. The winner received four tickets to a future game. During the second game of the Philadelphia series, a 7-year-old boy said he should be Fan of the Game because, "I like the Marlins, they're gonna win the World Series, and I really like Gary Sheffield." The crowd booed. You had to feel sorry for him. The little boy, that is.

Then Charles Johnson homered with one out in the bottom of the ninth inning and fireworks erupted from the leftfield seats. "Ya Gotta Believe!" flashed on the scoreboard, and *Don't Stop Believing* by Journey, the 1980s sleeveless rock band, blared over the loud speakers. The five hundred or so fans remaining in the park stood and applauded. Johnson's home run would have been meaningful if it had happened three innings earlier, when he struck out as the potential tying run in the bottom of the sixth, but it meant nothing with the Marlins trailing, 13-3. Had a team ever been mocked by its own stadium? *Don't stop believing? 13-3?*

The loss to the Phillies, who had dropped thirteen straight on the road, was immediately forgettable on most counts. Something old: Gary Sheffield popped up with men on base. Something new: Kevin Brown got hit hard. But three Marlins—Conine, Matt Whisenant, and Mark Kotsay—will likely remember the day five, ten, twenty, even thirty or forty years from now.

Conine: His wife Cindy gave birth to the couple's second child and first son, Griffin Riley, during the late afternoon. Conine arrived late, did not play. If the son is anything like the father, he will have been blessed with perfect posture. Conine sits, walks, and runs with his body straighter than any man alive. He has the perfect physique for country line dancing.

Whisenant: He faced five batters, didn't retire any of them, and walked four, in a dismal ninth inning that he might remember for a long time as the last time he pitched in the ninth inning of a close major league game. The worst move of Whisenant's life was getting hurt during the spring, because that gave Jay Powell the chance to reclaim his spot in the bullpen.

Anyway, Whisenant was walking batters like crazy, and then the Phillies started scoring runs like crazy, and Leyland turned to Conine on the bench and said, "By the time this baby's over, your kid's gonna be one."

Kotsay: Some day, he'll tell his children that in his major league debut, he threw out Gregg Jefferies with his first throw in the first inning of his first game, nearly took off Curt Schilling's head with a single to center in his second major league at-bat, and received a standing ovation. He also stood in centerfield through a steady rainstorm as water dripped off his cap. He'll remember all of that, including the 13-3 loss.

"Having my parents in the stands means a lot to me," Kotsay said. "My dad got to see my first big league hit."

It came sooner than anybody thought it would, including the Marlins. Kotsay, 21, was the Marlins' first pick in the 1996 amateur draft, and it's rare that any player, even a phenom, makes it to the big leagues in only a year. He wasn't even on the Marlins' forty-man roster because they didn't want to have to protect him in the expansion draft. But this was really a matter of desperation. Devon White was going to be out for another month, at least, and Leyland and Dombrowski felt they needed another left-handed bat in the order. Rather than look elsewhere, they talked it over for a week, conferred with farm director John Boles, and decided to take a shot with a left-handed centerfielder in their own organization.

That's how Kotsay, who planned to spend the entire season in Double-A and wasn't even counting on a September callup, ended up in a locker between Jim Eisenreich and Jeff Conine in the Marlins' clubhouse. Pretty heady stuff, although Kotsay didn't seem overwhelmed. During batting practice, Leyland thought he'd fool around with the rookie and asked, "Kots, did you play in college?"

"Yeah, I played three years," said Kotsay, who went to Cal State Fullerton, and was so impressive that he was named to the all-time College World Series team.

"Did you start?" Leyland asked.

"I did the first year," Kotsay deadpanned. "Not the last two." Then he walked away.

◆ ◆ ◆

One of the reporters suggested Cliff Floyd, with his huge upper body, should have chosen football over baseball, and Leyland shot back, "Football? He can't play two baseball games without getting hurt."

"Cliff says he'll be ready to play in a week," another reporter said.

"Well," cracked Leyland, "I hope he likes Carlos Tosca. He's not playing his way into shape here."

Tosca managed the Marlins' Triple-A team in Charlotte, North Carolina.

The ability, or willingness, of certain players to play with pain figured to have a large impact on the Marlins' fortunes over the next three months. Floyd needed to find a way to run all the way to first base without pulling a hamstring. White, who underwent an MRI that showed a torn muscle in his left leg, had to decide whether, at age 34 and with two World Series rings already on his fingers, he had the will or the need to risk further injury. Sheffield's thumb looked like it might never heal, and Castillo was at least a step slower since bruising his heel early in the season. But not much sympathy came from the manager.

"Christ," Leyland griped, "you have to play in a little pain."

◆ ◆ ◆

Bonilla was so impressive on and off the field, playing in pain, fielding his position, and dealing with the media, that the reporters in New York and Baltimore probably wouldn't have recognized him. Take this incident that in cither of those two cities would have escalated into a controversy that lasted for days. He arrived at the ballpark Saturday afternoon and caught local TV reporter Steve Shapiro poking through his locker and swinging one of his bats. Bonilla couldn't believe the nerve, but managed to smile as he good-naturedly bellowed at the TV guy.

"You can't go through my things!" Bonilla yelled out as Shapiro moseyed away. "This is my stuff! Nobody invited you!"

Then he summoned equipment manager Mike Wallace.

"Wally, come here," Bonilla said. "Can you believe this? The man was going through my locker!"

Ron Colangelo, the publicity director, walked over.

"I haven't had an outburst in years," Bonilla said, almost laughing. "I'm due for one. Maybe my power will come back."

A few minutes later, Wallace emerged from his office and hung a sign over Bonilla's stall: MEDIA MEMBERS BEWARE! STAY OUT OF MY LOCKER.

Bonilla walked back toward the trainer's room, shaking his head and looking over his shoulder toward Shapiro. "The man was going through my locker!" He still couldn't believe it.

◆ ◆ ◆

A frighteningly intense late afternoon thunderstorm threatened to cancel the Marlins' annual photo day with the season ticket holders, and one of the players—not a usual suspect—was so overjoyed by the news that he let out a holler and yelled, "Kiss our ass, fans, you sweaty fat fucks!" When the rain stopped after a half hour, a decision was made to go on with the show, and it was a telling scene to watch the fans running across the field to the picture-taking stations, while the players reluctantly trudged out to do their duty.

It's an amazing thing, but a lot of major league ballplayers still haven't grasped the connection between the paying public and their multi-million-dollar salaries. You'd think they'd welcome any opportunity to thank the people who have made them so lavishly rich, and you'd be wrong. What made this worse for the Marlins— and the PR staff that was trying to make them look good—was that another team in town, the Panthers, had this fan/money thing down pat. The relationship between the Panthers and their fans was so strong, the players frequently credited the fans for their success. They signed hundreds of autographs after every practice. When Brian Skrudland, the team captain, left the Panthers after four seasons, he wrote an open letter to the fans that appeared in the local papers.

Leyland staunchly defended baseball players and insisted they're better than their image, but it's the attitude that can be so annoying. Most of the Marlins acted as if they were doing the fans a favor when they signed autographs or posed for pictures. Then there's the Autograph Police, the security guards stationed near the dugouts who can make autograph hunting a very unpleasant experience. It's bad enough for a child to get blown off by a millionaire baseball player who brushes by without even an acknowledgment. The situation is worse when some $10-an-hour rent-a-cop admonishes the child for calling out to the player.

"Don't yell at the players!" the Autograph Police scold. "They'll come over if they want to."

Little kids can be pretty persistent. Conine might be standing next to the batting cage and it's clear that he is about to step in and take his swings, but the kids will be yelling out, "Hey Jeff! Hey Jeff!"

"Don't yell at the players!" the Autograph Police chide.

A fan might place his program and pen on top of the dugout.

"Don't put your things on top of the dugout!" say the Autograph Police.

Players come out for infield practice, and start playing catch.

"They can't sign now, they're practicing!"

A player finally consents to sign. Eager, excited fans are reaching over the dugout.

"Mr. Eisenreich will sign one autograph at a time!"

The Autograph Police are the designated on-the-field protectors of the players, and they are so enthralled by their authority they squeeze out every ounce they can. Of course the Autograph Police are merely following their marching orders, which can be traced through a maze of authority and right back to the players. The thing is, this is nothing new. The players' disdain for the fans goes back decades and decades, probably to the start of organized baseball. The "rubes" is what turn-of-the-century players, called them. In the 1990s, they have progressed to "sweaty fat fucks." Wonderful.

On the other hand, as Gary Sheffield slowly walked toward his station on photo day, it was easy to understand his seeming reluctance to mingle with the same people who had been booing him for the past two days. Then again, you can have a $61 million contract, or you can have sympathy from the public, but you can't have both.

◆ ◆ ◆

Maria Leiter sat in a suite behind Section 201 and was queen for the day. She did several TV interviews, spoke with a few local columnists, and had been wired for sound by *This Week In Baseball.* The occasion: Her two sons, Mark and Al, were going to pitch against each other for the first time in their major league careers, Mark for the Phillies and Al for the Marlins.

"I don't know how I'm going to watch, but I guess I'll have to," she said.

But nobody, not even Maria Leiter, was looking forward to this more than the brothers, who flew in twenty-five family members for the occasion. Al is three years younger than Mark, and remembered when they were growing up and watching the Niekro and Forsche brothers pitching on TV.

"It's something that Mark and I had always talked about," Al said. "I've pitched in a World Series, I've pitched in an All-Star Game, I've thrown a no-hitter, but to be a part of this is a big thrill for both of us. We've both had our share of heartache and struggle."

Six times previously they had come a day apart from meeting, and now they were finally on schedule. Actually, they weren't originally, but Mark talked manager Terry Francona into allowing him and Curt Schilling to switch days. Al knew better than to ask Leyland to change the pitching rotation, especially during a pennant race. Francona didn't mind. The Phillies were thirty-one games out of first.

And then it rained.

And it rained. And rained. And rained some more. It stopped raining, then started again.

At 9 o'clock, the game was postponed. Five minutes later, pitching coach Larry Rothschild walked up to Leiter and told him Alex Fernandez would start Sunday afternoon's game against Mark.

Leyland's explanation: Leiter had already warmed up. He didn't want to change his rotation.

Actually, Leiter warming up had very little to do with it. Leyland simply didn't want to change his rotation.

"Six other times we're one day apart, now we're right on the day and it rains," said a disappointed Al as he stood in front of his stall. Leiter can see the silver lining behind any cloud—even one over Pro Player Stadium—and he didn't lose his smile as he spoke. He refused to second guess Leyland, even though he clearly didn't think warming up for fifteen minutes was reason enough to push back his next start another five days.

A few hours later, he was sitting in a nearby restaurant, having a beer and trying to forget his disappointment.

"I'm not very happy with my manager," he said sadly.

◆ ◆ ◆

Billy the Marlin, the team mascot, had his fifth birthday party before the final game of the Phillies series, and he was joined on the field by several other mascots for the celebration. Billy, Hugh Manatee, Slugger, Orbit, Stanley C. Panther, and Billy's furry, big-beaked mother and father were together, hugging and kissing. The manager and his coaches, sitting in the dugout and watching the spectacle, thought it was the most ridiculous thing they had ever seen on a major league field, and it was hard to argue with them.

"Hell, you would've thought it was *Ted Williams, This Is Your Fucking Life,*" Leyland said.

Speaking of ridiculous things, for the second time in a week Leyland went on the record with something he had previously insisted was off. This time it was about the possibility of building a retractable roof stadium for the Marlins, and Leyland—who originally didn't want to be quoted because he didn't want it to sound as if he was lobbying for a new stadium—said, "If ever there was a place to have a dome, it's South Florida. I think it's going to be very important for the franchise."

He said this after the third game in four days against Philadelphia was delayed by rain, this time for an hour and a half. Again, it was hard to argue with him. The paid attendance was 26,860, pretty small anyway for a summer Sunday. Only about half of the people who bought tickets bothered showing up.

◆ ◆ ◆

And on the subject of ridiculous things, Sheffield came to bat for the second time in the fourth inning, having homered to lead off an eight-run outburst, and relief pitcher Reggie Harris threw two straight pitches out of the strike zone. Then Sheffield swung for the fences and missed a chest-high fastball over the middle of the plate. So what did Harris do? He threw the same pitch, chest-high. Sheffield tomahawked the ball into the club level seats in leftfield for a three-run homer. Two home runs by the same batter in one inning had been done only thirty-seven times previously in major league history.

Here's how messed up Sheffield's head had been. One of the main things on his mind was the grand slam he had taken away by the rainout in the second game of the Yankees series. That had been nearly a month ago. It really wrecked him.

"When you go through what I've been going through all year, and everybody brings up the contract and things like that, and you're trying to win ballgames, and we're in second place, nobody wants to talk about the second place we're in," Sheffield said. "They want to talk about individual stats, and this is not an individual game. It's been a tough season. Then when I go out and do something well in a big series, I get up for the series, and do something that gives us a chance to sweep the World Champions, and then they take it away from you, it drains you inside. It's just more what could have been. A lot of times you have to block those things out, and it's a little difficult for me to do that."

In this game, for reasons unknown even to Sheffield, he was focused, able to block out distractions. He had spent a week looking at videotapes of himself in 1995 after Mike Carr, the team's video coordinator, noticed that Sheffield held his hands differently that season. Two days earlier, Leyland saw that Sheffield looked a little more relaxed, which was an amazing observation on the manager's part. Sheffield does everything slowly. He walks slowly, spends a long time showering after games, takes his time getting dressed, and barely breaks into a jog when he goes to the outfield between innings. A man couldn't look more relaxed. Of course Leyland was talking about demeanor in the batter's box, where Sheffield really had looked tense, especially after a called strike he didn't agree with. On Sunday, Sheffield felt relaxed. Zoned-in. Oblivious, really.

"When I went up there again, I didn't even realize it was the same inning," he said of his two-homer fourth.

But bad came with the good, as Sheffield is always willing to point out. He hit a home run in Atlanta and injured his thumb. He had two hits in New York and got thrown out of the game. This time he was rounding second base on a triple by Moises Alou in the sixth inning when suddenly he felt a spasm in his right hamstring. Sheffield clutched his thigh as he hobbled into third and walked home, and on the Marlins bench players were saying, "It's a cramp. It's a cramp." Leyland was thinking, *I've heard that before.* Sheffield left the game and his injury turned out to be a cramp, not a pulled hamstring. Nonetheless, he would have to miss a game or two, just when it looked like he was about to break out.

That'll teach him to run hard.

◆ ◆ ◆

Russ Morman is the all-time minor league home run king, but he has bounced around the minors for fifteen seasons because he's one of those guys who kills Triple-A pitching, but can't hit in the majors. Anyway, with Sheffield day-to-day, the conversation came around to who might take his place in rightfield if he had to go on the DL, and one reporter asked, "Is Morman ready?"

"Ready?" Leyland said incredulously. "He's forty-one fucking years old!"

Everybody in the room, including Leyland, burst out in uncontrollable laughter.

With Sheffield unavailable and the Marlins facing Jeff Juden, the Expos' 6'8" righty who dominated them in two previous starts, Leyland loaded his lineup with lefties and came up with this improvisation: Cangelosi, RF; Renteria, SS; Kotsay, CF; Bonilla, 3B; Eisenreich, LF; Zaun, C; Conine, 1B; Abbott, 2B; and Rapp, P. Four bench players, a rookie, and the No. 4 starter.

"This fucking lineup'll probably get shut out on two hits," Leyland decided as he looked over the lineup card in his office. Then he paused. "I like it."

For five and a half innings, it looked like Leyland's comment might be near the mark. Rapp was struggling again and, with Juden dominating, the Expos took a 4-0 lead to the bottom of the sixth. Then Bonilla hit a mammoth two-run homer into the rightfield picnic area—his first left-handed homer as a Marlin in Pro Player Stadium—and the comeback was underway. The Marlins tied the game with two in the seventh and won it in the twelfth on Eisenreich's ground ball through the legs of the third baseman.

Eisenreich had three hits, and the bullpen pitched like it had in the first half of the season, but Bonilla was really the story. He probably shouldn't have been playing, his left wrist was bothering him so terribly, yet he managed to hit one out to the deepest part of the park. The fence in right-centerfield is so far away that Bonilla wasn't sure it was gone and ran as hard as he could just in case, but the ball kept going and landed halfway up the picnic area.

"This was huge," Bonilla said. "This was a big win."

Bonilla, dressed in standard-issue jeans and blue T-shirt, sat in front of his locker for a long time after the game and felt so tired he was in no hurry to leave. The incident with the TV reporter the other day was still on his mind, and Bonilla was happy with how he had handled the situation. He recalled the time during his second season in New York, after reporter Bob Klapisch had written a book about the Mets' stormy 1992 season. Klapisch got a little too close to Bonilla's locker for his own good, and Bonilla threatened to "show him the Bronx." It's the incident and quote most associated with Bonilla.

"With the Klapisch thing, he wrote that book and he was standing around like nobody could touch him," Bonilla said. "With this guy, it was different. I was mad and I let him know it. If I had my wallet or my money in the locker, I would've been all over him."

Maybe, maybe not. The warning to the media was still hanging above his head, but in this season, with his image under repair, it seemed like a friendly joke, not a threat.

◆ ◆ ◆

The day after getting hurt, Sheffield said he would be available to pinch hit, but on the other hand might have to go on the DL. That made no sense to his manager.

"I don't understand that shit," Leyland said. "'I feel like I can hit, but I might have to go on the DL.' What's that shit? That's what I call a wugwump. There's wug on one side of the fence, and wump on the other."

◆ ◆ ◆

Gregg Zaun was sitting around before the first game of the Expos series trying to remember the last time he had started two games in a row for the Marlins, and couldn't come up with one because it had never happened. Then he went out and committed a passed ball, allowed a stolen base, popped up three times, and struck out once.

"Remind me of one thing," Leyland said the next afternoon. "Never to play Zaun two days in a row again. When he's horseshit, he's horseshit. I won't play him two games in a row." Pause. "As long as I have an ass."

Leyland liked Zaun's effort, but sometimes questioned his head. Zaun is a decent hitter for a catcher, with below-average defensive skills. He's also a bit of a showboat. Earlier during the season, Zaun created a scene in the clubhouse by throwing a chair across the room and yelling, "I can throw a chair, but I can't throw a ball to third base!" During spring training, Zaun told the coaches he was staying late for extra batting practice against the pitching machine, then turned out the lights and left a few minutes after he thought they were gone. They shook their heads at his gall while admiring his desire to make an impression. Something must have worked because Zaun made the team.

Against Montreal, Zaun sprinted towards the dugout and dove for a ball that was at least ten feet out of his reach. His body bounced off the artificial dirt, the ball bounced into the dugout, and Leyland shot him a look that said, *What the hell is wrong with you?* The crowd applauded Zaun's hustle, when it was really nothing more than showboating. As far as Leyland was concerned, he might as well have waved to the TV cameras while he was diving.

Naturally, Charles Johnson was back behind the plate for the finale of the two-game series, but it really didn't matter. "Bulldog" Dustin Hermanson, the pitcher the Marlins gave up in the Cliff Floyd deal, stretched his streak to nineteen consecutive shutout innings against his former teammates and allowed only five hits in a 5-0 win.

The Bulldog made the Marlins look bad. It recalled a day in early March, when Hermanson was throwing batting practice and the Marlins standing around the batting cage were so impressed they said, "We got that for Quilvio Veras?" So they weren't surprised by Hermanson's dominance.

By the way, the game was so hopeless for the Marlins, Whisenant pitched the ninth inning. He retired the side in order.

◆ ◆ ◆

Kurt Abbott was standing near the dugout signing his autograph on the back of a jersey as Leyland watched from the bench.

"That's A-B-B-O-T-T," Leyland called out helpfully, breaking into a grin, then turning to reporters and nodding his head. "He's my man."

John Cangelosi walked by.

"Hey, Cangy!" Leyland said.

"Yeah?"

"You're playing today."

"I know," Cangelosi answered with a quizzical look, then kept walking. He had seen the lineup card an hour earlier, as Leyland must have known. Every player checks the lineup card when he arrives at the ballpark.

When Abbott was done signing, Leyland waved him over.

"Hey, Abby!"

"Yeah?"

"You're not playing today."

"I know that. You told me that before," Abbott said. "You told me after the last time in Los Angeles. 'Abby, you will never again play against Nomo.'"

The manager was in a good mood. He had just spent ten minutes playing ball with Gary Sheffield's 3-year-old son, Gary Jr. The little boy is cute as can be—a mini version of his father. Pretty good athlete, too. Leyland decided to teach him how to hit and handed him one of Gary Sr.'s big baseball bats. It was longer than the kid. Leyland kept showing him how to choke up, but Gary Jr. kept sliding his hands down the bat. Then Leyland pitched to him underhanded and Gary Jr. showed pretty good power to all fields. Gary Sr. sat on the bench and watched. Leyland and Gary Jr. never stopped smiling.

"C'mon, Gary, it's time to rest," Sheffield told his son after a while.

Gary Jr. smiled at his father, then went on playing.

A few minutes later: "C'mon, Gary, it's time to rest."

Gary Jr. just ignored him.

It was a good day overall for the Marlins. Kevin Brown pitched a one-hitter and the Marlins beat the Dodgers, 5-1. The Dodgers, a pre-season choice to win the NL West, arrived in Miami with eleven wins in their past twelve games and a .349 batting average in July. The middle of the order—Mike Piazza, Eric Karros, Raul Mondesi, and Todd Zeile—came into the series with seventy-eight home runs, fifty-one more than the entire lineup Leyland put out on the field.

Brown said he wasn't aware of the Dodgers' recent productivity until a reporter told him after the game, and it was easy to believe him, considering his ability to block out all distractions. Leyland had had the rare opportunity to watch Brown from a different angle, on TV, during the All-Star Game, and was impressed by the look of intensity on his face, even for a meaningless game. He saw that same look against the Dodgers.

"He's a tenacious guy," Leyland said. "That's T-E-N-A-C-I-O-U-S."

The manager was Hooked on Phonics all day.

◆ ◆ ◆

Baseball has a lot of rules and many of them have no effect on what happens on the field, but matter on the scorecard. Some of them don't make much sense, until you think hard about them.

Charles Johnson went into the first game of the Dodgers series having committed no errors in five hundred fifteen chances. In the fifth inning, Raul Mondesi of Los Angeles singled, then tried to steal second. Johnson threw hard and low, and the ball bounced into centerfield. As Mondesi rounded second, he bumped into Luis Castillo, and umpire Bob Davidson awarded him third base because of the interference. An error on Johnson, right? If his throw hadn't gone into the outfield, Mondesi never would have attempted to go to third. That's what everybody thought, including Johnson and official scorer Doug Pett.

But Julio Sarmiento, the Marlins' assistant director of publicity, suspected otherwise, so for the next fifteen minutes, he and director of publicity Ron Colangelo poured through the baseball rulebook trying to save Johnson from being charged with an error. They finally found what they were looking for on Page 91: If interference is called, the scorer cannot assume that the fielder wouldn't have thrown out the runner at third base. The interference supersedes the error.

So Johnson's record remained clean because the assistant director of publicity knew the rules. Even Johnson was unaware of the scoring change until after the game, and he was surprised because the catcher is almost always charged with the error when a throw goes into the outfield and the runner takes an extra base.

"I didn't look at the scoreboard," Johnson said. "Automatically, I knew it was my error."

Baseball's evidence that life isn't fair: Realistically, Castillo didn't deserve the error, although Kotsay, playing centerfield, might have had a good chance at throwing out Mondesi at third. And there had been other times when Castillo or Edgar Renteria saved Johnson's throws from going into the outfield.

"I've made some tough plays and the ball was short-hopped, it skipped off the grass, and they'd come up with the ball and make the tag," Johnson said. "I tip my hat to those guys."

Johnson was being too modest. Zaun was throwing to the same second baseman and shortstop, but he had committed eight errors in three hundred fewer chances. No catcher in baseball history had gone through an entire season without committing an error or a passed ball, and Johnson had a chance at being the first. If he did, he'd owe an assist to the assistant PR guy.

◆ ◆ ◆

The New York Mets fired general manager Joe McIlvaine, even though the team was ten games above .500 and one of the surprises of baseball. McIlvaine was criticized for being an absentee GM, who was always off scouting minor leaguers. There were times when former Mets manager Dallas Green would be asked the whereabouts of his general manager. He'd shrug his shoulders and say, "You tell me."

It brought to mind the scene a few weeks earlier at Shea Stadium, when McIlvaine was standing behind the batting cage talking with Dave Dombrowski. Dombrowski had an underachieving team on one of the highest payrolls in baseball. McIlvaine had an overachieving team on a lesser payroll. Who could have guessed that McIlvaine would be the first to go?

Fact: McIlvaine pitched for Leyland in Clinton, Iowa, of the Midwest League in 1972.

"What kind of pitcher was he?" a reporter asked before the first game of the Dodgers series.

"Not very good," Leyland recalled.

Dombrowski never will be accused of being an absentee GM. He rarely misses a home game and can always be found in his office, upstairs in the general manager's suite, or in the press dining room on game days. After a game you might find him walking past the clubhouse with assistant GM Frank Wren following a few steps behind, or coming out of a meeting with the manager. Dombrowski and Leyland talk every day about minor leaguers, players on the major league rosters, and possible trades. Sometimes they just talk.

Of course, part of Dombrowski's job is keeping track of the minor leaguers, and he'll skip an occasional road trip to watch the Single-A team in Melbourne, Florida, the Double-A team in Portland, Maine, or the Triple-A team in Charlotte, North Carolina. Although he's never more than a phone call away and carries the standard executive's power pack of beeper and cell phone, Dombrowski likes being with the team. Many years ago players considered it a bad sign when the GM came along on a road trip. It meant somebody was about to get traded or sent down to the minors. These days, it's expected. Dombrowski wants to form his own opinions about how players are performing. He never knows when an injury might force him to call up a player from the minors, and he likes to make the decision in person, rather than by phone.

When he goes on the road, Dombrowski brings along his office essentials in a large trunk. He'll stay in the same hotel as the team and set up shop in a large, lavish suite. GMs travel in style, but they rarely have time to enjoy their luxury. Dombrowski will sleep in one bedroom and unpack his office supplies in another. That's where he spends most of his time. A large living area with couches, tables, chairs, a TV, and a VCR, might be used to conduct meetings or perhaps hold an impromptu press conference.

Days on the road follow a set pattern for Dombrowski. In the morning, he might receive a large overnight envelope containing all of the previous day's mail. Most of the morning is taken up with going over the mail, catching up on paperwork, and talking to his scouts, managers, and opposing GMs. The period from a few weeks before the All-Star break until July 31, the trading deadline, is the peak period for trades, and Dombrowski might speak to a few GMs a day, either over the phone or at the ballpark. Contending teams are always trying to add a player or two for the stretch run. Non-contending teams want to unload large contracts or players that are about to become free agents.

Around noon, Dombrowski will change into his running clothes and head downstairs for a jog around town, or maybe a workout in the hotel's athletic club. Then, after lunch, he'll make a few more phone calls and do some more work before heading out to the ballpark at around 5 p.m. for a 7 o'clock game. He watches the games from the press box or from a special suite for visiting teams. When the game ends, he goes downstairs and chats with the manager, and then might finish his day by pouring over the results from minor and major league games.

Dombrowski is youthful looking and approachable, but it's unwise to be fooled by appearances. He says what he wants to say, and often has a roundabout way of not answering questions. A few weeks earlier in Boston when Sheffield was fined for his remarks about the umpires, Dombrowski had conducted an on-the-field press conference during which he was asked several questions, but didn't give clear answers to any of them.

REPORTER: You don't expect it to happen again?

DOMBROWSKI: This particular situation is closed.

He answered every question in a similar manner. More recently, he and Boston Red Sox General Manager Dan Duquette headed a committee that studied media access in Major League Baseball. Their immediate goal was barring media clubhouse access from the time batting practice began until ten minutes after a game. That's exactly what baseball—a sport desperate for any exposure it can get—doesn't need. Less access equals less free press. Their ultimate goal was barring media clubhouse access entirely, forcing reporters to rely on colorless pre- and post-game press conferences.

Perhaps the image of GMs as gruff, old Branch Rickey-types who do whatever they want behind closed doors really hasn't changed at all.

◆ ◆ ◆

Fashion designer Gianni Versace died Tuesday, July 15, when he was gunned down in front of his mansion in Miami's South Beach, so Moises Alou showed up on Wednesday wearing a lime-green Versace shirt and purple Versace jeans.

"And, I'm going to South Beach later on," Alou said.

Versace clothes are so expensive they're usually worn only by actors, actresses, socialites, and other extraordinarily wealthy people, such as Major League Baseball players. Actually, most major leaguers don't have such extravagant taste that they walk around in Versace jeans. You won't find many players wearing Levi's and Lee's, but you will find a lot of Calvin Klcins, Polos, and Tommy Hilfigers, which makes them no different from ordinary upper bourgeois. Gary Sheffield never wears jeans. Bonilla, Leiter, Saunders, and Conine wear them all the time.

Conine prefers the regular guy look: blue jeans, polo shirts, and a pair of dock shoes. He blends in with the crowd. During the series in New York, Conine and his father took the No. 7 train every day from Grand Central Station to Shea Stadium, and only a few times did anyone realize he was a Major League Baseball player. Those who did said a few words, then left him alone. Conine was like any other passenger on the New York City subway system.

"They probably don't even recognize the Mets," Conine said.

That's not to say Conine isn't different from other regular guys. Most men hand out cigars when they have their first son. On Thursday, Conine gave out Hershey's Mr. Goodboy—as opposed to Mr. Goodbar—candy bars with Griffin Riley Conine inscribed on the wrapper.

The players realized they were keepsakes. Nobody ate them. Or tried to smoke them.

◆ ◆ ◆

Gregg Zaun walked into the clubhouse and said out loud to nobody in particular, "Can somebody please tell me what's the point of tank-top undershirts? They don't look good. They don't prevent underarm sweat. What's the point?"

Nobody answered because nobody had ever considered the question. Zaun has a unique way of looking at a lot of things. He loves movies and during the season wrote a monthly movie column for ESPN SportsZone on the Internet. One month the topic was "Gregg Zaun's Top Five Date Movies," which loosely translated meant "Gregg Zaun's Top Five Movies To Impress Upon A Woman Your Sensitivity And Get Her Into Bed." Wrote Zaun about *Father of the Bride*: "Unless your name is Franc, the wedding coordinator, you're probably not crazy about weddings. Women love them. They dream about weddings. People tell brides they look like princesses. It's the culmination of everything for them. This day should not go unexploited. That's why this is the classic date flick; she'll think you are as excited about weddings as she is. Shank! Nevertheless, use this movie as a tool, guys. Tell her you can't wait to see her walk down the aisle in that white dress. You'll appear charming and sensitive; she'll find you irresistible."

123

Zaun got engaged during the season and, whether he was at home or on the road, kept a framed photo of his fiancée in his locker. She joined him in Boston for the series against the Red Sox and, before one of the games, Leyland called Zaun into his office to tell him he was playing the next day.

"By the way," Leyland said. "I met your fiancée."

"Yeah, she told me," Zaun answered.

"She's a beautiful girl," Leyland added. "You'd better marry her before I send your ass down to Charlotte."

◆ ◆ ◆

Sheffield resurfaced in the finale of the Dodgers series. In the sixth, he put on a batting helmet and swung a bat in the dugout, close enough so that Leyland couldn't miss him. The next inning, with the Marlins leading 6-5 and runners on first and second, Sheffield climbed the dugout steps and received a standing ovation as he walked toward home plate.

He had an interesting at-bat. With the count two and one, Sheffield looked at a knee-high fastball across the middle of the plate. Eric Gregg, the home plate umpire, called strike two. Sheffield dropped his shoulders and looked back at Gregg as if to say, "Are you kidding?" Normally this season, Sheffield's mind would have been so messed up by the call that he would have struck out. Instead, he drove the next pitch into centerfield for a two-run single that turned out to be the key hit in an 8-7 victory.

Bad news for Whisenant: The relief pitcher pinch-ran for Sheffield when position players were available.

First signs of spring: Everybody hit, just like in March. Right-handers hit the ball to rightfield and left-handers went to leftfield. Johnson and Renteria each had three hits, even Castillo had a two-run single. Leiter pitched six strong innings. The bullpen tried, but failed, to blow a big lead.

Leiter hadn't pitched since July 4, which gave him plenty of time to think about what had gone wrong during a first half in which he had a 5.02 ERA. Missing the start against Philadelphia gave him more time to think.

"The most disappointing thing for a pitcher is to not feel like you're in command and not have the concentration and relentless attitude that goes with every pitch," Leiter said, repeating one of his common themes. "I'm going to try to make a little pact with myself, no matter what. If I give up a home run, I'm going to get back on the rubber and maintain that aggressive attitude. I don't care if I give up runs or not, I want to feel like I'm in control and going after the hitter, relentlessly."

He'd have to convince his manager. Although Leyland might have been right in removing Leiter for a pinch-hitter with two on and none out in the sixth, it's hard to believe he would have done the same thing with Kevin Brown or Alex Fernandez on the mound. Leiter had thrown one hundred six pitches, not a high count for him, and could have laid down a bunt to set up the top of the order. But Leyland didn't feel comfortable with Leiter pitching or bunting. Remember, this is the guy who supposedly ruined his no-smoking vow in under two hours.

Watching the two men interact was humorous. Leyland would walk past Leiter during batting practice and yell out, "Leiter"—hard on the "L"—to which Leiter would simply respond in a half-mocking, half-good natured way, "Leyland"—hard on the "L." Then they'd keep going in opposite directions without saying anything else. Sometimes they'd look at each other as if they were from different worlds and, in some ways, they were. Leyland is the old-time baseball man with the clubhouse mentality and raw sense of humor. When Leiter talks, he sounds like a kindly young school teacher explaining a lesson to a student, or even a patient telling his problems to a psychologist.

Leiter walked only three and threw a lot more strikes than balls against the Dodgers, so perhaps a turning point in his relationship with Leyland was approaching. Maybe next time Leyland would let Leiter pitch against his brother.

◆ ◆ ◆

The Knitting Lady finally came out of mourning: She wore teal and orange, Miami Dolphins colors. It must be football season already.

◆ ◆ ◆

Here's how fast a reporter can fall from a manager's good graces: Thursday afternoon, Leyland was taking his usual good-natured shots at Gregg Doyel of *The Miami Herald* and offering that one day he would let Doyel take a few swings during batting practice.

Two hours later, Leyland called Doyel into his office. When Doyel arrived, Leyland was holding a copy of that day's *Herald,* in which Doyel had written that the Marlins were trying to trade Pat Rapp so they could make room in the pitching rotation for Livan Hernandez. Doyel had based the story on conversations with unnamed sources within the organization and quoted Hernandez's agent.

"Where the fuck did this come from?" Leyland asked.

"What?" Doyel asked.

Leyland showed him the paper.

"You can see I quoted his agent," Doyel said.

"You talked to the agent. So what?"

"I talked to two other people in the organization and they confirmed it."

"I want to know who they are," Leyland demanded.

"I can't," Doyel answered. "Just like you won't bad-mouth a player in the press, I won't tell you who said something off the record. I just won't do it."

Leyland was getting angrier by the second, and his voice rose to the point where he could clearly be heard down the hall.

"Well let me tell you one fucking thing!" Leyland screamed. "The next time you put something like this in the paper, I better fucking know who's telling you. Now get the fuck out!"

Doyel turned to leave, but Leyland wasn't finished.

"This is just the kind of horseshit that can tear up a club from the outside," he shouted.

"Jim," Doyel started.

"Get the fuck out!" Leyland ordered.

Leyland hadn't cooled down nearly five hours later, even though the Marlins won the game. He hesitated for a good fifteen seconds before mumbling a few words in answer to one of Doyel's questions, then said to the group during a pause in the questioning, "If you have any more questions, ask them. Otherwise, leave. I wanna eat."

The next day at 3:30 p.m., Ron Colangelo walked into Leyland's office and told him the media was ready for its daily session with the manager. Leyland angrily replied that there would be no more daily meetings in his office, and that if the reporters needed him for anything, they could find him in the dugout during batting practice. Leyland was there, as promised, but he was short with his answers and didn't engage in his usual small talk.

The funny thing about it was that the *Herald* story turned out to be absolutely correct.

◆ ◆ ◆

There's a great side to being a major league ballplayer: You play games for a living and make a lot of money. And there is a bad side, too: You can get traded to any team, anywhere, at any time.

Let's say, for example, you are Pat Rapp. It is Friday, July 18, 1997, prior to the ninety-fourth game of your fifth season with the Marlins. You have been with the franchise since Day One—there are only two others who can say the same thing, Alex Arias and Jeff Conine—but today as you take batting practice with the rest of the pitchers, you know that your scheduled start tomorrow night might never happen. You have been talking with your agent, and he's been telling you that the Marlins have been shopping you around.

So at 5:25 you are standing in the clubhouse when you see Jim Leyland, Dave Dombrowski, and Frank Wren go into the manager's office and close the door, and you have an idea that they are talking about you. You take a seat in front of your cubicle and you stare at the TV set, but you really aren't watching what's on because all kinds of thoughts are going through your head. *Have they traded me? Where am I going?* You have your left hand on your chin, then you cross your legs, then you uncross them, then you switch to your right hand on your chin, then you cross your legs again, and you are looking very unhappy. You have a wife, two sons, and a home in South Florida, and you don't want to leave.

But Matt Rosenthal, the assistant clubhouse manager, walks over and shakes your hand, and you are now pretty much certain of your fate. Then pitching coach Larry Rothschild calls you into the manager's office, and there is no doubt why they want you. Behind closed doors you find out you have been sent to the San Francisco Giants, a first place team, in exchange for two prospects. The manager and the general manager say they are sorry to see you go and thank you for your effort, and eight minutes later when you leave the meeting and walk out into the clubhouse, you are not surrounded by teammates anymore. They are ex-teammates. So you make the rounds, shake hands, and say your goodbyes. Now you have a little smile on your face, because it beats crying, which is what you really feel like doing.

Outside in the dugout, Dombrowski is breaking the news to the press, and what you don't hear him say is that he doesn't know too much about the players the Marlins are receiving, or that he isn't concerned about replacing you in the rotation with rookie Livan Hernandez, because, "How many games has Pat won for us? Four. How many games has Livan won for us? Two." Nor do you see Conine sneak a peek at a reporter's notes and crack, "My name's not on there. Good." Because when you get right down to it, the Marlins aren't really too sorry to see you go, and your teammates are happy it's not them.

Then you talk to the Florida media for the final time as a Marlin, and probably come pretty close to the truth when you say, "Every year you're in the papers mentioned with trades. It took five years, but they finally found somebody to take me." You don't smile when a reporter says, "You were traded from a second place team to a first place team," because you'd rather stay with the second place team. You have been through all of the losing years. Now you'd like to be around for the end of the winning year, and when you are asked whether there is a good side to this, you can't come up with a single thing, other than that another team wants you.

Back in the clubhouse, the equipment manager is already clearing out your locker and placing your things in boxes and a duffel bag, so you sit and talk for a while with Kevin Brown and Mark Hutton, and shake Felix Heredia's hand. At 6:45 your teammates walk out to the field because the game is about to begin, and shortly afterwards you leave the clubhouse for the final time. This used to be your home, it's not anymore, and you know in your heart the Florida Marlins' only concern now is that the door doesn't hit you on the way out.

◆ ◆ ◆

Now let's say you are Jim Leyland. It is the sixth inning of a game against the San Diego Padres the same night, and you are sitting on the bench steaming mad because your team is trailing the Padres, 5-1, and maybe you made a bad move by giving Luis Castillo the green light to swing with the count 2-0 and the bases loaded. Between innings you walk into the bat room for a cigarette, but your spikes don't take well to the wet floor, and suddenly you find yourself splayed out on the floor with pain shooting from your knee and ankle. And this is a pretty embarrassing situation, because you are The Great Manager Of A Major League Baseball Team, and you are supposed to be in complete control.

So you are helped off the floor and back to the clubhouse, but after an inning, you decide to gut it out and walk back to the dugout. On your way a reporter from the Associated Press, who wandered down from the press box to find out what was going on, spots you and yells out, "Jim, what happened?" and you answer with a look that can kill. But an inning passes, and the pain is unbelievable, so you limp back to the clubhouse for X-rays.

When the game ends you are sitting at the desk in your office answering questions from the media, and when somebody asks you how your ankle feels, you say, "It hurts like hell." You will undergo an MRI the next morning, but you are not going to get a lot of sympathy from the people around you. You have angered a lot of people over the past few days—browbeating co-workers and beat reporters who were only doing their jobs—and now everybody's going to find out how well The Great Manager plays in pain.

◆ ◆ ◆

Or maybe you are Alex Fernandez, pitcher for the Florida Marlins, and you have just allowed four runs in the third inning to the San Diego Padres. You get back to the dugout and you are so angry with yourself that you are cursing out loud, but it's about to get worse. In the next inning Mandy Romero, a 29-year-old who toiled through ten minor league seasons—nearly eight hundred games—before starting in his first major league game tonight, hits a solo home run, and it's all more than you can stand.

You leave the game after the fifth inning, trailing 5-1, and when you get back to the clubhouse, you pick up a baseball bat and attack a water cooler, leaving it misshapen and broken beyond repair. But you are not finished, so you march back to your locker and smash in the wall between your two cubicles. By the time you are done, the carpet is littered with splinters, there's a hole in the wall, and a strip of wood is missing. Your locker looks like it has just been attacked by termites. Termites with baseball bats.

After the game, you are asked about Romero, who also comes from Miami but will make about $6,850,000 less than you do this year, and you answer, "Congratulations this time, but it won't happen again." But you can be sure that on this night, Mandy Romero's locker looks nothing like yours.

All of which is to say that Friday, July 18, 1997 was a very good day to be Mandy Romero, but not a very good day to be Pat Rapp, Jim Leyland, or Alex Fernandez.

◆ ◆ ◆

Leyland aftermath: He suffered a severely sprained ankle and torn ligaments, but wouldn't require surgery. He would be able to sit on the bench, but he wouldn't be able to hit fungoes, and there was no way he was going to limp out to the mound and make pitching changes. He had too much pride for that.

Team physician Dan Kanell wanted him to wear a large support boot, but Leyland snapped, "I'm not wearing no boot."

Nevertheless, Tommy Sandt and John Wehner presented him with an oversized teal boot, which sat unused beneath his desk. They wrote "Jim Leyland" on the wrapper.

"Assholes," Leyland grumbled.

Charles Johnson saw the original accident and said Leyland flew three feet off the ground.

"He was moaning," bench coach Jerry Manuel said. "I turned around and saw him lying on the floor. I thought he had a heart attack."

Said Leyland: "I think Jerry Manuel had the lineup card out of my pocket before I hit the ground."

The next day Leyland was walking with a severe limp, and as he made his way across the clubhouse from his office, the players couldn't help commenting.

"You all right, Jim?" Johnson asked.

"Yeah," Leyland replied sharply. "I'm fine."

Kevin Brown broke into a smile as he watched the manager limping.

"You're walking like Fred Sanford," he said.

Fred Sanford was Red Foxx's character in the TV show *Sanford and Son*. He had a severe case of hemorrhoids.

◆ ◆ ◆

Pat Rapp aftermath: He flew to St. Louis, started Saturday night against the Cardinals, and pitched his typical game: five innings, three runs allowed, four walks, a no decision. He also got hurt, pulling a muscle in his side, and had to be placed on the disabled list. So he got out of Florida in one piece, but didn't make it much further.

Hernandez pitched the same night for the Marlins and fared far better than Rapp had in any of his starts this season: six innings, no runs, only one hit allowed, in an 8-5 victory.

"You could see he threw pretty well this spring," pitching coach Larry Rothschild said. "He needed to firm up his slider and his curveball a little bit. I always thought his slider was going to be his better pitch, especially control-wise, and he worked on it a bit in the minors and did a good job."

Rapp's $1.125-million contract doesn't sound like much when a team has a payroll of $49 million, until you realize that it was one-eighth of the entire Pittsburgh Pirates' payroll. Dombrowski didn't hide the fact that the Marlins hadn't stopped looking for pitching help. Rapp's departure opened up another roster spot and gave Dombrowski some money to work with. Leyland also didn't hide his desire for another starting pitcher.

"I think a couple of things will happen," he said.

He didn't offer any names, but he certainly had several in mind. For the past week, Leyland, the coaches, Dombrowski, Wren, and the scouts had spent late hours in the manager's office, talked about what they needed, and mulled over possibilities. With the July 31 deadline approaching, there was no time to sit still.

◆ ◆ ◆

Players from the Marlins' Gulf Coast League rookie team attended Sunday's game and were on the field during batting practice. They were spread out in front of the dugout and Bobby Bonilla looked them over and said, "Look at all these big mothers here to take away my shit!" Then he went down the line and shook hands, and every once in a while he stopped and said, "Are you the mother fucker that's gonna take away my shit?"

The rookies nodded and laughed, and Bonilla laughed along with them, even though he had spoken the truth. Just about every player starts out in the rookie leagues. Fifteen years ago, Bonilla was playing in the Gulf Coast League and hitting only .228, so the idea that one of these kids would one day be playing for the Marlins and making millions of dollars wasn't merely possible, it was likely.

◆ ◆ ◆

Four fans sitting in the field level seats down the leftfield line got a little restless during the third game of the Padres series. First the two men got into a fight and security guards broke it up. Then their girlfriends started throwing punches, and when one of the security guards got between them, one of the women started whaling on him, too. The crowd reacted like it was the best action they had seen all night, which it was.

Not much else kept them interested. The Marlins lost to the Padres, 3-0, even though Saunders allowed only three hits in six-plus innings.

The thought of the day came from Leyland, who when talking about the Marlins' inability to win big and string together strong offensive performances said, "We have to get pepped up to go and get ready for that bonus round." He meant the playoffs, if the Marlins got there.

On Monday afternoon Kevin Brown got knocked around for eleven hits—he also injured the middle finger on his pitching hand—and the Padres beat the Marlins, 10-2. Everything went wrong. Conine left four men in scoring position. The Padres stole five bases on Charles Johnson. Castillo bobbled a routine grounder. The only bright spot came when Cangelosi, the outfielder, pitched a scoreless ninth inning of relief. Although his seventy-eight-mile-per-hour fastball would have been passed on Florida's Turnpike, he was the only one of four Marlins pitchers to not allow a run. The crowd gave Cangelosi a nice ovation when he walked off the mound after the ninth and Cangelosi doffed his cap. Bonilla, smiling broadly, offered a good-natured shove from behind.

"I've relieved four times in the majors," Cangelosi said afterward. "And you can write this down: Zero point zero zero ERA."

Meanwhile, the Braves had won. The Mets had won for the fifth straight day. The Marlins led the Mets by only one game in the loss column after finishing the homestand with six wins and five losses. And Leyland said, "We looked like we were playing in cement."

◆ ◆ ◆

Sheffield celebrated his return to the lineup on Monday by shaving his head and beard, but keeping a goatee. Alex Fernandez thought that made him look like a serial killer.

"Hey, Sheff!" Fernandez called halfway across the room. "You look like Cunanan!"

"Who?"

"Cunanan. You know, the guy that killed Versace."

Bonilla poked his head around the doorway near Fernandez's locker and warned, "You'd better have your driver's license with you, Sheff."

Andrew Cunanan was the suspected killer of fashion designer Gianni Versace. Recent pictures of Cunanan showed him with a full head of hair, a mustache, and no goatee. They also showed that he was white and looked nothing like Gary Sheffield.

Sheffield went out and hit a home run. Cunanan was still at large.

◆ ◆ ◆

Leyland hadn't snapped at anyone for days after his fall and seemed somewhat humbled. The team doctor ordered him to wear the surgical boot, so he put it on. An MRI showed that the ligaments were torn worse than believed, and Leyland said, "It scared me a bit, to be honest."

Then on Monday afternoon, with the reporters gathered around him in his office, Leyland was asked a question about his temper and said, "I don't yell at home—too much. I usually take it out on you guys. Doyel in particular. Don't take any offense. I don't mean anything by it. There's a lot of pressure on all of us and sometimes we all overreact a little bit. I know you guys have a job to do and I appreciate that. And if you do your homework and get something, then God bless ya."

It sounded like an apology.

◆ ◆ ◆

A few years ago the Marlins hired a consultant to advise them on the best starting time for their summer Sunday home games. Judging by this homestand, there is no good time to play baseball on any day during the summer in South Florida. Four of the eleven games were delayed by rain and the twelfth was rained out. The front office had known for months the homestand was a slow seller. With the weather not helping, the Marlins fared a little worse than they expected: the average of 25,240 for 11 games dropped their season average by a thousand to 28,762.

From all appearances, local sports fans had yet to get excited about the pennant race. But wait: The Marlins' attendance increase over 1996 was growing with every game, despite the disappointing turnouts, and was by far the biggest gain in the majors at more than thirty percent. Advance sales for the rest of the season were strong, and Jim Ross projected the Marlins would average more than thirty thousand a game in August and September.

The biggest obstacle—besides the lack of a retractable roof—could be found about ten miles up the road in nearby Davie, where the Dolphins had begun preseason football practice. Each day, more than six thousand fans had packed the bleachers and an adjacent parking garage, just to watch the team go through its drills. No games. Just drills. On Saturday, the Dolphins would play their first pre-

131

season game, and from then until late December, they would dominate the attention of South Florida sports fans.

Really, the only chance the Marlins had at the box office was to win and win big. And that just wasn't happening.

NATIONAL LEAGUE EAST STANDINGS

	W	L	Pct.	GB
Atlanta	63	36	.636	—
Marlins	**56**	**41**	**.577**	**6**
New York	56	42	.571	6.5
Montreal	52	45	.536	10
Philadelphia	29	67	.302	32.5

10

Root Canal

July 22, 23 at Cincinnati
July 25, 26, 27 at St. Louis
July 28, 29, 30 vs. Cincinnati

Cindy Conine woke up Monday morning, July 21, picked up the Fort Lauderdale *Sun-Sentinel,* and couldn't believe the headline on the front page of the sports section: "Daulton might be a Marlin." The first thing she did was read the story. The next thing she did was show the newspaper to her husband.

"Have you heard anything about maybe getting Darren Daulton?" she asked him.

"No," Jeff Conine said.

"Well, according to the paper, he's traded here, and you lost your starting job."

Up until that point Conine hadn't heard anything about a Daulton deal, and neither had his agent, Michael Watkins. Daulton to the Marlins was one rumor that hadn't made the rounds, and Conine—despite his .198 batting average since April 26—had never imagined his job might be in danger because of two bad months after four very good years.

But it was, and Conine didn't need anyone to tell him that. Daulton was a catcher who had converted to first base because of knee injuries. He batted left. Conine batted right. All along, the Marlins had expressed their need for a left-handed power hitter, and here he was: Darren Daulton of the Philadelphia Phillies. This wasn't the nicest wakeup present Conine could have received, but it was about to get worse.

The deal was done by the time Conine arrived at the ballpark. Daulton, who had the right to veto the deal because he was a ten and five man—ten years in the major leagues, five with the same club—had given it his blessing, and outside in the dugout, general manager Dave Dombrowski was announcing the trade to the media.

What disturbed Conine most was that nobody had said a word to him, not Dombrowski or Leyland, even though he was the man most left in limbo by the deal. Daulton knew where he was going. Billy McMillon, the Marlins' half of the deal, knew where he was going. But as Conine stood in front of his locker—steel-jawed, blue eyes staring straight ahead, legs planted, arms folded across his chest, his father standing just ten feet away—he had no idea what the immediate future might bring.

"Nobody's said anything yet," Conine said. "Hopefully somebody will say something to me before the day's over with."

Conine patiently answered questions for a few more minutes and the betrayal he felt was obvious from the look in his eyes and his answer to a reporter who asked, "Was the fact that you were hitting seventh in the lineup something you first heard from us, too?"

"That's something I heard from you as well," Conine said.

In fact, Leyland hadn't said much about anything important to Conine all season. Although Leyland resented the fact that the media had crowded around Conine's locker in the spring shortly after he announced the Marlins' two-time all-star would bat seventh this season, Leyland had never bothered telling Conine face-to-face. Once again, he was left to figure things out for himself.

"Have you talked to Conine yet?" a reporter asked Leyland before the final game of the Padres series.

"Why would I talk to Jeff about it?" Leyland shot back.

"Well, you have a guy coming in that will play a little first."

"That's a lot of speculation on everybody's part," Leyland said. "I haven't talked to anybody about anything."

Speculation wasn't necessary. Daulton had played three positions in his major league career: catcher, first base, and rightfield. He couldn't catch because of his bad knees. He wasn't going to play rightfield; Gary Sheffield already had that position. That left first base—Conine's position. This much was clear to everyone, including Conine: Either he would be traded or get the short end of a platoon with Daulton, who as a left-handed batter would play against all righties.

After four solid years as a Marlin in which he never batted below .292, Conine had been tossed aside because of two bad months. Of course, he didn't like it. This was obvious because Conine, who always kept bags of beef jerky in his locker, both to eat and hand out to reporters—it was his way of staying on their good side, he joked—wasn't handing out any.

"No jerky today, boys," Conine said.

Leyland still hadn't spoken to Conine by the end of the afternoon. Cindy Conine drove her husband to the airport to catch the team's flight to Cincinnati for what they knew could be his last road trip as a Marlin. Dombrowski was on the flight, too, and didn't say a word to Conine. Meanwhile, the Marlins were working on a deal that would send Conine to the Kansas City Royals in exchange for Jeff King, who played for Leyland in Pittsburgh.

Mr. Marlin, as Conine had become popularly known, went to bed that night with no idea what might happen over the next few days.

◆ ◆ ◆

In his thirteenth season, Darren Daulton, 35, had become a curiosity around Major League Baseball. Having survived nine knee operations, a near-fatal car accident in 1991 with teammate Lenny Dykstra, and an apparent retirement in 1996, he had improbably began displaying some of the form that had made him a three-time All-Star. Daulton's ability to overcome injuries, undergo numerous surgeries, play in pain, and run out every groundball as if the World Series depended upon it, was also a curiosity, considering that most ballplayers don't do that sort of thing.

"One of the Philadelphia coaches told me that in thirty-seven years of baseball, he was the toughest, hardest playing guy he had ever seen," Leyland said.

Whether or not he would be an improvement over Conine remained to be seen, because at the time Daulton was hitting .264 with eleven home runs and forty-two RBIs, numbers that were better, but not considerably, than what the Marlins were already getting from Conine. What Daulton figured to supply, however, was an intangible that isn't seen too often in baseball: leadership.

That's not a knock against the leadership qualities of Major League Baseball players. It's just a fact of the game. Baseball is not a sport in which fearless captains lead their teams into battle like in hockey or football, so leadership often means nothing more than standing up in the clubhouse after a tough loss and saying what needs to be said, or at least something that sounds good. Bonilla had tried that a few times, but wasn't entirely effective. Not that Leyland minded.

"Oh, I don't believe in that leadership stuff," he growled one day. "That bullshit is so overrated, it makes me sick."

But count Jim Eisenreich among the believers. Eisenreich had spent four seasons playing with Daulton in Philadelphia and counted him as a friend, which was something he couldn't say about a lot of people in baseball. He had watched Daulton getting in the face of a teammate who needed a dressing down, or calling team meetings, and suspected the Marlins could use a little attitude. What Eisenreich didn't know was that just a few weeks earlier, Daulton had closed the door to the visitor's clubhouse in Atlanta and chewed out his last-place Phillies teammates. This leadership thing was something he had down pat.

In stepped Daulton, whose reputation was legendary for reasons unrelated to baseball, too. His first wife was Lynne Austin, a former *Playboy* Playmate and the spokesmodel for the Hooters restaurant chain. There is a famous photograph of Daulton running in the outfield in Clearwater, Florida, the spring training home of the Phillies, past a billboard featuring his former wife's likeness. About ninety percent of the male race didn't know how he could go on living.

But he rebounded spectacularly and in 1995 married his second wife, Nicole, a strikingly beautiful brunette. Both are in magnificent physical condition—Darren with his muscular arms, chest, and back, and matinee idol looks, Nicky with her high cheekbones and thin, well-toned physique. When they're walking together, through a hotel lobby or down the street, they look like something out of a fitness pageant. Heads turn.

Darren and Nicky Daulton spent a lot of time together. Nicky rarely missed a game and joined her husband on most road trips, something most married players would never encourage or allow. She is a born-again Christian. He became born again after meeting her, and talked often and openly about his "blessed" station in life.

Daulton had expected to get traded before the July 31 deadline, because he would become a free agent after the season and the Phillies didn't want to lose him for nothing, but he hadn't heard anything about a trade to the Marlins until the eighth inning of the Phillies' game against the Pirates Sunday afternoon in Philadelphia. When he returned to the clubhouse after the game, Phillies president David

Montgomery was waiting to tell him that a deal had been reached with the Marlins. All it needed was his approval.

Daulton had a mixed reaction to the trade. He was excited over the prospect of playing for a pennant contender, yet at the same time he knew that his career, which started in Philadelphia, would not end in Philadelphia. So while he was thinking, *Yes,* when told about the trade, he didn't say yes right away.

"My wife and I have a lot of friends in Philadelphia. We were very comfortable there," Daulton said. "It had been our home for a lot of years. You think you know what to do or say when something like that happens, then it happens and you don't know what to do or say."

Not that it was total upheaval for Daulton. He and Nicky had sold their house in Philadelphia the year before, when he played in only five games and painfully realized his career might be over, and purchased a new one in Clearwater, across the state from Miami. After a night of talking and crying, Daulton told the Phillies that the trade was OK with him.

So there was Nicky, who stood with her husband on the field at Veterans Stadium in Philadelphia as they waved goodbye to the fans. It must have been a hard pill for Phillies fanatics to swallow, losing two of their favorites in less than a year—first Eisenreich, then Daulton—but Daulton made the transition in a matter of minutes. When he called the Pro Player Stadium press box Monday afternoon to arrange a conference call with the media, the first question he asked Ron Colangelo was, "Are we winning?"

And the first questioned he answered was, "What position do you want to play?" Daulton said, "DH," which his knees and Conine wished could have been true. There is no designated hitter in the National League.

◆ ◆ ◆

By the way, Leyland said, you know my tirade at Shea Stadium prior to the All-Star break? I didn't really mean it.

That was the one in which he had turned red-faced, stripped naked, and ranted for ten minutes.

"We've been talking for a while about the addition of a left-handed bat," Leyland said while discussing the Daulton trade. "That's why I tried to downplay it when Sheff said we could use a left-handed bat. I didn't want to tip our hand, because several teams were interested in Daulton and I wanted to downplay it."

He also told reporters: "I've been honest with you and I won't lie to you. There are only certain things I'm at liberty to tell you."

◆ ◆ ◆

With Daulton's arrival, Matt Whisenant was designated for assignment and, between tears, he said, "I have some advice for anybody who is reading this on this club: Don't get hurt. Do yourself a favor and stay off the DL."

He might have been on to something. Last week, Cliff Floyd had been sent down to Charlotte for rehab, and Dombrowski said he didn't know whether Floyd would be back.

Designated for assignment meant that the Marlins had seven days to either trade Whisenant or release him. After that, he would be placed on unconditional waivers and subjected to claim by any team that could use a 26-year-old lefty with a ninety-five-mile-per-hour fastball who can't get anyone out. But the chances of him remaining in the Marlins organization were remote, nearly impossible. After five years with the Marlins—and only 2⅔ innings in the big leagues—Whisenant knew he was gone.

And he was: On July 29, Whisenant was traded to the Kansas City Royals for a minor league catcher.

◆ ◆ ◆

Conine had the conversation he had been waiting for with Leyland on the afternoon of the first game of a two-game series in Cincinnati. It went as he expected, which is to say, badly. Leyland told Conine he hadn't been mentioned in any deals for a pitcher, but had been mentioned in a deal for Kansas City's Jeff King. So there was a good chance Conine wouldn't be around after the July 31 inter-league trading deadline.

Conine had already figured out the rest of what Leyland told him: If a trade wasn't made, he would platoon at first base with Daulton and be used as a late-inning defensive replacement. Conine would play against lefties, Daulton would play against righties. And if Conine had bothered to look at the statistics, which surely he had, he would have seen that up until that day, the Marlins had played twenty-one games against lefty starters and seventy-five games against righties.

All of which meant Conine wasn't even a part-time first baseman. He was a temp.

◆ ◆ ◆

Then Conine went out and had two hits, a home run, and two RBIs in the series opener, and Leyland said, "You never know what motivates somebody." That could have been taken as an insult, depending upon your point of view. The implication was that Conine needed a kick in the butt.

Speaking of kicks in the butt, Leiter looked as if he wanted to send Leyland flying when he got removed in the sixth inning with the Marlins leading, 3-1. He had thrown only one hundred eighteen pitches. Then Leyland ended up looking bad when Felix Heredia allowed five runs in the seventh inning and the Marlins lost, 7-6.

Leiter on his manager's seeming lack of confidence in him: "From spring training on, it's been one thing or another. I go to spring training with a bad back and go through rehab and all that bullshit. That wasn't good. Then five starts into the season, I hurt my knee."

Smart man, Leiter. Criticizing Leyland wouldn't have done him any good at all.

Daulton was in the starting lineup the next night against righty Mike Morgan, and the Marlins won, 8-1, behind another strong outing by Alex Fernandez who—

accorded the respect Leiter had not earned—was allowed to throw one hundred forty pitches in eight innings. Daulton tripled and bore in hard to break up a double play. Conine, in his new role as temp, replaced him for the last two innings.

◆ ◆ ◆

And a final word about the Daulton deal: It was an amazing move, considering that a month earlier Huizenga proclaimed he had made a mistake by overspending during the off-season. By adding Daulton, the Marlins had increased their payroll by $1.9 million—the prorated portion of Daulton's $5-million-per-year salary. Combined with other moves the Marlins made and would make, they would climb from seventh in overall salary to fourth.

Huizenga had said he wouldn't shy away from doing whatever it took to win, and here was the proof. In fact, Huizenga had phoned Dombrowski several times and urged him to trade for whatever players he needed, regardless of salary. A few more pitchers. A hitter or two. Anything.

"We were going for broke," Huizenga said. "We wanted to win the World Series."

◆ ◆ ◆

Leyland was harping on a report in *USA Today,* which had Conine being shopped around for a pitcher.

"I've talked to Dave Dombrowski every day and not once has Jeff Conine been mentioned in a deal for a pitcher," Leyland said. "It's just another case of people writing about gossip."

The Marlins weren't looking to trade Conine for a pitcher, but they were looking to trade him for infielder Jeff King. The deal fell through, mostly because the Royals decided they didn't want to trade King. That made Conine a happy man, although the trade deadline was still eight days away and he knew anything could happen. He wasn't passing out the beef jerky just yet.

◆ ◆ ◆

Alou, Castillo, and Renteria were dancing in the aisles to loud Latin salsa music during the bus ride from the St. Louis airport to the team's hotel when Alou turned down the volume and addressed his teammates.

"I just wanted to tell you guys that I've played on teams before that didn't let the Latin players play our music," Alou said. "But you guys do, and we appreciate that. That's what makes us a team. And that's why we're going to win the World Series."

If only the Expos, Alou's previous team, had known this key to baseball success: salsa. Makes you wonder why they bother with managers and general managers. And $5 million leftfielders.

◆ ◆ ◆

The first thing the Marlins should have done when they arrived at Busch Stadium was get down on their knees and kiss the field. Not that they should have been so happy about being in St. Louis, where the temperature was around one hundred degrees all day Friday, July 25. But the good news was that the artificial turf at Busch had been ripped up two seasons ago and replaced with real, live grass. So the temperature on the field for the games Saturday and Sunday was only one hundred twenty degrees, while in Cincinnati, the city they had just left, the temperature on the plastic grass was one hundred fifty degrees.

Grass or turf, the weather in St. Louis was pretty close to what one might expect on a bad day in hell. High heat, high humidity. Worse than South Florida because there wasn't any wind. Many of the players on both teams were complaining about the conditions except, of course, for one man.

"It's hotter here than anywhere in baseball," Leyland said. "I like it. I'd rather be hot than freezing."

Leyland, bum ankle and all, had played eighteen holes of golf Friday morning despite the stifling heat. He wasn't quite fit for the outing. Leyland hit one shot way off into the rough and when he asked third base coach Rich Donnelly, his golf mate, "What shot do you hit from over here?" Donnelly replied, "I don't know. Nobody's ever had to hit a shot from over there."

The heat didn't bother Livan Hernandez, either. He pitched 6⅔ innings and got the win, 5-4. Nor did it bother Dennis Cook, who pinch-hit in the ninth inning and hit a home run.

But the heat was getting to the Marlins. There was no doubt about that.

◆ ◆ ◆

On Saturday, the Marlins didn't do much of anything, except lose as quickly as possible and drink a lot of Gatorade: twenty-five gallons, as opposed to the seven they usually drink. It was a good day for the people at Gatorade, as well as the Cardinals.

Here's a fun fact: If the weather is ridiculously hot or ridiculously cold, count on Gregg Zaun being in the lineup. It happened on that afternoon in Chicago when the weather was frigid. It happened in Philadelphia when the temperature on the plastic turf was one hundred sixty degrees. It happened again in St. Louis.

"There was a time when I didn't want to play day games," he said. "Now I love to play anytime I can."

The truth of the matter is that most starting catchers don't play in day games after night games, so there was no Zaun Conspiracy at work here.

◆ ◆ ◆

The weather conditions were similar Sunday afternoon, as was the result: Kevin Brown fell apart after Luis Castillo made an error in the third inning and the Marlins called it a day after falling behind, 5-1. They lost, 6-4, and when the game ended, they rushed back to the cool of the visitor's clubhouse. When the door closed behind them, Darren Daulton stood up and held his first meeting as a member of the Marlins.

Daulton had watched most of Sunday's game from the bench and didn't like what he saw. So he let his teammates know it: They had to start showing the same intensity and emotion against weak teams they had shown against good teams. He felt there was too much of a laid-back atmosphere in the clubhouse, and warned his teammates that if they didn't change, they wouldn't make the playoffs.

"It's like a country club in here," Daulton said. "You guys have a masseuse. You have people washing your cars for you. When I was with Philadelphia and we came here to play Florida, we didn't give a shit about how much money you guys were making. We wanted to beat your ass."

His teammates listened and pitched in a few comments of their own. After a few minutes, the clubhouse doors opened, and an outsider would have never known that something semi-meaningful had just happened.

"He said one thing about when I'm up, I don't need a pat on the back, but when I'm down, I need a pat," Eisenreich revealed. "He wanted everybody to come together and support each other."

It might have seemed a bit presumptuous, a player who had been with the team for less than a week holding a meeting, but nobody seemed to mind. Daulton had arrived with the reputation as a player who would do that sort of thing. Besides, he already had Bonilla's backing, and that counted for something. What might have counted for more is that Daulton is huge. His shoulders are huge, his arms are huge. Even his face is huge. The man has a big face and big hair. You do not tell Darren Daulton to sit down and shut up.

"We have to respond," Sheffield decided. "When a guy does his job and says what had to be said, we have to go out and produce."

The Marlins would be fortunate if that was all it took. If they went on to win the pennant, they would look back upon Daulton's meeting as a turning point. If they didn't, it would be only the first of many players-only meetings.

◆ ◆ ◆

Goodbye, Mark Hutton. Hello, Craig Counsell.

Craig Counsell?

"I don't know a fucking thing about him," Leyland said, controlling his excitement over the new arrival. "I don't even know how to spell his fucking name."

It's C-O-U-N-S-E-L-L. Second baseman. Bats left, throws right. Graduated from Notre Dame with a degree in accounting. Father played in the Minnesota Twins organization. About six feet, 170 pounds soaking wet. Twenty-seven years old. Looks about 14, especially when he's wearing his uniform. In jeans and a polo shirt, he can pass for 21. Maybe. If the bar is having a slow night. Was considered the best second baseman in the Pacific Coast League, but had only one career at-bat in the majors. Missed most of the 1996 season with a fractured right shin. Buck Showalter, who would manage the expansion Arizona Diamondbacks, had been telling people that Counsell would be his second baseman. The trade changed nothing, because it was unlikely the Marlins would protect him in the expansion draft.

Counsell walked into the clubhouse for the first time Monday afternoon, July 28, and everyone thought the Marlins had hired a new batboy. After about a day or two, Leyland knew this about Counsell: "I like him. I like him a lot. He's a dirtball."

Leyland likes dirtballs, players who work hard and aren't afraid to get their uniforms dirty. His favorite players on the Marlins were dirtballs. On Monday, Leyland went up to Counsell and said, "What kind of player are you?" and Counsell answered, "I'm a blue-collar guy. I'm not always pretty out there, but I get the job done."

As for poor Mark Hutton, the man who led the Marlins' staff in home runs allowed per at-bat was going to Colorado, hitter's heaven. He figured to last about a day.

◆ ◆ ◆

The two straight losses to the Cardinals bothered Leyland so much that after the second loss he said, "The intensity is just not there. It's like we're walking on eggs. At the first sign of adversity, we cave in. I'm very, very disappointed." Then he said it again: "I'm very, very disappointed."

The next afternoon before batting practice at Pro Player Stadium, Leyland was back on the same theme, which included the following supporting points, in order of appearance:

1. "We're acting like we're having a goddamn root canal."
2. "Shit, this is what it's all about."
3. "I ain't no goddamn rah-rah, you know, Saturday fucking pep rally for a football team."
4. Baseball is like going fishing.

"You go to the goddamn pond twenty days and you don't get a bite, you go to another goddamn pond," Leyland said. "Try something else. That's the way I look at it. It has nothing to do with Gary Sheffield. I'm sick of hearing everybody pointing to Gary Sheffield. I'm not pointing to Gary Sheffield a goddamn bit. I'm talking about the team. If you want it, there it is, but you have to pay for it."

If asked, Gary Sheffield probably would have preferred that Jim Leyland did not mention Gary Sheffield's name every time he said that he wasn't pointing at Gary Sheffield. But Jim Leyland did not ask Gary Sheffield.

Leyland also said he would not hold a team meeting, but would speak to players one-by-one during batting practice and in his office. Then he went around the field and spoke with Jack McKeon, who manages the Cincinnati Reds, and Lenny Harris, who plays for the Reds, and Joel Youngblood, who's a coach for the Reds. When he got back to the clubhouse, the first thing he did was call in players, starting with Bonilla.

A few minutes later, Bonilla and Moises Alou were sitting on a couch in the clubhouse discussing the team's problems.

"Where's our fire?" Bonilla asked.

"We don't know how to kill," Alou said, holding up his fists like a boxer. "We don't know how to knock a guy out when he's bleeding. We keep sitting around, waiting for other guys to come out of their slumps. We're waiting for things to happen when we should be making them happen."

Bonilla tried to make things happen by getting two hits and getting robbed of a third, then running out a grounder as hard as he could. But Alou muffed a fly ball to leftfield, Jay Powell allowed two home runs, and the Marlins lost to the Reds, 4-0, despite eight shutout innings by Leiter. Afterward, Bonilla sat glumly in front of his locker with one hand on his chin while he sucked on a beer, Powell made no excuses, and Sheffield offered a clue.

"Everybody's kind of tense here," he said. "I don't feel that looseness we had in spring training. I don't know if we're trying to feel each other out, or what, or it's just a combination of each other's personalities, but as a bunch by now we should've come together."

He had no idea why they hadn't, nor did Leiter, who completely disagreed with Sheffield's diagnosis.

"I don't feel tight," Leiter said. "But I can only speak for myself."

Obviously, the Marlins themselves weren't sure what their problem was.

◆ ◆ ◆

Devon White had told Leyland before the road trip he would be ready to come off the disabled list when the team came home, so Leyland called him Monday morning and asked whether he preferred going down to the minors for rehab or getting right back into the lineup. White said he was ready to play, but would be willing to go to the minors.

"Do you honestly think you're ready to play?" Leyland asked.

"Definitely," White said.

"That's good enough. You're playing centerfield tonight and leading off."

White's return from the DL seemed a little hasty, considering only two weeks earlier he was supposedly a month away from returning. A skeptic might have said Darren Daulton's presence was enough to embarrass anyone into playing in pain. Not that White wasn't hurt. He was. Badly enough so that the trainer and team doctors agreed he shouldn't be playing. But when you look to your left and see Daulton, who stretches for thirty minutes before every game and barrels over catchers, even though his knees have been torn to shreds, it can be kind of humbling.

Maybe that's what leadership is all about.

White's return meant Kotsay would go back to Double-A Portland and the Marlins had lost their gamble: Kotsay wouldn't have had to be protected in the expansion draft if he wasn't called up, and now that he had been, the Marlins would lose a player they wouldn't have lost otherwise.

And the good news for fans sitting down the first and third base lines at Pro Player Stadium was Castillo had been sent down to Triple-A. Leyland said it was the best thing for Castillo, because he could work on his hitting. Castillo was asked by reporters if it was for the best and said, "A little bit yes, a little bit no." He sounded like he was trying to convince himself.

Of course, Leyland and Dombrowski didn't ask for Castillo's opinion. The fact was, Castillo couldn't hit big league pitching and everybody knew it, especially his teammates. They'd sit on the bench watching Castillo struggling to hit a ball out of the infield, knowing that after slicing a few foul balls into the lower level seats and nearly taking off a few heads, Castillo would ground out meekly to third base. It bothered them, knowing their leadoff hitter had very little chance of getting on base.

So it was White for Kotsay, Counsell for Castillo. Basically, the Marlins were trying a new pond.

◆ ◆ ◆

Leyland was angry because the *Palm Beach Post* and *Miami Herald* both reported he had held a closed-door meeting after the final game in St. Louis. This misunderstanding was easy to understand for two very good reasons:

1. The doors to the visitor's clubhouse in St. Louis were closed after the game. Thus: Closed-door.

2. When the doors opened, Leyland said to the reporters, "This is what I just told the players . . ." Thus: Meeting.

Of course, Leyland hadn't held a meeting, closed-door or otherwise. Daulton had.

"The media has everything backwards," Leyland said on Monday, sounding a bit agitated. "I had no clubhouse meeting at all yesterday. I read in the paper where I had a closed-door meeting. I had no meeting whatsoever with my team yesterday."

A few minutes later, he said, "I'll emphasize one more time. I did not have a closed-door meeting. I want to announce that to the world."

And a few minutes after that he said, "I did not have a meeting yesterday."

Then Bonilla walked past the dugout and said, "They giving you a hard time, Skip?"

To which Leyland responded, "I'm telling them about that big meeting I had yesterday, but I don't remember ever having one."

Bonilla smiled, said nothing, and walked away.

◆ ◆ ◆

Dombrowski called a press conference Tuesday afternoon to say he wasn't planning on making any moves before the midnight Thursday trading deadline, other than a minor "tweak" here or there. Conine was so comforted by the general manager's words he looked up at the clubhouse clock, placed his right hand on his chin, and said, "Let's see, there's still fifty-six hours left. A lot can happen."

Conine was right. Anyone who believes a word a general manager says during the week before trading deadline is in dire need of a reality check. Dombrowski might look innocent enough with his blue eyes, boyish face, and dimpled chin, but it's a general manager's nature not to say anything unless it's in his own best interests, in this case preventing wayward trade rumors from distracting the team. And Dombrowski is one of those GMs who doesn't offer much to the writers, on or off the record.

Naturally, Dombrowski had left open the possibility of another general manager calling him and making a deal—perhaps something considerably more than a tweak, perhaps a major tweak, or a grab—which meant his little press conference was meaningless. And a day later, he would be talking to the Chicago White Sox about right-handed reliever Roberto Hernandez and coming so close to a deal that Leyland would be waiting by the phone for a call.

Conine had spent a good part of the past week considering the possibility of being traded and was prepared to leave if a trade was made. But he was by no means resigned to the possibility.

"It's our home and it would be the biggest pain in the butt to pick up and move out of here," Conine said. "But, also, it's part of the game."

◆ ◆ ◆

Another part of the game for the players is not liking what they read in the newspapers or see on TV. Bobby Bonilla was watching TV Tuesday afternoon when he heard a sportscaster say the Marlins had hit rock-bottom the night before when they were shut out by John Smiley. It perturbed him.

"That's a hard comment," Bonilla said. "You got to be able to recognize when a guy pitches his ass off, and when I went home I thought Smiley pitched a helluva game. You have to credit the opposition."

Bonilla didn't hear his manager just about confirming the TV report on the Marlins' pre-game radio show: "Hopefully we bottomed out." Leyland said that. All four words. In that exact order. "Hopefully we bottomed out." Which is about as close to "rock-bottom" as you're going to get. After all, the bottom is the bottom. Actually, if Bonilla had thought harder about it, he would have realized that hitting rock-bottom was good. Once you're there, the only way to go is up.

Another part of the game: Occupational hazards are everywhere. On the field. In the dugout. In the clubhouse. Out on the street. In the garage. Alex Fernandez went home Monday night and was playing with his son, chasing him through the garage when . . . *Wham!* Fernandez slammed right foot first into a step machine. He grabbed his toe, hopped around for a while, and screamed out a few choice curses. It didn't feel very good. When he arrived at the ballpark Tuesday, Fernandez had his toe X-rayed and found out that nothing was broken. Not that it would have stopped him anyway.

"I was gonna go," he said. "It wasn't a question. I would've gone out there on crutches."

Then he went out without crutches, pitched eight strong innings, and beat the Reds, 7-1. Counsell had his first major league hit while his mother and father looked on, The Couch Guys had three homers—two for Alou, one for Bonilla—and Fernandez stopped a Marlins' three-game losing streak for the second time in a week.

Fernandez on the upcoming Braves series: "I don't give a shit if it's the Cincinnati Reds or the Atlanta Braves. We have to win fucking games right now."

He said this while standing in front of his locker with a pair of flip-flops on his feet. He had no bandages on his toes and there was no apparent swelling.

The Braves won, so the Marlins remained seven and a half back.

144

◆ ◆ ◆

The Darren Daulton Decibel Level was established after the game. It is very loud. By order of Dutch Daulton, the music in the clubhouse must be turned up to ear-piercing, wall-thumping levels after a win. Kurt Abbott enjoyed it so much that he yelled out, "Would somebody turn down the fucking music?" Abbott's plea couldn't be heard across the room; you had to be standing right next to him.

This was completely different from how things were after a loss, when the stereo was off and the players behaved as if they had just suffered the most devastating anything of their lives. They sat in front of their stalls with blank, devastated looks on their faces, or they lingered in the trainer's room or the clubhouse dining room, and spoke in hushed tones. Nobody smiled or joked, including the media relations staff, which didn't dare make eye contact with the players. They might have been laughing and joking during the elevator ride down from the press box to the clubhouse, but once they entered those doors . . . *Whoosh!* Instant mourning. Even the media played along. They asked questions as if they were interviewing the loved ones of recently departed. It's really nothing more than a reflex reaction: When athletes lose, they tend to bite. Nobody, especially a reporter, wants to get bitten.

After a loss, the manager picks at his food and answers questions as shortly as possible. After a win, like this one, he answers a ringing phone by saying, "Hello, President Clinton. How are you? Can I call you back? I've got a press conference." And smiling all along.

Meanwhile, you can hear the thump-thump-thump of rap music bouncing off the walls and players are milling all about. All four TVs are tuned to the Braves game, appetites are healthy, and, suddenly, for a night at least, all is right with the Marlins' world.

◆ ◆ ◆

Just in case anybody missed it, before the final game of the Reds series, Leyland said: "I did not have a closed-door meeting in St. Louis. There was no closed door and there was no meeting of any kind."

No closed door. No meeting. Got that?

◆ ◆ ◆

A flasher won the Fan of the Game competition. The woman announced it was her birthday and said she had a treat for all the men who came to the game to check out women. So she lifted her T-shirt—she had a bathing suit top on underneath, thank goodness for the family-friendly Marlins—and won four tickets to a future game. Her competitor, a man, got booed.

That display put an end to the Fan of the Game competition in the *mano a womano* format. Fearing a total exposure by an overzealous fan, the in-game entertainment staff decided to simply choose a winner at random, rather than go through the "Why I Should Be The Fan Of The Game" speech and the attendant hazards. So Fan of the Game went the way of Karaoke Night and You Rate The Record.

Still alive, however, was the lucky program contest, in which the questions included such baseball classics as, "What is the telephone number for the Marlins' community relations department?"

The answer, in case you didn't know, is 305-626-7267. Of course, the only way to know that was by buying a program, which was the whole idea behind the contest.

The ultimate prize for all this, as the final Fan of the Game winner showed, was the chance to be seen on the video screens by twenty thousand people. People will go to great lengths for their moment of fame. One night, a shirtless, obese man in the upper level kept dancing to the between-innings music in the hope of being shown on the scoreboard. He had one eye on his jiggling belly, another eye on the screen, and fans kept yelling at him to put his shirt on and sit down. But the man was shameless and kept right on dancing. Fortunately for the rest of the crowd, he was never shown on the screens, proving that even the Marlins' in-game entertainment crew had standards of decency.

◆ ◆ ◆

Alou hit a three-run homer in the finale of the Reds series, a 6-0 Marlins win, and Leyland summed up his team's two-game home run spate by saying, "We hit a couple the last couple of days that you can't catch. As a manager, there's no way to predict when that might happen, there's no way to defense it. It's just runs on the board and nobody can do a damn thing about it to prevent it. That's just the way it is. Ball leaves the ballpark. Nobody has a chance to make a great play."

No wonder he's considered the best manager in baseball.

◆ ◆ ◆

Devon White made a spectacular play in the top of the fourth inning. The Reds had one on and two out when Eddie Taubensee drove the ball high and deep to centerfield. White got a good jump on the ball and retreated, side-pedaling quickly, and when he reached the warning track, he jumped, reached out his glove, slammed shoulder-first into the wall, and caught the ball against the yellow stripe at the top of the wall.

What second base umpire Frank Pulli didn't see was the ball rolling free after White's glove hit hard against the artificial dirt. White quickly shoved the ball back into his glove, but by that time Pulli had made the out sign. White laughed as he jogged off the field to a standing ovation.

"That ball, was it high on the fence?" White said later. "I don't know. Well, it's one of those plays. I thought I caught the ball, but when I hit the ground . . ."

White stopped right there and smiled, because there was no way he was going to admit that he had dropped the ball.

"Shit happened," White decided. "I hit the wall hard and it didn't give. When I hit it, I didn't know if I was hurt or not. It kind of jarred me."

White wasn't hurt, but you never would have known it by looking at him after the game. He had big ice packs against each thigh and his left leg was completely wrapped. He would wear a walking cast for plane trips and hope he'd be able to make it through the rest of the season without getting hurt again.

"It's spring training for me," he said. "This is a precaution. We have, like, fifty-seven games left, hopefully eighty games. Hopefully. I can't afford to go down again."

Livan Hernandez pitched eight innings and allowed only three hits to go 5-0. And the Braves boarded a plane for South Florida, leading the Marlins by 7½ games.

◆ ◆ ◆

Loud heavy metal music was playing on the clubhouse stereo when Daulton arrived at Pro Player Stadium for the first of a four-game series against the Braves. He walked over, turned off the CD, and tuned the radio to a news station.

And that's what clubhouse leadership is all about.

NATIONAL LEAGUE EAST STANDINGS

	W	L	Pct.	GB
Atlanta	69	39	.639	—
Marlins	**60**	**45**	**.571**	**7.5**
New York	60	46	.566	8
Montreal	54	51	.514	13.5
Philadelphia	32	72	.308	35

11

Love on the Rocks

July 31, August 1, 2, 3 vs. Atlanta
August 4, 5 vs. Houston
August 6, 7 at Pittsburgh
August 8, 9, 10, 11 at Atlanta

The eagerly awaited twelve-day stretch of eight games against the Braves had arrived, and no splash of reality could spoil the fun. South Florida had never watched a pennant race in person, and even if it wasn't watching a real one now, with the Marlins 7½ games back, it could at least make believe. The newspapers were packed with news of the big series, and Braves relief pitcher Mike Bielecki asked, "Which big series?"

So the Braves were in Miami for four games, and Don Smiley and Dave Dombrowski were excited, because they knew it was the Marlins' last chance to get back into the pennant race, and Jim Ross was excited because at least three of the four games would be sold out. But it was Leyland, of all people, who offered perspective.

"This series is more important for us than it is for them," he said.

The math was easy: If the Marlins won all four games, they'd be 3½ games back. If they won three out of four, they'd still be 5½ back. If they split, or worse, any ideas of a pennant race were mere hallucinations and would likely remain that way. The pennant race, if it had ever existed, would have been over. Or, as Chipper Jones of the Braves so eloquently put it, "This is a chance to put the nail in the coffin."

Knowing this, the Marlins were careful to not say anything that might incite the Braves or wake them from their post-All-Star-break slumber. Except for Gary Sheffield, bless his soul. He was asked on the afternoon of the first game of the series if he admired the Braves.

"No."

"Are they a good example?"

"To what?"

"To a team that's trying to get as good as they are."

"No," Sheffield said. "We're not intimidated. We're capable of beating them, and we know that."

Sheffield also said it was very important for the Marlins to win three out of four games because with each win "you move up in the standings."

Nobody could argue with that.

◆ ◆ ◆

It was to be the biggest series in Marlins history.

"They don't have a lot of history," Braves pitcher Tom Glavine pointed out, laughing.

Nobody could argue with that, either.

◆ ◆ ◆

More than the Braves was on the Marlins' minds Thursday, July 31. The trade deadline loomed hours away at midnight, and although there hadn't been a lot of talk over the past few days, a deal remained possible. Last season the Marlins had made a trade nine minutes before the deadline, so the players were a little apprehensive.

There was a lot of questioning going on in the Marlins' clubhouse, mostly from Kurt Abbott, whose name hadn't been mentioned in trades at all. But Abbott wasn't entirely certain he would last the season in Florida, so for what must have been the hundredth time he walked up to a reporter and asked, "What do you hear? Think I'll make it through the season?" Maybe he just wanted to feel wanted.

Leyland was sitting in his office at 2:30 in the afternoon when Dombrowski called to relay a trade proposal, but that was the last he heard of it. By 4 o'clock, Leyland was certain a trade significantly larger than a "tweak" would come about and told reporters, "There'll be lots of action tonight."

"On or off the field?" he was asked.

"Both."

But judging by Dombrowski's activity during the evening, there wasn't much going on at all off the field. He casually ate dinner in the media dining room with assistant GM Frank Wren and not once did his cellular phone ring. When the game started, he sat in his box behind home plate and only twice all night was he on the phone. And when the game ended, he and Wren didn't go to the manager's office—where they might have discussed prospective trades with Leyland—but right to their offices. Leyland holed up in Dombrowski's office from 11:15 to midnight, and the phone rang only three times. Each time, it was the same GM from the same team calling. Leyland went home.

Other teams were more active at the deadline. The Cardinals got Mark McGwire, who decided the National League was OK with him as long as he was playing for his former manager, Tony La Russa. Roberto Hernandez ended up in San Francisco. Dombrowski, who had already traded for Daulton and Counsell, and made room in the pitching rotation for Livan Hernandez by trading Pat Rapp—addition by subtraction, by any measure—stood pat. They were the same team Friday morning that they had been twenty-four hours before.

◆ ◆ ◆

Saunders pitched seven shutout innings, Daulton singled home Renteria with the only run of the game in the fourth inning, and the Braves had one on with two out

149

in the eighth inning when Leyland summoned Nen from the bullpen. Under just about any other circumstances, Dennis Cook would have been allowed to finish the inning, but Leyland knew that if the Braves won, his team would have been 8½ games behind and out of the pennant race by August 1. Nen struck out Jones, then retired the side in order in the ninth and the Marlins won, 1-0.

One down, three to go. Then there's the rest of the season. Said Leyland: "This isn't college football where you have a pep rally on Friday night and a bonfire. You have to grind it out night after night."

The crowd at Pro Player Stadium, which numbered only about twenty-five thousand out of the 30,559 paid, sounded like it was attending a college football game. There was an inexplicable air of intensity that started with the first pitch and built up throughout the game to the point where, by the seventh inning, the atmosphere in the field level seats was feverish. For a change, everybody seemed to be watching the game, not Billy the Marlin or the Jumbotron screens, not talking to their neighbors or planning a between-innings getaway to the concession stands, which were unusually quiet while the game was going on.

It was probably the most exciting baseball game in South Florida since opening day in 1993, and when it was over Bonilla was talking about Daulton and Daulton was talking about Bonilla and Conine was talking about Counsell and everybody was talking about Saunders, who was 3-0 against the Braves. And when asked about the pressure of the next three games, Daulton said, "The pressure is something I haven't thought of until you brought it up. So thank you for bringing it up. I probably won't get any sleep tonight."

◆ ◆ ◆

At least two Marlins didn't sleep at all that night. One was Saunders, who found out at 3:30 in the morning that his wife, Joyce, was in labor with their first child. The other was Leyland, who Saunders called a few minutes later for permission to leave the team and join his wife in Maryland.

"Congratulations. See you when you get back," said Leyland, who could have lived without the wakeup call.

Saunders' baby was born, a girl, while he was on the plane, completing one of the happiest twelve hours of his life.

◆ ◆ ◆

Greg Maddux vs. Kevin Brown was the pitching matchup Friday night, but home plate umpire Larry Vanover managed to steal the spotlight with an odious performance in the eighth inning. Vanover was correct when he called Kenny Lofton out for running out of the base path, but he missed by about half a foot on a called third strike against Alou. Alou was ejected for cursing at Vanover, then dropped his bat and walked away. And Vanover, in a typical display of umpire arrogance, kicked Alou's bat after him.

Three batters later, Abbott asked Vanover if a strike was called because the ball was in the strike zone or because he didn't check his swing. Vanover answered and Abbott laughed. Vanover got in Abbott's face, inciting Leyland to rush to the defense of his player.

"What did he do?" Leyland asked Vanover.

"He laughed."

"He can't laugh?" Leyland said. "What the fuck can he do?"

Answer: Whatever the fuck Vanover wants him to do. Most modern day umpires walk around with their sphincters clutched so tight it's a wonder they can pull themselves away from the lavatory long enough to work a game. A few decades ago, the difference between umpires' and players' salaries wasn't dramatic, but now the gap is astronomical. That could be one reason umpires love showing off their control over the players. Imagine the power trip, making a piddling seventy-five grand a year and telling multi-millionaires what they can say and do.

Another reason is that umpires see themselves as a much-maligned group. Several years ago, the players refused to support the umpires' strike in the only way they could have, by walking out themselves. And in 1996, when umpire John McSherry died, Cincinnati Reds owner Marge Schott showed her sympathy by sending the umpires a basket of recycled flowers. It was a beautiful gesture.

Of course, one might say that none of this should have anything to do with the umpires doing their job fairly and properly, but let's face it. When you're maligned, you're maligned.

But the Marlins survived Vanover's show of strength. Abbott stayed in the game and singled to center, then Devon White singled to right, driving home Counsell to tie the game at two.

Back on the subject of "What the fuck can he do?": Leyland had gone through a starting pitcher, four relievers, and almost all of his bench when the Marlins came up in the bottom of the twelfth. Johnson doubled to the gap in right-center, so Leyland sent out Zaun to pinch-run. Nothing wrong with that, except Zaun was the last position player on the bench. And why didn't Leyland use Cook as a pinch-runner instead?

"He can't run the goddamn bases," Leyland said. "He can't do nothing."

So—all together now—WHAT THE FUCK CAN HE DO?

Well, he can hit.

After Counsell sacrificed Zaun to third, Leyland had Cook pinch-hit for Powell. The gamble worked. Cook, who had been three-for-three as a hitter, blooped a single to right, and scored Zaun with the winning run.

But that still left the burning question: Even if Cook couldn't run better than Zaun, wasn't Zaun hitting and Cook running a better option?

"What was I gonna do? I was outta soap," is all Leyland would say.

As for Cook, he was extremely hesitant to discuss his hitting, and for a pretty sensible reason.

"Let's put it this way," Cook explained in his good ol' boy Texas drawl. "No pitcher likes to give up a hit to another pitcher. I haven't swung the bat in seven years until this year, but I feel when I come to the plate, I can make contact. But you don't want to make it seem like you think you can hit."

It turned out hitting was something Cook had thought about quite often. All the time, in fact, when he was sitting down in the bullpen whiling away the innings.

Instead of watching the hitters, like pitchers are supposed to do, Cook often watched the pitchers and asked Zaun, "What does this guy throw?"

"We oughta get him in the lineup every damn day, at least until somebody can get him out," Brown decided. "But don't put that in the papers or else the secret gets out."

The secret was safe with Brown. And about four million other people.

◆ ◆ ◆

Gary Sheffield is not Superman. He made that clear before the first game of the Braves series, when asked how he felt about the fans booing him for half-heartedly running out ground balls and lackadaisically fielding fly balls.

"They think I'm Superman," Sheffield complained. "Any time a ball drops in front of me, I'm supposed to catch it, and any time a ball goes over my head, I'm supposed to catch it. I could say I'm injured and I shouldn't be out there, but that's what I get for being out there."

Of course, the fans could be excused for not realizing that Sheffield was injured. He never ran out ground balls in the first place.

Although Leyland pointed out Sheffield was wise to not run out grounders he had no chance of beating out, he had broached the subject with him in the past, before Sheffield hurt his hamstring. According to Leyland, Sheffield said he wasn't even aware of what he was doing—or wasn't doing—so Leyland decided that Sheffield's lack of hustle wasn't laziness, it was just a bad habit that many ballplayers had fallen into.

"Jeff Conine doesn't run out groundballs, either, and nobody says anything about it," Leyland pointed out.

Actually, the fans were starting to lose their patience with Conine, too. They booed him a little when he struck out in the fourth inning of Saturday night's game, a lot when he struck out in the seventh inning.

Meanwhile, Sheffield was having a good night. He singled in the first, singled in the third, hit a flyball to the warning track in the sixth, and crushed three foul balls. He felt relaxed at the plate, said he was seeing the ball well. But then in the eighth inning, Sheffield ran out a grounder to shortstop and pulled up past first base, holding his left hamstring. He left the game and later said, "I don't know how much rest it needs. If I rest fifteen days, they can't promise me it'll feel better. I don't think it's as serious as the last time."

Of course, he had heard that before this season. Twice before. His powers of healing weren't what he hoped they would be. And, of course, he wasn't Superman.

◆ ◆ ◆

The Marlins lost, 4-2, Saturday night and Leyland got thrown out of the game for arguing a call with home plate umpire Tom Hallion in the ninth inning. The scene was comical. First, Mark Lemke laid down a bunt and Charles Johnson pounced on the ball and threw to second for the apparent forceout. But Hallion ruled Lemke had fouled the ball off of home plate.

Leyland tossed out a few choice words from the bench, then charged up the dugout steps screaming. He heard a pop in his bad leg as he stormed toward the umpire, and later said that even if he had fallen flat on his nose, he would have kept on arguing. When he got there, he threw his glasses to the ground, stomped his feet a little bit, and asked Hallion, using the most colorful language in his vocabulary, what had happened. First, Hallion said that he had called it foul right away. Then he ejected Leyland, who stuck around a few more minutes more to get his money's worth.

Leyland hadn't cooled down at all after the game ended. He sat at his desk and gave short answers to every question and refused to discuss his run-in with Hallion. Then a reporter wondered why he hadn't used Daulton as a pinch-hitter in the eighth inning when the Marlins had the bases loaded with the tying run on third and Chad Fox, the Braves' rookie right-hander, was throwing pitches five feet outside the strike zone.

After considering the question for about a second, Leyland glared at the reporter as if he was about to bite his head off, and then answered: Fox was struggling with his control, and if Leyland brought in a lefty to pinch-hit, Braves manager Bobby Cox would have brought in veteran left-hander Alan Embree to pitch to Daulton. Righty vs. righty—Fox vs. Abbott—was the preferred matchup over lefty vs. lefty— Embree vs. Daulton. Leyland wasn't going to make the first move. Or the second one, either, because if Cox had brought in Embree, he definitely would have stuck with Abbott.

But the next question was, "Jim, were you confident that if you stayed with righties, he'd keep Fox in the game?"

Which pretty much was all Leyland needed to hear before offering a more explosive analysis of the situation.

"You know, I want to tell you guys something," Leyland snapped. "You don't know a fucking thing about baseball. You got a young kid out there who just threw eight out of nine fucking balls to Conine and Johnson, that might fucking hang one to Abbott, who's got all kinds of power. If I bring in the fucking left-hander, they're going to bring in Embree. I'm taking my chances that fucking kid's gonna get a little nervous and not be able to fucking throw a strike, or get behind and lay one in. And that's why I didn't do that. I just explained that. I'm not fucking going to sit here and fucking explain strategy every night."

Not surprisingly, that was the final question. Outside in the clubhouse, there weren't many players around for follow-ups. The Marlins had fallen 6½ back once again.

◆ ◆ ◆

Edgar Renteria had a pleasant surprise waiting at his locker when he arrived at the stadium Sunday afternoon. A Colombian TV morning show was planning an away-from-the-ballpark feature on Renteria, so its very attractive female host, wearing something very skimpy above the waist, was there to ask if he'd be willing to shoot pool with her for the show. Of course, the smiling Renteria said yes.

She hung around and talked to him for a while and after a few minutes, Livan Hernandez, whose locker is on the other side of the clubhouse, walked over, pulled up a chair, sat down, and smiled. By that time, every player in the room had their eyes turned in the direction of Renteria's locker. Then Darren Daulton, whose locker is in the opposite corner of the clubhouse, walked across the room carrying a towel over his arm and a glass of water, like a waiter. Daulton handed Renteria the glass.

"Is everything all right, sir?" he asked.

Renteria nodded. Then Daulton patted Renteria's forehead with the towel.

"Just let me know if you need anything else, sir," Daulton said.

Renteria nodded again, and all of the players who had been watching this scene broke out in laughter. Meanwhile, Renteria and the woman kept talking, living proof that athletes occasionally enjoy dealing with the media.

The Marlins players seemed to have a thing for Colombian women. One time, an extraordinarily attractive Colombian woman, wearing a short skirt and a midriff-baring top, was sitting in the photographers' booth next to the dugout during batting practice, and several players went out of their way to walk past her. Bonilla spotted her and kept yelling out, "Co-LUM-bee-AH!" and she'd just smile and nod her head. Then a few minutes later, Bonilla dragged Devon White into the dugout so he could see the sights and White complained, "You dragged me all the way out here to see her?" And Bonilla yelled out, "Co-LUM-bee-AH"

◆ ◆ ◆

Conine was telling Abbott how unhappy he was with a column in the *Sun-Sentinel* that traced the Marlins' loss the previous night to his at-bat with the bases loaded in the first inning.

"According to the *Sun-Sentinel*," Conine complained, "I lost the game for us last night by flying out in the first inning."

Conine wouldn't have been any happier had he heard what his manager said a few minutes earlier. It was pointed out to Leyland that Conine hadn't shown much patience in a first inning at-bat against Denny Neagle, and Leyland agreed.

"Jesus Christ," Leyland grumbled. "He's hitting .407 against him with two home runs. First fucking pitch, he swings."

"But you have to give him a chance to get out of his slump, right?" somebody asked.

"He ain't gonna get out of it," Leyland snapped. "He's all fucked up."

Conine, who had been hitting .227 since April 25, was hitting .350 since the Daulton trade.

Much higher on Leyland's list of favorite players was Livan Hernandez, who had carried out such manager-friendly acts as asking Leyland how his foot felt. Leyland had said he could count on one hand the number of players he'd managed in his career that he disliked. He definitely liked Hernandez, especially the young pitcher's confidence. The look in his eyes, the way he carried himself.

154

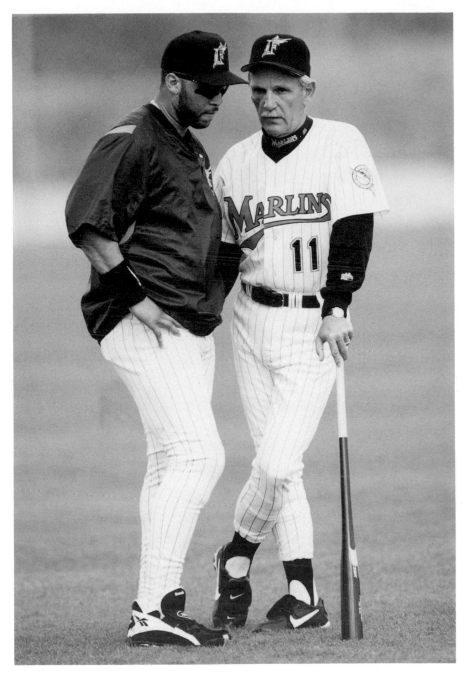

Gary Sheffield, the Marlins' $61 million slugger, frequently sought out shoulders to cry on during a frustrating 1997 season, and sometimes turned for consolation to manager Jim Leyland. "You don't criticize a team when they lose," Leyland said. "That's when they need support. In fact, I'm more apt to get on their ass when they win."

Owner Wayne Huizenga, who once described himself as a "fat, bald-headed rich guy," knew the risks when he approved the Marlins' $49 million payroll. But the real pressure was on general manager Dave Dombrowski, who went on a record-setting spending spree with his boss's cash.

When free agent pitcher Alex Fernandez wasn't working hard at taking off excess weight, he was throwing fastballs past opposing batters or mooning passersby.

Finding ways to kill time during frequent rain delays was an art form all its own. So Bobby Bonilla would go roller-blading through the hallways of Pro Player Stadium (left) or Jeff Conine would play cards with Antonio Alfonseca, Kurt Abbott, and Cliff Floyd (clockwise from top right) in the clubhouse dining room.

First baseman Jeff Conine, otherwise known as Mr. Marlin, was with the team from the beginning, when he was selected in the 1992 expansion draft. "I've seen it all," Conine said. "But we can't look at this season like we have to win back the fans and save the franchise. We have to worry about winning on the field. Everything else is out of our control."

"Bite me," pitcher Kevin Brown (right) once told a reporter. But most of the time, the intense, surly Brown looked like he was about to bite someone. Gary Sheffield's relationship with the media was far more amicable, even though the big stick he carried didn't cause much damage to opposing pitchers.

Bad times, good times. Alex Fernandez and his wife, Lourdes (above), had a hard time controlling their emotions when it was announced that Fernandez would miss the rest of the playoffs with a torn rotator cuff. But the Marlins had Cuban refugee Livan Hernandez. His pitching performance in Game Five of the National League Championship Series was one of the best in post-season history.

Outfielder Moises Alou (left) was the Marlins' most consistent hitter during the regular season and a standout during the World Series.

"Ooooh, that feels good going down the back of my leg!" Bobby Bonilla (below) enjoys the rewards of victory with clubhouse attendant Matt Rosenthal and TV announcer Jay Randolph after the Marlins clinched the Wild Card in Montreal.

Watching . . . hoping . . . "the ball got through." Edgar Renteria, the Marlins' best clutch hitter all season, wins the World Series with a single in the bottom of the eleventh, then gets mobbed by his joyous teammates after one of the greatest Game Sevens ever played.

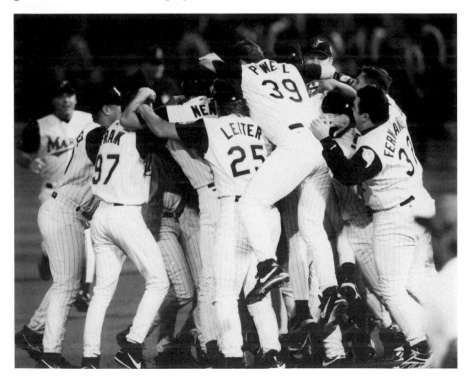

"I like a young player who isn't afraid to talk to the manager," Leyland said. "He acts like he wants to come home for fucking breakfast. On the next road trip, I'll probably have a new roommate."

A few days later, a story appeared in *The Miami Herald* detailing Hernandez's "rough road" in defecting from Cuba to the United States, and the accompanying photo showed Hernandez sitting on top of his Ferrari. The article was making the rounds in the Houston Astros clubhouse, and Luis Gonzalez said, "Rough road? What do you mean rough road? My whole family is from Cuba and they've never seen a Ferrari."

Imagine if he had known that Hernandez, at 22, not only owned a Ferrari, he also owned a Mercedes S-500 and a Range Rover sport utility vehicle.

◆ ◆ ◆

One of the reporters pointed out that Devon White looked rested and Leyland said, "He should be rested. He's had more rest than Rip Van Winkle."

◆ ◆ ◆

Alex Fernandez, the Cuban American whose locker was next to Hernandez's, pitched the finale of the Braves series in front of the third straight sellout crowd at Pro Player Stadium. Overall, it had been a strong weekend from a public relations standpoint for the Marlins' front office, which was hoping the excitement of four games against the Braves would be a catalyst for ticket sales the rest of the season.

Leyland was mindful of this, too, and had an eye on the Dolphins, who were playing an exhibition game in Mexico City the next night. Then he considered the consequences of a Marlins loss on their talk radio airtime and decided, "I hope we win, so they won't be talking about a field goal in Mexico tomorrow."

The Marlins did win, 8-4, with their Bomb Squad lineup: Cangelosi for Alou, Zaun for Johnson, and Eisenreich for Sheffield, Daulton in the lineup against a right-handed pitcher. They scored seven runs in the first three innings and White finally broke out with four hits and three RBIs.

Another indication of how important the Marlins considered this series: Nen came in for the ninth inning with the Marlins leading by four runs, even though he had pitched the previous three nights. Leyland wasn't taking any chances. With dark thunderclouds rolling in from the west and a rain delay just minutes away, Nen set down the side in order, striking out two.

Leyland was so happy with the win he could barely contain his smile. His upper lip kept twitching as he tried not to smile, then he finally gave in. Fernandez decided, "Tomorrow's as big a fucking game as this one." White, responding to Chipper Jones' pre-series "nail in the coffin" comment said, "I've won two rings. I know what it takes to get there. Just play ball and don't blab your mouth."

On this night, the Marlins couldn't stop blabbing.

◆ ◆ ◆

Tuesday was moving day for the Leyland family. Katie Leyland was flying back to Pittsburgh with the two kids, so on Monday, August 4, the manager brought his 5-year-old son, Patrick, to work. He sat in his rocking chair, bouncing Patrick up and down on his lap, and said, "Hey, that's my boy," and Patrick said back, "Hey, that's my dad." The apple doesn't fall far from the tree in this family. Leyland asked his son, "What did you think of your kindergarten teacher?" and Patrick twisted his hand back and forth at the wrist and muttered, "Shaky." The kid had learned his lines well.

A little while later, Leyland was helping Patrick put on his baseball socks and asked, "Do you wanna wear 'em like your dad?" Patrick nodded. Leyland tugged on the socks for a few minutes, pulling them up to the boy's knees, then folding them down inside-out. Finally, Leyland said, "You gotta learn how to dress. You gotta learn how to put these on. I'll be twelve feet under by the time you're old enough to wear these for real."

Then Leyland took Patrick outside and hit fungoes to him behind the batting cage. Leyland couldn't stop smiling, and neither could his son.

◆ ◆ ◆

A member of the Marlins' front office staff was speaking on the phone one afternoon with somebody from Universal Records, who suggested the Marlins listen to a song by the ska band Reel Big Fish. The song contained the following chorus:

Everybody's doing the fish.
Yeah! Yeah! Yeah!
Everybody's doing the fish
Yeah! Yeah! Yeah!

Key word: Fish.

In all fairness to Reel Big Fish, the lyric *Everybody's doing the fish. Yeah, yeah, yeah,* isn't much different from *She loves you, yeah, yeah, yeah,* and that sold a trillion records for The Beatles. Nonetheless, people of less vision might have deposited the tape into the nearest trash receptacle and forgotten the whole thing, but not the Marlins. They decided to turn it into—as PA announcer Jay Rokeach exulted nightly—"the dance craze that's sweeping South Florida." So, with Billy the Marlin leading the way, the new "Fish" dance was introduced to Marlins fans.

Unfortunately for the Marlins' in-game entertainment staff, nobody was doing The Fish, unless you counted Tommy Sandt. The first base coach danced his version in the clubhouse prior to Sunday's game against the Braves. Backstroke, breaststroke, plus a funny looking move in which you point your left arm out, place your right hand perpendicular to the top of your head, and wiggle your body. Sandt had it down pat and with plenty of rhythm. If the in-game entertainment staff had been aware of Sandt's performance, they could have taped it, shown it on the stadium screens, and had everybody doing The Fish, instead of staring at Billy the Marlin and friends doing The Fish.

156

Anthems can pull a team together. The 1979 Pirates had *We Are Family.* The 1997 Marlins now had *The Fish.* On Monday, the Marlins defeated the Astros, 4-1, and when the clubhouse doors opened, *The Fish* was blaring on the stereo and Zaun was dancing in time. And a few days later Felix Heredia walked onto the team bus grinning and singing, in his thick Dominican accent, "Everybody doosing The Fish. Yeah, yeah, yeah. Everybody doosing The Fish. Yeah, yeah, yeah."

So it was catching on, with the players and coaches if not with the fans.

◆ ◆ ◆

Renteria had breakfast with the Colombian TV host. At 4 o'clock in the afternoon. On the baseball field. Right next to the Marlins dugout. She wore a black Marlins jersey, very tight, of course, and he wore his baseball uniform. The table was covered with a colorful cloth and had flowers in the middle. Renteria and his hostess dined on *arepas* and orange juice. Renteria wasn't the only one who found the scene quite amusing. So did his teammates, who kept walking by and laughing.

◆ ◆ ◆

The conversation came around to watching the out-of-town scoreboard during a pennant race, and Leyland said, "I get a big kick when people say, 'Do you scoreboard watch?' Well, Jesus Crickets, it's up there in big neon signs! Where I sit in the dugout, you can see the whole board, and I don't stop when I get to Atlanta."

On Tuesday night the out-of-town scoreboard read PIT 5, ATL 4 when the Marlins came to bat in the bottom of the ninth inning, trailing the Astros, 5-4. Renteria, who by that time hadn't even digested his breakfast, walked to lead off the inning. Sheffield singled and Abbott replaced him as a pinch-runner. A walk to Daulton loaded the bases, then Alou blooped a two-run single to right, winning the game and setting off a celebration that would continue hours later on the Marlins' flight to Pittsburgh. They were a joyous bunch.

Sheffield stormed out of the dugout, lifted Alou, and gave him a big hug. Later he said he could have lifted Alou over his head, he was so pumped up. The crowd of 25,483, most of which had stayed to the end, kept cheering even as they made their way down the circular ramps and to the parking lot. They could be heard from inside the clubhouse. Alou said it sounded like a crowd in a pennant race. And Bonilla said, "I was going to have to put that L.A. label on South Florida, but they stayed tonight. There was limited beach ball action."

He was referring to the beach balls that got bounced from fan-to-fan in the lower level whenever the game got boring, and sometimes even when the game got exciting. South Florida fans also were in the habit of doing the wave at the most inappropriate times, such as bases loaded, two out, full count, close game. Those habits were broken for one night, at least.

But the game the Marlins had gained on Atlanta was lost right back in Pittsburgh. Brown beat the Pirates, 12-3, on Wednesday. Leiter lost to the Pirates, 5-1, on Thursday. Meanwhile, the Braves were beating the Cardinals two straight, and the Marlins went to Atlanta trailing by 5½ games.

157

◆ ◆ ◆

The Atlanta skyline had undergone a subtle change since the Marlins last visited in mid-May, and the change became less subtle the closer one got to Turner Field. Atlanta-Fulton County Stadium, across the street from The Ted, had been blown to smithereens by a demolition crew, its shell tumbling down like dominoes from the impact of a TNT blast. A craterful of Atlanta-Fulton County Stadium rubble had been left behind, and certainly a few thousand people, at least, must have commented that it looked better dead.

Atlanta itself looked a bit dead, too, on Friday before the first game of the series. The sky was cloudy and gray, a cool wind had blown in, and rain threatened. Atlanta in August is usually hot and muggy, almost unbearable, so cool and dreary was a major improvement. Then Turner Field filled to capacity by gametime, and against the gray backdrop, the scene looked like it could have been October and the National League Championship Series.

A few hours before the game, Leyland asked a Braves official whether he could meet Jane Fonda, but as it turned out, Fonda and her husband, Braves owner Ted Turner, didn't attend the game. Maybe the series wasn't so important after all.

◆ ◆ ◆

Gregg Zaun had talked his way into Leyland's doghouse. Zaun's problem was reporters loved quoting him because he always had well-thought-out opinions on the subjects of the day—inter-league play (he's against it), league realignment (he's against it), the designated hitter (he's against it), pitchers throwing at hitters (he doesn't understand it)—and willingly shared them. That's unlike most major league players who, twenty-seven years later, are still living by the baseball axiom quoted by Jim Bouton in the book *Ball Four*: "He's a helluva guy. Wouldn't say shit if he had a mouthful."

Of course, you can say whatever you want if you're a superstar like Ken Griffey Jr. or Greg Maddux. Backup catchers aren't supposed to express themselves, especially when their manager is an old-fashioned man who lives by baseball axioms. So Leyland, genuinely furious and frustrated by his inability to get his message across directly to Zaun, told the writers a story.

"Did you ever hear the story about the bird that fell into a pile of manure?" Leyland started, leaning over his desk and sounding like somebody's grandfather gone mad. "A pile of shit. There's bad weather and everything, and it's fucking cold and everything, and he's down there in his fucking shit and boy, he's warm and everything, and boy, he's real cozy, just laying in that shit, feeling real comfortable and everything's perfect, and the fucking bird's whistling and he's really happy. Then a fucking cat came over and ate the mother fucker. And the moral of the story is, when it's fucking warm and you're comfortable and everything's going all right, keep your fucking mouth shut. That's the moral of that story. It's a good story for Gregg Fucking Zaun. Don't draw any fucking extra attention to yourself.

"He's a dumb mother fucker. I mean, you gotta be dumb if your manager pleads with you about three or four times, 'Keep your fucking mouth shut,' and you don't. Then he's gonna tell me afterwards that he fucked up. I said, 'Well, you ain't gonna fuck up again. It'll be the last fucking time.' His ass will be out of here in a heartbeat."

The players had already been alerted to Leyland's displeasure with Zaun. One day Zaun was talking to a group of reporters when Bonilla walked up, waved his finger, and scolded, "Watch yourself, Z." Before the first game of the Braves series, Leyland sat in the dugout between Bonilla and Daulton, and again launched a tirade against Gregg "Fucking" Zaun, who was not present. Daulton and Bonilla just laughed. Later, a reporter asked Moises Alou a question, and Alou suggested, "Why don't you ask Zaun?"

But that wasn't going to happen because the beat reporters heard the message loud and clear: Protect Zaun by not talking to him, unless he hits a grand slam to win the World Series. Whether Leyland was punishing Zaun, or just didn't feel like using him, was hard to tell. Zaun would make one appearance in this series, as a pinch-runner. He never batted, never caught.

◆ ◆ ◆

The reading material in the visitor's clubhouse at Turner Field included *Field & Stream, U.S. News & World Report,* a copy of the Victoria's Secret catalog, and a few very worn copies of *Hustler* magazine, both of which long ago had become so frayed their covers had fallen off. On the list of which magazines had been getting the most attention, it looked like *Hustler* by a nose, or whatever, over the Victoria's Secret catalog, with *Field & Stream* third and *U.S. News & World Report* trailing by a wide margin. The majority of visiting players who passed through Atlanta had a far better chance of naming the *Hustler* Honey for August 1997 than they did of identifying the vice president of the United States.

One of the most colorful features in *Hustler* is the Asshole of the Month, and if the Marlins had a vote, they undoubtedly would have chosen Chipper Jones. The Braves' third baseman had been in severe violation of baseball's "Wouldn't Say Shit If He Had A Mouthful" rule and had recently angered the Marlins with some of his comments.

Jones is a 25-year-old power hitter with country boy looks. Braves fans love him because he plays with a lot of emotion and hits a lot of home runs. The Marlins couldn't stand him because he always had something to say. It wouldn't have been so bad if Jones was a veteran, but he was in only his third major league season on a team of veterans, and here he was acting like the spokesman for the Braves.

The quote that really bothered the Marlins was uttered by Jones after the four games in Miami. This is what he said: "They took it to us this series, but if everything stands pat until next weekend at Atlanta, I'll take my chances. It's not beyond the realm of comprehension that we can sweep them there."

That quote doesn't sound so inflammatory, but remember, this is baseball and these are baseball players. Wouldn't say shit, and all that.

When an equipment company representative brought a few bats into the Marlins' clubhouse, one of the players picked up a bat, swung it a few times, and asked, "Whose bat is this?"

"Chipper Jones'" the equipment rep answered.

Hearing that, the player dropped the bat to the floor, then squatted over it as if he was defecating.

◆ ◆ ◆

Most people tracked Charles Johnson's sudden emergence as a hitter back to the All-Star Game, when he sat in the National League clubhouse surrounded by the best players in the world and realized he deserved to be there. It gave him confidence. The irony was that Johnson wouldn't have been there if not for Braves manager Bobby Cox and Mets catcher Todd Hundley; Hundley got hurt, Cox chose Johnson as his substitute, and from that moment on Johnson was hitting .397.

"It was a good boost for me, but I'm not saying that's the sole reason," Johnson said. "Before the All-Star break, a lot of people didn't notice that I was starting to drive the balls a little better. Centerfield. Right-center. I was staying on the ball a lot better. I had a little momentum before the All-Star break, then after the All-Star break it just kept going."

Johnson is one of those players you can't help rooting for because he is such a gentleman. He is big and imposing at 6'2", 220 pounds, but he speaks gently, patiently, and always with a smile. There was no difference in Johnson's attitude when he was hitting .226 or .270. He quietly went about his business, never avoided the media after a bad day at the plate, and was always careful to credit his teammates for his success.

Johnson was also one of the most powerful hitters on the team. That sounds odd because he had never hit more than thirteen home runs in a season, but no Marlin—other than Kurt Abbott, another unlikely suspect—could hit the ball further. The Marlins had held a home run hitting contest for charity back in June and Johnson won, hitting several balls into the upper deck.

So it wasn't surprising Friday night when Johnson hit a two-run homer to straight-away center in the fourth inning, depositing the ball into a TV camera stand and tying the game at 2-2. Then, in the seventh inning, Johnson walked with the bases loaded to force home what turned out to be the winning run in a 6-4 Marlins win. The Marlins were 4½ behind.

◆ ◆ ◆

Dennis Cook was pitching in the seventh inning Friday night with the Marlins leading, 6-2, and Pat Corrales, the Braves' first base coach, had umpire Mark Hirschbeck check the ball for scuff marks. Then, with Kenny Lofton on first base and Jeff Blauser at the plate, Corrales had Hirschbeck check again. Blauser hit Cook's next pitch into the leftfield seats for a two-run homer.

Cook retired the next two batters to end the inning, and as he walked off the mound, he turned and yelled at Corrales—something about Corrales' mother, something about Corrales' sexual habits. He later fibbed, "I don't know what I said," but it wasn't hard to guess. Corrales didn't remember his response, either, but later insisted, "I'm not trying to rattle him. You don't see me hollering at Robb Nen or anyone else, do you?"

The umpires, by Corrales' request, had checked baseballs thrown by Cook the previous weekend in Miami, too, and found nothing then, either. But the video-tapes were telling: Cook was using his finger nails to dig in and raise the seams on the balls. That's not allowed according to major league rules, so the Braves showed the tapes to crew chief Bruce Froemming. Froemming showed them to Leyland. Leyland showed them to Cook, and told him to change the way he rubs up his balls, or words to that effect.

Leyland also told Corrales where to stick his rules in a diatribe that bordered on the comedic. As Leyland saw it, Corrales was violating the rules, too, by stand-ing far outside the coach's box.

"If you're going to be a rules purist, then be a rules purist," Leyland said angrily. "Follow the rules yourself. If you're a rules purist, then get in the goddamn coach's box. That's in the rule book, but I don't bitch about it. But if you're gonna be harp-ing on the rules every goddamn day, then abide by them yourself. Standing five, six feet out of the coach's box, trying to steal signs every night. Get in the god-damn coach's box.

"But he's right on the rule. I want to make that perfectly clear. Pat Corrales is right on the rule. You can't deface the ball. But it's not like the rules are made for everybody else and not for you. The rules are made for all of us. If you want to pull that silly shit and draw attention to yourself, then do what you're supposed to do yourself. I mean, don't throw stones if you live in a glass house."

Then Leyland put on his glasses, pulled out a rule book, and opened it directly to the section pertaining to coach's boxes. He had the pertinent passage underlined in pen and read it aloud, as if he had been waiting for this moment. Which, of course, he had. He had been planning this little speech all morning.

Leyland sounded as if he was going to call the Braves on the coach's box rule in Saturday afternoon's game, but he didn't. Maybe it was because Marlins coaches Tommy Sandt and Rich Donnelly stood far outside the coach's boxes, too.

Question: What's worse, doctoring a baseball, or standing a few feet outside the coach's boxes? Most people would probably say doctoring a baseball, but, of course, Leyland isn't most people.

◆ ◆ ◆

Baseball players have a universal method of taking penance after a loss. First, the offending player will place a stool in front of his locker. Then he'll drape a towel over his head. Then he'll sit down, facing into the locker, and place his elbows on his knees and his hands on his cheeks. For added emphasis, he might shake his head a few times, mutter a few curses, anything to make it thoroughly clear to team-mates, coaches, the managers, and the media, that he couldn't possibly feel worse even if his agent had just been run over by an armored car.

161

Sometimes there's no way of knowing whether the player feels worse about what he did to the team or what he did to himself, such as in the case of Marlins relief pitcher Rob Stanifer, who had been up and down from the minors all season. Stanifer, still dressed in his uniform, was assuming the position after the Marlins' 4-3 loss to the Braves Saturday afternoon. The Marlins were leading, 2-1, in the bottom of the sixth inning when Stanifer relieved Livan Hernandez. Javy Lopez, the first batter he faced, singled home the tying run. Then Stanifer allowed two more hits and a suicide squeeze. By the time the inning was over, the Braves were ahead, 4-2. Stanifer's sinker wasn't sinking, but his longterm major league prospects were.

Eisenreich and White struck out in the top of the ninth inning with the tying run at third base and the winning run on second, so they couldn't save Stanifer. Another bad outing or two and nobody would be able to save Stanifer.

◆ ◆ ◆

A tough day at the ballpark turned into a tougher night at the hotel. Leyland returned to his room after the game and went right to bed at 5:30 p.m. When he woke up four hours later, he called room service for a grilled cheese sandwich and a chocolate shake. The chocolate shake came fine, but the grilled cheese sandwich was a grilled *cream* cheese sandwich. Who ever heard of a grilled cream cheese sandwich? Then he flipped through the TV channels, couldn't find anything to watch, and went to bed.

The next morning, he called room service and asked for a pot of coffee with two cups—one for him, one for Rich Donnelly—a newspaper, and a pack of cigarettes. Leyland was soaking his foot in the bathtub when the phone rang. He jumped out of the tub, rushed across the bathroom all soaking wet, and picked up the receiver. It was room service to tell him that a pack of cigarettes would cost five dollars. "Fine," Leyland grumbled. He wasn't happy about it. Thought they were trying to rip him off.

A few minutes later, the waiter arrived with one cup, not two, which got Leyland even angrier. The waiter was standing in the doorway waiting for a tip, but Leyland wagged his finger at him and said, "You made a big mistake. Now you go downstairs and take two dollars out of that five dollars from the pack of cigarettes. You just blew a ten-dollar tip."

Leyland got to the ballpark early Sunday for a 1:10 game, but was miserable because his ankle, which had been feeling better, was hurting him again.

Punch line: Grilled cream cheese sandwiches are on the room service menu at the Marriott Marquis in Atlanta. Room service cigarettes really do cost five dollars. So it was a rough day for Leyland, but an even rougher day for some poor stiffed waiter.

◆ ◆ ◆

The Braves scheduled a press conference Sunday afternoon to announce the signing of pitcher Greg Maddux to a new contract. All kinds of gigantic numbers were being thrown about for the four-time Cy Young Award winner, and back in the

Marlins' clubhouse Conine deadpanned, "It'll be a lot of money. I betcha it'll be at least a million a year."

He was joking. This figured to be a replay of the Sheffield press conference, only bigger. After all, if Sheffield, who had never so much as led the National League in home runs or RBIs was worth $10 million a year, what was Maddux worth? Conine's actual prediction of between $55 million and $60 million for five years was closer to reality: The contract was for $57.5 million, making Maddux the richest player in baseball history, exactly what he wanted to be all along.

"It was important for me to make sure that pitchers are paid like everyday players, because we're just as valuable," Maddux said. Bobby Bonilla nearly choked on his cigar when he heard that.

"He's not the best player," Bonilla insisted. "He's the best pitcher. I'll give him the MVP if he goes 35-0, but you can't compare a guy who plays thirty-five games with a guy who plays one hundred sixty-two."

Naturally, the next question for Bonilla was, "Who is the best player in baseball?" His response was interesting. Bonilla said it was Barry Bonds, his friend and former Pittsburgh Pirates teammate. Then he added, "If Nike was to do the same thing to Barry as Griffey, people would think Barry was the best player. What about Griffey do you know? What side of Barry do you know? It's that Nike went out of its way to promote Griffey."

This wasn't a revelation. Anybody who has watched TV or read a magazine over the past five years knows Nike has become the image maker in sports. But it was refreshing to hear a multi-million-dollar athlete admit the images created for athletes aren't always true.

Of course, Bonilla knows that as well as anyone. And by the way, he wears Nike.

◆ ◆ ◆

Renteria and Sheffield each drove in a run in the top of the tenth inning to give the Marlins a 4-2 victory Sunday afternoon and afterwards C. Jones of the Braves, who felt not so chipper at all, said, "You could say we're choking, you could say we're nervous, but the bottom line is we're just not getting the job done."

Jones' teammates saw his comments in the newspaper the next day and didn't like what they read. The key word was choking. In sports, you can think it, but you can't say it. Just a few months earlier, Terry Murray had coached the Philadelphia Flyers hockey team to the Stanley Cup finals, and got fired because he dared to suggest that his team had choked. Since No. 3 hitters that are batting .312 with nearly one hundred RBIs can't get fired or benched for saying the wrong thing, the Braves went after Jones verbally.

"If he thinks we're like that, maybe he should be captain," spat Javy Lopez.

Strong words, but they could have been stronger. What he should have done was tell Leyland's bird story.

When you got right down to it, choke wasn't an inappropriate word to use when describing the Braves, who in the 1990s had reached the World Series four times and won once. In 1996, they had a 2-0 lead on the Yankees and didn't win another game. There was a lot of pressure on this team to get there again, and win this time, which was obvious from walking into the Braves' clubhouse after the loss. It was not a pleasant atmosphere.

Bobby Cox sat in his office with his feet up on the desk and his hand on his chin. The major difference between Leyland after a loss and Cox after a loss is that while both men use the word "fuck" a lot, Cox uses it as a higher percentage of total words spoken. Leyland at least tries to use it as a part of complete sentences. Relief pitcher Mike Bielecki talked about being suicidal because he just gave up the winning runs and Jones, red-eyed and speaking in a hushed tone, said "Maybe we'll use the ride home to vent a little bit."

Jones' comment should have been taken as a warning and broadcast on all traffic reports that night. It's frightening to imagine a sports car-driving baseball player venting on I-75 in downtown Atlanta. The damage would be horrific. Fortunately, no major accidents involving baseball players were reported that night.

The Braves took losing much harder than the Marlins, probably because they were so used to winning. When the Marlins lost, one or two players, maybe the losing pitcher and the hitter who made a key out, sat staring into their lockers. When the Braves lost, half the team assumed the mourning position and reporters walked around using their pens to take the players' emotional temperatures.

"You don't make plans for October vacations in this clubhouse," Jones said, referring to expectations that the Braves were supposed to be in the World Series every year. For a team that had been winning so much, the players didn't look like they were having much fun. They looked like they needed a vacation.

◆ ◆ ◆

The Braves won, 2-1, in the final game of the series Monday night, August 11. Brown misplayed a couple of ground balls in the sixth inning and Heredia made the critical mistake of walking leadoff hitter Ryan Klesko in the bottom of the ninth with the game tied, 1-1. Then, with one out and the bases loaded, pinch-hitter Danny Bautista hit a fly ball to rightfield that Sheffield had to back up on. He did, but not fast enough. Sheffield caught the ball while still moving backward, and his throw home sailed over Johnson's head. Klesko scored. Afterward, Heredia, Brown, and Sheffield, all vied for a share of the blame, but Leyland credited Atlanta.

"This is the ultimate organization you're talking about," he said. "They're the eggs Benedict."

◆ ◆ ◆

Sheffield had been talking the "winning is all that matters" line for months, and there was good reason to believe he wasn't merely voicing the company line.

"All my buddies got rings at home: Dwight [Gooden], Tino Martinez, Derek Bell. I just want a ring," he said. "That would satisfy my whole career." In other words, Sheffield wanted to show off his jewelry.

Meanwhile, Leyland was insisting Sheffield had shown signs of breaking out of the slump, but he sounded like a manager supporting a mentally fragile player. Against Atlanta, the hardest balls Sheffield hit were foul by ten or twenty feet, and he didn't reach the warning track once. By the final game Monday night Sheffield was back to his old tricks: Taking close pitches and arguing with the umpire. With forty-five games remaining, it was clear Bonilla, Daulton, Alou, and the pitching staff would have to carry the Marlins. Help from Sheffield couldn't be depended upon.

◆ ◆ ◆

So, here's the catch.

Those eight games in twelve days between the Marlins and Braves?

The post-season tension?

The sellout crowds?

The sad clubhouses? Chipper Jones venting on the ride home? Leyland kneeling all game long on the dugout steps as if it was the seventh game of the World Series? Stanifer and Heredia taking penance and Brown assessing the importance of the loss Monday by saying, "At the end of the season, I'll let you know."

None of it really mattered very much.

As long as the Marlins qualified for at least the wild card, there wouldn't be much difference between their route to the World Series and the Braves'. The post-season format for the 1997 season—as pre-ordained by the geniuses in Major League Baseball's home office—gave home field advantage to the Central and Western Division champions for the first round of the playoffs. The Braves and Marlins, no matter which order they finished in, would open the playoffs with two games at home, and then play three, if necessary, on the road.

Leyland admitted this—"As long as you get to post-season play, it doesn't matter"—although he never acted as if he really believed it.

But these eight games were not without meaning in South Florida, where people were finally paying attention to the Marlins. Television ratings had soared. SportsChannel Florida had a record viewing audience for Monday night's game, and in some cases, ratings for the eight games had doubled from numbers posted early in the season. By the day, fans were buying tickets by the thousands for the remaining games, and the final four home games of the season against the Mets were nearly sold out. Crowds of more than twenty-five thousand would attend each of the nine games on the next homestand and, for the first time, there was real, live pennant fever in South Florida.

The players, coaches, and managers appreciated the backing. At least they said they did. Bonilla called the four home games against the Braves "great for South Florida" and said he could feel the fans' support. Sheffield talked about how nice it was to have the fans behind the team, if not him, for a change, and Leyland was unusually effusive when discussing the sellout crowds and the way they acted. He said it was important, exciting. It meant a lot.

"It has to be a marriage," he said. "We're playing our asses off for them. We're in this together."

165

But this fans/team relationship thing was something Leyland didn't have quite down pat. He was sitting in the dugout at the Astrodome on Wednesday, one night after the Marlins lost to the Astros, 13-2, and his anger was obvious. Then Mike Phillips from *The Miami Herald* walked over.

"Mr. Sheffield's not in the lineup tonight," Phillips offered by way of a question.

"So?" Leyland responded. "We got a day off tomorrow and he's been fucking hurt. It makes sense. Who gives a fuck what the lineup is?"

"I know how you feel about lineup questions," Phillips said, "and ninety-nine percent of the time we don't ask. But when Sheffield isn't in the lineup, the fans want to know."

And Leyland barked, "The last thing I care about is the fucking fans."

Leyland went on to point out, in an obscenity-filled explanation, that Devon White and Charles Johnson weren't in the lineup, either, and that Sheffield had been hitting .083 against Astros starter Shane Reynolds.

But by that time, he had already put a damper on the marriage.

NATIONAL LEAGUE EAST STANDINGS

	W	L	Pct.	GB
Atlanta	75	47	.615	—
Marlins	**69**	**50**	**.580**	**4.5**
New York	67	53	.558	8
Montreal	60	59	.504	13.5
Philadelphia	42	75	.359	30.5

"My Groin Has No Comment"

August 12, 13 at Houston
August 15, 16, 17, 18 vs. Pittsburgh
August 19, 20 vs. Chicago
August 22, 23, 24 vs. St. Louis
August 25, 26, 27, 28 at Chicago
August 29, 30, 31 at Toronto

There was no end in sight to Leyland's summer-long rage. The games against Atlanta had lifted the team's spirit and sparked excitement over a pennant race, but Leyland's sour mood deepened. That Wednesday night in the Astrodome, he was angry at Phillips for asking about his lineup. He was angry at radio announcer Joe Angel for asking him on the air whether the Marlins were "flat" in the 13-2 loss to the Astros. He hated questions about the team being "flat." They fell under his category of "silly shit."

Nonetheless, those were forgivable offenses. The real source of his anger was Leiter, who Leyland felt had made him look like a fool Tuesday night by hiding a groin injury. His displeasure didn't abate after an 8-6 victory over Houston, or two days later when the Marlins returned to Miami for the start of a four-game series against the Pirates.

Leyland insisted on being unreasonable, which would have been fine. Managers reserve the right to be unreasonable because they have the final say on most matters. But this time, Leyland strayed over the line into an area where he didn't have the final say, and ended up in a screaming match with his boss, general manager Dave Dombrowski.

Actually, it was a pretty one-sided screaming match, because Leyland was doing most of the screaming.

Leiter had pulled the groin muscle in the third inning of the first game of the Houston series, but didn't tell anyone about it until after the fourth inning. By the time Leiter decided to be forthcoming, he had already allowed seven runs and infuriated his manager.

The next day, Leyland was sitting in the visitor's dugout, grumbling about Leiter's "horseshit" performance, and complaining that Leiter made him look like an idiot by keeping him in the game.

"We don't need any fucking heroes," Leyland announced. "We're in a pennant race."

As for Leiter's immediate future, Leyland was sure about one thing: If Leiter couldn't make his next start, he'd go straight onto the fifteen-day disabled list.

"And you can take that to the fucking bank," he guaranteed.

Leyland meant every word of what he said, and nobody, he decided, was going to get in his way, even Dombrowski. The victory that night didn't change his mood, nor did a day off. When Leiter reported to work on Friday, August 15, with his groin still aching, Leyland decided to place him right onto the DL, no questions asked.

The problem was that placing players on the DL isn't the manager's decision, it's the general manager's. Leyland wanted to go right over Dombrowski's head and make the move on his own, and he didn't care about protocol. All he cared about was exercising his power and punishing Leiter for hiding the injury. But Dombrowski said it was his call. He wanted to have Leiter throw on the sidelines, then consult with the pitcher, the pitching coach, and team doctor, before making an educated decision. Besides, there was no reason to hurry.

When Leyland heard this he lost whatever composure he had left and began shouting at Dombrowski. As Leyland ranted, Dombrowski listened, shocked that his manager would speak to him in such a disparaging manner.

"If you want to manage the team, you manage the team," Leyland finally threatened. "Here, you take the fucking lineup card."

"Go ahead, leave," Dombrowski calmly replied, knowing fully that Leyland had no intention of quitting. The manager was acting like a 12-year-old who tells his parents, "I hate you," and threatens to run away from home. Leyland, Dombrowski knew, wasn't going anywhere, except to the bullpen to watch Leiter throw. And that's where he went, later in the afternoon.

The bullpen session didn't go well for Leiter. He felt OK when pitching from a full windup, but experienced a stabbing pain in his groin every time he pitched from the stretch position. Nonetheless, he felt he could get away with missing only one start and avoiding the DL. Leyland disagreed, and animatedly made Leiter aware of his feelings. It was quite a scene, Leiter standing on the mound, while Leyland paced, ranted, and raved with arms waving.

A decision was finally made by Dombrowski and Leyland in concert to place Leiter on the fifteen-day disabled list and recall a pitcher from the minors. The other option—keeping him off the DL and taking a chance that Leiter would have to miss more than one start—didn't make sense to them, especially in a pennant race.

"This is better for the team and better for Al," said pitching coach Larry Rothschild.

Leiter wasn't at all convinced of the self-benefits. "My groin has no comment," is what he said before throwing in the bullpen, and he still hadn't changed his mind.

◆ ◆ ◆

With Leiter on the disabled list, pitcher Antonio Alfonseca was called up from Triple-A Charlotte to take his place. Alfonseca apparently had no trouble getting along on minor league meal money: His pear-shaped upper body didn't look any slimmer from when he had last been with the Marlins in mid-June. Alfonseca was only 25, but with his sleepy eyes and sun-worn skin he could've easily passed for 50. He is the kind of athlete a sportswriter loves; nobody can poke fun at a scribe's physique when men who look like Alfonseca are paid good money to be athletes.

The most unusual thing about Alfonseca, other than his rather imposing size of 6'6", 235 pounds, is that he was born with six fingers on each hand and six toes on each foot. His nickname is "Pulpo," which is Spanish for octopus. When Leyland met him for the first time in February, he shook Alfonseca's hand and, he said, "felt something funny crawling up my arm." It was Alfonseca's additional digit, which hadn't moved an inch.

◆ ◆ ◆

The Marlins made a trade on August 12, sending Rick Helling to the Texas Rangers in exchange for left-handed relief pitcher Ed Vosberg. The Rangers got Helling and the Marlins got Vosberg, despite Major League Baseball's strict post-trade deadline restrictions, because nobody else wanted them. Simple as that.

◆ ◆ ◆

Jim Eisenreich said something that didn't make much sense, although it wasn't entirely his fault. Ballplayers often try to explain why things happen, when they really have no idea. The problem is, they're always being asked to explain streaks and slumps, so they have to come up with something.

Here's what Eisenreich came up with when asked about the Marlins' supposed upturn in intensity. He said it after the Marlins beat the Pirates, 6-5, on Friday by scoring two runs in the bottom of the ninth inning: "You heard the Skipper say a couple of weeks ago that we bottomed out against Cincinnati that one game. We'd just been dead, dead fish in the water. We knew the Braves were coming in and we played them with playoff-like atmosphere. We continued that through our road trip and tonight again. Just because we're down in the ninth inning, we fight and claw and scratch and do everything to try to get a run and try to win a game. We have enough good players, and we hadn't been playing with intensity.

"We had a great spring training, and I think everybody expected us to come out here like in spring training, and it's a lot of pressure. We, as players, probably took it the wrong way and tried to do a little too much, instead of just kind of playing our game. It probably took the Braves to kick us in, and we all knew that, we just didn't know how to do it, and we just needed a big game. We're playing with more intensity. We're having fun. There's music playing in here."

OK, so according to Eisenreich, the Marlins were trying to do a little too much before, which was bad, but now they were playing with more intensity, which was good. They started fighting and clawing in the late innings. Fine, except that all season they had been winning one-run games and rallying in the late innings. As for the music, supposedly the sign of a happy team, well, music played in the clubhouse after every win all season. It just got turned up a bit after Daulton arrived.

169

The fact of the matter is that nobody knows why teams suddenly click. They just click. It just happens. No metaphysical explanations are necessary. But, of course, the people who cover the team daily need a reason for everything and the players, who are usually searching for answers themselves, manage to come up with something. It makes baseball sound more cerebral.

That afternoon, a discussion had come around to the concept of baseball teams looking flat, and Abbott said: "You mean is everybody on the bench hung over from the night before? We don't have a lot of drinkers on our team. What it means is that the other pitcher basically shoved it up our ass."

Baseball teams are successful when they shove it up the other team's ass, unsuccessful when they have it shoved up their ass. Shoving with more intensity doesn't do them much good.

The next night, Francisco Cordova and the Pirates did the shoving, 10-5. So much for the Marlins having fun. The music wasn't playing, either.

◆ ◆ ◆

Abbott had been suffering from a sore throat and an upper respiratory ailment so bothersome it was taking him two hours every night to fall asleep. He felt so sick there was nowhere he would have rather been than in bed, but on Friday he had pinch-hit and Saturday he would play two innings in leftfield. Abbott was asked whether he would have been better off sitting out a few games, and, after spitting some virus-infected saliva onto the dugout floor, said, "What am I supposed to say? 'No, I can't play?'"

Well, maybe. Wasn't it Leyland who said, "We don't need any fucking heroes?" Of course, Leyland had also once said, "Christ, you have to play in a little pain." So you could understand the confusion.

◆ ◆ ◆

Actual Lucky Program Contest question: "Who is playing 'with all the ability in the world?'"

The answer, as if you didn't know, was Edgar Renteria. It could be found on page 57 of the August edition of the Marlins' program, and anyone who didn't know the answer without peeking, well, they just hadn't been paying attention, had they?

Similar frivolity was on display every game day at Pro Player Stadium. There was Muscle Boy, a skinny fourth-grader sitting in the first row who pulled off his shirt and went into a Hulk Hogan posing act whenever the Village People song *Macho Man* was played: Showing off his biceps, puffing out his chest, kissing his arms. It was cute the first or second time, maybe even the third time, but long before the twentieth time there was no greater urge than to strangle the kid. By mid-August, Muscle Boy had even worn thin with the team's promotional staff, and they were ready to put the kibosh on his act. Actually, their biggest concern was he would start demanding tickets, or, even worse, a share of the gate.

Other Pro Player Stadium fan/characters included Willie and The Professor, a Willie Nelson near-look alike and his friend who sat in the leftfield corner and waved to the camera once a game; The Golden Girls, two silver-haired senior citizens sitting in the upper deck who wore Marlins shirts and danced on cue; and young women with large breasts and small clothing, whose appearances on the video screens lasted until they realized they were on the video screens. When they waved, the camera ducked. Voyeurism for the baseball set.

And The Fish was just not going away. Never. Not in the near future, perhaps not in this millennium, maybe not in your lifetime. This much could be said about the Marlins' in-game entertainment and promotional staff: When they latched onto an idea, they stuck with it. They backed it with all the support that a franchise supposedly losing $30 million a year could muster.

For two days, they loaded Billy the Marlin into a van and visited the beaches in Miami and Fort Lauderdale, where they had everyday folks—preferably muscular men in abdomen-caressing bathing trunks and busty young women in bright-colored string bikinis—dance crazily to The Fish. They taped the impromptu performances, created a video, and began showing it every time Billy and friends came out onto the field to do The Fish. So right up there on the screens were more people doing The Fish on video than had ever done it in person at Pro Player Stadium.

This was, basically, a prime example of the advertising style known as "monkey-see, monkey-do." At first, most fans simply stared at the screens and hooted every time the bikini girls came on, but after a few days, more of them started doing The Fish, perhaps figuring that if these pretty tanned people on the video screens could do it, so could they. A few more showings and it figured that everybody *would* be doing the fish, just like the song said.

But nothing happening inside the Stadium matched the unintentional humor entertaining drivers traveling north on Florida's Turnpike. On the west side of the road stood a gigantic Marlins billboard featuring Gary Sheffield and these words: "MR. BALL, MEET MR. SHEFFIELD."

Somebody should have had the decency to take it down or change the message, if only for Sheffield's sake. By mid-August, after a game in which Sheffield left another three or four runners in scoring position and hit a few more weak grounders and popups, the best attitude was to take it as comic relief. Lit brightly at night, for all the people streaming north from the stadium to see, it was better than anything David Letterman or Jay Leno were offering.

◆ ◆ ◆

It was hard not to feel for Sheffield as he struggled mentally with his season-long slump, and it was impossible not to admire him for the work he did with his pet charity project. RBI—Reviving Baseball in Inner Cities— is a youth baseball and softball program sponsored by Major League Baseball and designed for disadvantaged children who can't afford to play in Little League or pay programs.

Prior to this season, Sheffield's contributions to the Marlins' RBI program were mostly monetary, but in 1997 he decided to start giving his time, too. Of course, baseball players have more money than most people, but they have the same hours in a day as anyone else, and time is often their most prized gift.

171

During the season, Sheffield gave clinics, motivational speeches, and often dropped by the fields—the one in North Miami was named after him—just to talk with the kids. More than anything, he wanted to be a role model for these children, and show them that if he could become successful, so could they.

Sheffield had grown particularly attached to the 13- to 15-year-old all-star team that won the regional championship and earned a trip to the RBI World Series at Coors Field in Denver. This was a dream come true for all of the players, many of whom had never been outside South Florida, and a chance for Sheffield to do something more. He asked Reebok, one of his sponsors, to supply uniforms so that the players could feel like professionals, then he invited the players out to the stadium, spoke to them individually, and gave another motivational speech. He spoke, and they listened attentively.

Then, when the team went to Colorado in early August, Sheffield asked Stacy Ostrau, the front office staffer who caringly oversaw the program for the Marlins, to call him with daily updates. He was in Tampa on an off day when he found out that the team had won the championship. He was so excited he decided to buy rings for all of the players. Their success was one of the highlights of his season.

"I was like them," Sheffield said. "It's what I've been through. When you're 14 or 15 years old, you don't know what you're capable of. I show them different ways to look at baseball. Baseball is life in some ways, but it's not life itself. Seeing them keeps everything in perspective and never lets you get a big head."

Then he was asked, "Are any of the players as good as you were?"

"They're as good as I am now," Sheffield joked. He was keeping perspective.

◆ ◆ ◆

Wayne Huizenga sat in the owner's suite Sunday and watched the Marlins' 10-2 victory over the Pirates. It was a rare visit by Huizenga, who had attended games frequently until he announced his intention to sell the team, but since then no longer found room for baseball in his busy schedule.

The conditions were perfect for an appearance by the owner: sunny skies without a hint of rain in the forecast, and a big crowd of 38,221. Just that afternoon, Mark Geddis, the Marlins' director of communications, was saying that if he and the rest of the front office staff had their way, Huizenga would show up only when the stadium was packed and the weather was good. But during the first few months of the season, Huizenga kept showing up on rainy weeknights when there were often less than fifteen thousand people in the house. Then he decided to sell the team. Most likely it was a coincidence, but maybe it wasn't. Seeing is believing, and all that. What Huizenga saw on many of those May and June nights—plenty of empty seats, fans getting soaked by torrential downpours before they had time to find shelter—wasn't very pretty.

Not that a big crowd and good weather could change his mind. "I'm still trying to find a buyer," Huizenga said in the clubhouse later. "We just haven't found one yet."

In addition to owning the team, Huizenga also owned the stadium, the clubhouses, and the furniture within them, which is why he could sit on one of those cozy leather recliners without hearing a peep. Anyone else did it and the players screamed bloody murder . . . through the PR guy, of course . . . by way of the club-house manager.

Anyway, Huizenga was talking about his AutoNation used car dealership and inadvertently supplied a clue as to why the Marlins' front office workers were so anxious to impress the owner. He sounded like he was trying to sell a car, extolling the virtues of his product, then pointed out that buyers didn't have to worry about getting hassled over price, because the salesmen received the same commission whether they sold a Porsche or a Chevy Nova.

"But we have a great incentive program," the billionaire added. "If they don't sell enough cars, they get fired."

Huizenga laughed at his own joke which, of course, wasn't a joke at all. It was an expression of his business philosophy, and anyone who worked for Huizenga, whether selling cars or baseball tickets, knows it.

◆ ◆ ◆

Players only on the couches and reclining chairs is one clubhouse rule. Another is no cellular phones, but it isn't a Marlins rule, it's a Major League Baseball rule that stems from 1989, when Pete Rose was banished from baseball on suspicion of gambling. Major League Baseball wanted to erase the perception that players and managers might be calling their bookies before or during games, so it ordered the teams to remove all clubhouse and dugout phones with direct outside lines. Now if a player, coach, or manager wants to make a phone call, he has to go through the Stadium operator, who logs all calls. The proliferation of cellular phones made it easy to circumvent the rule, so MLB decided to ban them from the clubhouse, too.

Of course, the rule is ridiculous. It accomplishes nothing. Anybody who really wants to make a bet can call his bookie before arriving at the ballpark, or merely ask a friend or relative to make the call for him. The rule is routinely ignored by every team in the majors. Walk into any clubhouse and you'll see players on their cell phones. The only time the rule is enforced is when a member of the media tries to use a cell phone. Then an equipment manager or clubhouse boy will pipe up with the friendly reminder, "No cell phones in the clubhouse." And meanwhile a player sitting a few feet away is yapping away with his wife, children, or agent.

Management had its special privileges, too. Many days, Leyland would sit in his office reading the racing form and have Javy Castro, one of the clubhouse attendants, run bets for him at a nearby racetrack. When post time neared, Leyland would again summon Castro, who would call the track and have the P.A. announcer leave the line open so Leyland could hear the call of the race. One afternoon, Leyland asked the announcer about a first-time starter he had bet on.

"He's all lathered up," the track announcer said.

"He's all lathered up, hey?" Leyland said.

That wasn't a good sign.

"Your horse has four bandages."

"He has four bandages, does he?"

Considering that most horses have only four legs, that wasn't a good sign, either. The horse lost. If he had won, the clubhouse attendant would have been right back across the street cashing the ticket. After all, you can't have a man wearing a baseball uniform and spikes walking through a racetrack, can you?

◆ ◆ ◆

Kirt Ojala was called up from Charlotte to replace Leiter and start against the Pirates on Monday, August 18. Ojala, 28, had spent eight years in the minors without ever getting summoned to the majors and was wondering whether it would ever happen. Then, Saturday afternoon, he was walking around the outfield in Scranton, Pennsylvania, wearing camouflage and getting ready to do some climbing in the cliffs behind the stadium, when manager Carlos Tosca called him over and said, "I don't want you to get hurt. You're going to Florida."

"He just blew my top," Ojala said.

After trading Dustin Hermanson, Mark Hutton, Rick Helling, and Pat Rapp, the Marlins had no choice but to dip into their minor league system for an emergency starting pitcher. As the age-old baseball saying goes, you can never have enough starting pitching, and here it was, proof positive. They decided upon Ojala, for better or worse. He didn't exactly receive ringing endorsements.

From pitching coach Larry Rothschild: "He's a lefty."

From Leyland: "I don't know who the fuck he is. I don't know whether to be scared or not."

Ojala started the season in the Cincinnati Reds organization and was dealt to the Marlins in a minor league trade. That's why Leyland never saw him during the spring. He is a changeup pitcher who, like most lefty changeup pitchers, admires Tom Glavine. And he graduated from the University of Michigan with a degree in psychology.

The Marlins have a team psychologist, but you can never have too many shrinks around a major league clubhouse. There were 38,221 psychologists at the stadium Sunday afternoon practicing all kinds of motivational techniques on Sheffield. They cheered him loudly after he flied out to the warning track in the first inning, which might have been their way of saying, *Baby steps, Sheff. Baby steps.* Then they went back to booing him after he struck out in the third inning; positive reinforcement for a positive action, negative reinforcement for a negative action. And they chanted "Gah-ree! Gah-ree!" when he came to bat leading off the fifth inning. Sheffield walked.

The next night, Ojala made his debut and lasted all of 3⅔ innings before Leyland couldn't take anymore and removed him. If Ojala had glanced over his shoulder at the start of the fourth inning, he would have noticed that Alfonseca was already warming up in the bullpen, even though at the time Ojala had only allowed one run and hadn't committed Leyland's cardinal sin of walking batters.

The Marlins planned on using Ojala just one more time before returning him to Charlotte, although they might have been better off keeping him around and using him for a different job. Ojala's locker happened to be located equidistant—give or take thirty feet—between Sheffield's stall and the manager's office.

Undoubtedly, he would have been far more valuable to the cause by putting that psychology degree to work.

◆ ◆ ◆

The crowd of 30,200, by far the Marlins' largest Monday night crowd of the season, gave the Marlins a season total of 1,773,538 after sixty-one dates, surpassing their total attendance for the entire 1996 season. It was a nice accomplishment that came as no surprise: The Marlins had gone over two million tickets sold by July 1 and sold their 1,773,538th ticket on April 25.

Perhaps as significant was Bonilla's discovery of a new insect indigenous to baseball fields: The sand flea, as in, "I fucked it up. I wish I could say I got a sand flea caught in my eye." He said that after committing two errors—one throwing, one catching—in a 7-2 loss to the Pirates in the series finale. Years ago, in his more immature days, Bonilla might have tried to sell the sand flea excuse.

◆ ◆ ◆

The next night, the Marlins continued their quest to disprove the theory of momentum in baseball by beating the Cubs, 8-1. Bonilla hit a grand slam and Fernandez got his sixteenth win, so the Marlins bounced back quite nicely.

Leyland on Fernandez's clubhouse and bench demeanor: "Alex is one of the biggest agitators we got on the team, and on the day he is pitching, he's a prick."

Proud of it, too. Fernandez was always messing with somebody on the bench and his voice could often be heard booming across the clubhouse prior to games. As for proof of Fernandez's agitation, his locker and the water cooler still hadn't been repaired from his tirade a month earlier. It was a lasting reminder of Fernandez's temper.

◆ ◆ ◆

The talk of the clubhouse and the front office on Wednesday was a column in *The Miami Herald* by veteran sports editor Edwin Pope, who carried some influence in South Florida. The column, which Pope stressed was based entirely on personal opinion, urged fans to go out and watch the current version of the Marlins before it was too late.

Pope wrote: "The richest Marlins—Gary Sheffield, Bobby Bonilla, Moises Alou, Devon White, Al Leiter, maybe even Alex Fernandez and Kevin Brown, probably manager Jim Leyland—won't be around, despite no-trade clauses for Sheffield, Fernandez, and Alou. It's cold logic: You're losing around $30 million with a $49 million payroll. Cut payroll to $20 million, you might break even."

The players didn't like the column because they viewed it as negative and unnecessary while they were in a pennant race. Front office staffers didn't like it for much the same reason, although they should have been overjoyed by Pope's message to buy tickets now. Only one person, it seemed, liked what was written.

"I think it was a helluva article, if you wanna know the truth," Leyland said. "I thought it made sense. I thought he showed pretty good foresight. But I do think he went overboard to try to make his point. You can't just get rid of salaries."

As for his own future, Leyland reiterated what he had said a few months earlier, after Huizenga announced his intentions of unloading the team: "I'll be back next year, and you can take that to the bank."

Of course, he had said that once before, nearly a year earlier, when Pirates owner Kevin McClatchy announced payroll cuts for the 1997 season, and Leyland said he'd honor the final four years of his contract. Leyland changed his mind less than a month later and ended up with the Marlins.

This time, Leyland's concern wasn't about a new owner cutting payroll. The way he saw it, the cuts couldn't be too drastic because of no-trade clauses in several of the higher-paid players' contracts. Even if there were cuts, the Marlins had a strong enough farm system to remain competitive. His biggest worry was of a new owner getting involved in the day-to-day managing of the team, like George Steinbrenner has always done with the Yankees.

Leyland had thought about the possibility of an intrusive new owner. That's why he had Huizenga add an escape clause to his contract. He didn't want an owner's bratty little kids running around the dugout and making a nuisance of themselves— although little kids ran around the dugout all the time at Pro Player Stadium—or some know-nothing telling him what to do. Even know-somethings, like Dombrowski, were given little breadth with Leyland.

"I'm not going to be sitting there asking Bing Crosby's son whether it's OK to bunt," Leyland growled. "But I'll tell you this: After I leave here, I'll be home in Pittsburgh. I won't be managing."

Leyland sounded like he meant that, too, but only a few weeks earlier, he was talking about this being his final contract and how his next managerial job would be with his son's Little League team. You could almost imagine the scene: *Leyland on the sidelines at a town park, watching soft ground balls going through the legs of 12-year-olds, daydreaming about the days of grilled cream cheese sandwiches in fancy hotels, and telling a reporter from the local weekly, "Remind me never to play Goldberg two games in a row."*

There are two scenarios for Leyland. One has him ending up a crusty old manager like Casey Stengel, using his baseball bat for a cane and barking out his baseball wisdom. Another Old Professor with a cigarette in one hand and a cup of coffee in the other.

The other scenario, the one of Leyland rocking on a porch and watching his children play while a Major League Baseball game is going on somewhere, is as hard to envision as Bing Jr. saying, "Jim, it's time for a squeeze play," and Leyland responding, "Yes sir."

◆ ◆ ◆

Livan Hernandez's locker was diagonally across the clubhouse from Javy Castro's, so one day a reporter walked up to the pitcher and asked, "Livan, how do you feel looking across the room and seeing Castro?"

At first, Hernandez didn't know what the reporter was talking about, but then he looked and saw the name CASTRO on the nameplate above the clubhouse attendant's locker. Seconds later, as if on cue, Castro walked by.

"Hey, Javy," Hernandez called out in Spanish. "Which of Fidel's families are you from?"

Castro looked at Hernandez as if he was crazy, then kept walking.

Hernandez, smiling slyly and holding a black magic marker, then strode across the room and wrote the initial F.—for Fidel, the Cuban dictator—on the nameplate above the clubhouse attendant's locker. Javy Castro didn't find that funny at all and quickly erased the F. with a towel, while Hernandez laughed.

The truth was, Fidel Castro was no laughing matter to Hernandez. It was Castro, not the one hundred twenty miles of ocean between Hernandez's apartment in Miami Beach and the shores of Cuba, that separated him from his mother. When Hernandez stood on the balcony of his oceanfront apartment, staring at the glistening, turquoise Atlantic down below, he would resist the thought that his family lived across those waters.

"I can't, because if you start doing that, you just get sad," he said through a translator. "It can get depressing."

At times when he was really lonely or depressed, Hernandez would call his mother three times a day. One month his phone bill was more than $1,200. But Hernandez was aware all along of the emotional and monetary price for defecting, and he supported his family by sending money back to Cuba through intermediaries.

In the clubhouse, he relied upon Alex Fernandez, Jerry Manuel, and Dennis Cook for support and help in learning English and adapting to the United States. He frequently dined at singer Gloria Estefan's restaurant in Miami Beach and hung out with the valet parking attendants. Even when Hernandez took a walk by himself, people who recognized him would come up to him and just start talking. Hernandez never shooed them away.

"Whether they're rich or someone without a home, I treat them all the same," Hernandez said. "I'll buy them dinner if they need it. I feel like I'm like every other person and I want to share what I have. My mother taught me that way."

For whatever reason, the people Hernandez met on the streets weren't coming to the ballpark. Here was a genuine Cuban defector—as opposed to Fernandez, a Cuban American born in Miami—and rookie sensation, but only 18,323 had come out to watch his sixth straight victory a few weeks earlier. Even Fernandez, who was supposed to be a drawing card for the Latin community, attracted less than twenty-five thousand for each of two straight starts in July.

So the Marlins took action and heavily advertised the back-to-back starts by Fernandez and Hernandez in the two-game Chicago series. Advertisements in *El Nuevo Herald* trumpeted, "The Rhythm Continues," and featured the pitchers' names in big, block letters. The results were encouraging, but not great. On both nights, fans in the outfield seats waved Cuban flags. Fernandez's start on Tuesday drew 34,720. Hernandez's start on Wednesday attracted 28,003. He struggled and won, 6-5, and improved to 7-0.

Still, South Florida had a long way to go before it could match Los Angeles in its adulation of ethnic heroes. In the 1980s, sellout crowds packed Dodger Stadium for almost all of Mexican Fernando Valenzuela's starts. For two Cubans who had won a combined thirteen straight games, Pro Player Stadium remained nearly half empty.

This fact was not lost on local radio personality Hank Goldberg, who has one of the strongest opinions in the South Florida market. Goldberg spent hours on the air wondering why Latin Americans weren't turning out to watch Hernandez, one of the hottest rookies in the major leagues, and reached his usual conclusion that Miami was a bush-league sports town.

Actually, on most nights, about thirty-three to fifty percent of the crowd at Pro Player Stadium was Latin American, which was about equal to the percentage of Latin Americans in the South Florida population. Goldberg was right, though: When Hernandez pitched, logic said the stadium should have been packed with singing, cheering Cuban Americans.

The Marlins' efforts to draw from the Latin community were so intensive they would win an award for Hispanic marketing, beating out twenty-nine other nominees. Their office in Miami was located right in the heart of the Cuban community, a few blocks away from the famous Versailles restaurant where President Clinton appeased the Cuban American community every election year by eating flan at 1 o'clock in the morning.

Maybe that was the secret.

◆ ◆ ◆

Moises Alou was batting in the third inning Wednesday night when he fouled a pitch off the plate. It bounced back—*Ta-ting!*—right smack into his groin. Alou fell to the ground and remained there for several minutes, while his teammates on the bench tried, but failed, to control their laughter.

Bonilla: "We thought somebody shot him from the top of the stadium. We thought a sniper got his ass."

Well, not exactly his ass, but close enough.

Anyway, Alou got up and, before continuing his at-bat, walked back to the dugout. And where did he go from there?

"I went to the bathroom," Alou said, "to see if I still had a dick."

He did. Even more of one than before, in fact.

"I'm fine," Big Mo insisted, "except for my swollen cock head."

Alou was relating the details of his physical ailment a few days later at about the time Bonilla showed up for work and walked past Alou's locker. So Dave O'Brien of the *Sun-Sentinel* couldn't resist the opportunity to announce, "Hey, Bobby, this guy's got a swollen cock head."

And Bonilla shook his head slowly and said, "That's a beautiful thing. He's gonna make some woman very happy."

Presumably, some woman would be Alou's wife who, Moises said, was the first one down to the clubhouse after the game.

"But she didn't care about me," Alou said forlornly. "She cared about her."

Punch line: Alou wasn't wearing a protective cup. Most outfielders don't wear cups, most infielders do. Bonilla, especially.

"I don't have hands like those two guys," Bonilla said, pointing to where Renteria and Counsell were sitting. "I got on all kinds of shit. I got soccer pants down there."

Just in case you were wondering, Alou finished the at-bat by popping out to second. The strange thing was that Alou was smiling as he walked back to the plate after checking his personal equipment.

"It was embarrassing," he said. "I got hit in the dick."

It had been a tough homestand for the Marlins' groins. First Leiter, then Alou. Nearly Sheffield, too. The Marlins won, 6-5, over the Cubs, and Sheffield hit a two-run homer, his first since August 1, but he also flipped over the bullpen fence while chasing a foul popup. Had the fence been a few inches higher, Sheffield would have suffered a fate similar to Alou's. Instead, he went tumbling head over heels and landed on his chest.

◆ ◆ ◆

Also surviving a confrontation Wednesday was Bob Becker, the Marlins' producer of in-game entertainment. On that particular night, the in-game entertainment emanating from the stadium speakers included a taped voice screeching, "Everybody just calm down!" when Cubs manager Jim Riggleman argued a call in the ninth inning with first base umpire Terry Tata.

Not very funny, but nothing to lose your mind over. Unless you're Jim Leyland. Red-faced with anger, Leyland stormed back to the clubhouse after the game and summoned Dombrowski and Don Smiley to his office.

Smiley wasn't available, but Dombrowski was, and Leyland let him know, loudly, that what had happened was an embarrassment to the ball club. His primary concern was that the Cubs would use the insult for motivation when the Marlins played in Chicago the following week. Of course, that would have meant the Cubs overreacted, too. Then he demanded—loudly—that Dombrowski fire Becker, and Dombrowski replied—loudly—that there was no way he was doing any such thing. Leyland was as angry as he had been over anything all season. Dombrowski, disturbed by the intensity of the manager's outburst and his second act of insubordination toward the GM in less than a week, was powerless to pacify him.

Instead, Dombrowski walked to the umpires' dressing room and apologized to Tata, who was unaware that anything had happened. Then he walked over to the Cubs' clubhouse and apologized to Riggleman, through Cubs GM Ed Lynch. Riggleman accepted, although he didn't think the incident—if it could be called that—was anything to get worked up over, either. Becker, near tears, immediately apologized to Dombrowski and wanted to apologize to Leyland, too. But Leyland didn't want an apology. He wanted Becker fired.

By the next morning, news of the incident had swept through the Marlins' front office, resulting in two points of view.

The most popular: Leyland had popped his cork and overreacted.

The least popular: Leyland had popped his cork, but was right. Most managers would have reacted the same way to an opposing manager being shown up.

Dombrowski, by the way, agreed with the popular view.

Perhaps it was best Thursday was an off day and Leyland had time to relax with his wife and children, who were down from Pittsburgh. When he returned Friday morning, he was in a better mood to accept a face-to-face apology from Becker, who had realized his mistake a split second after his finger touched the play button. All heads remained attached to all bodies and, by Friday night, everybody had finally "calmed down."

◆ ◆ ◆

Leyland's insubordination toward Dombrowski was telling, but not surprising. In the Becker situation, as in the Leiter situation, Dombrowski wasn't the target of Leyland's anger, but had found himself caught in the firing line. Most managers would never think of yelling at their general manager in such a crass manner, but Leyland wasn't like most managers, and Dombrowski wasn't like most GMs.

On paper, the Marlins' pecking order read Huizenga, Smiley, Dombrowski, Leyland. In reality, although Dombrowski hired Leyland, he really had no power over him. Huizenga and Smiley had been close friends with Leyland for years. Although Dombrowski was friends with Leyland, too—he had stayed at Leyland's house in Pittsburgh while attending the funeral for Carl Barger, the team's first president, in 1992—his relationship with Smiley and Huizenga wasn't nearly as tight. Dombrowski, not Leyland, was the outsider.

When asked whether he expected Leyland to return for the 1998 season, Smiley responded, "I hope so. I love him like a brother." Smiley spent hours in Leyland's office, just visiting, smoking cigarettes, and watching TV. It is extremely rare in any sport for the president of a team to be so close with the manager. In many cases, they have no contact at all.

So the hierarchy was all messed up, and Leyland knew there would never be any serious backlash for yelling at Dombrowski. If the $89-million Marlins fell far short of their potential, Dombrowski, not Leyland, would get fired. The only damage would be to Leyland's reputation.

Even so, Dombrowski couldn't allow Leyland to get away unscolded with these two incidents. He called Leyland into his office, pointed out the manager's inappropriate behavior, and demanded an apology.

"What's going on here, Jim?" Dombrowski demanded.

Leyland did apologize, but it meant nothing in the grander scheme of things. On the Marlins' power chart, the manager still had the edge over the GM that had hired him.

◆ ◆ ◆

The Cardinals came to town on Friday, August 22, led by Mark McGwire with his big arms, big mustache, and big bat and Leyland predicted, "He won't hit one five hundred thirty-nine feet like Galarraga. I can assure you that shit won't happen again."

Bonilla was less certain and stuffed his pants with a little extra protection, just in case the 6'5", 250-pounder got a hold of one and aimed it at him. That was more likely than not to happen at least once over the weekend. McGwire had been so impressive since being traded to St. Louis that people were buying season tickets in August for a team with almost no chance of making the playoffs. They wanted to watch McGwire. Bonilla didn't.

"I already told Saunders, 'Don't go hanging him any fucking changeups,'" Bonilla said. "I ain't wearing Zaun's mask."

"You'll be playing deep?" somebody asked.

"I will be playing extremely deep."

Not deep enough, as it turned out. Not nearly deep enough. For proper placement Friday night, Bonilla would have had to have placed a piece of Velcro on his posterior and attached himself to the tarp in the upper deck of Pro Player Stadium. Neither of the two balls hit by McGwire posed any danger to Bonilla, who was standing approximately three hundred fifty feet away from where they landed.

The first, off Tony Saunders, measured five hundred feet. The other, against a one-hundred-miles-per-hour fastball by Robb Nen, measured four hundred sixty-two feet. The Marlins lost, 7-3.

"I've never seen bombs like that in thirty-four years of professional baseball," Leyland said.

McGwire is an awfully intimidating figure. Before the game, Leyland had been saying that he didn't want his pitchers watching McGwire take batting practice, and related a story about a former Pittsburgh Pirates pitcher named Vicente Palacios.

"We're playing in Wrigley Field, and he's gonna pitch that day, and I told the trainer, 'Look, the wind's blowing out. Whatever you do, don't let that fucker come out on the field for batting practice, ours or theirs,'" Leyland recounted. "So we're halfway through batting practice and I look over and say, 'Fuck, he's out here.' So I went over to him and I said, 'How do you feel?' And he said, 'I feel good, but those hitters, they feel better.'

"And the fucker goes out there and shuts 'em out, and to this day, I don't know how it happened."

None of the Marlins' pitchers watched McGwire take batting practice Friday afternoon because there was no batting practice; the grounds crew was still changing over the field from the Dolphins' pre-season game the previous night. But a few thousand fans showed up late Saturday afternoon and McGwire put on a batting practice show, hitting seven of ten pitches over the fence, including one into the upper deck.

At that time, the Marlins were safely back in their clubhouse, watching the Little League World Series on TV, and Jim Eisenreich said of McGwire, "You know what it's like? It's like putting one of us in that park." He was pointing to the game on TV.

◆ ◆ ◆

The one constant within the clubhouse all season had been the players' total reluctance to publicly question the manager's decisions. Now, that might sound like common sense, but up in New York, Mets catcher Todd Hundley was snapping back at manager Bobby Valentine after Valentine had questioned his sleeping habits. The closest any Marlin had come to questioning Leyland was Daulton. On Saturday, he wondered out loud on TV whether the Marlins had made proper decisions in pitching to McGwire the night before. Then he stopped just short of questioning Leyland's lefty-righty switches with him and Conine. On Friday, for example, Daulton had three hits and two RBIs, but with the Marlins trailing, 4-3, Leyland went with the lefty-righty percentages anyway and pinch-hit Conine.

"I have my thoughts on that," Daulton mused, "but I just work here."

Daulton then went out and scored all three runs in the Marlins' 3-0 victory over the Cardinals Saturday night. He was also replaced by Conine in the seventh inning.

◆ ◆ ◆

Conine, on the other hand, had the politically correct thing down pat. Asked about being used as a defensive replacement, rather than a regular, Conine said, "It's not a role I'm used to, but it's a role I . . ." He stopped right there. Then he paused for a few seconds and collected his thoughts. Finally he finished the sentence with, "gotta get used to." He had exactly the right idea.

◆ ◆ ◆

Counsell was reserved about hitting his first major league home run—even better, a grand slam—in a 7-1 victory over the Cardinals on Sunday, but the crowd wasn't. They urged him out for a curtain call and he reluctantly obliged.

The fans had begun to get the hang of rooting in a pennant race, or a playoff race, or whatever the Marlins were involved in. They chanted Bonilla's name prior to an at-bat in the seventh inning, awarded Ojala with a standing ovation, never stopped cheering for Counsell, their new favorite, and even did The Fish. At least half of the crowd of 28,713 did, anyway, which was a drastic improvement over the pre-Fish video days.

The Fish video, by the way, had undergone several additions since its previous showing, including the editing-in of dancing grounds crew members and several other hyperactives.

"It's a work in progress," Jim Ross informed of his pet idea, which had already received national attention on the MTV web site and in *Rolling Stone* magazine.

On another in-game entertainment front, Cardinals catcher Mike Difelice was thrown out of the game for vehemently arguing a called third strike with home plate umpire Scott Potter, and nobody up in the scoreboard operators' booth cued-up the *Everybody just calm down!* clip. Too bad.

◆ ◆ ◆

Let it be known that on Monday, August 25, while the Marlins were in Chicago, newspaper delivery was officially cut off at the home of Jim Leyland in Parkland,

Florida. "I don't read the papers after August 25, when the pennant race starts," Leyland said.

And there you have it: The groundhog not seeing his shadow is the first sign of spring, Leyland no longer reading the newspapers is the first sign of a pennant race.

Presumably, he would stick to his no-newsprint vow longer than he did to no nicotine, no caffeine.

Whether or not the Marlins actually were in a pennant race could be debated. After going 6-3 on the homestand, they trailed the Braves by four games with thirty-four remaining. Since the All-Star break, they had made up a grand total of 2½ games. Since leaving Atlanta two weeks earlier, they had made up 1½. They hadn't been closer than three games back since late June.

For their part, the Marlins were convinced they had the Braves in their sights. They cared, deeply, about how the Braves fared each night. A week earlier, Tony Saunders was watching the Braves play the Cardinals on the clubhouse TV. When the Cardinals didn't score in the bottom of the tenth inning of a tied game, Saunders turned and walked out of the clubhouse muttering about "the fucking Braves." On Sunday, Daulton arrived at the stadium, glanced up at the TVs, and jokingly asked, "What game is this?" Of course, it was the Braves, whose games were always on.

Then Smiley, sitting in the manager's office, flipped to the Wisconsin-Syracuse football game on TV—Wisconsin is his alma mater—and Leyland said snidely, "You don't mind if we watch the Braves, do you?"

The Braves game it was.

◆ ◆ ◆

Cheryl Rosenberg, of the *Palm Beach Post,* wasn't present, but she was on Leyland's mind as he spoke with four reporters in the visitor's dugout at Wrigley Field prior to Monday night's game.

"Which of you guys," Leyland asked, "have fooled around with Cheryl?"

The reporters, all male, were dumbfounded. Dave O'Brien, from the *Sun-Sentinel,* asked Leyland, "What is *wrong* with you?" And the conversation moved along to a different topic.

◆ ◆ ◆

The Marlins opened the four-game series by losing to the Cubs, 3-1, but Livan Hernandez came back a day later and won his eighth straight decision, 11-0. The only alarming moment for the Marlins came in the third inning, when Ryne Sandberg of the Cubs tried to steal second and Charles Johnson's throw skipped into centerfield. Seemingly, there went Johnson's chance of becoming the first catcher in major league history to go through an entire season without committing an error or a passed ball.

But Johnson wasn't concerned. He had already heard the umpire call strike three for the third out of the inning. The throw didn't count. No error.

"Sometimes I just like to get a throw in," he explained.

◆ ◆ ◆

You have to like Gregg Zaun, even if you're Jim Leyland. The late August edition of Zaun's ESPN SportsZone movie reviews featured his "Top Five Chick Flicks," and Zaun wrote: "It has come to my attention that our female users, especially one named Fluffy, are a little offended by how sexist my column is. So I'm offering an olive branch, if you will, with a piece written especially for you feminists out there. Put out the flames of your brassiere bonfire, and listen to this. This one's for you, Fluffy."

Zaun's top five chick flicks were *Steel Magnolias* ("Total chick flick."), *Boys on the Side* ("I didn't buy Whoopi Goldberg as a lesbian."), *Beaches* (Al Bundy's least favorite movie; Zaun might be the only baseball player in the world who likes Bette Midler), *An Affair to Remember* ("Timeless, even though it was done way before I was born"), and *Thelma and Louise* (Driving off the cliff at the end was "a sissy thing to do.").

Leyland had yet to extend his olive branch to Zaun, who rarely started. Perhaps Zaun's crowning moment of the season was pinch-running for Johnson in the ninth inning of Wednesday's game at Wrigley Field, with the Marlins trailing, 3-2. Daulton singled to left, scoring Conine, and Zaun tried to score, too. He should have been out by ten feet, but the throw was a little off-line, and Zaun made a beautiful hooking, head-first slide to avoid the tag. The Marlins won, 4-3.

A week earlier, Leyland had been discussing Charles Johnson's chances of winning the Gold Glove and, just out of the blue he said, "I don't know. Zaun might vote for himself." Players don't vote on the Gold Glove, managers and coaches do. In all fairness to Zaun, it was a cheap shot by Leyland.

The Marlins had also asked Zaun to appear in the season highlights video they were preparing, although not in the traditional sense for scoring game-winning runs and throwing out baserunners. The idea was for Zaun to carry a camera onto the team plane and film a day in the life of a traveling baseball team. Zaun liked the idea, but said it would have to be cleared with the manager. The manager said no. Leyland also said no to a camera crew sitting in on a pre-series pitchers meeting. So at least he wasn't singling out anybody.

Zaun had participated in an on-line chat session on ESPN's SportsZone and when asked about realignment he said, "We'll leave realignment to the owners." So the message from Leyland had finally come through loud and clear. Good ol' Gregg Zaun. Wouldn't say shit if he had a mouthful.

◆ ◆ ◆

After splitting four games with the Cubs, the Marlins resumed inter-league play Friday, August 29 with a three-game series in Toronto. The visit to SkyDome—billed as "The World's Largest Entertainment Centre"—gave Don Smiley the opportunity to stand on the field, look up, and see what he wanted most: A retractable roof.

SkyDome is a monstrosity, a big, cement hunk with plastic grass and artificial dirt, planted on the edge of downtown Toronto. The stadium features a hotel with views of the field, several restaurants, and mini-McDonald's passing for concession stands. In SkyDome, fans have the opportunity to eat the most expensive french fries in the major leagues and Big Macs that cost more than decent seats in some ballparks. The way SkyDome treats baseball, you'd think Canadians were getting revenge against Americans for stealing hockey.

But it has that roof, a big, beautiful, retractable model that opens or closes in twenty minutes and keeps out rain, snow, and cold weather.

"I don't know about the place," Smiley decided, "But I like the roof a lot."

Smiley not only liked the roof and wanted one, but had long ago decided the Marlins couldn't survive in South Florida without a retractable roof stadium. There were too many rain delays, potential rainouts, and too many nights when the threat of rain hampered attendance. He had realized, along with the fans, that nothing in all of sports is more boring than sitting through a two-hour rain delay. There's only so much bad food, $4.50 beer, and *This Week In Baseball* a person can take.

Getting a stadium built was the second part of Smiley's plan. The first part was putting together an investment group—twenty or more owners at somewhere around $5 million to $7 million apiece—to buy the team from Huizenga. And that's what he had been doing since the All-Star break, going around, trying to scare up some money, and seeing if it was possible to save the franchise from the inside-out.

"The developments dictated, 'Hey, why don't you take a run at it?'" Smiley said. "I know how to operate the team. I helped fill out the expansion application and helped bring baseball to South Florida. I just want to take a crack at keeping it here, even if that means working night and day to get it done. If I'm not successful, I'll feel bad about that, but I'll never feel like I didn't try."

So, he started knocking on doors. After creating a list of likely candidates, he phoned each person to find out if they had any interest in becoming part owners of a major league team. That reduced his list to about fifty people. Then he met with the interested parties, one-by-one, and explained the terms of the deal.

Naturally, they had a lot of questions for Smiley, and the first was, "Why would we succeed where Huizenga failed?"

Smiley's answer to that question centered on the stadium issue. His strategy was to put together a group of businessmen with enough political power and influence to get a stadium built for them.

"If you have a group of people asking for support, that's much different than one individual," Smiley said.

By early September, it was clear South Florida's baseball future hinged on Smiley successfully implementing both parts of his plan. There had been no local offers to purchase the team. If Smiley couldn't put together a group, Huizenga would likely sell the team to outside investors, who would move it to another city. Even if Smiley's potential group did buy the team, there was no guarantee the Marlins would remain in South Florida, unless a local government built a stadium for them.

"If that doesn't get done, we'll have to deal with the alternative, and the alternative is to move the team," Smiley said.

As for the 1998 season, it didn't matter whether Huizenga or Smiley's group owned the team. Player payroll would be reduced significantly, perhaps by $20 million, as the Marlins relied more heavily on the strong minor league system they had developed over their five seasons. The wild free-agent spending of the previous winter would not be repeated for a long time, if ever. The 1997 Marlins were a one-season creation.

◆ ◆ ◆

Just in case Smiley's plan didn't pan out, there was the Marlins Relocation Search Committee, which was formed to find a city outside South Florida that might want a baseball team. The Marlins Relocation Search Committee wasn't a real committee, nor was it associated with the Marlins who, according to Huizenga and Smiley, weren't looking for a place to relocate. It was the creation of the *New Times,* an alternative weekly out of Miami that came up with the amusing idea of doing the Marlins' dirty work for them.

The Marlins, by the way, did not find it amusing.

Among the cities receiving letters were Providence, Rhode Island; Fresno, California; Portland, Oregon; Gary, Indiana; Nashville; Biloxi, Mississippi; and Kokomo, Indiana. When the mayor of Nashville phoned the Marlins' Pro Player Stadium office, rather than the Relocation Committee headquarters—which were located in the editorial office of the *New Times*—the Marlins caught onto the ruse and had their lawyer write the paper a threatening letter. The *New Times* responded with a phone call, during which the following conversation took place:

MARLINS ATTORNEY: Why didn't you say in the letter that you were with the *New Times*?

NEW TIMES: Well, people might not have called us back.

ATTORNEY: Why did you say you were authorized by the Florida Marlins to gauge interest in the team relocating?

NEW TIMES: We never said we were authorized. We said we were empowered.

ATTORNEY: All right, empowered. Why did you say that you were empowered by the Florida Marlins to gauge interest?

NEW TIMES: We didn't say we were empowered by the Florida Marlins. We just said we were empowered.

ATTORNEY: Now you sound like an attorney. So who empowered you?

NEW TIMES: We always believed that empowerment starts with the self. So in that sense, we empowered ourselves to gauge interest.

After a few more threatening words from the attorney, the Marlins Relocation Search Committee was disbanded. Temporarily, at least.

◆ ◆ ◆

In a preview of life in a retractable roof stadium, the Marlins won all three games from the Blue Jays. Leiter, who had pitched three full seasons for the Blue Jays, returned to boos and pitched six shutout innings in an 8-0 victory. The next night, Fernandez won his seventeenth game, 4-1. In the finale, an 8-3 Marlins victory, Hernandez became the first rookie since Whitey Ford in 1950 to start a season with a 9-0 record.

Cuban historical baseball sidelight: Santiago, the old fisherman in Hemingway's *The Old Man and the Sea,* had heard of Joe DiMaggio, but Hernandez had never heard of Whitey Ford. If Hernandez had done his research, he would have learned Ford is the all-time winningest pitcher in Yankees history. So Hernandez, although he didn't know it, was in pretty good company.

NATIONAL LEAGUE EAST STANDINGS

	W	L	Pct.	GB
Atlanta	85	51	.625	—
Marlins	**80**	**55**	**.593**	**4.5**
New York	73	62	.541	11.5
Montreal	67	68	.496	17.5
Philadelphia	50	82	.379	33

13

That's Over. O-V-E-R.

September 1, 2, 3 vs. Orioles
September 5, 6, 7, 8 at Los Angeles
September 9, 10 at San Diego

September arrived along with the Baltimore Orioles for the Marlins' final three inter-league games of the season. The Orioles had the best record in the major leagues, and it wasn't unreasonable to think Marlins vs. Baltimore was a World Series preview. Pro Player Stadium would have big crowds for all three games.

The Marlins had opened a lead of six games over San Francisco in the wild card race while the Mets, who had chased them into early August, had fallen seven games behind. The Mets' woes were predictable: Their pitching had fallen apart and a trade with the Cubs turned out to be a disaster.

Less predictable were the Mets' clubhouse problems. For months they appeared to be a close-knit, overachieving team, but then the losses piled up and manager Bobby Valentine moved into the headlines, first by questioning catcher Todd Hundley's sleeping habits, then by feuding publicly with pitcher Pete Harnisch.

Valentine had never been capable of overcoming his run-ins with the players, while Orioles manager Davey Johnson seemed to thrive on them, as if it was his style: Keep things interesting, keep the players on their toes.

Management by confrontation is a style contrary to the one preferred by Jim Leyland, whose record was nearly clean in twelve seasons of big league managing. Never had he scrapped with a player in the media, nor had a player ever called a radio station to criticize him. Barry Bonds, the one player he did briefly engage in a public dispute in Pittsburgh, always went out of his way to visit Leyland whenever the Giants were in town. Certainly, Leyland had managed a handful of players whom he didn't care for and who didn't care for him—even a few on the Marlins—but they would have never been foolish enough to identify themselves publicly. For good reason.

Leyland's network of friends in baseball spreads wide and includes some of the most respected people in the business: Huizenga, White Sox owner Jerry Reinsdorf, Gene Lamont, Tony La Russa, Bobby Cox, and Joe Torre. Many of those he can't count as friends respect his opinion, so his power and influence extend far beyond his own clubhouse. When a friend such as Don Zimmer or La Russa came to Miami, Leyland often spent as much time during batting practice on the visiting team's side as his own.

Leyland's strengths are his hard work and thorough preparation, keeping his players happy, and instilling a team concept by keeping everyone involved. There is a well-thought-out reason for everything he does on the field. Almost every player on the Marlins was playing at least a few times a week, relief pitchers were rarely overused or underused, and every player knew that he was of some value to the team. Leyland promised during spring training that it would take all twenty-five players or more to win, and he was true to his word.

Even Conine had resigned himself to being a part-time player, and a team player, too, as long as winning was the reward. He got to spend more time than he wanted on the bench, watching Leyland, and marveled at how the manager would always be a step ahead of the game, telling coaches to remind players of this and that. Frequently, what Leyland had warned them about would actually happen.

"He was always prepared and he was always reminding us to be prepared," Conine said.

On one hand, it was easy to see why Leyland's teams in Pittsburgh came close, but never reached the World Series. Leyland is a jittery man whose presence is by no means soothing, and that can rub off on his players. During the first four months of the season, up until the eight games against the Braves, the Marlins were a tight, nervous team, a reflection of their manager. After a game in June that the Marlins won after nearly wasting a big lead, Leyland said he was looking forward to an easy win so he could relax. When the Marlins finally did win big one night, Leyland was asked whether he enjoyed the game.

"No," he answered.

"Do you ever relax?"

"To be honest, no. Maybe one time, early this season."

His personality was revealed when he admitted he didn't like the suicide squeeze because "every time I put it on, it feels like a thousand years before the play happens." In other words, Leyland didn't like the apprehension. He hadn't used the squeeze all season. He rarely attempted double steals. Leyland was at his most daring when he played his Bomb Squad of bench players. He took his chances at the racetrack.

Although the players rarely spoke about Leyland, most of them liked and respected him. They didn't see, or didn't care about, Leyland's run-ins with the media and treatment of front office staffers, his crass behavior and remarks, his Jekyll and Hyde personality. Leyland scored high on the factors most important to players: He let them play and usually made the right decisions. He supported them when they lost and when times were tough. He treated them like adults and didn't make a lot of rules.

"Yeah, I have a curfew," Leyland said a few weeks earlier in Atlanta. "But I can also tell you this: In the last eighteen years I've managed, I haven't done a bed check, and I ain't gonna start now."

Bonilla, the staunchest Leyland supporter on the team, often said he liked Leyland as a manager because he left him alone and let him do his job. That was all.

189

"In all the years we've been together, he really doesn't say too much," Bonilla said, hardly describing a surrogate father and son relationship. But Bonilla also revealed the depths of his respect for Leyland when he said, "I know our manager would like to win a World Series, and I'd like to be there with him."

With twenty-seven games remaining in the regular season, Leyland's chances were as good as they had ever been. The tense atmosphere around the team had loosened with the arrival of Daulton and Counsell, and the players were finally looking upon the pennant race as an enjoyable challenge, rather than a life-or-death ordeal. Even Floyd, who returned to the team on September 1 with the annual expansion of major league rosters, felt the change.

"Everybody's relaxing," Floyd said. "I expected to come in and see everybody tense."

Well, not everybody was relaxing. The Marlins beat the Orioles, 10-4, in the first game of the series Monday, but afterward Leyland looked as nervous as he had been all season. The Marlins had retained their six game lead over the Giants, while moving a game closer to the end of the season, but for Leyland, the end wasn't in sight.

"It looks like we're there," he reminded everyone, "but we're not."

He would never allow himself to relax and, yet, that's exactly what he wanted his players to do. Somehow, even if wasn't of his own doing, he had achieved that goal. But Leyland had been in this situation before, with a talented team on its way to the playoffs, capable of winning it all if it got a few breaks here and there. He had never won, had never even been to the World Series, and now he was facing another test with a team that was built to win. No wonder he was so high-strung.

The next morning, after sleeping on the couch in his office, Leyland ended his newspaper fast by reading the sports sections of the local papers.

"I couldn't help it," he explained. That came as no surprise at all.

◆ ◆ ◆

Floyd hit a three-run homer Monday in his first at-bat since returning from the minors and the next morning was a guest on the local sports talk radio station. So Leyland commented, "The guy's got one home run in eight months and they got him on Oprah Winfrey."

◆ ◆ ◆

Of course, there was a rain delay of one hour, forty-six minutes in the bottom of the second inning.

"Inter-league rain," Jim Ross called it, remembering clearly the rain that spoiled the Yankees series in June.

Most of the sellout crowd stayed through the rain delay and got to see Devon White hit a grand slam in the bottom of the sixth inning, but when the game finally ended at 9:30, White was in no mood to bask in the media glory of his accomplishment.

"It's been a long game," White said, "and that means it's time for me to go home."

And then Devon White, friend of the media, just walked away, leaving a group of stunned reporters staring into their notebooks.

◆ ◆ ◆

Inevitably, every time there was a long rain delay—which only seemed like every night—the talk the next day would be about the need for a retractable roof stadium. On Tuesday, Leyland expounded upon his vision: The budget retractable roof stadium. Kind of like a bed and breakfast for the stadium set.

"If I was involved, it would be something like Wrigley Field, a smaller stadium without all the gingerbread, and a retractable roof. New but old," Leyland said.

Gingerbread?

"Gingerbread," he explained. "Bars, hotels, restaurants, fancy sky boxes. The things you don't need. I don't think."

While they were at it, a ban on free-agency and a rollback of the major league minimum salary to $10,000 a year might have been a good idea, too.

◆ ◆ ◆

The Marlins beat the Orioles, 3-2, Tuesday in a game that was memorable for several reasons. In the first inning, Rafael Palmeiro of Baltimore drove a Kevin Brown fastball down the rightfield line and halfway up the fence. But that's not how first base umpire Bruce Froemming saw it. He saw the ball go over the fence. So he missed the call by only five feet. At least he had the grace to admit his mistake the next day. Froemming had watched the replay after the game and was horrified by what he saw.

Of course, not admitting his mistake would have been all the proof anybody needed that Froemming was legally blind.

Then in the seventh inning, with the Marlins trailing 2-0 and not doing anything against Orioles righty Mike Mussina, Bonilla came to bat and bunted, of all things. It was a beauty, right down the third base line, and Cal Ripken Jr. was playing far too deep to have any chance of making the play. Bonilla chugged as hard as he could to first base and when he got there, Palmeiro, his former teammate, grabbed him in an armlock and patted him on the head. Alou hit a two-run homer to tie the score and Renteria won it on a single in the tenth.

After the game, a replay of Bonilla's bunt was shown on the clubhouse TVs, and Bonilla's teammates were razzing him about his running style: Arms churning, legs lifted high, going as fast and hard as his 240-pound body would allow him to go. And Bonilla, who also watched and laughed, struck a statuesque pose like a football player running and said, "That's my Heisman style."

◆ ◆ ◆

Here's a touching scene: After many home games, Craig Counsell walked out to the players' parking lot with his father, John, on one side, and his mother, Jan, on the other. Jan and John Counsell lived year-round in Fort Myers, on Florida's west coast and, until this season, they had seen no more than ten of their son's minor league games in five years. And now they had seen ten games in two months.

It was easy to spot Jan and John Counsell in the hallway outside the clubhouse after games. Besides being the oldest people there—most of the players had wives, girlfriends, and children waiting—they were also the ones with the widest smiles. They would drive from Fort Myers every night, then drive back after the game, about a four-hour round trip. Craig, who had no idea where he would be playing in 1998, and had a good idea it wouldn't be Miami, was living by himself in a Fort Lauderdale hotel.

"They're the only people I know down here," Counsell said. "It's one of the great things about playing here, that my Mom and Dad get to see me."

Even better was that John and Jan Counsell got to see their son hit .340 and become a crowd favorite because of his hustle and fine fielding at second base. Even his manager liked him.

◆ ◆ ◆

Leyland revealed Wednesday afternoon he planned on bringing up a pitcher from the minor leagues for Friday night's game in Los Angeles. He wouldn't, however, reveal the pitcher's name, or offer any clues.

"His name is pitcher," he said. "That's P-I-T-C-H-E-R."

And Steve Wine from the Associated Press asked, "Does he have ten fingers or twelve?"

Antonio Alfonseca, the only twelve-fingered pitcher in the organization, was already up with the Marlins and faring quite well with a 2.38 ERA in eleven innings. He had relieved Saunders in the fifth inning of Monday's game with two on and one out, allowed only one of the runs to score, then pitched a scoreless sixth inning. Leyland just couldn't figure out how he was doing it.

"He doesn't know what the fuck he's doing out there," Leyland said. "He has no idea. None. He just gets up there and throws."

Then he paused.

"He's better off that way."

By the way, P-I-T-C-H-E-R turned out to be S-T-A-N-I-F-E-R.

◆ ◆ ◆

The roof above the visitor's dugout collapsed before the bottom of the third inning of Wednesday night's game against the Orioles. A member of the Bleacher Brigade bounced up and down on top of the roof, teasing the fans with the promise of free T-shirts, when a thirty-foot portion broke off. Incredibly, nobody was hurt because most of the Orioles on the bench had just gone onto the field for the bottom of the inning. It took twelve grounds crew members to cart off the fallen slab, and Orioles pitcher Mike Mussina later said, "If anybody had been sitting at the end of the dugout or standing there, they'd be $100 million richer. If they lived."

The incident shattered Dave Dombrowski's long-standing belief that, if he left his box between innings and went downstairs for a cup of coffee, the stadium would look exactly the same when he returned as it did when he left. It reminded him of the time in 1979, when he was working for the Chicago White Sox, and owner Bill Veeck held Disco Demolition Night at old Comiskey Park. Dombrowski left the press box between games, but when he returned, he looked out and saw a huge bonfire of burning vinyl records where shortstop used to be.

"The press box there was all the way at the top of the stadium and I remember thinking, 'This place is gonna burn down,'" Dombrowski recalled. "I was trying to figure how I was going to get out of there alive. They finally put out the fire, but there was this big ditch at shortstop and we had another game to play. Bill was down there on the field trying to convince the umpires that we could play."

Veeck, one of baseball's all-time great promoters and talkers, failed to convince, and the White Sox forfeited the game. Since then there have been no more Disco Demolition nights anywhere in baseball and no bonfires on the field between games.

There are, however, Bleacher Brigades, at least at Pro Player Stadium. Basically, the Bleacher Brigade is what happens when you take a bunch of aerobics instructors, dress them up like forest rangers, and turn them loose in a ballpark with slingshots and T-shirts. Although it appeared from their frantic, frighteningly hyperactive behavior that they had all ingested some marvelous combination of illicit drugs, all of them had been subjected to stringent, pre-hiring drug testing. The fans, however, had not been, and they habitually reacted to the mere sight of the Bleacher Brigade as if there was nothing in the world they wanted more than a cheap cotton T-shirt with the Marlins logo on the front. They reacted like Pavlov's dog to a dinner bell.

◆ ◆ ◆

Sheffield hit a home run in the bottom of the ninth inning to beat the Orioles, 7-6, Wednesday night and complete a sweep of the best team in the American League. At first, Sheffield thought he had hit the ball too high, but then it kept carrying, and suddenly the Marlins were only 2½ games behind the Braves. As Sheffield trotted around third base, he saw his teammates waiting for him at home plate and broke into a wide grin, then he pumped his fist and fell into their arms.

"It was one of the best times of my life," Sheffield said.

It was one of the best times in franchise history. The Marlins felt like champions, their confidence had soared, and later Dombrowski was asked what he thought about inter-league play.

"Let's just hope we have some more of it here this year," he said.

He was talking about the World Series.

◆ ◆ ◆

The biggest problem facing the Marlins when they arrived at Dodger Stadium Friday afternoon, September 5, was the lack of entertainment in the visitor's clubhouse. No stereo. Bonilla and Daulton discussed the problem, then dispatched assistant equipment manager Matt Rosenthal to the nearest appliance store. After the game a nice, shiny new boom box was sitting in the Marlins' clubhouse.

It went unused. The Dodgers beat the Marlins, 7-4, on an off night for Fernandez and a shaky night for Sheffield. The Dodgers, trailing 4-3, had two on and one out in the fifth when Todd Zeile lofted what appeared to be a harmless fly ball to right-field. But Sheffield turned the wrong way, then stumbled going back to the wall, and turned the potential out into a two-run single.

Afterward, Leyland refused to condemn Sheffield, but Fernandez, when asked whether Sheffield should have caught the ball, answered, "What do you think?" And then he said, "I knew he didn't hit it well. It was a fly ball." Sheffield blamed it on his latest injury, a bad back, which he said he suffered on a check swing earlier in the game. Right then, the scene would have been perfect if Leyland walked by and barked, "We don't need any fucking heroes," but he didn't.

◆ ◆ ◆

The Marlins blew a 5-0 lead Saturday afternoon and lost to the Dodgers, 9-5. Cliff Floyd had his career day with two two-run homers, and the interview requests from Letterman and Leno, not to mention Oprah, figured to be pouring in any minute. Besides that, it was a dismal afternoon for the Marlins.

The highlight of the game came afterwards. A Korean TV reporter covering Chan Ho Park, the Dodgers' Korean pitcher, wandered into the Marlins' clubhouse and, with cameras rolling, asked John Cangelosi the following question: "Which Dodgers pitcher is the easiest to hit?"

Now there's a question no baseball player in any frame of mind would ever dare answer, especially with the Dodgers looming as the Marlins' possible first-round playoff opponent, so Cangelosi didn't answer the question. Instead he said bluntly, "That's a stupid question." And Kevin Brown, standing in the next locker, told the reporter, "Fuck off." He was extremely proud of his response. He kept boasting about it. Every time a teammate walked by, he'd re-tell the story.

It was a bad day for the Marlins, but a good day for sarcasm. Alou was asked whether he lost an eighth inning flyball in the sun and said, "No, I lost it right in the fucking moon."

Resiliency was proving to be the Marlins' greatest asset. The loss was a damaging one because the Braves would win later and extend their lead to four games, but the Marlins handled it well. The clubhouse was quiet for ten minutes after the game, until Devon White walked over and turned on the stereo. Bonilla sang, players joked and made dinner plans for the evening, and only one of them sat in front of his locker with his head hung: Dennis Cook, who was icing down his arm after a poor performance. The Marlins no longer treated each loss as devastating, as they had during the first four months of the season. They had learned to relax and enjoy the pennant race.

The same could not be said of their manager, who with the first of September had instituted a new rule prohibiting reporters from interviewing players during batting practice. He didn't want them distracted. He also didn't like it when a crew from the cable TV station Comedy Central showed up at Dodger Stadium Saturday morning to film comedy bits with Zaun, Bonilla, and Sheffield. The show went on—the Dodgers refused to participate—but not before Leyland expressed his feelings about such "goofy shit."

Then the Fox Network, which was televising Saturday's game, wanted Zaun to wear their helmet cam, which offers viewers a catcher's-eye view of the action. Leyland's reaction was, "No, let Piazza wear it." Piazza, the Dodgers' catcher, did not wear the helmet cam, which was fair enough. But Leyland had allowed Charles Johnson to wear the helmet cam earlier in the season, so it was easy to believe that Leyland's refusal had less to do with the device itself than with his reluctance to allow Zaun an afternoon in the spotlight.

◆ ◆ ◆

Sign of status: Most major league clubhouses are built for twenty-five players, so roster expansion on September 1 can lead to a crowded situation, especially at Dodger Stadium, where the visitor's clubhouse is narrow to begin with. The Marlins made room by cramming three temporary wire lockers into the middle of the clubhouse and assigning the stalls to Mike Wallace, the equipment manager, Marcelino Lugo, the bullpen catcher, and Kurt Miller, the pitcher. That's good company for the equipment manager and the bullpen catcher, bad company for the pitcher.

Leyland was being careful about how he used Miller. The 25-year-old right-hander had undergone elbow surgery the previous December and pitched only twenty-seven innings in the minors all season, so he wasn't in condition to pitch several days in a row. A week before, Leyland had replaced the struggling Miller with Ed Vosberg in the middle of an at-bat and later explained, "I didn't know Vosberg could get out of it, but I knew for sure Miller could not." Vosberg got out of it.

Miller's hard times continued Saturday. He entered in the eighth inning with the score tied and allowed the game-winning home run to Todd Zeile, which pushed his ERA to 13.50. Miller wasn't feeling too good about himself as he sat alone in the dugout after getting removed from the game, and nobody consoled him. Nobody except Leyland, who walked to the opposite end of the dugout and patted him on the shoulder. Suddenly, Miller felt less alone.

◆ ◆ ◆

Tony Saunders not only lost his spot in the pitching rotation because of his performance in a 9-5 loss to the Dodgers Sunday afternoon, he jeopardized his chances of pitching in the first round of the playoffs. Saunders, who hadn't beaten any team but the Braves all season and hadn't lasted past the sixth inning since August 10, allowed seven runs in 1⅓ innings, and afterward said, "If I keep pitching the way I am, they gotta do something, because they can't keep putting me out there."

Saunders wasn't surprised the next day when Leyland called him into his office and told him he would miss his next start.

"He seemed relieved," Leyland said.

That's exactly how Saunders seemed Monday evening before the final game of the Dodgers series. Ever since the series in Atlanta, he had been trying to figure out what was going wrong and, as he called it, "beating myself up." His teammates had tried to support and encourage him. After Saturday's game, Daulton and Leiter came by his locker and said, "Pick us up, Tony," but then he went out the next day and let down his teammates again. The way Saunders saw it, the team was in a pennant race, and here he was stuck in this disturbing psychological funk.

"We're trying to win a pennant and I'm going out there every fifth day and getting my ass kicked," Saunders said, breaking into a sardonic grin. "My whole life, this is the worst I've been. This is flat bottom. You want respect from your teammates and lately I haven't been earning it."

Although most of his teammates considered him to be a cocky rookie, Saunders is among the most honest and self-deprecating athletes you'll find anywhere. Even in July, when he was allowing one or two runs a game and losing because the Marlins didn't give him any support, Saunders blamed himself. And in August, when things really deteriorated, he started bringing his problems home, which was a real change because until then he and his wife had never talked baseball. She wasn't much help.

Nobody was. The best answer Leyland could offer was support and a way out.

"He needs a buddy right now," Leyland said. "I'm not going to go have dinner with him or anything, but I am going to be here for him. You don't criticize a team when they lose. That's when they need support. In fact, I'm more apt to get on their ass when they win."

As for the playoffs, although Saunders' chances of pitching in the first round were diminishing, he figured to get a start against the Braves, the one team he had dominated, if the Marlins played Atlanta in the National League Championship Series. The way Saunders saw it, the situation could have been worse.

"Hey, I'm still here, ain't I?" he said. "I'm still in the major leagues."

He didn't sound too confident about his long-term prospects for that, either.

◆ ◆ ◆

The Marlins tried, but failed, to blow another big lead Monday night. They took a 4-0 lead in the first inning on home runs by Sheffield and Alou, but Brown wasn't having his best game and the lead had been cut to 5-4 after eight innings. Then Conine hit a three-run homer in the ninth and the Marlins salvaged one game against the Dodgers.

The conversation after the game came around to whether these four games were a precursor of what might happen if the teams met in the first round of the playoffs and, naturally, both sides were mixed in their opinions. Dodgers manager Bill Russell thought his team had sent the Marlins a message, but if it had, the Marlins didn't get it. Or so they said.

◆ ◆ ◆

Leyland broke his rule about not publicly criticizing a player. The Marlins gave Leiter a 6-0 lead over the Padres in San Diego Tuesday night, but he couldn't hold it, even against a Padres lineup that was missing Tony Gwynn and Wally Joyner. The Marlins eventually lost the game, 7-6, in thirteen innings, long after Leiter had departed with a 6-4 lead, and later Leyland wasn't concerned with the fact that the Marlins managed only two hits in the final nine innings.

"We let them back in the game," Leyland said as he picked at his food. "If you're the starting pitcher, you gotta bury that fucking game." Then he looked long and hard at a reporter and said it again: "You gotta bury that fucking game."

In all other cases all season, Leyland had defended his players by saying things like, "That's baseball," or pointing out something else that had gone wrong in the game, but he was in no mood to defend a pitcher who walked the leadoff man with a 6-0 lead and did it again with a 6-2 lead. But you had to wonder if he would have made the same comment if the pitcher was Brown or Fernandez. Then again, Brown and Fernandez had not blown 6-0 leads this season.

Leiter's teammates weren't any softer on him. A reporter pointed out that the Marlins shouldn't have allowed the Padres to come back, and Daulton said, "Especially against that lineup. No Gwynn, no Joyner."

The Marlins had been wasting leads all road trip: 3-1 and 5-0 against the Dodgers, then 6-0 against San Diego, and their pitching staff, which had carried them all season, was slumping. Naturally, Leyland noticed. The next afternoon, he was sitting in the dugout talking to Edgar Renteria when pitching coach Larry Rothschild walked by.

"How ya doing, Larry?" Leyland said.

"Fine," Rothschild answered.

"If we score seven runs tonight, think you can fucking hold it this time?"

Leyland said it with a smile, but clearly he was only half joking.

◆ ◆ ◆

Bonilla was sitting in the clubhouse prior to Wednesday night's game and the conversation came around to the Most Valuable Player balloting. Bonilla couldn't understand how the Marlins, who had the second best record in the National League, didn't have an MVP candidate, so he began campaigning for Alou.

"We don't even have a mention of a guy," Bonilla said. "That's what's really bothering me, not to have any of our guys mentioned. There was a lot more pressure on us than any other team."

Bonilla didn't expect Alou to win the award, not with Mike Piazza of the Dodgers and Larry Walker of the Rockies each batting over .350, but the way he saw it, MVP meant Most Valuable Player to a team. Alou was batting close to .300 with one hundred seven RBIs, even though the Marlins lacked a productive leadoff hitter for most of the season.

Bonilla stated his case, a few reporters and TV guys nodded in agreement, and the subject was never brought up again.

◆ ◆ ◆

The pennant race ended, for all intents and purposes, Wednesday night in San Diego. The Marlins didn't give Fernandez seven runs, they only gave him two, and although they tied the game in the eighth inning on a double by Bonilla, they lost it in the bottom of the ninth when Vosberg allowed his first run as a Marlin in eleven appearances. The Braves beat the Dodgers for the second straight night and extended their lead on the Marlins to 6½ games with only eighteen remaining. Over. The Marlins knew it, and afterward they offered what sounded like a retrospective on the season: The Braves had beaten the teams they were supposed to beat, the Marlins hadn't. Now they had to worry about holding on for the wild card spot.

The road trip had been a total loss for the Marlins. They left South Florida trailing the Braves by only 2½ games and feeling good about sweeping the Orioles. But the pitching had broken down, the hitting hadn't come through when it had to and, finally, the breaks hadn't gone their way. In the bottom of the ninth of the second game in San Diego, Steve Finley was barely grazed by a fastball, giving the Padres runners on first and second, then Gwynn bounced a single just past the outstretched glove of Renteria for the winning run.

"We went out to the west coat and got our asses kicked," Bonilla said. "No hidden secrets. Every once in a while, shit happens, and shit has been happening all week."

They couldn't wait to get home.

NATIONAL LEAGUE EAST STANDINGS

	W	L	Pct.	GB
Atlanta	91	54	.628	—
Marlins	**84**	**60**	**.583**	**6.5**
New York	79	66	.545	12
Montreal	73	72	.503	18
Philadelphia	58	85	.406	32

14

"That'll Get You an Atta Boy"

September 12, 13, 14 vs. San Francisco
September 15, 16 vs. Colorado
September 17 (2), 18 vs. Philadelphia
September 19, 20, 21, 22 vs. Mets
September 23, 24, 25 at Montreal
September 26, 27, 28 at Philadelphia

Manager's day off: The Marlins' plane touched down at Fort Lauderdale-Hollywood International Airport at 9 a.m., then Leyland drove home and slept for a few hours. He got up and tried to play golf with third base coach Rich Donnelly, but the rain got in their way. By that time, Leyland was in a bad mood, so he went home and, with his wife and children up in Pittsburgh, played housekeeper. He dusted the house, vacuumed the floors, and did the laundry. Then he watched a college football game on TV and went to sleep.

The next day, Leyland hosted the Marlins Managers Annual Luncheon in Little Havana, although hosted is a strong word to describe what he did. In reality, he was dragged there. He said he had a good time, but he didn't like the fact that only two other people from the front office came with him, and he certainly didn't like being placed in a non-smoking section of the restaurant. Every ten minutes, he had to get up and step outside for a cigarette.

Then Leyland gave a speech in English—"with a little Spanish thrown in just to tease them," he said—and, as usual when he does this kind of thing, charmed everyone in the room. He told stories about his times as a manager in Venezuela. When a balloon popped, he joked that he thought "somebody was trying to shoot me because of the road trip we just had."

Leyland is a pro at giving speeches to large groups of people. One of Tony La Russa's most vivid memories is of Leyland wearing a hideously bright, canary yellow tuxedo as the MC of the White Sox's coming home dinner in Sarasota back in 1983. There was Leyland, up on the dais with his small, thin body and fuzzy mustache, telling jokes while wearing a Don Knotts outfit and cracking up the room. Give him credit, the man is shameless.

199

Later at the ballpark, Leyland was asked whether the team needed the day off, and he was quite adamant in his reply that it didn't. "If anyone's tired out there, there's something wrong with them," Leyland said. "I'm not tired."

Tired of days off, maybe, but he didn't have to worry about filling any more of them. The Marlins had no more for the rest of the regular season.

◆ ◆ ◆

Charles Johnson broke the major league record for consecutive errorless games by a catcher Friday night, September 12, with one hundred sixty. It might be the most boring record in all of sports, unless you're the catcher's wife or his father. Johnson himself didn't seem overwhelmed by the feat. A few days earlier in San Diego, he had been talking about the record and asked, "How close am I?" Then he held up his left hand and said, "I honestly don't know, on my grandfather's grave."

Catchers have fewer chances to make errors than any other player on the field, and on Johnson's record night, he fielded one popup and didn't have a single opposing runner attempt to steal. The crowd of 30,964 at Pro Player Stadium wasn't exactly holding its collective breath in anticipation, and offered no recognition of his feat when Johnson batted in the ninth inning.

But after the game, a large crowd of reporters gathered around Johnson's locker and waited while Charles and his father embraced warmly. The force of that hug must have been enormous. All it takes is one shake of Charles Johnson Sr.'s hand to know where his son got the strength to throw out runners from his knees and hit batting practice home runs into the upper deck. Reconstructive surgery on the bones in the shaking hand feels like the only option after getting caught in C. J. Sr.'s vise-like grip.

Johnson's father is a high school teacher in Fort Pierce, Florida, and Tuesday night he had stayed up late, far past his normal bed time, to watch his son's game from San Diego. He was a nervous wreck all night. The Padres kept getting runners on first, and when Quilvio Veras walked in the fifth inning, Charles Sr. was certain he would try to steal second. Veras stayed put. Then, in the thirteenth inning, Steve Finley did steal second, and Counsell had to prevent Johnson's throw from bouncing into the outfield. The game finally ended at 2:45 a.m. in the east, and Senior had to get up two and a half hours later to teach school.

Charles Sr. wasn't nearly as nervous Friday night, although he had no idea why. It might have been from being around his son, who always appears cool and never shows any signs of nerves, especially when he is playing.

"I always tried to teach him, never to be afraid to make a throw," Charles Sr. said. "You can't be afraid out there."

Another thing Charles Sr. taught C. J. was to accept good and bad the same way, with an even approach. So as Charles Jr. stood patiently and answered one question after another, smiling kindly but otherwise showing no emotion, Charles Sr. watched from a few feet away and nodded. He couldn't have been prouder.

◆ ◆ ◆

South Florida's tepid response to the wild card race was thirteen thousand empty seats on a pleasant Friday night for a game against a team directly behind the Marlins, the San Francisco Giants. But not to worry. Outside the stadium, the Marlins' players' wives sold black and teal maracas for charity in what a press release called an attempt to increase "team spirit and excitement for post-season play." And Leyland snapped, "Why are they selling pom-poms? We haven't won anything yet."

Then the Marlins went out and lost to the Giants, 1-0, as Livan Hernandez suffered his first major league loss, through no fault of his own. An error by Conine led to the only San Francisco run. The loss was the sixth in seven games for the Marlins, who no longer reacted calmly to defeat. Team spirit was low and the pom-poms hadn't worked their magic.

After the game, the clubhouse doors closed for fifteen minutes, and Daulton again addressed the team. Then Bonilla grabbed a bat, walked down to the indoor cages, and took batting practice for forty-five minutes. It was the classic response to late-season turmoil: Hold a meeting, practice harder.

Another classic response to late-season turmoil is hold no meetings and practice less.

Or hold no meetings and practice harder.

Or practice less and hold meetings.

The effectiveness of any of these methods was impossible to judge, because teams had won and lost by trying any of the four. What they're doing is playing mind games with themselves.

"It's all speculation," Kevin Brown agreed. "You do it because you think it's going to help and the only way to know is to do it. This game has its ups and downs. We came off a huge high, playing so well, then coming home and beating Baltimore three times, and then we went out there on the west coast and, for whatever reason, we got bad breaks. The thing is, you want to make sure that no one's leaving anything at this point in time. Everybody's got to give everything they've got, so we said, 'Let's not leave anything hanging. If we go down, let's go down fighting. If we win, let's win it busting our asses, and forget the bad breaks we've had.'"

The next afternoon, Brown pitched a three-hitter, White hit two home runs, Alou hit a 458-foot homer into the second deck, and the Marlins won, 8-1. Whether the team meeting had anything to do with their success was impossible to judge, but the Marlins weren't asking questions.

◆ ◆ ◆

Zaun walked into the dugout forty-five minutes before Saturday afternoon's game, looked up into the seats, saw a mostly empty stadium, and decided, "You know where they oughta move this team to? Charlotte, North Carolina."

Fortunately for Zaun, the manager wasn't around to hear that remark.

Unfortunately for the Marlins, the stadium never filled up. Only 30,311, the Marlins' smallest Saturday turnout of the season, showed up on a beautiful, pleasant afternoon. Nobody, particularly vice president of sales and marketing Jim Ross, could figure out why attendance was so low for a game against a possible playoff opponent, although reasonable excuses included the lack of a giveaway item, and the University of Miami football team's home opener against Arizona State. Either way, a contending team shouldn't have to give things away in mid-September, and Miami football hadn't been a big draw in years.

BIG CLUE: *Jim Ross flashback, early July: "The jury is out on whether fans get captivated by a wild card race. It hasn't been the case yet in other cities."*

Well, guess what? South Florida was no different.

Unaffected by the small crowd was the sale of maracas; more than fifteen hundred had been sold on Friday and Saturday. Also unaffected was Don Smiley's optimism about putting together a group of investors to buy the team. "Whit" Hudson, Huizenga's brother-in-law, had recently identified himself as a possible investor and Smiley had just returned from a trip during which he tried to round up a few dozen more.

Anyway, Smiley was sitting in the media dining room, talking about his trip, when somebody jested, "I've got five dollars in my pocket. What'll that get me?"

"That'll get you an atta boy," Smiley responded. "And a thanks for your concern."

The Charlotte suggestion was not passed along, although it was not unreasonable. Don Beaver, a businessman from nearby Jupiter, had been leading a group of fifty to bring a major league team to North Carolina, and they didn't care whether it was an expansion team or an existing team. Their focus at the time was on the Minnesota Twins.

Beaver had not inquired about buying the Marlins, nor had he been asked to become a part of Smiley's ownership group. He did, however, make a point of expressing his support for Smiley's efforts. So atta boy, Don. Thanks for your concern.

◆ ◆ ◆

Charlotte was looking better every day. With the Dolphins playing on the road against the Super Bowl champion Green Bay Packers, only 28,610 showed up on Sunday for the finale of the Giants series. The Dolphins game came on TV at 1 p.m. and ended at about 4. The Marlins game started thirty-five minutes later, plenty of time for anyone who cared to make it to the ballpark. Obviously, not a lot of people cared.

◆ ◆ ◆

Nonetheless, maracas sales continued along at a healthy pace. The problem was that the maracas—as one Marlins front office employee helpfully pointed out—didn't make a lot of noise. Quiet maracas. The manufacturer had skimped on the beads, so although people in the stands were shaking their maracas, there was very little sound coming out of the maracas. It would have taken forty-two thousand fans, all holding maracas, to make the noise of one good Brazilian maracas band.

◆ ◆ ◆

Sheffield hit a 447-foot home run into the upper deck Sunday and the Marlins had a 5-3 lead going into the ninth inning when things started getting hairy. The Giants loaded the bases against Robb Nen, who was having a hard time throwing strikes, and scored a run on a misplayed groundout, bringing up Barry Bonds with the potential winning run on second base and two outs.

That forced Leyland into making a decision. He could have walked Bonds and had Nen face power-hitting Jeff Kent with the bases loaded, or he could have allowed Nen to pitch to Bonds, who Leyland called the best player he'd ever seen. Neither option was appealing, but the way Leyland saw it, Nen wasn't throwing a lot of strikes. The last thing he wanted was Nen falling behind 2-0 on Kent, then having to throw a fastball down the middle of the plate. He let him pitch to Bonds, then sat back and hoped. It was the most difficult decision he made all season.

"I was praying," Leyland said. "I was sitting there holding my breath saying, 'Please don't let these mother fuckers second guess me all night long.' That's a hard feeling to have in that situation. I fuck up a lot as a manager. I make a lot of mistakes, but the thing that's really screwed up is when you're kicking yourself in the ass."

The mother fuckers Leyland was referring to were the media, because he knew that if Bonds hit one out of the ballpark, everybody would ask why he didn't walk one of the best power hitters in baseball. So afterward, with the beat reporters gathered around him in the office, Leyland asked each one what they would have done. Most said they would have walked Bonds and let Nen take his chances with Kent. Leyland decided the rest were liars.

Leyland's decision turned out for the best. With the count one-and-one, Bonds sent a towering popup toward the third base seats. Bonilla raced over, reached far into the stands and around the body of a fan, and made the game-ending catch.

By the way, a rain delay in the fourth inning lasted more than an hour, and only about ten thousand fans remained when the game continued. Three people were sitting in the section where Bonilla caught Bonds' popup, so bad weather and fan apathy helped the Marlins this time. If there had been more people, he would have had a hard time reaching through the crowd. But there was no crowd.

◆ ◆ ◆

Bonds had the chance to win the game for the Giants because Abbott, playing second base, bobbled a possible double play grounder, missing out on the force play. Leyland wasn't so sure Abbott would have had the out, anyway, even if he fielded the ball cleanly.

"He might have got him," Leyland said. "He also might have hit Billy the Marlin. Abby's paws were shaking. He couldn't drive a hot buttered needle up his ass."

◆ ◆ ◆

Sheffield was so excited about hitting a home run, his first into the upper deck at Pro Player Stadium, that afterward he promised, "If we get to the playoffs and I'm playing well, I can carry us the rest of the way."

Whether that quote would join, "I could go out and do what Tony Gwynn does, but I chose to have the whole package," in the Sheffield quote scrapheap remained to be seen. After a season of feeling bad, he had a right to finally feel good.

◆ ◆ ◆

Mike Carr, the video coordinator, hand-delivered the Colorado Rockies' lineup to the manager's office Monday afternoon and Leyland playfully made as if he had just seen a ghost. The Rockies had Ellis Burks, Larry Walker, Andres Galarraga, Dante Bichette, and Vinny Castilla in the two-through-six slots, accounting for one hundred seventy homers, more than the entire Marlins team.

"Jesus Christ," Leyland sighed.

"Goddamn," he cursed, burying his head in his hands.

"I've got like six pitchers that might call in sick tonight."

Then a reporter pointed out that Fernandez, the Marlins' starting pitcher, figured to keep the game close.

"That's right," Leyland agreed. "If he pitches good, we got a chance. And tomorrow . . . Ojala.

"I just might take my first night off."

◆ ◆ ◆

By Monday night, September 15, the Marlins' front office staff was asking, "Where have all our fans gone?" As if they didn't know: Their fans were home watching *Monday Night Football.* The paid attendance was 19,148, the smallest since August 4, and those who didn't show up couldn't have been home watching the game, unless they owned high-powered, X-ray telescopes capable of penetrating the walls of Pro Player Stadium. The game wasn't on TV. All those people who sang "Let's go Marlins!" as they exited the stadium after the games against Baltimore were gone.

This was no time for an attendance slump. Public sale of tickets for the first round of the playoffs would begin Saturday morning and the people in charge were less certain than ever that the games would sell out. Jim Ross had visions of fans wrapped around the stadium waiting to buy tickets, and another vision of only a few people on line.

He feared the worst. Here were the Marlins, approaching their first playoff appearance in franchise history, and all anybody in South Florida wanted to talk about was whether Jimmy Johnson tried too many trick plays in the Dolphins' loss on Sunday. Leyland had listened to the call-in shows Monday afternoon, figuring he'd hear some talk about the Marlins, but all he heard was hour after hour of calls from football fans.

Then Boog Sciambi, the host of one of the shows, walked into the manager's office, and Leyland sarcastically reminded him, "You know, the Marlins are still in town."

◆ ◆ ◆

Lessons in media relations: Daulton committed two errors at first base in the eighth inning Monday night and helped turned a 3-1 deficit into a 7-1 blowout, but after the game he didn't hide in the trainer's room or take a long shower or dawdle in the clubhouse dining room. Instead, he had publicity director Ron Colangelo direct the media to his locker. Then he blamed himself for the loss.

"We were in the ballgame until the inning when I singlehandedly took us out of it," Daulton conceded politely. "I'll talk to the pitching staff tomorrow and tell them to try to get the balls hit to the other side."

Presumably, by the other side, he didn't mean the other side of the world, which was about where Galarraga's seventh-inning home run nearly landed. For the second time this season, he blasted the ball into the upper deck, four hundred fifty feet from home plate and just ten rows below the giant Jackie Robinson sign he had nearly punctured three and a half months earlier.

Afterward, Alex Fernandez, the victim of three Rockies solo bombs, pointed out that "they all count for one," which was true. But sometimes it seems as if they should count for two.

Fernandez, as Daulton had done, patiently spoke about his performance for five minutes, but then Michelle Kaufman from *The Herald* asked, "Alex, as a player who is from Miami, are you surprised that there were only nineteen thousand fans here tonight?" And Fernandez, without missing a beat, said, "I don't care to answer that stupid question. I don't give a fuck about the fans here."

Bad choice of words. Fernandez had resisted attendance questions all season, and didn't like being the poster boy for Latin American attendance at Marlins games. The next day, after the radio call-in shows had some fun with his comments, Fernandez claimed he meant to say, "I don't care about attendance, especially after I just lost a game." Of course, it was entirely possible he said exactly what was on his mind. Who knows?

The real question was: Did the fans care about Alex Fernandez?

The best way to find out was by driving south on I-95 to the Little Havana section of Miami and taking a ride down *Calle Ocho*—Eighth Street—into the most heavily populated neighborhood of Cubans in the world, outside of Cuba. There, you'd find few, sometimes no, indications that the hometown pitcher was on anyone's mind. You'd see an occasional person wearing a Marlins jersey, and sometimes it had the name FERNANDEZ on the back. Just as often, the name on the back was CASTILLO or RENTERIA or any of the other Marlins.

Fernandez, like most of the Marlins, would get autograph requests whenever he went out for dinner, but he was never besieged. He could walk the streets without being bothered, although never without being recognized. On the nights when Fernandez pitched, the coffee houses of Little Havana weren't jammed with Cuban cigar-smoking men crowded around the television. No more, at least, than when he wasn't pitching.

Fernandez's impact on attendance at Pro Player Stadium was hard to gauge. When they signed him, the Marlins hoped he'd be good for an additional five thousand fans every time he started. The Marlins' overall attendance had increased by seven thousand per game, and their Hispanic season ticket sales had tripled. But remember: The Marlins also signed Moises Alou, a Dominican, and planned on an all-Latin middle infield of Renteria and Luis Castillo. Once the season started, attendance wasn't higher on nights Fernandez pitched than when he didn't pitch.

"The first thing I thought when Alex was signed was that we were going to have a full house every night," Sheffield said.

Well, at least the luxury box Fernandez had bought for his family and friends was full every time he pitched. Other than that, Fernandez's pitching nights weren't special occasions at Pro Player Stadium. He had pitched in front of two sellout crowds, including one for a game against Atlanta, which would have been sold out no matter who pitched.

So the fans did care about Fernandez. Just no more than they cared about anyone else.

◆ ◆ ◆

The bases were loaded with two outs in the ninth inning Tuesday night, and the Marlins trailed the Rockies, 6-5, when Bonilla came to bat against Jerry DiPoto. DiPoto hadn't allowed a home run in sixty-five innings and all Bonilla was trying to do was single in the tying and winning runs.

There are unforgettable moments in every team's season, and this would be one of the best for the Marlins. Bonilla was batting from the left side, and the right-hander DiPoto threw one inside pitch after another. The count was two-and-two, DiPoto kept making his pitches, and Bonilla kept fouling them off. Five of them.

Bonilla chased the next pitch and sent a high, rising fly ball to rightfield. Larry Walker, the rightfielder, turned to watch, and Bonilla stood at home plate pointing his bat skyward. He knew the ball was gone. It landed deep in the rightfield seats for a grand slam, and Bonilla joyously raised his arms and skipped away from home plate. His teammates rushed out to meet him, and the crowd of 21,990 exulted.

Bonilla was mobbed at home plate and he practically carried his teammates back to the clubhouse, but when they got halfway there, they had to drag him back, because the crowd was begging for a curtain call.

"I don't think anybody's feet hit the ground," Conine said. "When he hit it, everybody just jumped straight onto the field."

The grand slam not only won the game, it also won $10,000 for a man in the crowd as part of a local newspaper's "Million Dollar Pitch" promotion. And Bonilla, still smiling a half hour after the game, said, "You can't say I don't give anything back to the community."

◆ ◆ ◆

John Cangelosi, who stands 5'8" and walks a lot, drew a key walk in the ninth inning Tuesday, and Leyland helpfully pointed out, "He's only two-foot-three. It's not like Kareem Abdul-Jabaar is standing up there."

◆ ◆ ◆

Saunders tried the Check Your Brain At The Door theory of pitching in his return to the starting rotation Wednesday night and discovered, as he suspected, that sometimes the best thoughts for a pitcher are no thoughts at all. Saunders' post-game analysis of his outing could be summed up thusly: If it was possible for a pitcher to have a frontal lobotomy and retain the motor coordination necessary to pitch, he'd be the next Cy Young.

According to Saunders, in the eleven days since his last start in Los Angeles, he hadn't thought at all about his spot in the pitching rotation being on the line, or possibly lost for good. Instead of thinking about what went wrong in his last four starts, he thought about . . . well, nothing at all. "I said, 'I didn't care who was hitting,'" Saunders said. "I didn't care what the situation was. I didn't care what the count was. I just said, 'Here's my stuff,' plain and simple."

Fortunately for Saunders, the batters he was facing were Mike Lieberthal, Rex Hudler, Billy McMillon, and Bobby Estalella of the Phillies, not Galarraga, Walker, Bichette, and Castilla of the Rockies. He allowed one run in six innings and the Marlins beat the Phillies, 5-2, to salvage a split of a doubleheader.

"My stuff has been there," Saunders insisted. "I just haven't thrown strikes."

Saunders' explanation wasn't universally sound. Those were strikes, of course, that the Rockies and Marlins had hit over the fence the night before, so the philosophy of a pitcher throwing strikes has its drawbacks. But Saunders didn't have to worry about putting any extra thought into his next outing. It would be against the Phillies, too. Throwing strikes would suffice.

◆ ◆ ◆

After making two errors Monday night, Daulton didn't play Tuesday, then made an error on the first ground ball he handled Wednesday. So for those of you keeping score at home, that was three consecutive errors on three consecutive ground balls. Statistics on those types of things aren't kept, but Daulton must have been close to a record for first basemen.

Again, after the game, Daulton willingly faced the media, which this time included his old friends from Philadelphia, and one of the questions was, "Do you think you'll be back next year?" Daulton took a deep breath and responded, "You picked the wrong time to ask me. If we won, it would've been a better time to ask me. I'm in retirement mode right now."

Sadly, it looked like Daulton would remain in retirement mode for a while. Although he had been an important addition for the Marlins, he was a liability in the field, and it was doubtful any American League teams would want a designated hitter who batted .269 with thirteen home runs.

Daulton had certainly given this season his best effort. Dombrowski remarked that every time he left the manager's office at 2:30 in the afternoon, Daulton was usually the first player coming into the clubhouse. The Marlins were not an early arriving team, but Daulton was an early arriving player. He loved being at the ballpark—during the early 1990s, he often slept in the clubhouse—and was living through a dream season: From retirement, to arriving at spring training without any guarantee of a job, to getting a spot in the Phillies' lineup when Danny Tartabull got hurt on the first day of the season, to getting traded to a World Series contender.

"You can't get a better script than that," Daulton said. He couldn't wait to see the final scene.

◆ ◆ ◆

The Giants played the Dodgers Wednesday night and just from watching on TV you knew something special was happening in San Francisco that wasn't happening in South Florida. The Dodgers entered the series two games ahead of the Giants, and the crowd noise rose and fell with every pitch. Meanwhile, the Marlins were headed towards their first playoff appearance, but they'd hardly been in a pennant race, or even a wild card race. They hadn't been less than 2½ games behind the Braves or less than three games ahead of the Giants or Mets since August. So maybe that's why people weren't coming out to the ballpark.

On Wednesday, the paid attendance was 26,305, but there were never that many in the ballpark at any time, not even close, and less than two thousand were present when the first game started at 4:05 p.m. This was not a good sign at all for baseball's future in South Florida and worrisome thoughts were humming through the minds of the Marlins' front office staffers. *Maybe South Florida would never be a baseball area. Maybe these people just don't like baseball.*

◆ ◆ ◆

On the good side, the Marlins had sold their entire supply of maracas. The South Florida market for silent maracas had proven to be very good, indeed.

◆ ◆ ◆

The search for the manager's missing buttocks began on September 18, when Zaun played his second game in a row against the Phillies.

Leyland flashback, July 15: "I won't play him two games in a row, as long as I have an ass."

To Zaun's credit, he didn't make Leyland regret the decision. He had four hits and threw out three runners trying to steal in two games, and Leyland said he did "a helluva job." It was the strongest compliment Zaun received from his manager all season, but Leyland also said, "I'll play Charles tomorrow. I don't want to push my luck with Zaun."

Nonetheless, it was a far cry from, "He's a dumb mother fucker."

Being no dummy, and aware that additional major league jobs would be available next season when the expansion teams began playing, Zaun had been working for months on his defense with the Marlins coaches. One pitched, another played second, another coached, and Zaun worked on his throws. Not surprisingly, Zaun's main problem was he wasn't waiting for pitches to come to him. He was going after them before they reached his glove. This idea of Zaun as impatient is not a reach. In Wednesday's second game, he hit a ball to the wall in left-centerfield and decided to stretch a double into a triple, even though Rich Donnelly was giving him the stop sign from the third base coach's box. The play was close, but Zaun was safe.

"It was a stupid play on my part," Zaun said. "I shouldn't have done that with two outs. Rich didn't say anything to me, but I asked him if it was close. I didn't get thrown out at third, thankfully."

Thankfully is right. Zaun certainly would have heard about it had he been out, especially if the Marlins went on to lose the game. They didn't. They also won Thursday, 8-2, over the Phillies, on another strong outing by Brown, who won his sixth straight. Once again, Bonilla, Sheffield, Johnson, and Alou didn't play, which came back to the question of why Zaun played two games in a row: Because Leyland knew the wild card race was over and his primary job was resting players for the post-season.

So, he canceled batting practice.

The players weren't required to show up until 3:35 for a 4:35 game.

A quick check confirmed that Leyland's buttocks were right where they had been before, tucked in between his lower back and his thighs. His brain, too, had not moved an inch.

And only 16,677 fans showed up at the ballpark. October couldn't come soon enough, yet there was one piece of unfinished business remaining: The clinching of the wild card spot.

◆ ◆ ◆

The complete transcript of an actual pre-game discussion between Leiter and his manager:

"Hello Al."

"Hello Jim."

◆ ◆ ◆

Nen threw a high, inside ninety-eight-mile-per-hour fastball in the ninth inning Friday that Carlos Baerga of the Mets swung at and missed. Charles Johnson missed it too, and the ball landed at the backstop, allowing a run to score.

At that moment, the action shifted from the field to the press box, where official scorer Sonny Hirsch suddenly found himself in the uncomfortable position of having to award Johnson his first passed ball of the season.

All eyes turned to Hirsch, who hesitated to make the call. The game, a 5-2 Marlins win, ended one batter later and Hirsch still hadn't made his call. By that time, the beat writers were getting antsy, because they wanted to file their stories with the news of Johnson's first passed ball. But Hirsch wanted to be absolutely certain before making a decision, and asked to see a replay.

This especially angered Dan Graziano of the *Palm Beach Post,* who confronted Hirsch in the press box lobby and demanded, "Make a call!"

"If you don't mind, I was watching the replay," Hirsch explained.

And Graziano responded, "Why? You never watch the replay for your other horseshit calls."

Naturally, Hirsch did not appreciate a reporter questioning his integrity as score-keeper of the Great American Pastime, and an angry, obscenity-laced argument ensued. It was capped off by this exchange of ideas:

"Fuckhead."

"Assbreath."

Hirsch finally ruled it a passed ball, and later one of the anchors on ESPN's *SportsCenter* commented, "They must have been beating up the official scorer in Miami over that call." The man had no idea how close he was to the truth.

The Marlins agreed with the call, although Daulton, the former catcher, wondered if Johnson had lost sight of the ball when Baerga swung. Johnson said he had, but not for that reason: He had taken his eye off the ball for a microsecond, long enough for him to lose it.

Although Johnson insisted he had never thought or worried about completing the season without committing a passed ball, it was obvious he would have liked to have done it. After answering a few questions about the passed ball, Johnson was asked about Leiter's performance. But his eyes glassed over as he discussed Leiter, and he kept going back to the passed ball. Of course it bothered him. The no passed balls/no errors record was gone. He could have been the first.

◆ ◆ ◆

Tickets for the first two playoff home games went on sale Saturday morning. These events generally attract a few crazies who camp out overnight so they can be the first in line. Like Linda Sloven, a 53-year-old mother of three and devoted fan from Year One, Day One. She happily told the story of the time when she arrived at 6:30 in the morning to get hockey player John Vanbiesbrouck's autograph. The signing wasn't scheduled to begin until 4:30 in the afternoon.

"And you think I'm crazy now," she said.

Psychologists say that behavior learned in childhood often carries over into adult life, and that was obviously true of Ms. Sloven, who as a child in Toronto camped overnight with her parents for tickets to an Elvis Presley concert. They got them, she never forgot it. And here she was, dressed in shorts and a T-shirt, wearing sneakers, a backwards cap on her head, a fanny pack around her waist, and equipped with all the essentials: A beach chair, a sleeping bag, flashlights, candles, bottled water, and a barbecued chicken. She was first in line at 4:30 p.m. on *Friday*, seventeen and a half hours before the ticket windows opened.

Sloven wasn't the only one waiting. About a half dozen people stayed through the hot, sticky night. By 5 a.m., people started showing up by the hundreds. The Marlins served bagels, orange juice, and coffee, and there were at least five hundred people waiting when tickets went on sale at 10 a.m. The line snaked into the parking lot.

The Marlins had the foresight to open forty-one ticket windows, so the line moved smoothly and quickly as fans caught their first dose of playoff fever. That was evident from the fiery reaction of several fans who walked away from the windows holding up their tickets and letting out loud, guttural, inner-animal-type screams of "Playoff tickets! Yeeeeeaaaahhhh!"

"Playoff tickets! Yeeeeaaaahhhh!"

Holding three of those tickets, but not letting out any primal screams, was Linda Sloven.

"I wouldn't sell them for anything," she said. "I wouldn't even sell them for a thousand dollars."

How about $2,000 and a barbecued chicken?

"No," she said. "I wouldn't sell them for anything."

Better seats were available, but Sloven purchased three tickets in the upper deck, ten rows up, seats she could have had without waiting over night. Not that she cared about that. She was happy as can be.

"A lot of people don't know this, but if it's a day game, it's a lot cooler upstairs," she explained. "And I passed out once downstairs, anyway."

The entire scene made a happy man out of Jim Ross, who after a week of sub-par crowds was thrilled about seeing evidence of playoff excitement. By the end of the day, nearly fourteen thousand tickets had been sold.

◆ ◆ ◆

Sheffield returned to the lineup Saturday afternoon, bad back and all, and nearly didn't make it through the first inning. Brian McRae of the Mets hit a fly ball to deep rightfield and Sheffield raced back, never slowing down even when he reached the warning track before flinging himself shoulder first and with all his energy into the fence. The ball easily cleared the wall for a home run, Sheffield ended up on the ground for several minutes, and the only reasonable explanation for the way he played the ball was that, after a tough season, he had tried to commit suicide.

◆ ◆ ◆

Fernandez was suffering from the flu but pitched anyway Saturday and got hit hard, 7-3.

Hmmm. We don't need any fucking heroes?

Not exactly. Leyland didn't think twice about starting Fernandez, who afterward said of his illness, "That's no excuse. I sucked." And Bonilla, when asked if the team was aware of Fernandez's sickness, stuck his tongue firmly in cheek, smiled, and said, "I had no idea. That just goes to show you what a true, gutsy individual he is."

◆ ◆ ◆

Kevin Brown showed up before the third game of the Mets series sporting his new haircut, a very short, combed-forward style that had become very popular.

"This is the George Clooney look," Brown offered.

And Leiter, unsure whether his teammate looked more like Clooney or Jim Carrey, said, "It's more like the *Dumb and Dumber* look."

◆ ◆ ◆

The Marlins thought their hopes of clinching the wild card hinged on them winning and the Dodgers losing Sunday, but then Dave Dombrowski walked into the media relations office early in the day and asked Ron Colangelo, "Can we clinch on the field if the Giants lose?"

They sat down with a pen and paper, figured out the math, and decided that the combination of a Marlins victory and a Giants loss would be enough. Because the Giants game started at 4:05 and the Marlins game started at 4:35, the Marlins could clinch the wild card on the field, rather than while watching the Dodgers game, which started at 8 p.m., on TV.

The players weren't aware of this new fact until they arrived at the ballpark, and most fans weren't aware of it at all. That could have made for an entertaining scene had the Giants lost and the Marlins won: The players would have been dancing all over the field, the fans would have been watching in total confusion, and the public address announcer would have had to say something like, "Oh, by the way, we just clinched."

Armed with the new information, the clubhouse staff immediately put twelve cases of champagne on ice and placed rolls of protective plastic on top of the stalls, to be rolled down in case of a celebration.

They needn't have wasted their energy. The Giants won. The Marlins lost to the Mets for the second straight day, 2-1, as Rick Reed outpitched Kirt Ojala in front of 44,176, the largest home crowd of the season.

In case you're wondering, Pro Player Stadium hadn't grown; the blue tarps had been removed from the top rows of the upper level seats.

◆ ◆ ◆

The South Florida chapter of the Baseball Writers' Association of America hands out a Good Guy award each season to the player who is the most cooperative with the media, and this season's winner, in a landslide, was Bobby Bonilla. Imagine that, Bobby Bonilla—who in New York was arranging media tours of the Bronx and who in Baltimore threatened to shove his shoe up a reporter's ass—a friend of the press. Will wonders never cease?

Wow, they're gonna have fun with this in New York, was the first thought that crossed Bonilla's mind.

Bonilla had grown into his role as team spokesman during the season. At first he seemed uncomfortable in the role, but then he embraced it to the point where he encouraged reporters to seek him out for assessments on the state of the team. Sometimes he made sure everybody knew what was on his mind, like on Sunday after Ojala lost to the Mets and was surrounded by reporters at his locker. "The man pitched his balls off," Bonilla yelled out, as heads turned.

Not that Bonilla didn't have his rough spots, most of which were saved for the TV cameras. He loved giving the TV reporters a hard time, and often peppered his remarks with curses, just so the reporters would have to go back and either edit

212

out the bad words, bleep them over, or not use them altogether. He especially liked playing games with a young female reporter from a local station. On Sunday, Powell and Stanifer had both dropped relay tosses, so the reporter, with camera rolling, asked, "Did the miscues in the game have an effect on the team?"

"You mean did the pitchers fuck up? Yeah, they fucked up!" Bonilla said, smiling broadly.

"Well . . ."

"Just say it. No miscues. They fucked up. Shit happens."

The other TV reporters laughed because Bonilla had said absolutely nothing they could use on the air. Even if they bleeped out the curses, they would have been left with, "You mean did the pitchers up? Yeah, they up!"

Bonilla knew this perfectly well and laughed, too. Then he said, "If you wanna come to this locker, you gotta be prepared." Above him, the warning sign to reporters was still posted. So not everything had changed.

◆ ◆ ◆

The conversation came around to the anticipated post-season media circus, and Fernandez was asked whether he planned on changing the way he went about his business.

"Fuck, no," Fernandez said. "I'll be a media shithead, just like I've been before."

He said it with a smile and a justified sense of pride.

◆ ◆ ◆

Pre-game clubhouse scene on Sunday: Bill Beck, the director of team travel, handed out strips of playoff tickets—division series, NLCS, and World Series—to the players, coaches, and clubhouse men. Two apiece, courtesy of Wayne Huizenga, who also bought two strips for each full-time employee in the front office.

The players took their tickets and tucked them neatly in their lockers. And Leyland walked by hurriedly with his head down and never looked up. He had no use for playoff tickets when his team still hadn't clinched the wild card.

◆ ◆ ◆

The Dodgers lost their game Sunday, which meant that all the Marlins had to do was beat the Mets Monday to clinch the wild card spot. It also meant a lot of very nervous people were walking around Pro Player Stadium. The people in charge of ticket sales were nervous because they knew it would look bad if they didn't have a big crowd on clinching night, and they knew the team hadn't drawn well on Mondays all season.

Of course, the manager was nervous. Leyland was walking around in one of his grumpiest moods of the season, partly because he was sick with a virus, and partly because he hated all of the commotion over the possible clinching. The beat writers tried talking with him before batting practice and barely got a word out of him. Then he refused permission to the local TV stations to cover the post-game clubhouse celebration live. For the fourth straight day, the clubhouse was closed to the media for a period during the afternoon, ostensibly so the players could stretch. They had been stretching outside all season, and closing the clubhouse was a violation of major league rules.

Then assistant athletic trainer Kevin Rand snapped at a reporter for trying to speak with a player who had stopped to get a drink during batting practice. *The assistant athletic trainer?* The next thing anybody knew, the stadium janitors would be copping an attitude.

Well, close. Even the Travis Bickle, *Taxi Driver*-like character who guarded the home dugout at Pro Player Stadium was touchier than usual, which is saying something. One of the Triple-A coaches and a female reporter were playing catch near the dugout, and he didn't like that. So Travis, between nervous twitches, told them to "take your act somewhere else," then walked away cursing under his breath.

Actually, there was some debate over whether the dugout security guard better resembled the fictitious sociopathic near-assassin in *Taxi Driver,* or the Michael Douglas character in *Falling Down,* the one who walked into a fast food restaurant after breakfast time, demanded breakfast anyway, and opened fire when told that he could only have lunch.

Said one of the Marlins front office employees about Mr. Bickle: "If we gave him a gun, and told him to use it whenever he felt it was necessary, there'd be at least twenty dead people every night."

On this night, he fit right in. Although Leyland was almost certain the Marlins couldn't blow their big wild card lead, every possible negative scenario had raced through his mind. He refused to discuss the playoffs, or anything except Monday night's game, including his pitching rotation for the upcoming series in Montreal. He was totally focused, in a Napoleon-with-a-baseball-bat disturbed kind of way, as he hit fungoes in batting practice and smoked more than usual.

The same couldn't be said of the players, who were one hundred percent confident and already looking forward to the post-game celebration. The scene on the field would be a "dog pile," Conine said. After the loss Sunday afternoon, Bonilla was smiling and guaranteeing the Marlins would win one of their final seven games.

"I like our chances," he said.

The champagne was still on ice. The protective plastic wrap remained atop the lockers. TV stations set up their cameras outside the clubhouse. The beat reporters, figuring a post-game celebration in the clubhouse would make interviewing the players difficult, asked the players hypothetical post-clinching questions *before* the game, and the players went along and answered. They talked about how they would celebrate and acted as if there was no way they could lose to the Mets that night.

◆ ◆ ◆

Then they went out and got killed, 10-3. Hernandez pitched his worst game of the season, allowing nine runs in 2⅓ innings, and the Marlins trailed 9-1 after three. The crowd of 29,234, considerably fewer than the front office had hoped for and embarrassingly low for a game in which the Marlins could have clinched their first playoff berth, booed the home team several times.

It was an awful performance by the fans, a terrible performance by the Marlins, but a great performance by Leyland, who sat and steamed in his corner of the dugout for most of the game, stretched out and sipping from a cup of water. Then, during his post-game session with reporters, he showed why he doesn't hold team meetings. There's no need to when, as he did prior to the All-Star break, he can send messages through the media. So Leyland started out slowly, and built up steam.

The theme of his speech was I'M VERY DISAPPOINTED. That must have been the theme. He said it nine times. Runners-up were variations of fuck and shit, each of which he said seven times but, of course, even in baseball, can't be the theme of a speech.

Excerpt One: "Guys should worry about what's going on right now, and we have too many guys that are spokesmen who don't know what the hell they're talking about, if you want to know the truth. You know, they're trying to act cool, talking about this, talking about that, instead of bearing down and taking extra BP and getting ready to win a ballgame."

Excerpt Two: "If they don't know what we have at stake, then they got problems. They should do less bullshitting with you guys and more action on the field. That's what they should be doing. They're laying on their ass talking to the media, when they should be out there working their ass off."

Excerpt Three: "They better go out there and take care of their business instead of bullshitting with you guys and talking about this and talking about that and falling into that bullshit that you guys have been baiting them for a fucking week about the playoffs and all that shit, and then the fuckers go out and sit there and comment about it. They'd better get their fucking mind on what they're doing."

Excerpt Four: "I'm sick and tired of people walking around here with forms for post-season play and all that shit when they haven't done nothing yet."

Excerpt Five: "I'm very disappointed. Very disappointed. And I don't give a fuck who knows it, either, and that goes for the fucking veterans as well as the rookies. They got all the fucking answers, walking around like they've done something. They haven't done shit."

And Bonilla, hearing about his manager's comments, shook his head and said, "If we don't win, we're gonna have a long winter. It's gonna be real long."

Almost as long as their flight to Montreal. They landed at 3:05 in the morning and, after clearing customs and making the forty-five-minute bus drive from the airport to the hotel, didn't get to sleep until after 5. They were fortunate. The Expos, who had just lost in Atlanta and watched the Braves celebrate their clinching of the division title, didn't get home until 5:30 a.m. Tuesday's game figured to be a fair fight.

◆ ◆ ◆

Montreal is no place to clinch a playoff spot, but it would have to do for the Marlins. Olympic Stadium is a hulking domed cement mass in the middle of other hulking cement masses that were the venues for the 1976 Summer Olympics. It looks cold. Dreary.

The best thing the Marlins had going for them Tuesday, September 23, was Kevin Brown, who had been their best pitcher by far since the All-Star break and hadn't lost since July. Brown was good, not outstanding, and threw one hundred twenty pitches in six innings—a Leiter count—but he left the game with a 4-3 lead because of Charles Johnson's run-scoring single in the fifth.

The score remained the same into the eighth inning, and the Expos were batting with five outs to go, when Julio Sarmiento, the Marlins' assistant director of publicity, went down to the bathroom next to the Marlins' dugout. While he was standing there, Jim Eisenreich walked over and took the stall next to him. Sarmiento couldn't figure it out: Eisenreich kept staring at him for ten seconds.

"OK, what?" Sarmiento asked.

"That sweater," Eisenreich said, pointing to Sarmiento, "doesn't stand a chance. No chance."

He was talking about the post-game clinching party.

◆ ◆ ◆

Conine, the original Marlin, had entered the game in the eighth inning as a defensive replacement for Daulton, and came to bat in the ninth inning with Sheffield on first base. What Conine had been doing a lot of lately was hitting home runs after entering the game for defense, and he did it again. The Marlins had a 6-3 lead.

Nen threw only strikes in the bottom of the ninth. Mark Grudzielanek grounded out to Conine, Joe Orsulak grounded out to Counsell, and Jose Vidro grounded to Counsell, again, for the final out.

The Marlins walked to the mound to congratulate Nen and calmly exchanged high fives. Dombrowski, sitting in the lower seats, punched his fist in the air, stood up, shook hands with traveling secretary Bill Beck, and, smiling tightly, watched the subdued celebration on the field. The managers and coaches shook hands in the dugout. The few thousand fans remaining from the crowd of 9,400, the smallest to watch a Marlins game all season, turned their backs and walked away. The Marlins headed back to the clubhouse.

◆ ◆ ◆

The most important part of clinching a playoff spot is knowing what clothes to wear for the celebration. For the Marlins, their outfits included caps with "WILD CARD" on the front and T-shirts with the slogan, "25 Men, One Goal." So they got back to the clubhouse, changed into the nice new clothes that they were about to destroy, and got into the spirit of the celebration the moment they saw the plastic wrap covering their lockers. It was like telling children, "Go ahead. It's OK to fingerpaint the entire house."

The second most important part of clinching a playoff spot is knowing what to pour and what to drink. You *drink* Dom Perignon champagne and Presidente beer. You *pour* $8.99 bottles of Freixenet champagne and cheap Bud Light over your teammates' heads.

Drink Dom and Presidente.

Pour Freixenet and Bud Light.

Also, pour Gatorade. Leiter dumped an entire bucket of Gatorade over Fernandez's head. Fernandez enjoyed the shower, which brings up another important part of clinching celebrations: The more champagne and beer that winds up on the floor, the better time everybody has. Very little drinking went on in the Marlins' clubhouse; that would be saved for later.

Mostly, the players smoked cigars and poured. They screamed. They said things like, "This is a great feeling," and "This is only the beginning," and "We don't wanna stop here, we wanna keep going," and it didn't matter who said what, because everybody said everything and none of it meant anything, except that the time-honored tradition in all sports is to spray and pour until you run out, then go out and buy some more.

"Ooooh, that feels good going down the back of my leg," said TV announcer Jay Randolph, who was walking around the room conducting interviews while wearing a polo shirt that had been soaked to his skin with champagne.

And Jim Leyland, who had shown every other emotion known to man over the course of the long season, showed a new one. He cried. He stood in the middle of the clubhouse with a blue towel draped around his neck and graciously acknowledged former Marlins managers Rene Lachemann and John Boles as the players poured champagne over his head, too. His voice was hoarse and shaking, and it looked like he might break down into someone's arms any second.

He didn't. Instead, he composed himself, lit a cigar, and wiggled his hips to hip-hop music. Then he spotted Antonio Alfonseca, his twelve-fingered, twelve-toed relief pitcher.

"Hey, Pulpo," Leyland ran up and shouted with his right hand in the air. "Give me six!"

FINAL NATIONAL LEAGUE EAST STANDINGS

	W	L	Pct.	GB
Atlanta	101	61	.623	—
Marlins	**92**	**70**	**.568**	**9**
New York	88	74	.543	13
Montreal	78	84	.481	23
Philadelphia	68	94	.420	33

15

The Bonus Round

September 30, October 1 vs. San Francisco
October 3 at San Francisco

The Marlins partied their way through Montreal and Philadelphia, emerged from their hangovers Sunday night, and walked into another party. When their plane landed in Fort Lauderdale, five police cars waiting on the runway led them back to the hangar, where two fire engines, red lights blazing, formed an arc of spraying water for the plane to pass through. The hangar had been decorated with black and teal balloons.

The players got off the plane, walked down the ramp, and were met at the bottom by Huizenga and Smiley. The players' wives and families, along with Marlins front office employees were there, too, about a hundred guests in all. The players were handed gift bags of Dom Perignon engraved with the Marlins logo and "Congratulations 1997 Wild Card Champions." A small band played. Then Huizenga, Smiley, Dombrowski, and Leyland gave short speeches. Waiters circulated with hors d'oeuvres and champagne. Billy the Marlin shook hands and patted guests on the back. The band played on.

After about an hour, the party ended, and the players went home. Leyland, who didn't have anybody at home and was nursing a terrible chest cold, went back to the stadium and slept on the couch in his office. The next morning, he woke up and began preparing for the San Francisco Giants, come-from-behind winners of the Western Division after a close race with the Los Angeles Dodgers, and their opponents in the best-of-five-games Division Series.

The success of the season would be judged by what happened in October. On the field, the Marlins did no more and no less than what was expected of them. For $89 million in free-agent expenditures, Huizenga got a wild card team. In the stands, the fans came out on weekends, rarely showed in large numbers on weekdays, and yet the Marlins posted the largest attendance gain in baseball: 617,620 fans. Their total attendance was 2,364,387, just short of the thirty thousand average they said they wanted.

For the moment, the Marlins were calling themselves Wild Card Champions, which meant they were the best second-place team in the National League. Champions? Not quite. This wasn't exactly what Huizenga had in mind when he opened his wallet. Nor, really, was the home attendance: The Marlins had the fourth highest payroll, but the eleventh highest attendance.

When you got right down to it, the Marlins hadn't accomplished much.

◆ ◆ ◆

Winning had brought out the worst in T-shirt designers. In addition to "25 Men, One Goal," which had gained popularity among fans, there was Darren Daulton's "700 Players, 25 Rings, Get Focused," an allusion to the numbers of players in the major leagues and how many win World Series rings each season. Then there were "The Hunt For Teal October" T-shirts that the Marlins found at their lockers when they arrived at Pro Player Stadium for Game One of the Division Series against the San Francisco Giants.

The T-shirt makers lacked imagination. Better ideas that went unused included: "$89 Million, One Wild Card," "45,000 Tickets, Good Seats Available," "Multiple Personalties, One Manager," and "My Team Finished Second And All I Got Was This Lousy T-Shirt."

The playoffs were supposed to be a wonderful time for an area that had never experienced the thrill of baseball in October, and until five years ago had never experienced the thrill of baseball in any months but February and March. "Marlins fever is sweeping through South Florida," one breathless talking head exclaimed on a TV newscast. But the manager of a local sports merchandise store related the sad tale of how he had ordered two dozen Marlins shirts a month earlier and hadn't "moved a one of them."

That pretty much summed up Marlins fever.

"Only seventeen hours until the first pitch," our breathless talking head warned.

Two hundred fans attended a playoff rally in nearby Hollywood.

Two hundred. Passers-by might have thought it was a company picnic.

About two thousand tickets remained available for Game One. Fearing a sea of empty seats that would look bad on TV, the Pro Player Stadium crew carted out the blue tarps and reattached them to the last five rows of the upper deck, then closed off two more sections in the upper corners.

South Florida could hardly wait.

◆ ◆ ◆

All that celebrating, all that champagne over his head, all those late nights at the Montreal casinos, did a number on a drawn, haggard-looking Leyland, whose voice was hoarse when he spoke at the pre-series press conference the day before Game One and sounded even worse four hours before the game. He felt as bad as he sounded.

"Off the record," Leyland said, leaning forward in his chair up on the podium. "Totally off the record . . . They're treating me for walking pneumonia right now."

◆ ◆ ◆

What was Leyland talking about? Had he gone totally out of his mind? In front of about fifty reporters, with at least eight TV cameras rolling and people in the room whom he had never seen before, Leyland had become the first manager in major league history to go off the record—totally off the record—in the middle of a press conference.

There are limits to a manager's control of the media, and those limits are expanded during the post-season. The tunnel outside the clubhouse was roped off, creating two traffic patterns: One for the media and other outsiders, another for the team. Clubhouses were closed before each game, so the only way reporters could interview players was to grab them as they left the field after batting practice. If batting practice was canceled, the media would be out of luck. For the most part, the manager was available only in the controlled setting of the pre- and post-game press conferences, which are run by Major League Baseball. These press conferences are not good forums for small talk and follow-up questions. You can rest assured Leyland did not elaborate on which players he would not play "as long as I have an ass" during these formal gatherings. Nor did he utter any of his favorite four-letter words.

So the flow of information is controlled tightly, and any tidbit of interesting news—such as the manager has walking pneumonia—is cherished. For Leyland to think he could throw out a piece of news, then restrict its use, was ludicrous. Most of the media ignored the embargo, which was within their rights and ethics. There are, of course, reasonable limits to "off the record."

"Off the record. Totally *off the record. I'm fatally ill."*
"Off the record. Totally *off the record. I just murdered Zaun."*
"Off the record. Totally *off the record. The fix is in."*

Then again, maybe Leyland was suffering from Marlins fever.

◆ ◆ ◆

The main reason for post-season media restriction is to control clubhouse traffic and allow the players time to prepare and get focused for the game. Focus is very important in baseball. If a player isn't focused, he has no chance of succeeding, because he can be certain that the players on the opposing team are focused. Focus is the key.

Different players have different ways of getting focused, so by closing the clubhouse before playoff games, each player can prepare and get focused in his own way. Some work out, stretch, examine game tapes, or shadow bat. Many watch TV. Others eat ham sandwiches.

It's also important for focusing to begin early. A player can't, for example, start getting focused at 3:55 for a 4:07 game. That's not enough time. He needs to start focusing at least two or three hours prior to game time, if not earlier. Getting focused is not easy business.

During the years following the Pirates' loss to the Braves in the 1992 National League Championship series, Leyland decided the Pirates had been too accommodating to the media, and therefore not focused enough. Francisco Cabrera won that series for Atlanta with a two-out, two-run single in the bottom of the ninth inning of Game Seven, and nobody ever figured out which interview had cost Pittsburgh the pennant.

◆ ◆ ◆

The other reason Leyland restricted media access during the playoffs was that he didn't trust his players. He had seen how easily they became distracted during the two possible clinching games against the Mets, and was angry with the way they behaved, acting as if they had already won. He wasn't going to let it happen again.

On the subject of past mistakes, there was one lesson, at least, Leyland had learned from his three previous losing trips to the post-season: Staying calm and poised will get you nowhere. This time, Leyland planned on turning his emotion to his advantage. He and his coaches had watched the movie *Hoosiers* all three days in Montreal and, as usual, found it inspirational every time. During the season, he had kept team meetings to a minimum. Now he planned on holding them before every game, like the basketball coach in *Hoosiers.*

"It sounds corny, and my peers will probably laugh at me, but I think you can't do it over a one hundred sixty-two-game schedule, because it gets drawn out," Leyland said. "But when you get into a situation like this, you have to grab their attention somehow. It's silly. I admit that it's silly, goofy. But I tried to be calm and poised and all that shit like that and we lost. The only difference is that I have a better looking wife than Norman Dale."

Norman Dale was the *Hoosiers* coach who led a small high school to the 1951 Indiana state basketball championship with a victory over huge South Bend Central. Anyway, Coach Dale did all kinds of silly, goofy things to grab his team's attention, like hiring a drunk assistant coach, getting himself thrown out of games, and playing with only four players instead of five because his only remaining sub was on his shit list.

So the first silly thing Leyland did in the playoffs was point to his uniform and say to the players, "Look at the number on the back of my jersey. Eleven. That's how many games we're going to win."

What Leyland was saying, in a goofy, silly, corny kind of way, was, "We're going to win the World Series," because that's how many wins it takes—three in the first round, and four each in the NLCS and World Series.

By the way, Norman Dale is not married in the movie, although he does kiss Barbara Hershey's character passionately. If Leyland was comparing his wife to Barbara Hershey, it was an awfully nice compliment.

Come to think of it, if Leyland was comparing himself to Gene Hackman, it was an awfully nice compliment, too.

◆ ◆ ◆

On the day of Game One Sheffield said, "Every time I go up to the plate now I feel like I have a chance to do something big." He had hit .324 in September with five home runs, by far his best month, and was feeling better than he had all season.

He had also pulled on his new T-shirt, a dark blue tie-dyed number with the Superman crest on the front. It had been given to him by a fan earlier in the season, and Sheffield had been waiting until the playoffs to wear it. And there he was in batting practice, wearing the T-shirt and reaching the leftfield seats with a couple of swings. So now not only did the fans think Sheffield was Superman. Sheffield thought it, too.

The Marlins would have a hard time doing anything in the post-season unless their cleanup hitter started hitting like a $10-million man, or Superman, or whatever. Earlier in the season, Barry Bonds of the Giants told Sheffield, "Stay patient. When they finally challenge you, make them pay." And now Sheffield had a chance to use that advice against his friend. Maybe the fans could wait, but he couldn't.

◆ ◆ ◆

There's this thing about playoff games, and it's true in every sport: A playoff game makes you realize how meaningless and unexciting most regular season games really are.

The first playoff game in Marlins history was just like that. Jim Ross, the vice president of sales and marketing, had promised to tone down the in-game entertainment portion of the proceedings and was true to his word. Jay Rokeach introduced the players on both teams, then the national anthem was sung. Mis-sung, actually. "Whose broad stars and bright stripes" became the first line of the second verse, replacing "Whose broad stripes and bright stars."

Somehow, the Bleacher Brigade found its way onto the field, but that was the extent of the silly stuff. Oh, and Billy the Marlin did The Fish. And Muscle Boy pulled off his shirt, revealing a radio station's bumper sticker that had been plastered on his chest. It looked like a form of child abuse. Somebody should have investigated and had his parents arrested.

Plenty of seats were empty when the game started, partly because the game never sold out, partly because it was raining, and partly because a portion of the parking lot had been closed for a fireworks display. The lack of parking created a traffic jam, so after a while the front office made the sane decision and scrapped the pyrotechnics. People finally made it to their seats. By the time the rain stopped in the third inning, Kirk Rueter and Kevin Brown were engaged in an impressive pitching duel. Nobody needed the scoreboard's reminder that "This Is Tense," but apparently there were limits to In-Game Entertainment's self-control.

Teal and orange Marlins banners decorated the area behind home plate, hiding the rotatable advertising sign, and big Division Series logos had been painted on the field next to the first- and third-base lines. The seating areas were a sea of white Marlins T-shirts and teal Marlins caps. The crowd numbered 42,187—capacity was forty-five thousand—and there was always a buzz in the stadium, the sound of people talking and rooting. It's what a stadium sounds like when people are watching and caught up in a game. The sound was different from Game 155 of the regular season, when 44,176 showed up and seemingly never opened their mouths, other than to call the beer vendors. This time, you had to listen real hard to hear the beer vendors. And there wasn't a maraca to be heard.

◆ ◆ ◆

With Leiter pitching Game Two on Wednesday—and by this time nobody felt safe with Leiter pitching—the Marlins considered Game One to be a must-win, especially since the final three games of the series would be played in San Francisco. But when Bill Mueller homered to lead off the top of the seventh, the Giants had a 1-0 lead and the crowd had been silenced.

The Marlins weren't doing much against Rueter. Sheffield had done his job, taking two walks, but the Marlins stranded two runners with none out in the sixth. Then, in the bottom of the seventh, just when it looked like the Marlins might never score, Charles Johnson reached down for a 2-2 breaking ball, and hit it far over the auxiliary scoreboard in leftfield, tying the game.

"This is what it's all about," the players had kept telling us. After a season with very little meaningful tension, maybe it was.

◆ ◆ ◆

The Fish video was played on the video screens during the sixth inning, and the Marlins' bullpen pitchers used the opportunity to take a break from their focusing. When the featured attraction of the video appeared, a wiggling brunette in a blue string bikini, the pitchers stood up from their bullpen chairs and raised their caps in tribute. Then they sat down again. Then the wiggling blue-bikini-wearer reappeared, and they stood up and raised their caps again.

Dennis Cook was the leader of this bullpen tribute to blue-bikini-wearing brunettes, arousing concern that he had lost his focus. On that account, Leyland seemed to be taking a big chance when he removed the very focused Brown from the game with the score tied, 1-1, after seven innings and brought in the apparently unfocused Cook.

But Cook retired six straight batters in the eighth and ninth innings and proved that if a ballplayer has prepared himself sufficiently for a game, he can lose his focus for a while, then get it right back.

It ain't brain surgery.

◆ ◆ ◆

One more thing about that buxom, wiggling blue bikini-wearer, who had caused quite a stir in South Florida and inspired one newspaper to sponsor a Find The Blue-Bikini-Wearer hunt. Nobody knew exactly who she was, because when the video was made, the Marlins simply had those appearing in it sign release forms. There were no pictures to go with the release form, so the Marlins assumed the blue-bikini-wearer was an out-of-town tourist who had no idea how much excitement she had generated. But an ugly rumor going around the front office had the blue-bikini-wearer's age at only sixteen.

That's *One-Six*, two years under the legal limit. If this rumor was true, hundreds of thousands of men over the course of the season had been committing statutory ogling.

◆ ◆ ◆

With the scored tied at one, Conine led off the bottom of the ninth by singling off of reliever Julian Tavarez. Then Johnson squared to bunt and got hit on the right arm. He bent over in pain for several minutes, and at first it looked as if he had been hit on the hand. But Johnson stayed in the game, jogged to first base, and the Marlins had the winning run on second with none out. That's when Giants manager Dusty Baker called to his bullpen for righty Roberto Hernandez.

Back in late July, the Marlins had pursued Hernandez up until the trading deadline, only to drop out of the bidding when the White Sox held their mid-summer clearance sale and dealt him to the Giants, along with Wilson Alvarez and Danny Darwin. Hernandez had been one of baseball's dominant relievers over the past two seasons, but the Marlins weren't willing to pay the White Sox's price in prospects. The virtue of making, or not making, the deal would be played out over the next few batters.

So poor Craig Counsell, who had never seen a one hundred-mile-per-hour fastball in his life, was sent up to bunt against a man who threw one hundred-mile-per-hour fastballs.

"Have you ever seen a one hundred-mile-per-hour pitch coming at you?" Conine asked later, shaking his head in disbelief. He was glad that he didn't have to bunt, or bat, against Hernandez.

He did, however, have to get from second to third on the bunt, despite being one of the slowest Marlins. And Johnson at first wasn't exactly the Roadrunner, either. Counsell had to execute a perfect bunt.

Counsell fouled off the first pitch and looked at the next pitch for strike two. He glanced up at the scoreboard and saw that Hernandez's last pitch had registered one hundred miles per hour. He tried to erase the thought.

"You have to put it in your mind that you have to get the bunt down," Counsell said. "Obviously, he's not the easiest guy to bunt against, but you just have to do that. You expect yourself to do it. I feel like I should be able to execute every time."

Which he did. On the next pitch, Counsell laid a perfect bunt down the third base line, and the runners easily advanced. Eisenreich was intentionally walked, loading the bases, then Devon White hit a ground ball to second, and Jeff Kent threw home for the forceout.

But all that did was bring up Edgar Renteria, exactly the man the Marlins wanted up in this situation. Seven times this season, Renteria had delivered the game-winning hit in the Marlins' final at-bat. The coaches and players, when polled on who they most wanted at bat in a game-winning situation, almost unanimously chose Renteria.

Their confidence had a limit. Bonilla was so nervous he stood in the batroom, unable to watch. But there was Renteria, and there was Hernandez, throwing that one hundred-mile-per-hour fastball, and on a 2-1 pitch, Renteria slapped a soft line drive into rightfield. As the ball left Renteria's bat, Sheffield started the charge out of the dugout and the crowd, which was already standing, went silent for a moment. Then the ball landed cleanly, scoring Johnson from third and setting off a roar from the crowd and a wild celebration. Bonilla ran out of the batroom and hugged Leyland.

Sheffield, acting like Superman, hoisted Renteria onto his shoulders. The Marlins had enjoyed celebrations like this before during the regular season, but never had they meant so much.

"This is the best moment in my life," Renteria exulted. "People think because I'm young and I haven't been around I'm not able to do something like that. This shows I can."

After five regular seasons, it was the best moment in Marlins history.

◆ ◆ ◆

The post-game celebration didn't last long. After Sheffield carried Renteria back to the dugout, the Marlins whooped it up a little in the clubhouse for five minutes, then calmed down.

"We had a good time," Leiter said. "But we realize we're not done."

He cocked his head and smiled.

"We're still focused."

◆ ◆ ◆

Darren Daulton said after the first game, "I want to be the man." But he wasn't going to get to be the man because the Giants were using three straight left-handed starting pitchers in the series, and that meant Daulton would remain on the bench. Even if the Giants switched to a right-hander late in a game, Daulton wasn't going to replace Conine at first as long as the score was close. The memories were fresh of Daulton's three straight errors on three consecutive groundballs in September, and the Marlins couldn't afford his defensive shortcomings. Not in the playoffs, when one run could mean everything.

Daulton, however, had already made his contribution to the team. If he had done nothing more than hold that team meeting after that hot, depressing game in St. Louis on July 27, it would have been enough.

"This team spent a lot of money for a lot of guys with the intention of winning, but we didn't have a real team leader," Eisenreich said. "Bobby Bonilla tried to be a leader with his play on the field, but it wasn't quite the same thing. Dutch told us we had to play with more emotion and intensity. He got us together for the big series we had coming up against the Braves and the Orioles.

"I don't think anybody was surprised. I think it was something everybody was hoping for. We didn't know what we were doing. It was a turning point in the way that Jim Leyland had been trying to tell us the same thing since Day One of spring training, and now it was a teammate of ours saying it, and somebody that everybody respected. It didn't seem like that big a deal at the time, but we had all heard the hype about getting him, that he was such a leader, and he proved that leadership on the sixth day he was with the team. It really hit home with everybody."

Whether the meeting actually made a difference was difficult to judge. The Marlins were 58-44 at the time of the meeting, 34-26 the rest of the way, which is just about the same. But the players thought it mattered, so nothing else was important.

It ain't brain surgery.

◆ ◆ ◆

With security tightened at Pro Player Stadium, Travis Bickle, Dugout Security Guard, was more on edge than ever, and chewed out two police officers who wandered into the dugout—a restricted area. His twitch had intensified, his eyes had gone positively batty—little specks of pupils in a white sea of red veins. One of the reporters considered taking a mad dash through the dugout, just to see what might happen, but thought better of it. Travis would have nabbed him after one step and kicked him in the gut for good measure.

Another off-limits area was, believe it or not, the grass. A member of the Autograph Police politely asked a strayer, "Please don't step on the grass. The grounds crew doesn't want the grass getting flattened out." Nothing worse than flat grass for a playoff game.

◆ ◆ ◆

During the season, Leiter had pitched well against the Giants and Giants starter Shawn Estes had pitched well against the Marlins, so Game Two figured to be low scoring. It didn't happen that way. Leiter was gone after four innings, having allowed four runs and seven hits. Estes was gone after failing to retire a batter in the fourth, with the bases loaded and the scored tied at 4.

That put the game in the hands of the bullpens, where the Giants thought they had an edge with Hernandez and closer Rob Beck. The thing was, the Marlins had one of the best bullpens in baseball during the first half of the season, and when the playoffs started, Leyland improved the bullpen with the addition of one: Livan Hernandez.

Leyland had caught a lot of people by surprise when he announced his rotation for the series and revealed that Saunders, not Hernandez, would start Game Four against San Francisco. It had been widely assumed Saunders would pitch only against the Braves, who had accounted for three of his four wins. Instead, Hernandez was sent to the bullpen.

"We need someone down there who can go longer," Leyland said. "We haven't had a long guy in the bullpen all season."

None of the Marlins' relievers, other than Cook, were used to pitching more than two or three innings, and Cook hadn't been a long man in years. Even Hernandez, however, wasn't accustomed to this role. Since coming to the United States, he had started all but one of his fifty-eight minor and major league appearances. In Cuba, he was a starter. This season, he had never done anything but start.

Using Hernandez out of the bullpen couldn't have worked out better for the Marlins. He pitched four innings, allowed only one run, and received a standing ovation when he left the mound after the eighth inning, leading 6-5. The difference in the game had been a home run by Sheffield in the sixth, a rocket shot off of Julian Tavarez, and Nen was called on to finish off the Giants in the ninth. He didn't get the job done, though through no fault of his own.

226

Conine made an error. Stan Javier blooped a single to left. Nen struck out Jose Vizcaino and, for the third time this season, faced Barry Bonds with the game at stake.

The first time, back in June, Nen's shaky confidence was on the line after getting rocked by Colorado. Nen won.

The second time, in September, Leyland's decision to pitch to Bonds, rather than have Nen walk him and pitch to Jeff Kent, was on the line. Nen won again.

This time, Game Two of the Division Series hung in the balance.

Nen threw an inside fastball. Bonds hit a ground ball to short. Renteria fielded it cleanly and flipped to Counsell for the force. But Counsell's throw to first was in the dirt, and the tying run scored.

"I was so keyed up, so adrenalined up, that I wanted that inning to start over again and not have it be tied this time," Nen said.

He couldn't have that.

The Marlins would have to find another way to win in the bottom of the ninth.

◆ ◆ ◆

The situation could have been worse for the Marlins. They had won twenty-five games this season in their final at-bat, including sixteen in the eighth or ninth innings, and had the heart of their order coming up: Sheffield, Bonilla, and Alou.

Again, Baker summoned Roberto Hernandez from the bullpen. Stan Javier moved from center to right, and Dante Powell was brought in as a defensive replacement in centerfield. Down at third base, coach Rich Donnelly was thinking, *It happens every time. Every time they do a double-switch, the ball's always hit to the outfielder with the best arm.* That would be Powell.

When Sheffield led off the inning with a single and stole second on the first pitch to Bonilla, and Bonilla walked on a 3-2 pitch, Donnelly immediately started thinking about what he would do if Moises Alou got a hit.

"You try to pre-think it," Donnelly said. "I said to myself, *If it's a hit toward Powell, and it's not a one-hopper, then take a shot with Sheff.* I knew Powell could throw, but I also knew with Hernandez, you won't get too many chances."

Alou lined the ball sharply toward left-center. Sheffield, not knowing whether it would be caught, took a step back to second. Sheffield should have been watching Donnelly. When he realized the ball would drop in, Sheffield headed toward third, and Donnelly waved him around to score. Powell fielded the ball cleanly and threw home, and Sheffield was going to be out, by five feet or more. Donnelly, watching the play, could do nothing but hope. There was no reversing what he had already set in motion.

"I was just trying to tell the ball to slow down," Donnelly later said.

Then an amazing thing happened: Powell's throw hit the pitcher's mound and bounced straight up. Sheffield tripped clumsily over his own feet and dove into home. He soared and landed chin-first, chest-next, on home plate with the winning run. The throw never even reached the catcher. Over in the visitor's dugout, Baker slammed his cap on the floor, cursing the Giants' bad luck. Meanwhile, another mob scene, just like the one after Game One, was taking place near home plate. This time, Sheffield was in the middle.

◆ ◆ ◆

The Marlins looked like they had been through something far more draining than a playoff game. Leyland removed his cap at the post-game press conference, revealing a bright red rash across his forehead. Said Conine, "After the first two games at home, I felt like I'd been in a car wreck. It's tense. You're into every pitch. If you kept up this level of intensity for a hundred sixty-two games, you'd burn out."

Sheffield was emotionally and physically drained. After the game, he disappeared into the trainer's room for nearly a half hour. It wasn't his best game of the season—he had misjudged a fly ball in the seventh inning that cost the Marlins a run—but it was his most important: three hits, a home run, and scoring the game-winning run.

"He's doing well," Bonilla said. "He's just trying to make everyone forget about the regular season."

About forty-five minutes later, sitting in front of his stall, with his son tugging on his nose and planting kisses on his face, Sheffield looked like he had already forgotten.

◆ ◆ ◆

Don Smiley was standing in the Marlins' clubhouse and smiling like a little boy on Christmas Day, and not only because the Marlins were ahead two games to none. What made Smiley so happy was that he had invited several potential investors to both games and knew there was no better selling job than the one the team had done over the past two nights.

"I invited them because I wanted them to share in the excitement of post-season baseball," Smiley said. "They had pretty good seats."

One of Smiley's friends who attended the game had seats that were a little too good. His name was Paul Anderson, and he was sitting in the first row, next to the screen behind home plate, when Estes fouled off a pitch in the second inning. The ball headed straight toward where Anderson was sitting, a few yards from where Smiley was safely ensconced behind the screen, and Smiley's only thought was, *I hope nobody gets hurt by that.* But the ball struck Anderson right in the temple and he sat bent over while Marlins trainer Larry Starr attended to him.

Anderson, by the way, was not one of the potential investors, although Smiley could have kicked himself for not seizing the moment. Here was a man with money, dazed and confused, a little out of sorts because he had just been struck in the head by a baseball. Maybe suffering from a momentary loss of judgment.

"I don't know," Smiley cracked. "That might have been a good time to ask him for $10 million."

Anderson turned out to be OK. He was taken to a nearby hospital, then returned during the eighth inning wearing a batting helmet for protection. The crowd behind home plate gave him a standing ovation and Smiley didn't ask him for a dime.

◆ ◆ ◆

Game Three would be played at 3Com Park in San Francisco where, as Charles Johnson said, "you get to the ballpark and there's no wind at all, then by the fourth or fifth inning, there's wind all over the place."

The Marlins arrived in San Francisco early Thursday morning, October 2, and worked out late in the afternoon at 3Com Park. The wind, of course, was blowing all over the place, and the sun was shining all over the place, and Leyland detected that the Marlins seemed a little distracted. He detected this because many of the players were complaining about the wind and the sun.

Leyland responded by stealing a scene from Norman Dale. This one was from the final act of *Hoosiers*, when the Hickory High players walk into the gym where the state championship game will be played, and are overwhelmed by its size. Coach Dale has one of his players measure the height of the basket.

"Ten feet," the player says.

Then he has him measure the distance from the foul line to the basket.

"Fifteen feet," the player says.

"I think you'll find," Norman Dale says, "it's the exact same measurements as our gym back in Hickory."

Players smile. Background music swells.

Here's how Leyland handled a similar situation in semi-real life:

"Hey, Devo," Leyland said in front of all the players. "How far is it from home plate to first base?"

"Ninety feet," White said, laughing. He had seen *Hoosiers.*

"How far is it from the pitcher's mound to home plate?" Leyland asked.

"Sixty feet, six inches," White said, still laughing. The players laughed. They stopped complaining.

The only thing missing was background music.

◆ ◆ ◆

Down two games to none, the Giants would have to win all three home games, a task made more difficult by the fact that they would have to face Brown again in Game Five. If they got there, which nobody expected them to do.

The Giants' Game Three starting pitcher was Wilson Alvarez, a former teammate of Marlins starter Alex Fernandez with the Chicago White Sox. Alvarez, who was born in Maracaibo, Venezuela, and hadn't yet mastered the finer points of English, had appeared at a press conference two days earlier and concluded just about every sentence with the phrase, "What can I say?"

On Alex Fernandez, his Game Three opponent: "Me and Alex are good friends, but when the game starts, he's going to be the enemy. What can I say?"

On big game pressure: "I'm going to try my best. What can I say?"

On being a big-game pitcher: "I never said that. I let the people say that and I let my numbers say that. What can I say?"

The story goes that when Alvarez was twelve years old and growing up in Venezuela, his parents made him choose between school and baseball. He chose baseball and never again went to school.

Which simply proves, once again, this thing about baseball: It ain't brain surgery, but it's a great way to get rich quick.

◆ ◆ ◆

Cliff Floyd, who was left off of the Marlins' post-season roster in lieu of John Wehner, made the trip to San Francisco. He wore his uniform, but otherwise looked like a little kid who couldn't come out to play as he sat in the visitor's dugout before Game Three and watched batting practice.

"Whaddya think, Cliff?" a reporter asked him.

Floyd shook his head, sat down, and folded his arms across his chest. "I don't think," he said forlornly.

◆ ◆ ◆

More pre-game scenes. Jim Leyland stood at one end of the dugout and stared long, hard, and curiously toward the opposite end where Michelle Kaufman, a reporter from *The Miami Herald,* was involved in heated discussion, in Spanish, with Livan Hernandez. Kaufman had written a very long, very flattering story about Hernandez, that included one unflattering quote—from Livan himself—about Hernandez's alcoholic father. Kaufman walked away in tears. As for Hernandez, he wasn't going to pitch that night, anyway, so there was no concern about losing focus.

Jay Powell, surrounded by teammates, performed his hilarious imitation of Sheffield's batting stance: Legs spread, feet dug deep into the dirt, hips swiveling, circling the bat behind his head, chewing his tongue, head and shoulders snapping back as if he was trying to avoid an inside pitch, then a hard glare because the imaginary pitch was called a strike. Sheffield laughed harder than anyone.

A young Giants fan reached over the dugout roof and asked Moises Alou for an autograph, and Alou said, "I don't sign in post-season." Which was unusual because Alou was one of the Marlins who usually signed autographs, especially on the road.

The two managers, Leyland and Baker, chatted and laughed near the batting cage while the Giants took BP.

Bonilla lifted two batting practice home runs into the rightfield upper deck, and Daulton just missed the top level. The wind was blowing out, which looked like bad news for Fernandez, who allowed a lot of long home runs without wind.

Then Wayne Huizenga, wearing a jacket and tie, walked onto the field, joined by Wayne Jr., wearing a neck brace and a Marlins jacket. Soon they were surrounded by Dave Dombrowski, Frank Wren, Jonathan Mariner, Don Smiley, and Huizenga Holdings higher-ups Bob Heninger and Jim Cole. Huizenga, an admitted fair-weather fan, even when he owns the team he's rooting for, had jumped on the Marlins bandwagon.

If there's anything worse than a fair-weather fan, it's a fair-weather fan who owns the team.

Huizenga wasn't the only one who had jumped on the bandwagon. The Marlins, despite their failure to sell out the first two home games, were becoming more popular. Back in Florida that morning, tickets for Games Three, Four, and Five of the National League Championship Series had gone on sale, and nearly two thousand people were standing on line when the windows opened at Pro Player Stadium. For the Division Series, about fourteen thousand tickets were sold the first day; this time, thirty thousand were sold.

And everybody loves a winner.

◆ ◆ ◆

Then the Marlins went out and looked like anything but winners because Wilson Alvarez—What can he say?—was shutting them down easily. They managed only three hits and no runs through the first five innings, and it was a good thing Fernandez had his best stuff. It was also a good thing the swirling winds at 3Com had changed direction just before game time and were swirling in, away from rightfield.

Not that the wind at 3Com isn't always a problem, no matter its direction. At a team meeting the day before, Leyland reminded his players that when the ball was hit in the air, every player within reaching distance should give chase. Good move.

In the first inning, Bonds hit a popup behind third that the wind blew into a popup behind short. Bonilla couldn't make the play, but Renteria was right there and did.

"If Edgar stays at shortstop," Leyland said, "we're in trouble."

The wind was blowing all over the place. The game started at 5:07 local time, but as the sun set, the temperature dropped, and the crowd of 57,188 that nearly packed 3Com bundled up. The weather had become a factor, but a good one for the Marlins. Kent hit a homer to dead center in the fourth—even the wind couldn't stop that bomb—but in the next inning, shots to rightfield by Vizcaino and Brian Johnson that should have left the ballpark dropped into Sheffield's glove.

◆ ◆ ◆

The Giants still had their 1-0 lead with two outs in the sixth, when Alou lined a sharp single to centerfield. Conine, the next batter, singled off of third baseman Bill Mueller's glove. Johnson walked on a 3-2 pitch, and White came up with the bases loaded and two outs. With the game, and possibly the Giants' season, on the line, Baker walked to the mound and tried to calm Alvarez.

"I could see he was frustrated," Baker said later. "I told him to relax and concentrate on his target and not worry about who's hitting."

Baker walked back to the dugout. Over the next few days, the critics in San Francisco would say he should have brought Alvarez with him, but Baker had nobody warming up in the bullpen. He didn't think he had much reason to worry about the No. 8 hitter in the Marlins' lineup, who had hit .188 against lefties during the season.

Alvarez threw a ball and a strike, then White skipped out of the way of a low, inside fastball. If he allowed himself to get hit, the game would have been tied, and what happened next wouldn't have happened.

Alvarez threw a low, inside fastball. White, seeing his favorite pitch, swung, made contact, and sent the ball toward the leftfield corner, into the ever-changing wind. Leyland later said he had no doubt it was gone, but the northwesterlies blowing in from leftfield did their best to keep the ball in the park. Bonds raced back to the base of the wall and jumped. The ball landed in the second row of the metal bleachers for a grand slam, and the Marlins had a 4-1 lead.

Bonilla danced out of the dugout and led his teammates toward home plate. Then, as if they realized the game wasn't over and a mob scene at home wasn't called for, the Marlins veered off, stopped, and waited. White circled the bases calmly, because he also realized the game wasn't over, but when he reached the dugout, his teammates were there to mob him.

"I'm not a home run hitter," White said. "You know the pitcher is going to press a little to throw strikes. Sometimes we press as hitters, too. But on this occasion, I got the better end of the stick." The Marlins had three innings to go.

◆ ◆ ◆

Roberto Hernandez, the Marlin who wasn't, failed again. He allowed two runs in the eighth, and Dennis Cook took a 6-2 lead into the bottom of the ninth. Cook didn't last long. He walked leadoff hitter J. T. Snow, and Leyland summoned Nen from the bullpen.

A chill wind swirled through the stadium. The fans in the leftfield seats drummed up a conga beat by banging their feet in time against the metal bleachers. The scoreboard flashed, "Anything Can Happen," and several fans waved huge Giants flags. It had become a typical San Francisco night—cold and breezy and anything could happen.

Nen didn't have his best control and walked Glenallen Hill. The Marlins got the first out when Vizcaino reached on a force at second, and the second out when Nen struck out Brian Johnson on a low fastball. Everyone in the ballpark was standing, including the players in both dugouts.

With two outs and runners on first and third, Nen lost his control again. Damon Berryhill, the pinch-hitter, worked the count to 3-1. If he walked, the tying run would have been at home plate. Fans in the centerfield seats threw toilet paper onto the field. Nen waited for the grounds crew to finish its work, rubbed up the baseball, and placed his right foot on the rubber. His next pitch was a fastball—his best pitch—and Berryhill grounded to second. Counsell fielded it cleanly, threw to first for the out, and the Marlins had the first series win in their five-year history.

Of course, they celebrated. Renteria jumped on top of Counsell and Conine, who were soon mobbed by all of their teammates, first Johnson, then Sheffield, then everybody else. The crowd ignored the Marlins and applauded the Giants. And in the background, Leyland walked briskly over to the Giants' dugout and shook hands with Dusty Baker and the Giants coaches. It looked like a very nice gesture.

◆ ◆ ◆

The Marlins ran back to the clubhouse and continued their celebration behind closed doors. According to major league rules, they were supposed to open the clubhouse immediately following the game, but Leyland decided to defy authority.

"I want them to enjoy it," Leyland barked.

But twenty-five minutes later, Leyland still hadn't opened the clubhouse, and the reporters and TV people outside were getting impatient. They pleaded to National League vice president Katy Feeney, who demanded that Leyland open the clubhouse.

"Fine," Leyland grudgingly conceded. "Open the fucking thing."

Because reporters and cameras weren't allowed inside, nobody knows exactly what was taking place, other than a lot of hollering and champagne pouring. This much is known: When the doors finally opened, Huizenga was standing near the entrance, smiling widely and dripping wet with champagne from head to toe. And later, still smiling, he said, "They were sticking it down the back of my trousers, and I was giving it right back."

◆ ◆ ◆

And about Leyland's post-game gesture: Baker appreciated it and said so.

Leyland also appreciated his gesture and also said so, in the clubhouse later on, even though nobody had asked him about it. Then, just as he was explaining why he did what he did, Antonio Alfonseca walked over and dumped the contents of a can of beer over his head.

◆ ◆ ◆

This celebration stuff was getting a bit ridiculous. First there was the Wild Card celebration, now the Division Series celebration, and if the Marlins won the World Series, there would be two more celebrations. In all other sports, teams celebrate once, when they win the whole thing. Only in baseball do eight teams out of twenty-six pour champagne over each other's heads, then four more after the first round of the playoffs.

What set apart this celebration from the one in Montreal was the presence of Barry Bonds, mustard, and milk, in that order. First, Bonds strolled down the hallway from the Giants clubhouse, turned left into the Marlins clubhouse, spotted his friend Bonilla standing near the doorway, and gave him a big hug. Bonds told Bonilla that he loved him. Bonilla told Bonds that he loved him, too.

A few minutes later, Bonds made his way over to Leyland, who was standing against a table in the middle of the clubhouse, smiling yet controlling his emotions. Bonds grabbed his former manager and pulled him tight into his chest. Leyland's hands started shaking, his face turned red, and tears flowed as Bonds whispered sweet nothings into his ear.

"I love you man. You're the best, man," Bonds whispered, and the more he whispered, the harder Leyland cried. He left Leyland sitting there a blubbering mess with tears dripping down his cheeks and his right hand shaking as it held a cup of beer.

This was a good thing, because up until Bonds showed up, nobody was crying, and although there was a lot of pouring going on, there wasn't that raw emotion every celebration needs. Sheffield also got a hug from Bonds and some good advice.

"Enjoy the moment, little brother, and keep the same focus you had against us," Bonds whispered. "You can carry this team. You can take it all the way to the World Series. I love you."

Sheffield sure looked like he was enjoying the moment. He had a right to after batting .556 in the series and reaching base ten out of fourteen times. He sat in the middle of the joyous clubhouse, puffing on a Cuban cigar and drinking from one of the few bottles of champagne Alfonseca hadn't poured over anyone's head. There were ice packs on his right shoulder and left thigh, but he didn't look or sound like he was in any kind of pain.

"Is that a good cigar?" he was asked.

"I don't know," Sheffield said, "and I really don't care."

It was about then that the milk and mustard started flying. The Marlins had run out of champagne and beer, so a few of the players, Alfonseca in particular, found the next best things, milk and mustard, and started pouring them over people's heads. Mustard, of course, doesn't flow quite as freely as milk, so that experiment was quickly quashed, but the milk pouring continued. The most unfortunate victim was a team photographer, who had two gallons of milk poured over her head as Alfonseca chased her across the room. The way she figured it, better her head than the expensive camera she was holding in her hand.

Ten players sat in the trainer's room smoking cigars and drinking beer, and finally, after about an hour of this, Bonilla walked through the clubhouse waving his arms, and broke up the party by shouting, "OK, shower up! Let's go!"

It was just as well, because by that time, even the milk supply had been exhausted.

◆ ◆ ◆

Later on, several Marlins were hanging out in a restaurant at the Parc 55 hotel, when Leyland walked in, took a seat at the bar, and ordered a drink. Standing nearby was Dan Le Batard of *The Miami Herald,* along with a female friend and two of her female friends. One of them, a provocatively dressed blonde wearing a tight, cleavage-revealing top, turned around and started talking to Leyland, and the first thing he did was admonish her for the way she was dressed.

"It's disrespectful," Leyland scolded.

"Would you believe I'm an M.D.?" she asked.

"Would you believe I'm the manager of a baseball team?" he said.

"Baseball's boring," she said. "I like basketball."

The woman proved she was an M.D. by pulling out her business card and showing it to Leyland, but Leyland had no way of proving to her that he was a major league manager.

"You really don't know who I am, do you?" Leyland asked again.

"I believe you, I believe you," she insisted, although unconvincingly.

Leyland kept trying to convince her that he was somebody famous, and all the time she had her back turned to a bank of TV sets airing highlights from the Giants-Marlins game. Then Leyland's face appeared on all of the TVs and the woman's friends shouted out, "Look! Look!"

Finally, she turned around and saw that the person sitting in front of her was the same person on TV. And she still wasn't impressed.

"I told you," she said. "I don't like baseball. It's boring. I like basketball."

The Marlins' bus left for the airport a few minutes later.

◆ ◆ ◆

Even Leyland wasn't sure how impressed he was by the victory. Sure, he was proud of the team, which had won a playoff series faster than any expansion team in history, but he had a hard time expressing his pride. Now that the Marlins had won something, they weren't sure exactly what they had won, other than the right to play the Braves in the National League Championship Series.

"Well, now we're the division champions, or the Division Series champions, or whatever," Leyland said a few days later. "Don't ask me what the heck we are."

16

One of Our Pitchers
Is Missing

October 7, 8 at Atlanta
October 10, 11 vs. Atlanta

According to a *USA Today*/CNN/Gallup Poll, twenty-three percent of fans who cared said they hoped the Braves won the World Series. But if the pollsters had bothered talking to Major League Baseball players, the results would have been far different: The Braves were the most hated team inside of baseball.

"Do me a favor," J. T. Snow of the Giants said to Jeff Conine while standing on first base during a pitching change in the ninth inning of Game Three. "If you win this, go kick the shit out of the Braves. And shove it up Chipper Jones's ass."

Jones had gained a reputation for having the biggest mouth in baseball and the Braves had gained a reputation for being the most arrogant team in baseball. This arrogance was expressed by pitcher John Smoltz when he commented on the Marlins making their first appearance in the National League Championship Series.

"Their feeling has to be greater than ours," Smoltz said. "Not to take away from our feeling, but we've been here so many times, we have nothing to gain. They have everything to gain."

Smoltz could be excused for his forgetfulness. It was true the Braves had reached the NLCS the last five times that there had been an NLCS, but they only had one World Series win to their credit. Not only could the Braves be considered baseball's Team of the '90s, they were baseball's Chokingest Team of the '90s.

Chipper Jones flashback, August 2: "You could say we're choking, you could say we're nervous, but the bottom line is we're just not getting the job done."

Well, for the Braves, now was the time and the Marlins wanted nothing more than to follow J. T. Snow's instructions.

It was personal. Publicly, the Marlins proclaimed their respect for the Braves. And they did respect the Braves. They just didn't like them.

The Marlins remembered how aloof and smug and confident the Braves were during the eight-game stretch of games in July and August, when the Marlins won five of eight. When asked about the Marlins' regular season dominance of Atlanta, Greg Maddux responded, "Who really cares?" The Braves seemed so workman-

236

like, they almost came across as inhuman. They pouted over losses and didn't celebrate victories, as if they always expected to win.

"You don't make plans for October vacations in this clubhouse," Jones had said.

Of course not. They're too busy losing in the World Series.

Leyland, who along with Bonilla had lost twice with the Pirates to Atlanta in seventh games of the NLCS, in 1991 and 1992, denied he had bitter memories of those losses—even the Cabrera game—but those closest to him, like Rich Donnelly, knew otherwise. Leyland couldn't have forgotten. People were reminding him of it all the time.

Leyland had no intention of repeating history. After the Marlins eliminated the Giants, he told his coaches, "We will beat Atlanta." He was sure of it.

The problem was, the Braves had three Cy Young Award winners—Maddux, Glavine, and Smoltz—and a 20-game winner, Denny Neagle. All Leyland had was a feeling.

◆ ◆ ◆

Well, just wait a minute with that theme of Big Bad Braves vs. the Lovable Young Marlins, because it didn't quite work. The idea of the fifth-year expansion team challenging the mighty Braves sounded appealing—like something out of *Hoosiers*—but it was misleading. Leyland was asked about being the sentimental favorite and said, "The only people I might be a sentimental favorite with are my wife and my mother."

He had that right. The Braves' payroll was now a half million dollars lower than the Marlins. Nine of the current Marlins, including three-fifths of the starting rotation, had been bought through free-agency over the past two seasons. The Braves had only six free agents and of them, only Maddux was an impact player. The rest of the team had been built through the amateur draft and trades. And the Braves planned on keeping their high-priced players. According to Huizenga, the Marlins were just renting theirs.

So just to set the matchup straight, this wasn't exactly David vs. Goliath. Or Hickory High vs. South Bend Central. It was Ted Turner vs. Wayne Huizenga, a couple of billionaire owners showing off what they had bought.

◆ ◆ ◆

Leyland announced his pitching rotation on Monday, a day before Game One at Turner Field: Brown, Fernandez, Saunders, Brown again, Leiter, Fernandez, and Brown again. And Daulton, when informed that Brown would pitch in Games One, Four, and Seven, said, "He definitely did not mention two, three, and five?"

The idea was for Brown and Fernandez to pitch five of the seven games, even though Brown would pitch twice on three days rest, something Leyland hadn't asked any of his pitchers to do all season.

"I felt this gave us our best chance," Leyland said. "Brownie's well rested, he hasn't been pushed real hard, and he was very receptive to it. I feel good about it.

But let's face it: When they know they have Maddux, Glavine, and Smoltz, they're not feeling too bad, either."

The rotation had taken shape swiftly. The way Leyland told it, he had jotted down a few ideas, then talked it over with pitching coach Larry Rothschild during the plane ride from San Francisco to Florida after Game Three of the Division Series. Then they told Brown.

Which prompted a member of the Marlins' traveling party to ask, "Was that before or after Leyland passed out for six hours on the plane?"

◆ ◆ ◆

Atlanta had taken on a few subtle changes since the Marlins last visited in early August. Most of the rubble had been cleared from the pit of Atlanta-Fulton County Stadium and all that remained was the lower cement shell. The transformation from stadium to parking lot was proceeding quickly. About forty thousand computer conventioneers had invaded the city, turning Atlanta into a hotel price-gouger's dream. Inside Turner Field, red, white, and blue bunting decorated the facades, the grounds crew manicured the field, and security guards prepared for the media invasion that comes with every National League Championship Series.

"Don't step on the grass!" a security guard warned, sounding eerily like the Pro Player Stadium Autograph Police.

Over in the visitor's clubhouse, the coffee table reading material had been updated. There was a fresh copy of *Penthouse's High Heels,* with cover and staples intact. Also, new issues of *Esquire, Sport,* and *Hunter.* The Marlins obviously weren't about to chance losing their focus just to ogle magazines-full of naked party girls, because Dennis Cook sat down in one of the leather couches and read *Hunter* and Tony Saunders pushed aside *Penthouse's High Heels* and dug into a golf magazine.

The Marlins were ready.

◆ ◆ ◆

Just to clarify matters, Leyland said, "Somebody's gonna win four games and when they do, they're going to the World Series."

Then the teams really took off their gloves and started firing shots at each other.

"This is what you play for," Conine explained.

"It's an entirely brand new ballgame," Braves manager Bobby Cox offered.

"They're good," said Bonilla, assessing the Braves.

"This is the playoffs," C. Jones reminded.

"Atlanta is the team to beat," Brown said. "There's a rivalry."

And, in case anybody forgot, Maddux pointed out, "Seven games and you need four wins."

Then you get to the World Series.

◆ ◆ ◆

Leyland had a closed-door meeting Monday with his players that lasted about a minute, and a longer closed-door meeting with National League vice president Katy Feeney. The NL wanted to make certain Leyland didn't close the clubhouse for twenty-five minutes after a game, as he did in San Francisco.

Leyland prevailed on one point. Feeney agreed he was within his rights by restricting the media from interviewing players during batting practice. So on Tuesday, October 7, before Game One, when Dan Le Batard of *The Miami Herald* was talking to Moises Alou during batting practice, Leyland walked up behind Le Batard, tapped him on the leg with his bat, and grumbled, "Dan, we're working."

Alou went back to what he was doing, which was walking around doing nothing, and most of the Marlins kept on doing what they were doing, which was standing in the outfield and shagging fly balls. They must have been getting focused.

◆ ◆ ◆

In The Attack of the Killer Clichés, Charles Johnson—who never has much of anything to say to the media, but is always willing to say it—said this when asked how much confidence the Marlins had gained from beating the Braves during the regular season.

His response went, in this order, verbatim:
1. "This is a totally different ballgame . . .
2. "Everything starts at zero . . .
3. "You can't focus on what happened during the season at this point . . .
4. "We have to turn the page and keep going, . . .
5. "come out today and execute . . .
6. "and do the things we've been doing all year to win."
Six clichés. Count 'em. Six. C. J. was in post-season form.

◆ ◆ ◆

Conine was talking about the Game One matchup between Maddux and Brown, and said, "If they're both on, they're gonna get everybody out. It's as simple as that."

It would have been that simple for Maddux, except Fred McGriff, his first baseman, missed an easy grounder by Conine in the first inning, loading the bases, and C. Jones, who was nursing a sore ankle, allowed Moises Alou's ground ball down the third base line to skip over his glove, scoring three runs. The crowd of 49,244, went dead silent because it realized a 3-0 deficit against Brown was trouble.

The Marlins had three unearned runs in the first inning, then Kenny Lofton raced all the way back to the centerfield fence for a drive by Sheffield in the third inning, only to watch the ball bounce off his glove. Before the inning was over, the Marlins had two more unearned runs, and Alou had four RBIs in the first three innings.

Brown didn't have his best stuff, either, but it was good enough, and he left after six innings with a 5-3 lead. The bullpen took over, Cook, Powell, and Nen shut down the Braves on no hits the rest of the way, and the Marlins had the win they needed in Atlanta.

The Braves also lodged their first complaint: If they hadn't made those errors, they might have won the game.

Were they dreaming? The implication was that unearned runs didn't count as much as earned runs.

"Everybody talks about unearned runs," Bonilla said later. "Bottom line, it's a win."

◆ ◆ ◆

The win had its price for the Marlins. In the bottom of the sixth inning, Alou jumped as high as he could, but couldn't haul in a home run by Ryan Klesko. He suffered two injuries on the play, one to his left wrist as it banged against the fence, and one to his right hamstring. Alou felt more pain in his hamstring than in his wrist, so the leg got ice, and the wrist didn't.

Renteria also had a rough night. Three batters after Klesko homered, Michael Tucker slid into second and jammed one of his spikes into Renteria's left leg. As Renteria laid on the ground for three minutes, having his shin taped where it had bled, he said to himself, *I'm gonna stay in. The only way I come out is if I break my leg.* Renteria stayed in the game, batted in the seventh, and got hit by a pitch on his right foot.

Revenge came swiftly. With one out and Renteria on third, Conine hit a low fly to short rightfield. Tucker caught it on a dead run, and third base coach Rich Donnelly sent Renteria. The throw beat Renteria by five feet, and Javy Lopez had the ball in his glove when Renteria started his slide. Right then, Lopez knew he was going to get hit, he just didn't know where. Renteria came in with his right leg elevated and spiked Lopez in the groin.

"If he doesn't hit me in my groin, he probably hits me somewhere else," Lopez said later, showing laudable understanding. "It'd be even worse. He was gonna knock the crap out of me somehow."

The Marlins sitting on the bench didn't realize what Renteria had done until later when they watched the replay back in their rooms or down in the hotel bar. ESPN kept showing the play in slow motion, just so all of its viewers could see, frame-by-frame, exactly where Renteria spiked Lopez.

"I was surprised," Abbott said, stifling a laugh. "I'm like, 'Holy shit! He did get him in the nuts!'"

Abbott then offered a lesson in Protective Cup Science: "When you get hit in the cup directly, it doesn't hurt," he said. "It's the hits that come up from underneath that are gonna get you. It looked like he got him directly."

◆ ◆ ◆

A reporter asked Bonilla what the Marlins game plan was against Maddux, and Bonilla said, "Swing the bat."

And Leyland said, "The idea is to win four games, so that means we have to win three more."

◆ ◆ ◆

240

The Marlins' Game Two problems started in the morning, when a groggy Alou tried getting out of bed by pushing off on his left hand, and fell on the floor. Later, he tried taking batting practice and couldn't even grip his bat. So at 3 o'clock, a very sad looking Alou talked things over in the dugout with Leyland and Dombrowski, and decided he couldn't play. Eisenreich replaced him in the lineup.

Then, in the bottom of the first inning, leadoff hitter Kenny Lofton bunted, and Charles Johnson made the mistake of trying to throw him out at first, even though he didn't stand a chance. Johnson realized his mistake the moment the ball left his hand—too late—and his throw skipped past Conine and into foul territory. Lofton, a fast runner, raced to second, and Johnson was credited with his first error in one hundred seventy-five games. His timing couldn't have been worse.

As for starting pitcher Fernandez, he had felt fine while warming up in the bullpen, but apparently lost something during the walk to the mound. The velocity on his pitches was down by as much as ten miles per hour compared to his normal speed. Keith Lockhart tripled home Lofton, Fernandez struck out Jones and McGriff, but Klesko homered into the rightfield bleachers, giving the Braves a 3-0 lead.

Klesko was quite impressed by his home run. He must have been. He stood at the plate and watched its flight for about an hour and a half, then casually flipped his bat to the ground before jogging to first base. Then he spent about another hour and a half circling the bases. By the time Klesko touched home, most of the crowd of 48,933 had gone home and to bed, so there were only a few people remaining to watch the rest of the Braves' 7-1 victory.

OK, that's not how it happened, although that's about how it was described after the game to Fernandez, who didn't see Klesko's act. After two relatively uneventful games, there wasn't much for the reporters to write about, other than Renteria's adventure in Game One and Klesko's showboating in Game Two, and there was no harm in stirring up a little bit of bad blood between the two teams. Fernandez, who lasted only 2⅔ innings and allowed five runs, was tired of talking about himself and obliged.

"I don't appreciate that, and we'll take care of it," he said. "I wish I would've seen it."

Bonilla, standing at third base, saw Klesko's act. He didn't mind it, either. In fact, he might as well have walked over to the Braves' clubhouse and patted Klesko on the back. It's the strangest, and sometimes the most endearing, thing about Bonilla, the way he sometimes talks about a game as if he were an observer, rather than a participant. He acted that way after Galarraga's monumental blast at Pro Player Stadium in late May, and here he was again, admiring Klesko.

"I wasn't mad at him," Bonilla said. "You know, he was probably in the moment. The crowd got into it, it was a big hit. During the regular season, it's one thing. It's the post-season. The world's watching. I guess you're entertaining a bit. Trust me, if I get the chance, I'll be standing there my damned self. I'll be styling like a mother fucker."

So much for bad blood.

♦ ♦ ♦

Even Fernandez had other things to worry about besides Klesko's showboating. Like himself. "This was a horseshit effort," he said. "It happens. Not often, but it does."

The funny thing was, although Fernandez seemed upset over his performance, he wasn't nearly as angry or surly as he had been after other bad outings this season. For example, this time, he didn't smash a water cooler or summon the baseball bat-wielding termites to eat away at his locker, the way he had after that bad outing in July. He sat in front of his stall and calmly answered questions for an hour in two languages, English and Spanish, explaining himself over and over.

"I felt pretty good in the bullpen," Fernandez said. "I felt like I had my weapons. But there's no excuses. I can still make pitches, even if I don't have my best stuff, by locating."

"Can you take it on faith that you'll have your best stuff next time?"

"Absolutely," Fernandez said. "Absolutely."

Larry Rothschild was asked whether there was reason to be concerned Fernandez might have arm trouble or a tired arm, and here's what he said: "We're not going to worry, unless he has unusual stiffness tomorrow or another reason to think he has a problem. I only think he's going to get out of it. It's more surprising when he doesn't get himself going."

Fernandez felt the same way. At least he said he did.

◆ ◆ ◆

The surest way to get a rise out of anybody affiliated with the Marlins was to mention their payroll. Of course, they loved hearing about it back in February and March, when they were using their payroll to sell tickets, but now that they had won something, they didn't like hearing that they had bought their success. They seemed to think it somehow cheapened what they had accomplished.

Offered Leyland, the man who had left Pittsburgh because the Pirates weren't spending enough money to suit his needs, "All this payroll talk makes me sick, to be honest with you. When they were jumping around after beating San Francisco, you never would have known they made a nickel." He paused and smiled. "And if they dropped it, I would've been the first to pick it up."

Well, he would have had to beat Huizenga to the pile.

"The Mets' payroll was $45 million and they didn't make the playoffs," Don Smiley pointed out.

"Yeah, and half of their starting rotation was on the DL last season."

"So what? They're not here, are they? People don't realize how hard it is to get this far."

The funny thing about the Marlins' protests was that there's nothing wrong with buying a pennant. It's just that the idea is so new. During the first seventy years of this century, the owners had all the power and all the money, the players had none of the power and none of the money, and free-agency hadn't been invented. The alternative to free-agency and player movement is indentured servitude, which is basically how baseball used to operate. Now here were the Marlins acting as if they had done something wrong, when they had actually done exactly what they set out to do.

Is it fair that teams can buy a pennant? the media asked. Well, the system certainly wasn't fair in the 1950s, but it's a lot fairer now. Before Game One of the NLCS, union president Don Fehr was seen walking around the field, sporting a knowing smirk. He had reason to be happy. Four of the top five payroll teams in baseball were still in the playoffs, added incentive for teams to go out and spend more money on players.

For the Marlins, a fifth-year team, spending money was a shortcut to the level reached by the Braves, whose team included players they had acquired as early as 1984. Huizenga had needed an answer to his question: Could the Marlins attract bigger crowds with a better team? Many of their minor league prospects weren't ready, so they took the shortcut and spent money.

"Unless you have a high payroll, you're not going to play in the post-season, especially in the later rounds," Dombrowski said, sounding like the Marlins' sole voice of reason. "You can overcome so much with a large payroll. We wouldn't be as good a club if we had a $30 million payroll. But a high payroll doesn't mean you're going to have a winning club."

That's true. It's also true that having a low payroll means you're not going to have a winning club.

The bad part about free-agency isn't when a team goes out and buys players. The bad part, as Giants president Peter Magowan said, is when a team buys players, then decides halfway through the season it doesn't want those players anymore.

At least the Braves' most important players figured to be around for a while. Getting attached to specific Marlins players was like hiring an escort and calling her your wife.

◆ ◆ ◆

Well, at least $7 million worth of Marlins payroll wasn't going anywhere in 1998. As it turned out, Fernandez not only lost something on his way from the bullpen to the mound before Game Two, he had lost most of his right shoulder between September and mid-October.

Fernandez found out from the team doctor Thursday morning, October 9, that he had a torn rotator cuff in his right shoulder. Very few pitchers have ever recovered fully from rotator cuff surgery, and the best case scenario for Fernandez had him missing all of the 1998 season, then coming back for 1999. Even that was wishful thinking. The worst case scenario was that his career was over.

Fernandez had felt soreness in his right shoulder off and on for the entire second half of the season, but didn't bother telling anybody because he didn't think there was anything seriously wrong. His results for the final month of the season would indicate otherwise: Fernandez was 0-3 with a 5.23 earned run average. He felt fine during his start against San Francisco in Game Three of the Division Series—his fastball peaked at ninety-four miles per hour—and pitched well, but didn't feel right afterward. All pitchers experience some arm stiffness after they pitch. Usually, they recover before they pitch again. Fernandez didn't.

"In the first inning, I couldn't throw the ball," Fernandez said.

The Marlins didn't know this because Fernandez didn't bother telling anybody, although Leyland had an idea something might be wrong. He had walked into the trainer's room before Game Two and saw something unusual in Fernandez's appearance. He didn't know what it was, or why he felt that way, but something was wrong.

"It's just the manager in me that thought something," Leyland said. "I smelled something that wasn't quite right. Something wasn't right with our star pitcher. Alex has a real ferocious look on his face when he's going into combat, and that look wasn't there."

Not until after the game, on the plane home, did Fernandez finally say something to the team trainer and Leyland. The next morning, Fernandez went for an MRI, and the results were far worse than the Marlins could have imagined. Dan Kanell, the Marlins' team physician, called Dombrowski at 9:30 a.m.

"How's the news?" Dombrowski asked.

"Not very good," Dr. Kanell said.

Dombrowski thought Kanell was talking about Alou, whose wrist had been examined that morning. He had no idea Fernandez's injury was so severe.

Fernandez was shocked, too. Just before noon, he walked into Leyland's office, where the manager was sitting with Dombrowski, Rothschild, and Donnelly, and, on the verge of tears, said, "I just feel like I let you all down."

About an hour later, Fernandez and his wife, Lourdes, sat behind a table during a press conference as Dombrowski announced the injury to the media. Fernandez's eyes watered over as he stared into the distance. When Dombrowski said, "The Florida Marlins have some disheartening news to announce," Fernandez swallowed hard. His arms were folded across his chest. Dark pools of sweat formed under his armpits. Lourdes also stared straight ahead, and when her husband got up to speak, she pulled out a tissue and dabbed her eyes.

"I'm a little hard-headed," Fernandez said. "I feel bad for the organization and the team. I feel that I let them down by not being there for Game Six, but you can only do so much sometimes. I'm down, but not out. I plan to be back soon."

He also said, "I pitch every game like it was my last one." This time, maybe it was.

◆ ◆ ◆

An outsider might have wondered if somebody had died or was terminally ill.

The players, devastated by the news, voted to have Fernandez's No. 32 written in white on the left side of their caps, above the bill, in a tribute usually reserved for the dearly departed. Leyland said, "This is a family matter. It's hard to share the emotion with the public," and called it a tragedy for Fernandez and his family. Dombrowski, who had struggled to find the proper words when he made the announcement, decided that it was "a baseball tragedy."

Outside Pro Player Stadium Friday night, a local radio station had fans sign a gigantic "Alex Get Well Soon" greeting card, as if the pitcher was sick. At that very moment, Fernandez was moving around the clubhouse, ragging and inciting teammates, as usual, and nobody would have ever known there was anything wrong with him.

"I'm still an idiot, I guess," Fernandez joked. "I can't change that."

And a local newspaper story began, "Marlins fans, reeling from the loss of home-town hero Alex Fernandez to a torn rotator cuff, coped as well as could be expected before Game Three of the National League Championship Series."

As well as could be expected? What were they supposed to do, drive their cars into the nearest canal in distress over Fernandez's injury, or maybe chop off their right arms at the shoulder in a show of support?

There was no doubting the sadness of what had happened to Fernandez. Here was a 28-year-old pitcher in his prime, who had returned home to play for a World Series contender, and suddenly found himself facing the possibility that he would never—not this year, not ever—fulfill every ballplayer's dream of pitching in the World Series.

What made it worse was that Fernandez was a battler, a stubborn, intense pitcher who played every game as if it were his last, and probably got hurt for that very reason: He pushed his shoulder beyond its limit. Certainly, there are plenty of athletes who, after suffering an injury such as this, would take the money and run. Baseball players have guaranteed contracts and Fernandez still had four years, $28 million remaining on his. But to Fernandez, the money clearly was secondary to pitching and helping his team. His sorrow hadn't lifted the next night.

"I'm still in a state of shock," he said.

Yet, it's difficult to think in terms of tragedy when there's this cold, hard fact: If Fernandez never picked up a baseball for the rest of his life, he would still collect $28 million. Not a penny less.

Somehow, life would go on.

◆ ◆ ◆

Finally, there was this medical adventure concerning Kevin Brown, who was scheduled to start Game Four on Saturday. At about 5 o'clock on Friday afternoon, Leyland walked into the interview room and announced, "Kevin Brown will be here in a little while. He's getting worked on right now." And twenty minutes later, Ron Colangelo stepped to the podium and announced that Brown had come down with a viral infection and never arrived at the ballpark.

Well, those two conflicting pieces of information didn't make much sense to the highly cynical, highly suspicious New York reporters, who set off to find the exact whereabouts of Kevin Brown. Was he home, or were the Marlins hiding him somewhere?

One reporter could have sworn he had spotted Brown throwing in the Marlins' bullpen. The Autograph Police and Al Leiter insisted they hadn't seen Brown all day. The investigation intensified as Rothschild was called out of the clubhouse to explain that Brown was safe at home, where Marlins medical personnel had visited him.

During Game Three, NBC-TV reported that Leiter would start Game Four in place of Brown. After the game, Leiter, smiling as if he knew something, coyly refused to admit he was the Game Four starter. Then, when asked whether Brown would start Game Four, Leyland hesitated for a few seconds before saying that Leiter would start Game Four and Brown would start Game Five. As for the rotation for the rest of the series, he said he had no idea.

"I gotta go back to the pencil and paper in my office and see what makes sense," Leyland said. "That real tragedy with the Fernandez family just blew up in our faces."

There was that tragedy talk again. Finding a missing pitcher was one thing. Finding perspective during the NLCS was nearly impossible.

◆ ◆ ◆

Three road games—the Division Series clincher in San Francisco and the first two games in Atlanta—had done more to generate interest in the Marlins than anything the team had done at home all season. On Wednesday night after Game Two, the final Delta Airlines flight back to Fort Lauderdale was packed with teal-cap-wearing Marlins fans. The untarping of the upper deck at Pro Player Stadium was underway and nearly 54,000 fans would attend each of the next two games, setting Marlins attendance records.

This was no small accomplishment for the Marlins because Yom Kippur, the holiest day on the Jewish calendar, fell on the days of Games Three and Four. Maybe in Atlanta or Texas that wouldn't mean a whole lot, but it's significant in an area in which an eighth of the population is Jewish.

Many of the Jewish season ticket holders had complained about the scheduling to the Marlins, but their phone calls were neither plentiful nor properly guided. Major League Baseball, which really doesn't care about anybody's religion—Jewish, Catholic, Protestant, Muslim, or Hindu—is in charge of playoff scheduling, not the individual teams. And besides, Don Smiley said, "Most of these people don't go to temple all year, then they have to go once a year out of guilt. What're they gonna do, turn to dust? I go to church every Sunday, but on Christmas I can't get a seat."

Smiley had stumbled upon an intriguing point. The Marlins' attendance patterns were very similar to the ones experienced by organized religion. Good pews are available all year long, but become scarce for the major holidays. In the Marlins' case, good seats were available all year long until the playoffs, when everybody wanted a piece of the excitement. Smiley and his clergyman had more in common than they could have ever known.

◆ ◆ ◆

Leyland said, "I like to let the guys go out there and get lathered up a bit," after a late afternoon rainstorm canceled batting practice prior to Game Three and prevented outdoor lathering up.

The Marlins did their lathering up inside, as did the Braves. Among those getting lathered was Alou, who tested his wrist in the batting cage and reported that he was capable of playing. But Leyland didn't want to take a chance and started Cangelosi in left instead. Cangelosi had a lifetime batting average of .526 against Game Three starter John Smoltz, so the move made sense.

Cangelosi had an interesting history against Smoltz. In 1994, he was playing for the Mets, when teammate Ryan Thompson hit a grand slam off Smoltz. Thompson took his sweet time rounding the bases, and Cangelosi had the misfortune of batting next. Smoltz hit him with his first pitch, inciting a bench-clearing brawl, during which Mets coach Frank Howard stood on the perimeter and shouted at Cangelosi, "Go get 'em, kid!" Meanwhile, Cangelosi was at the bottom of the pile, getting pummeled by Braves' catcher Charlie O'Brien.

And speaking of Smoltz, Cangelosi later said, "He came after me because I'm short."

◆ ◆ ◆

With playoff intensity heightened, the pressure was obviously getting to Travis Bickle, Dugout Security Guard. His twitch had worsened still, and he was seen in the dugout tunnel three hours prior to Game Three getting chewed out by a high-ranking Marlins employee. According to sources within the Marlins, Travis Bickle's most likely assignment for the 1998 season would be up in the rightfield corner seats, far away from the players, far away from the media, far away from anyone who might think he was associated with the team.

◆ ◆ ◆

Against the backdrop of these numerous focus-ruining distractions, an actual baseball game was played Friday night. Pro Player Stadium was packed with loyal Marlins crazies and johnny-come-lately Marlins crazies—53,857 of them, the largest crowd for a Marlins game at Pro Player Stadium. They were joined by the usual array of post-season dignitaries, including Braves owner Ted Turner and his wife, actress Jane Fonda. They were quite a sight, Ted and Jane, sitting in the lower level wearing Braves caps and rain parkas. The Fish video was played and Jane mouthed the words as if she had been practicing.

Even the player introductions were eventful. Klesko, the new enemy of South Florida, received the loudest boos, Leyland received the loudest cheers, and the Marlins tipped their caps to Fernandez when he was introduced. The Florida Philharmonic Brass Ensemble squeezed out the national anthem and local hero Herbert Tarvin threw out the first pitch.

Tarvin is not a local hero on the order of, say, saving twelve people from a burning building, but he's sort of a hero nonetheless. Tarvin is a 12-year-old boy who gained national attention when an armored truck overturned in a poor, ghetto area of Fort Lauderdale, setting off a frenzy of money-grabbers. Young Herbert thought about it, then turned in the money he found.

The amount he returned was eighty-nine cents.

"Wait until you see who we have tomorrow," Jim Ross enthused.

Somebody who returned ninety-five cents, perhaps?

"Even bigger," he said.

New T-shirts were unveiled. "The Chop Stops Here," said one, a reference to the Braves' tomahawk-chopping fans. Two fans wore "Buck The Fraves" T-shirts, and it was a fair bet that they also owned a rusty, broken down pickup truck adorned with the bumper sticker, "If You Don't Like My Driving, Call 1-800-EAT-SHIT."

It was a perfect South Florida night for baseball. At exactly 8:14 p.m., with two outs in the first inning, a driving rainstorm sent thousands of fans scurrying for cover.

But, as we had all been assured over the past few days, life would go on. Which it did. The rain stopped. The game continued without delay.

◆ ◆ ◆

Tony Saunders had spent the previous two days denying he had any special mastery over the Braves, even though they had accounted for three of his four wins. He had also tried to make like pitching against the Braves wasn't the most exciting thing he had ever done, but then in a moment of weakness he admitted, "This whole season has been a dream come true for me. If you would have told me in the spring that I would be pitching in the NLCS, I would have said you were crazy. I grew up watching the Braves in post-season, and now I'm pitching against them in the NLCS. What could be better?"

Well, it might have been better had Saunders not been facing John Smoltz, who with ten post-season victories was one short of breaking the record he shared with Whitey Ford and Dave Stewart. This looked like a one-sided matchup: A rookie who had won four games all season against one of the best playoff pitchers in history.

Then Saunders went out, broke his main rule of pitching—throw strikes—and succeeded anyway. He threw first-pitch strikes to only three of the first eighteen batters he faced, yet the score was 1-1 after the fifth inning.

This was a significant accomplishment, because Saunders had been suffering from bronchitis for the past two weeks. Anyone who has ever had bronchitis knows it's hard enough to get out of bed, let alone pitch against the best team in baseball, and Saunders had lost twelve pounds. He couldn't even eat.

"It really got me in Atlanta," Saunders said. "But I wasn't too sick. I'll go out every fifth day whether I'm dying or not."

Not too sick? Saunders was using a respirator between innings.

And the Marlins were on life support. The Braves loaded the bases with none out in the top of the fourth and scored only one run. Saunders returned to the dugout and started throwing things, because he knew one run might be enough to lose against Smoltz. Six of the first nine Marlins batters had struck out.

There was no reason for optimism. The Marlins had just gone through three straight bad days: Alou's injury, followed by the loss in Game Two, followed by Fernandez's injury, followed by Brown's illness. Now they were trailing, 1-0, and they still didn't have a hit off of Smoltz. Pro Player Stadium was as quiet as a stadium with 53,857 fans can get.

◆ ◆ ◆

Then Sheffield came up, swung at the first pitch, and sent it on a high, arcing flight toward the scoreboard in left-centerfield. The ball easily cleared the clock on top of the scoreboard, and as Sheffield crossed home plate, he pointed to his mother, father, and three children, who were sitting in his suite.

Sheffield had been making promises all season, and finally he was coming through on them when the Marlins needed him most. As Bonilla said of Sheffield, "They won't remember what happened during the year. They'll remember what happens in this series." Sheffield was well aware of this, and had been the happiest Marlin during the playoffs: Bouncing up and down excitedly after hitting hard foul balls, constantly flashing his smile, and seeming more at ease than he had at any point during the season. And the home run was huge because, as Bobby Cox said, Smoltz had been "untouchable."

Saunders left in the sixth inning, after the Braves put runners on first and third with one out, and was satisfied with his performance because he felt he had pitched as hard as he could and as effectively as he could for as long as he could.

"I didn't hold anything back," he said. "I left nothing on the field."

Considering his physical condition, that was a good thing.

◆ ◆ ◆

Leyland summoned Hernandez from the bullpen. This might have been a scary situation for any rookie—or any manager—but no tension showed on Hernandez's face. Nothing showed on Hernandez's face as he walked toward the mound.

"I love pitching in front of a full house," Hernandez said later. "They can yell all they want and it stimulates me even more. The regular season helped me a lot. I feel like I just finished eating, and now I'm getting dessert."

Although his face belied nothing, Hernandez was filled with emotion. With No. 32 written on his cap, he felt as if Fernandez was out there with him. And Fernandez, who spent most of the game standing on the dugout steps, cheering on his teammates and pumping his right fist, felt the same way.

Hernandez allowed only one of the two runners to score. After striking out Jeff Blauser to end the seventh inning, Hernandez sprinted to the dugout and pumped both arms up and down, asking the crowd for more noise. And they responded which, at the time, seemed impossible.

◆ ◆ ◆

By then, the crowd was in a frenzy because the Marlins had scored four runs in the bottom of the sixth. Daulton, starting his first game of the playoffs, had come up with Sheffield on first, Renteria on second, and two outs and ripped a fastball to right field, directly at Andruw Jones. Jones is usually one of the Braves' most dependable fielders, and it looked like he didn't have to move an inch to his left or right to make the catch.

He should have moved back. Jones leaped in desperation, but the ball went over his head and to the wall, allowing Renteria to score the tying run.

"He makes that play routinely," Cox lamented.

Two batters later, Charles Johnson came up with the bases loaded. Johnson had never in his life gotten a hit off of Smoltz. He was 0-for-12 and had looked feeble striking out in his first two at-bats in Game Three. Cox was so confident of Smoltz's chances that he had intentionally walked White to load the bases, and the decision looked like it would pay off when Johnson lunged weakly to foul off a 2-2 pitch by Smoltz. Johnson did all he could to not throw the bat a hundred feet.

But on the next pitch, Johnson reached outside and pulled the ball towards the gap in left-centerfield. Klesko, the leftfielder, raced over and dove, but the ball got past him and rolled to the wall. All three runs scored and Leyland breathed a sigh of relief.

"I thought we had missed our chance," he said.

Conine replaced Daulton in the seventh and made a fine diving stop on a hard grounder by Lofton. Cook retired the side in order in the eighth. Nen, throwing strikes like he hadn't done all season, got three flyouts in the ninth to complete a 5-2 win.

After three days during which it seemed like everything had gone wrong for the Marlins, something had finally gone right. The Marlins had a two games to one lead.

◆ ◆ ◆

The good news was fleeting. Before Game Four, Brown, who looked drawn and tired, appeared at a press conference wearing a black sweatshirt. For Brown, whose typical clubhouse garb is shorts and a T-shirt, that was one sweatshirt more than he usually wears. If there was a good sign for the Marlins, it was Brown's attitude: He was as surly and short with his answers as he usually is when he's healthy.

REPORTER: How are you feeling?

BROWN: Better than yesterday.

REPORTER: What's wrong with you?

BROWN: I don't want to go into that.

REPORTER: Are you definitely pitching in Game Five?

BROWN: They'd have to shoot me to keep me from going out there.

REPORTER: Are you able to eat?

BROWN: I'm not getting into personal stuff like that.

Personal stuff? Brown acted as if somebody was asking him his underwear size . . . which, at the moment, seemed to be a few sizes too small.

But Brown was making himself sound better than he really was, because shortly after the press conference, he went home.

He wasn't the only ailing Marlin. Bonilla was suffering from the same flu symptoms as Brown: fever, nausea, chills. According to Leyland, several other Marlins weren't feeling well. They couldn't have picked a worse time to get sick.

◆ ◆ ◆

Actual semi-celebrity seen on the field during batting practice: actor Robert Wuhl, who plays a sports agent on the HBO sitcom *Arli$$*. Fantasy had invaded real life: Wuhl was there with a TV crew, filming the show's opening shots, in which he hobnobs on the field with athletes and famous people. When Leyland came walking toward him carrying a fungo bat, Wuhl tried his luck.

"How ya doing, boss?" he asked.

"Fine," Leyland said. And he just kept on walking.

◆ ◆ ◆

Actual 9-year-old boy seen on the field during Game Three: Muscle Boy. There he was, doing his steroid-induced muscle freak routine, alongside Billy the Marlin, and the crowd got a rise out of it, as it always did. So the Marlins hadn't been true to their word on this count. Rather than putting the kibosh on Muscle Boy's act, they had given him a newer, bigger, brighter stage than ever.

Muscle Boy was on the verge of becoming more famous than even Robert Wuhl. He went back to being 9-Year-Old Boy and missed Game Four to attend a friend's party, but he had already appeared on *The Late Show* with David Letterman and *Hard Copy*. On Monday, he would become a Marlins turncoat and appear at Game Five of the American League Championship Series in Cleveland.

In the surest sign of celebrity, Muscle Boy copycats were popping up all over. He was spawning other Muscle Boys. Any time a camera focused on a young boy in the crowd at Pro Player Stadium, the boy felt compelled to do *his* Muscle Boy routine.

But Muscle Boy's days as Muscle Boy were nearly over. His father had recently made a big mistake.

He had hired Muscle Boy an agent.

◆ ◆ ◆

Leiter was telling a story about his best moment in the 1993 World Series, when he struck out John Kruk with the bases loaded in the seventh inning.

"We had a one run lead and the fans were going crazy," Leiter recalled. "And, honestly, I put myself back in Clearwater, Florida, when we played the Phillies, and I looked in and said to myself, 'We're in spring training right now,' to relieve the magnitude of the situation and get it to a level where it wasn't a big deal. You know it *is* a big deal, but those are negative forces that cause you to do things you shouldn't do. And it worked."

Relieving the magnitude of the situation, as he put it, didn't work for Leiter in Game Four Saturday against the Braves. The Marlins lost, 4-0, on a four-hitter by Denny Neagle, and the game was over by the sixth inning. That was obvious because rather than watching their husbands get manhandled by the Braves, the players' wives got up, congregated in the promenade behind their home plate seats, and small-talked. Whatever they were discussing, it had to be more interesting than the game.

◆ ◆ ◆

But if those of little faith marry ballplayers, then those of lots of faith root for them. They pack their coolers with barbecued chickens and sandwiches and wait on line to buy tickets. Linda Sloven, domestic engineer, was back. After spending seventeen hours on line for Division Series tickets and twenty-four hours on line for League Championship Series tickets, she showed up at the Pro Player Stadium ticket windows Saturday, thirty-six hours before World Series tickets went on sale. She planned on sleeping out for two nights.

"You think I'm crazy, don't you?" she asked.

"Well . . ."

"I told my husband that I was going to wait on line. He said, 'Go ahead.'"

"Nice husband."

"My friends up in Toronto told me that if I make it, they'll buy me four tickets."

Make it? Did she expect to die before 10 o'clock Monday morning?

Then she muttered something about the ticket scalpers who were also waiting on line, and her concern about her own well-being became clearer. Ticket scalpers will do anything for a prime spot on line. Ticket scalpers, it must be pointed out here, are a form of life even lower than Dugout Security Guard.

Linda Sloven and the scalpers weren't alone on this night. By Sunday night, twelve hours before the windows opened, the line for tickets was nearly as long as it had been on the morning when Division Series tickets went on sale. Some kind of craziness was catching on, although exactly what kind of craziness was impossible to tell.

Besides, these people probably wouldn't have much use for those World Series tickets. At the press conference after Game Four, Leyland seemed uncertain when asked if he planned on using Brown in Game Five. Then he offered a clue to his intentions while discussing the pitching rotations for the remainder of the series.

"They have Maddux, Glavine, and Smoltz," Leyland said, giving the Braves' rotation in order, "and hopefully we'll have Hernandez, Brown, and Saunders."

It sounded like Brown wouldn't pitch until Game Six. It also sounded as if the wives were right. The series was tied, 2-2, but with Fernandez injured and Brown sick, the Marlins looked like a lost cause.

17

If They Don't Win
It's a Shame

October 12 vs. Atlanta
October 14 at Atlanta

The wonder of these playoffs was how the Marlins had transformed themselves from a $89-million rent-a-team with a greedy owner, a moody manager, and overpaid stars, into injured, downtrodden underdogs who finally, for the first time all season, had actual adversity to overcome. Not the, "I'm feeling the pressure of having to prove I'm worth my $61-million contract" adversity, but real injuries, real sickness, adversity.

A lot had to happen.

Alex Fernandez's right arm just about had to fall off.

Kevin Brown and Bobby Bonilla had to be stricken by a stomach virus that kept one of them in bed for his scheduled Game Four start and the other fighting off chills and other queasy feelings.

Moises Alou had to jam his left wrist against the fence going after a home run he had no chance of catching, but went after anyway.

Instead of Brown and Fernandez pitching three of the final four games, the Marlins would have Brown pitching only one of them, against the Braves, whose pitching arsenal included three healthy Cy Young Award winners and a twenty-game winner.

Brown had watched Game Four at home and went to sleep thinking he was going to pitch the next afternoon. Meanwhile, Leyland was meeting in his office with his coaching staff, discussing options for Game Five. The alternatives—none of them perfect—included starting Brown, even though he hadn't thrown since Tuesday and still wasn't feeling well.

Another option was starting rookie Livan Hernandez, who had pitched two innings Friday night. The third option was starting Felix Heredia, letting him pitch three innings, and piecing together a start by using the bullpen. That option was quickly scrapped.

The most attractive option was a fantasy.

"I can't pull a rabbit out of a hat and put Sandy Koufax in a Marlins uniform," Leyland said. "We have to improvise. That's life."

The way Leyland saw it, Brown was only going to pitch one more game anyway, so it might as well be when he was healthy. Starting Hernandez was risky. Although he had pitched well in the playoffs, he was coming off a poor September in which he lost all three of his decisions, and got hit hard by the only two teams that saw him twice, the Mets and Phillies. The Braves would be seeing Hernandez for the third time, including his relief appearance in Game Three.

Nonetheless, with Koufax unavailable, Leyland decided to go with Hernandez and hold Brown until Game Six. Rothschild had the unhappy task of calling Brown, who unsuccessfully tried to change the decision. The next morning, Brown showed up at the ballpark and attempted to convince Leyland he should pitch.

"It's not too late to change your mind," Brown said. Actually, it was.

Although . . . three hours before the game, Leyland was hitting fungoes during batting practice and noticed that the wind was blowing out hard to rightfield.

"I was totally paranoid about it," Leyland said. "They had six left-handed hitters in a row, every one of them capable of reaching those seats. I thought, *We've had some troubles, and everything is going wrong now. We usually don't get that kind of wind at Pro Player.* I thought nothing was going right."

He was exactly correct. Nothing was going right for the Marlins. The injuries. The sickness. Not even the wind.

◆ ◆ ◆

Leyland had found himself in a drastic situation, and all during the playoffs, drastic situations had called for . . . Norman Dale.

So Leyland slipped back into *Hoosiers* mode and recreated a scene from his favorite movie.

In this scene, from early in the season, Norman Dale has just benched Roy, his best player, for defying a team rule. Minutes later, another Hickory High player fouls out, and because there are only six players on the team, Roy assumes he's back in the game.

"Sit down," Norman Dale orders Roy.

"We only have four out there," Roy protests.

"Sit down," Norman Dale barks. "Sit."

The referee walks over.

"Coach, you need one more," the ref points out.

"My team," responds Norman Dale, "is on the floor."

Background music swells. Unknowing fans in the bleachers boo. Barbara Hershey and the drunk guy knowingly smile. Hickory loses by twenty points.

Here's how Leyland handled a semi-similar situation in semi-real life.

"We have no reason in the world to lay down and quit," Leyland told the players. "That's not what this team has been about all year. Let's keep fighting and find a way to win.

"Our team's on the field."

Later, Darren Daulton said of his manager, "He's the wackiest of all."

◆ ◆ ◆

Trainer Larry Starr was asked whether Bonilla and Brown caught their illness from the manager, and Starr said, "Viral things like this aren't really contagious, unless you exchange fluids, like from a cup." Which sounded kind of odd, because not only were Bonilla, Brown, and Leyland sick, but Saunders was sick, and several members of the Marlins' traveling party weren't feeling good, either.

Not that the Braves cared. Said Tom Glavine: "I don't know how much sympathy you're going to get this time of year from anybody."

The answer: None.

◆ ◆ ◆

Bonilla wasn't looking for sympathy. All he wanted was a hit or two. He had entered the series with a .187 average in three LCS appearances, and in the first four games against the Braves mustered up only one hit in fifteen at-bats and struck out six times.

"I wouldn't call it a slump," Bonilla said. "I hate that word."

"What would you call it?" a reporter asked.

Bonilla thought about it for a second, then shook his head. "I have no fucking idea," he said.

Bonilla was ready to try something new. He looked worn and tired. His body—first the wrist, then the Achilles—had been defying him all season, and now he was sick at the worst possible time.

"I haven't had a lot of success in the Championship Series," Bonilla said. "I don't know why. I guess shit happens. I'm ready to try my luck in the World Series."

◆ ◆ ◆

Ten or twenty years from now, hundreds of thousands of people might say they were at Pro Player Stadium on Sunday, October 12, when Livan Hernandez became the most popular player in Marlins history. The afternoon had started with so little promise. The Braves had their ace, Maddux, who had been preparing for this start since Wednesday. The Marlins had their rookie, Hernandez, who found out he was pitching the night before.

The wind was blowing out. The crowd, expecting the worst, was unusually quiet for the start of a playoff game. Many of them hadn't known Hernandez, not Brown, was pitching until they arrived at the ballpark. Several hundred fans, who obviously were aware, waved Cuban flags. Then Kenny Lofton lined Hernandez's second pitch down the rightfield line for a triple, Keith Lockhart walked, and Hernandez wandered around the mound as if he didn't know what to do next.

But Hernandez—who had faced more dire situations in his life, like running from a Mexican hotel to freedom two years ago, and nearly getting run over by a car in the process—was simply composing himself. Bonilla walked over and, in Spanish, told Hernandez to not give in to the hitters. Hernandez didn't give in. Chipper Jones struck out swinging. Fred McGriff struck out swinging. Klesko looked at a 2-2 pitch to end the inning, and Hernandez charged off the mound to a wild standing ovation.

Crazy things started happening. White, leading off the bottom of the inning, leaned his back knee into a pitch by Maddux, and was awarded first base. Cox argued, but home plate umpire Eric Gregg stood by his call.

Leyland: "Fuck, he wasn't trying to get hit. His knees are bad. He's old."

Said White, "The pitch was inside. I wasn't going to move out of the way."

With one out, Maddux fell behind Sheffield, three balls and no strikes. Bonilla, in the on-deck circle, was so anxious to get to the plate that by the time Gregg called the next pitch a ball, he was halfway there. Bonilla lined a single to center, scoring White, and when he got to first, he pumped his fists.

The crowd got louder as the afternoon continued. Hernandez allowed a homer by Michael Tucker to start the second inning, then retired six in a row. McGriff singled leading off the fourth, then Hernandez retired fourteen in a row, including eight on strikeouts. The placement on his pitches was perfect; just about everything he threw was on the outside corner, or nearby, and it was obvious Hernandez was pitching on a special day.

◆ ◆ ◆

The utility players made contributions, too. For Gregg Zaun, who hadn't yet appeared in the series, his contribution consisted of yelling, "Fuck, yeah!" about fifteen times during the game.

"Maybe more," Zaun conceded.

Zaun was the first person running up the dugout steps whenever anything good happened for the Marlins, and uttered his first "Fuck, yeah!" in the first inning, when Hernandez struck out Klesko to end the Braves' threat in the first. He was followed up the steps by Fernandez, and both of them were pumping their fists and leading the dugout cheers. Zaun was even more excited and hyper than usual, which is saying a lot. He had cut his sleep intake and barely got in five or six hours a night, he was so anxious to get to the ballpark. He couldn't have been any more into the series if he was actually playing in it.

"I would love to play, but this is C. J.'s time," Zaun said. "He's earned it."

Zaun was content. He had one of the best seats in the house.

◆ ◆ ◆

Hernandez's impressive performance, one of the best in playoff history, was wind-aided. The wind was coming from the mouth of Eric Gregg, and the noise accompanying that wind was, "Steee-rike!" on pitches that were six to twelve inches out of the strike zone.

Hernandez took perfect advantage of Gregg's charity and threw as few actual strikes as possible. The game came down to which pitcher, Hernandez or Maddux, would be dumb enough to throw a pitch over the plate. That turned out to be Maddux.

On a day when suddenly everything was going right for the Marlins, Bonilla got a break when he led off the seventh. Bonilla drove a rare hittable pitch by

Maddux to the rightfield wall, and Tucker raced back. He snow-coned the ball at the tip of his glove, but then his body struck the wall, and his glove struck the wall, and the ball bounced out. Tucker desperately tried to grab the ball before it hit the ground, but he couldn't, and Bonilla wound up on second.

Maddux and Conine, the Marlins' next batter, spent the next ten minutes waiting for Tucker to find his contact lens, which had fallen out on the play. Then Conine, who had been 0-for-13 in the series, singled to center, scoring Bonilla, and the Marlins had a 2-1 lead.

That was all Hernandez needed, especially with Gregg behind the plate. After the seventh inning, Hernandez told Larry Rothschild, "I'm going two more innings."

Said Leyland to Rothschild, "He looks great. As long as he feels good, he's out there for the game."

In the eighth, Blauser was called out on strikes on a low, outside fastball that missed the plate by six inches. Lofton thought he had walked on a 3-1 pitch, then actually did walk on a 3-2 pitch. The crowd was standing for Keith Lockhart's entire at-bat, which ended when Johnson threw out Lofton trying to steal second on a 2-2 pitch.

When the inning ended, Hernandez had thrown one hundred twenty-nine pitches, but Leyland didn't think twice about keeping him in the game. Only once all season, when Fernandez had a no-hitter going into the ninth inning in Chicago, had Leyland allowed one of his starters to pitch the ninth with a one run lead, but Leyland knew better than to pull Hernandez.

"There were fifty thousand people here," Leyland said later, "and I didn't want to get snipered."

Lockhart led off the ninth. Hernandez made him his fourteenth strikeout victim on a 1-2 pitch. Chipper Jones lined a 1-2 pitch up the middle, but Hernandez stuck up his glove and made the grab. That brought up McGriff, one of the best late-inning power hitters in baseball. McGriff looked at a pitch on the outside corner for strike one. The second pitch was a ball. McGriff checked his swing on the next pitch, but Gregg called it a strike. Then McGriff evened the count at two and two, and fouled off Hernandez's fifth pitch.

By this time, everybody in the stadium was standing and cheering, and when Hernandez got McGriff looking at a 3-2 pitch, Fernandez and Zaun led the charge out of the dugout and mobbed Hernandez. There was jubilation as if the series was over. The Elton John song *Livon* blared through the stadium. Leyland hugged Hernandez, then waved his cap to the crowd and pumped his fists. Hernandez smiled for the first time all afternoon.

The fifteenth strikeout set an NLCS record and was only two short of the postseason record held by Bob Gibson. Like Whitey Ford, Hernandez had never heard of him, either.

◆ ◆ ◆

The last out was Gregg's crowning moment, his ultimate contribution to the early evening drama at Pro Player Stadium. The final pitch, a lazy curveball to McGriff, missed the plate by maybe ten inches.

Gregg's performance was so bad that after the game National League officials took the unusual measure of summoning him to a press conference so he could explain his calls. He put on quite a show. Perfectly reasonable questions were asked and Gregg responded with perfectly unreasonable, flippant responses topped off by the kicker, "Next question." Most of his answers aren't worth repeating, other than the anecdote he supplied from the top of the eighth inning, when Lofton questioned a called strike.

According to Gregg, this is how the conversation transpired:

LOFTON: "E! E!"

Translation: "Eric! Eric!"

GREGG: "Same strike zone I've been calling all game."

Translation: "I've been calling them wrong all game."

LOFTON: "You're right."

Translation: "How can I expect you to start calling them right now?"

Offered Braves manager Bobby Cox, "He called 'em like he saw 'em, I guess. Most of our guys were coming back to the bench saying his pitches were six to twelve inches outside."

A reporter asked Gregg how much the strike zone had changed over the past twenty years, and Gregg responded, "The strike zone has been the same for a hundred years." With that answer, he lost whatever credibility he had remaining. "Next question." There were none, and the press conference mercifully ended.

Leyland and the Marlins' players hailed Gregg's performance as "the greatest press conference" they ever saw, which only meant that they admired his evasiveness. Gregg was outstanding, if you like watching supposed arbiters of a sport dishing out some of the largest and smelliest crocks anyone has ever seen, smelled, or heard. Leonard Coleman, the National League president, should have walked in and fired him on the spot. Instead, he waited for a private moment, then told him to shut up.

◆ ◆ ◆

In Gregg's defense, he was equally bad for both teams. And that was the Braves' comeuppance, because Maddux and other Atlanta pitchers had been benefiting from a wide strike zone for years. Finally, an opposing pitcher got the same treatment and Hernandez took advantage of the situation. Not that the Braves recognized this and didn't complain.

"They whine more than any team in baseball," said Marlins assistant general manager Frank Wren, lending another meaning to the Braves' moniker, Team of the '90s. They were the whiningest team of the '90s and the lead whiner was— you guessed it, could it have been anyone else?—Chipper Jones.

"I'm so damn mad right now, I can't see straight," said Chipper, who went 0-for-4 and struck out twice. "Some people work their whole lives to get to this situation, and when you're not allowed to do your job . . ." Jones' voice trailed off. He shook his head. The man was beside himself.

The Braves complained about the strike zone. They complained about White leaning into Maddux's pitch in the first inning. After Game Three, Jones and the

Braves had complained about the poor lighting at Pro Player Stadium. The way they saw it, or didn't see it, Pro Player Stadium was a football stadium with football lights. What they didn't know was that the lights at Pro Player had two settings: One for football, another for baseball. It didn't have a third for the Braves.

What they ignored was that the Marlins had hit .263 at home, eight points lower on the road. The bad lighting apparently hadn't bothered the home team.

Privately, the Marlins wondered not about Gregg's strike zone, but about the unnatural movement on Maddux's pitches. Maddux had long been suspected of throwing spitballs, and the Marlins weren't convinced that he didn't. Conine asked a group of reporters, "Did you see the movement on that ball he threw to Moises? It was like one of those trackballs. I've never seen a ball move like that."

Conine was asked how that was possible, so he grabbed a ball, held it up, and made believe he was blowing his nose on it. Then he held it in front of his mouth and hocked a loogie. He got his message across quite nicely.

◆ ◆ ◆

An hour after the game ended, Leyland was sitting behind the desk in his office, wearing a Marlins T-shirt and his uniform pants. His emotion from the game hadn't died down and the more he talked, the more it became obvious that he felt the series was over. He kept saying things like, "We still have a lot of work to do," and "We haven't won anything yet," but it sounded as if he was reminding himself, more than anybody else, that the Marlins still had to win one more game.

He insisted this wasn't an optimist talking. Leyland recalled a game several years ago in Pittsburgh, when the Pirates were leading 10-0 after two innings and he was sure they were going to lose.

"And we did," Leyland said. "Don't ask me why, don't ask me how. But I felt in spring training that we were the one team that had a chance to beat the Braves. When we were in spring training, they said we were a flop if we didn't get to the playoffs. We're one game away from getting to the World Series, and everybody says, 'You'll take that.' Well, I won't take that. I expect this team to go to the World Series. I expected it when I took this job and I expect it today as we sit here."

Leyland was talking quickly. He sounded nervous and excited and he was having a hard time keeping himself from smiling. Then he started jabbering about how this playoff business "is fun for Dave Dombrowski's wife, it's fun for Frank Wren's wife, it's fun for my wife, but it's not fun for me," and went off on a tangent about how his wife goes to the VIP party tent after home games, but he doesn't go, because he's always back in his office, "either happy as shit or pissed off. For me, this is work."

He had never disguised that fact. Friends, such as Rich Donnelly, had worried about Leyland over the past three weeks because he seemed more driven than ever. He was drinking too much coffee, smoking more cigarettes than usual, and spending too many late hours in his office, despite having walking pneumonia. And now Leyland, after arguably the biggest win of his career, was speaking so emotionally, repeating things he had said just a few minutes earlier, talking about how he had been watching *Hoosiers* twice a day, and comparing himself to Norman Dale.

Whew! Just listening to Leyland was exhausting. He talked about how he had called Tony La Russa earlier in the day, but La Russa hadn't returned the call, and "I'm a little pissed off at him, to be honest with you."

"But please don't make it sound like I'm saying this thing's over and I'm getting melancholy," said Leyland, who sounded awfully melancholy. "Because that's not what I'm talking about. I'm talking about how the heartbeat of this club is ticking the same right now."

He went on about one heartbeat and about Rene Lachemann, the Marlins' first manager, who had called him earlier in the day. He called out to Dave Dombrowski, who was sitting a few feet away, and tried to get his attention, but Dombrowski was too busy with a meat-like substance in gravy that was swimming in the middle of his plate. He hadn't heard a word.

"This is a great day for me," Leyland said. "I showed more emotion for the fans today, and I looked like a fucking Little Leaguer, but what the fuck is wrong with looking like a Little Leaguer once in a while? That was my way of saying, 'We're fucking trying our ass off for ya.'" Meanwhile, Dombrowski was sitting there with this big hunk of meat stuck to the end of a fork, then he bit a chunk out of it, and he needed a napkin to mop up the juices running down his chin.

Talk about your emotional scenes.

◆ ◆ ◆

Finally, Devon White put the Marlins' three games to two lead in perspective. "Hopefully we can take it on Tuesday," said the veteran of five League Championship Series, "but if not, I think it's going to go seven."

◆ ◆ ◆

The Marlins again lost track of Kevin Brown. When last seen, he was leaving the clubhouse Sunday night, wearing a blue polo shirt, shorts, and white sneakers. Everybody assumed he was on his way to the airport to join the Marlins for their flight to Atlanta, but the next morning, a man fitting his description was seen at Fort Lauderdale Airport preparing to board a commercial flight. A man fitting his description was also heard answering questions from a reporter as if he were actually Kevin Brown.

The intrigue heightened Monday afternoon when Dombrowski revealed that Brown was on the Marlins' flight. Then Leyland said, "I haven't seen him today. Yes, he traveled with us last night. And yes, he will pitch tomorrow."

Well, those answers didn't jibe with the thirty or so reporters who thought they saw Brown, or a man resembling Brown, on their flight that morning. One of them asked Dombrowski what tactical advantage the Marlins gained from hiding Brown's whereabouts, and Dombrowski responded, "He wasn't on the plane?"

The Marlins tried to clear up the mess a little later when publicity director Ron Colangelo announced, "Jim Leyland and Dave Dombrowski thought he was on the plane and they wanted you to know that they didn't know that he wasn't on the plane."

Part II of the official explanation was that, having missed the games on Friday and Saturday, Brown arrived at the ballpark Sunday without his bags because he didn't know the team was leaving that night. According to Colangelo, "*They* told him to go home and take a flight tomorrow."

This mysterious *they* turned out to be traveling secretary Bill Beck, who was designated by Leyland to take the fall for the Marlins' oversight. The final official explanation was that on Sunday, Brown had told Beck he wasn't flying with the team, but Beck never bothered relaying the information to Leyland.

Tough break for the Marlins: Monday was an off day, and the media was hungry for news. That night, and the next day, ESPN, along with the national and South Florida print media, ridiculed Dombrowski and Leyland, and branded them as liars, incompetents, or both. How could the Marlins have lost track of their star pitcher and starter for Game Six?

This had been a lousy week for the Marlins from a public relations standpoint. The first Brown disappearance, when Leyland said he was being worked on by the trainers, then said he was home sick, looked bad. Then several writers from New York complained to the National League about the Marlins' dugout being a restricted area. Neither the Giants nor the Braves had closed their dugouts during the playoffs.

"We can now label Leyland a raving phony," wrote Joel Sherman in the *New York Post*. "Here goes a guy who is forever talking about how no one is bigger than baseball and how important it is to sell the game. And then in the forum that generates the most attention, the post-season, Leyland has refused to make himself available before most games, limited access to his players, and made his dugout a restricted area. All are flagrant violations of major league protocol."

Leyland, under orders from National League president Leonard Coleman, had opened the dugout for Game Four, but he wasn't happy about it and reiterated that the players wouldn't be available during batting practice.

"All you do is take up space when the players are getting ready," Leyland told the media. "But if you want to be in there, be in there."

The New York writers hadn't wasted any time finding seats in the dugout. It was quite an amusing sight, those four New York reporters, including Sherman, sitting alone in the dugout before Game Four, as if they were trying to establish squatters rights. Poor, forlorn Travis Bickle, Dugout Security Guard, stood a few feet away and looked like he was about to blow a fuse, but couldn't do a thing about it.

At which point Leyland, who didn't want reporters in the dugout, walked over, sat down, and answered questions from the New York writers for ten minutes.

◆ ◆ ◆

Brown showed up at Turner Field Monday afternoon and looked a lot better than he had a few days earlier. The sweatshirt had come off and he was wearing his typical garb: Marlins T-shirt, Marlins shorts, and sneakers. He worked out with the team, ran in the outfield, and later admitted he had been disappointed when Rothschild called him a few nights earlier with the news that he wouldn't pitch on Sunday. Of his chances of pitching in Game Six, Brown said, "I'm throwing, unless lightning strikes me."

That set off some bells and whistles among the media corps, because it was only a few days earlier when Leyland pronounced Brown "ninety-five percent" certain for Game Five, and Brown insisted, "They'd have to shoot me to keep me from going out there." At this point in the series, nothing was taken at face value, especially concerning Brown. Reminded of the quote, Brown snipped, "Do you wanna see the bullet wounds?"

Brown's sarcasm and forthrightness are always welcome. He was asked if he was one hundred percent healthy and Brown, who majored in chemical engineering at Georgia Tech, said, "I don't do numbers."

Well, Brown obviously was in no mood to offer information or perspective. Actually, he was never in the mood to offer information or perspective. Brown was generally considered the most intense player on the Marlins, but it's very possible his teammates confused intensity with surliness and rudeness.

"He's grown, actually," Sheffield said. "I think he's lot better than he used to be. Before, you had to stay out his way because he was like a psychotic."

Like a psychotic? Sheffield was being far too kind.

◆ ◆ ◆

While all of this intrigue was taking place in Atlanta, good things were happening five hundred miles to the south at Pro Player Stadium, where Linda Sloven and the scalpers had finally been given the right to purchase World Series tickets. The line was enormous and snaked around the building and not until 4:30 in the afternoon, six and a half hours after tickets went on sale, did the line dissolve to the point where a person could simply walk up to the window without waiting.

Buyers were limited to fourteen tickets per game, but that was merely a technicality for the scalpers, who paid off the local homeless to stand on line for them. There were at least six homeless people on line, distinguishable by their scraggly beards, unwashed clothes, dirty blankets, and beatific smiles as they clutched, however temporarily, onto wads of hundred dollar bills. For a few hours, they were the richest homeless people in the world.

Then again, there was always the slim possibility that these homeless were buying tickets for themselves, in which case there figured to be several underdressed fans at the World Series games doing The Fish and holding up banners reading, "Go Marlins. Will Work For Food."

By 11 o'clock, all forty-nine thousand seats originally available for Game One had been sold, and a decision was made to untarp the sections that had been made available for the NLCS. By 2 o'clock, the Marlins called Major League Baseball and asked permission to untarp and sell the seats in the upper deck behind left field. Those seats had an obstructed view—it was impossible to see the last fifteen feet of left field from most of them—but at twenty bucks a pop, nobody in the MLB offices was about to complain.

Chances are the Marlins could have hung bleachers from helicopters hovering above Pro Player Stadium and MLB wouldn't have complained.

"They're better than 'just get me in' seats," Jim Ross pointed out. He had made the journey from his office to the upper deck seats and decided it wasn't unreasonable for a person to sit up there and watch a game. Don Smiley, however, did point out, "They're not obstructed view. They're limited view." There's a difference, you know.

The Marlins sold all sixty-six thousand seats for Game One by the end of the day, well over a hundred thousand tickets overall. And if they didn't make it to the World Series, Jim Ross would likely take another walk up to those left field upper deck seats and fling himself onto the field, distraught from the idea of having to issue millions and millions of dollars worth of refunds. It would not be a pretty sight.

Yet, it was an indication of how far the Marlins had come since selling only 19,148 tickets for a game against the Rockies in mid-September.

Either that, or it was an indication of how much headway the Marlins had made into South Florida's substantial population of fair-weather fans. And homeless people.

◆ ◆ ◆

"I've said all along that we have to win four games somehow," Leyland said. "That pretty much simplifies it all."

◆ ◆ ◆

"I mean, you know, you have to keep everything in perspective," Sheffield said.

◆ ◆ ◆

"We're ticked off," said C. Jones of the Braves. "We're definitely ticked off." They were ticked off about Gregg's strike zone, they were ticked off about the lights at Pro Player Stadium, they were ticked off about the way they had played, and they were ticked off about how exuberantly the Marlins had celebrated after Game Five. They had a lot to be ticked off about.

◆ ◆ ◆

Dave Dombrowski was ticked off. *Definitely* ticked off. He was sitting in the Marlins' dugout at Turner Field, one hour before Game Six, and what was going through his mind?

Well, he had his right leg folded over his left and he was reading with great interest the day's South Florida newspaper clippings. He would turn a page, read an article, shake his head, then say something to assistant general manager Frank Wren. At one point, he called over Ron Colangelo and pointed to a line in one of the articles. Leyland walked past and Dombrowski didn't even look up.

Dombrowski was reading the newspaper accounts of the Kevin Brown disappearance, and one story especially annoyed him. It was a column by Dan Le Batard of *The Miami Herald* in which Le Batard wrote, "Before the biggest game in franchise history, the Marlins somehow left South Florida and forgot to bring their best pitcher? Not a good dilemma, this one. Either Dombrowski and Leyland were lying or not terribly competent."

So there was Dombrowski, reading a column by a writer he didn't like in the first place, and getting angrier with each word he read. He was irritated, clearly incensed about his integrity being questioned. He paged through the clips and pointed out mistakes made by other writers in other articles. If they were allowed to make mistakes, why couldn't he? Dombrowski couldn't understand why his apology hadn't satisfied the writers, but what made him angriest of all was Le Batard's column.

"I usually don't read Dan Le Batard's articles," Dombrowski insisted. "He's a bad person. You can ask any of our players and they'll tell you that. It's universally known in baseball that he's a bad guy.

"Dan Le Batard is an asshole."

And that's what was going through Dave Dombrowski's mind one hour before the biggest game in franchise history.

◆ ◆ ◆

Turner Field was a sea of red foam tomahawks, which had been given out by the Braves to fans as they entered the stadium. It was an impressive sight, all of those red tomahawk-holding fans doing the Tomahawk Chop in unison, but the background music was unique: The sound of maracas. You couldn't hear it in the stadium, but you could certainly hear it on TV; a few dozen Marlins wives, shaking black and teal maracas and making quite a bit of noise. This time, the wives watched the game from start to finish.

◆ ◆ ◆

The Braves had considered asking Francisco Cabrera to throw out the first ball prior to Game Seven, if there was a Game Seven. They decided against it, they said, "out of respect" for Jim Leyland.

Their respect didn't keep them from plastering Cabrera's picture on the Jumbotron after the top of the third inning in a game called "Who Am I?" Portions of the player's picture were revealed block-by-block, showing Cabrera's entire smiling visage in giant living color.

And right there, on display for 50,446 fans and two teams, was the Braves' respect for Jim Leyland.

◆ ◆ ◆

The Braves weren't overly concerned about their situation. In 1991, they trailed Leyland's Pirates, three games to two, in the NLCS, and came back to win two straight shutouts. In 1996, they trailed the Cardinals, three games to two, and came back to win the final two games at home.

"We've done it before," Bobby Cox said, "and that reinforces in our little brains that we can do it again."

Game Six was played on a perfect October night, a typical post-season base-ball night. The weather was a cool fifty-six degrees with a fall sky and very little wind. The players in both dugouts wore windbreakers. The crowd was the largest of the season at Turner Field, and what most of them expected was nothing less than another Braves win, to be followed the next night by another.

Their expectations were quashed quickly. The Marlins scored four in the first inning off Glavine. Cox was beside himself in the dugout, because as wide as Gregg's strike zone had been in Game Five, that's how narrow Frank Pulli's was in Game Six. Bonilla drove in both White and Renteria with a single to left. With the bases loaded, Glavine hit Johnson on the left biceps and Sheffield scored another run.

Brown, who hadn't pitched in seven days and was recovering from the flu, didn't have his best stuff either. Back-to-back RBI singles by Lofton and Lockhart in the second cut the Marlins' lead to 4-3.

But strange things had happened all series, and they would keep happening in this game.

In the second, Johnson committed another error, his second in a week after not making one for over a year.

The umpire was blind. Pulli left the game after the fourth inning because of an irritation in his right eye. By that time, Glavine had already walked four. Then, with the strike zone having diminished even further, at least in Cox's eyes, Glavine walked two more in the sixth. By the time Cox finished scratching his head and yelling at new umpire Charlie Williams, the Marlins had a 7-3 lead.

Former St. Louis Cardinals manager Whitey Herzog on Williams' ball-strike calls: "It's lucky he only has two guesses."

Then the most unlikely series of events of the night, probably of the entire sea-son, took place in the Marlins' dugout after the sixth inning.

Leyland told Brown he was taking him out of the game.

Brown told Leyland he wanted to stay in the game.

Under any other circumstances, at any other time, with any pitcher, including Brown, Leyland would have told him to take a walk.

Leyland flashback, March 5, 1997: "I've never asked anybody when to go get a pitcher and I never will. I figure it out myself. If I'm going to screw up, I want to screw up the way I thought."

Brown was more determined than he had ever been in his life to stay in and let Leyland know about it. Loudly. Up close and personally. Brown practically barked in Leyland's ear and Leyland, instead of walking away, listened.

"I felt like the further I could go, the better it would be for the team," Brown said later. "I was already into the rhythm of the game and the crowd wasn't both-ering me. I told him, 'I think I have something left to give and if you'll let me go hitter-by-hitter, then I'll do everything I can.' If somebody gets on and you want to come get me, fine. When I approached it that way, hitter-by-hitter, it made sense."

Trusting Brown's instincts instead of his own turned out to be the best move Leyland made all season.

But as Brown went out to face leadoff hitter Kenny Lofton in the bottom of the seventh, Dennis Cook continued warming up. He had already been told, "If Lofton gets on, you're in the game."

◆ ◆ ◆

Cook never got into the game. Lofton struck out looking. The Braves went down in order in the seventh and the eighth. Brown was suddenly so dominant that Chipper Jones walked over to third base coach Rich Donnelly during the top of the ninth and said, "If I don't see you again, good luck. You guys played like hell. You deserve it." Responded Donnelly, who wasn't about to be jinxed, "It ain't over yet, big boy."

The Marlins went down in order in the ninth. Before the bottom of the inning, Don Smiley, sitting in the first row of boxes, looked to the sky and mouthed, "I don't believe it." Tucker led off the inning by popping out to Johnson and the Marlins were two outs away from the World Series. Brown had retired fourteen in a row. Then Blauser reached on an infield single and Greg Colbrunn singled softly to center. Brown avoided looking at Leyland.

"I figured he would take me out," he said. "I don't know what was on his mind to stay with me like that, but I'm glad he did."

Lofton flied to center for the second out, then Lockhart fouled off two pitches before singling to right, scoring Blauser with the Braves' fourth run. The fans, who had been quiet since the sixth, were standing and tomahawk chopping. With two on and two out, Chipper Jones came to bat as the potential tying run.

Three times in his career, Leyland had taken teams to the NLCS. All three times he had lost, twice to the Braves. Several times over the past week, he had been reminded of Francisco Cabrera. His usual response was that he had been "stupid for the past four years because Francisco Cabrera didn't hit the ball right at somebody." The Cabrera hit had happened five years ago, to the day.

This time, if the Marlins lost, he would have been called stupid for keeping Brown in the game, when Nen was warmed up in the bullpen. And having the game tied on a home run by Chipper Jones, the most hated of the hated Braves, would have been the most painful blow.

Jones gave it a rip. Brown's first pitch was higher than he had wanted it to be, and Jones took a mighty swing. He hit it foul.

On a 2-2 pitch, Jones hit a ground ball up the middle, past Brown. Counsell ranged to his right and made the play backhanded, then flipped the ball across his body to Renteria.

Renteria caught it barehanded, the Marlins were National League champions, and never again would Leyland have to answer questions about Francisco Cabrera.

◆ ◆ ◆

Next, bedlam. Brown walked off the mound toward Johnson and let out a scream he might have been containing for all of his thirty-two years. It was almost like his reaction after pitching the no hitter in San Francisco—a delay, then ecstasy—but this time he screamed louder, loud enough to be heard above his shouting teammates.

Brown and Johnson were mobbed, of course. Then Hernandez danced on top of the dugout, like victorious players do in Cuba, and high-fived with a small group of Marlins fans. Bonilla found his wife in the crowd and threw her a kiss. Leyland found his wife, then he and Bonilla hugged each other.

"I've been playing for twelve years, and this is the first time I'm going to the World Series," Bonilla said minutes later. "I'm glad it's with Jim Leyland."

◆ ◆ ◆

There were the typical clubhouse scenes. Huizenga was presented with the National League championship trophy, players poured champagne and beer over each other's heads, and the air was clouded with cigar smoke. There was hollering and drinking and plenty of pouring. There was a balancing of the financial ledgers.

"There's nothing better than this," Huizenga said. "I told Rick Rochon, who works for me, 'You just keep track and let me know when I've had fifteen million dollars worth of fun.' And he told me a little while ago, 'I think we're getting close.'"

Great. But just what did he mean by *fifteen million*? Didn't he mean thirty million?

◆ ◆ ◆

Bonilla was standing in front of his locker with ice wrapped around his left thigh. He had left the game in the bottom of the ninth, after fielding Blauser's infield single and feeling a pop in his hamstring, but for the moment, there was no pain. A bunch of high-pitched screams could be heard outside the clubhouse, and Bonilla yelled out, "Let 'em in." The wives burst through the doorway, and the clubhouse was more open than Leyland ever could have dreamed it would be.

◆ ◆ ◆

The players were smoking cigars and their wives and girlfriends were smoking cigars, and Daulton, standing next to his wife, Nicky, and discussing the Braves' distaste for the Marlins' post-Game Five celebration, said, "If they don't care to show any emotion, then that's fine. Maybe they're a little above that. But we're going to the World Series with a lot of emotion."

The Braves hadn't stopped their whining. Told that Lofton said the best team didn't win the series, Brown stared in disbelief and said, "I won't even give that a comment. Maybe the team with the most heart won."

◆ ◆ ◆

Daulton had only four at-bats in the series, but he didn't mind. His fairy tale season was getting better by the minute. Across the room, Conine, who with Arias was one of only two Marlins remaining from opening day 1993, reminisced about the Marlins' first spring training. He remembered the dilapidated field in Cocoa on which the Marlins played their home games and the time the Marlins shared a hotel with bagpipe conventioneers.

No Marlin could better appreciate this victory than Conine, who five years ago never dreamed a National League championship would come so soon. Even three months ago, he thought he had lost his job with the Marlins because of Daulton's arrival, but here he had played in all six games against the Braves, and all nine of the Marlins' playoff games so far.

Maybe the only person who could appreciate the moment as much as Conine was his wife Cindy. He held a bottle of champagne with one hand and his wife with the other. Cindy Conine couldn't control her emotions. She cried as she recalled the day in July, when she drove her husband to the airport for what looked like his final road trip as a Marlin.

"I remember saying to Jeff, 'Maybe if you get traded, it's the best thing for you, because you'll be able to play every day,'" she recalled. "We felt we'd been really lucky because we'd been with the same team for five years. He wasn't going to play every day, he'd barely play at all, just against lefties, so maybe at that point in his career it was better to go somewhere else.

"Now that I look back upon it, the one thing I said at the time was the worst thing that could happen was if he got traded and this team won in the playoffs, because Jeff had been a part of it for five years. That would have been devastating. But things have a way of working themselves out.

"I don't think we'll be here next year," she said. "I really don't. Who knows what's going to happen? They're going to dump salary. They're going to sell the team. But you can't worry about that. You have to live in the now."

◆ ◆ ◆

Dombrowski was living in the now. He had hugged his wife a dozen times, embraced every player in the room, and his shirt was soaked with champagne from the celebration. Then he stepped down from the podium, where he had been posing for pictures with the championship trophy, looked around the room, and shook his head in disbelief. He walked over to a reporter and whispered in his ear.

"Dan Le Batard," he said, "is still an asshole."

◆ ◆ ◆

Rich Donnelly, who had coached under Leyland for twelve years, stood in an uncrowded corner of the room, away from the celebrating. He sipped a beer and wiped tears from his eyes. He had been crying for most of the past hour.

There isn't a person in the world who thinks more of Leyland than Donnelly, nor anyone who spends more time with him, and his overwhelming emotion was happiness for a good friend.

"People will never understand what he did this year," Donnelly said. "To put this team together, and not by just getting a bunch of good players, but by forcing them to one heartbeat, like he said. They weren't together until the All-Star break. He forced them to be together. He drove them.

"There's a show called *Rawhide,* about a trail boss who drives those cattle through everything. Windstorms. Everything! Disease. Everything! And they got to where they were going. That's Jim. He drove them through injuries. We had call-ups, we had all kinds of things happen to us. We had expectations. In April, people were saying, 'Hey, you're gonna beat the Atlanta Braves,' and he said, 'What are you talking about? We haven't won anything yet.' They were saying how we were as good as they were. And for a year, now we are.

"This is Jim's team. Like in *Hoosiers,* when the team's on the floor with four guys. This team was on the field, without Alex, without Kevin. The team's on the floor. And he told the team in San Francisco, when the wind was blowing out the first night we were there, and he called over Devo and he said, 'Devo, how far is it from home plate to first base?' 'Ninety feet.' Jim said, 'That's what I thought. Same as Pro Player Stadium,' and they all cracked up."

Donnelly paused. He grinned. He wiped another tear from his eye.

"And Norman Dale lives," he said. "Hickory High has just beaten South Bend Central. And it's beautiful."

Unfinished Symphony

October 18, 19 vs. Cleveland
October 21, 22, 23 at Cleveland
October 25, 26 vs. Cleveland

The Marlins were headed to the World Series and South Florida had finally discovered baseball. The Huizenga team store on Fort Lauderdale Beach couldn't maintain its supply of Marlins National League Champions T-shirts and caps. All four World Series home games against the Cleveland Indians, the American League champions, had sold out the day after Game Six of the NLCS, which really was no great accomplishment because there is no surer thing in sports than a World Series sellout.

Fans wearing Marlins jerseys went food shopping in stores, where teal and black Marlins' cupcakes were selling like . . . well, cupcakes. "Marlins Mania: It's natural," read a headline in *The Miami Herald,* over a story that quoted a local sociologist as saying that by rooting for a baseball team, "we're seeking to fulfill ancient, basic human needs—to worship heroes, to commune with each other, to drink from a common well of emotion, to escape daily life's relentless grind, to revel in the grand human drama."

To create banners that read, "Go Marlins! Bite Me Indians."

To take your finger and write in a thick film of dirt on the back of an 18-wheeler, "Indians Are No. 2. Marlins are No. 1."

To stand in the dugout prior to the Marlins' first World Series workout and hear Leyland proclaim, "We have to win four more games. Cleveland has to win four more games."

And to watch Devon White, who had avoided the local media all season with such comments as, "I'm not here," when he was very clearly right there, spend a half hour talking to the national media.

"Look at Devon White," said a local beat reporter standing nearby. "I'm not going over there. Fuck him."

Early Thursday, a man was run over by a train while trying to hang a "Go Marlins" banner from a highway overpass in Miami.

Early Saturday morning, an intern with Major League Baseball died after falling off a hotel balcony, after he had attended the World Series gala.

World Series fever had turned fatal.

◆ ◆ ◆

But the World Series would be over in eleven days or less, and its long-term effects on the franchise were difficult, but not impossible, to quantify. Back in August, Jim Ross did a little research and found that teams generally experienced their largest gains in attendance the year *after* they made the playoffs for the first time, or for the first time in a while, and that the attendance growth was usually around two hundred thousand fans. That meant the Marlins could expect to draw somewhere around 2.7 million next season . . . if fans didn't react negatively to any fire sale of players that would take place during the off-season.

The fire sale, however, was now in limbo. The Marlins had magically undergone the type of transformation that, two years earlier, resulted in the Florida Panthers getting the new arena Huizenga so desired and said he required. The Marlins were politically correct. An editorial in the Fort Lauderdale *Sun-Sentinel* endorsed the building of a new baseball stadium with a retractable roof. New investors were stepping up to join Smiley's group, and the mayor of Miami backed a plan to build a downtown stadium as part of his re-election campaign.

Publicly, Huizenga was deflecting questions about whether he still intended to sell the Marlins. Privately, he was telling people he had every intention of selling for the same reason as always: He thought there was no chance of getting a new stadium built as long as he was the owner.

Maybe. Maybe not. On Friday, the day before the World Series, *Miami Herald* columnist Dan Le Batard wrote, "Like him or not, Huizenga is the perfect sports owner, giving his team money and getting out of the way, and the Marlins would be better off with him than with anyone else." And within the day, Huizenga was talking about possibly not selling the team if a new stadium was built, and not cutting payroll.

The thing was, despite the unprecedented ticket and T-shirt sales, there was no dramatic groundswell of Marlins fever in South Florida. Only seventy-five people greeted the Marlins when they returned to Fort Lauderdale from Atlanta. Back in 1996, when the Panthers reached the Stanley Cup finals, it seemed as if every car on I-95 and Florida's Turnpike was equipped with a team flag. Not so for the Marlins.

What seemed to be fascinating South Florida wasn't Marlins Fever, but World Series Fever, Big Event Fever. Maybe it would wear off when the Series ended, maybe it wouldn't. The Marlins were still trying to take hold.

◆ ◆ ◆

The name of the real savior of baseball in South Florida was Livan Hernandez, the MVP of the National League Championship Series and a sudden hero among Miami's Cuban community. With his performance in Game Five, Hernandez had become an overnight celebrity and, perhaps, the kind of drawing card the Marlins had hoped Alex Fernandez would be.

But on Thursday, October 16, after the Marlins' first pre-Series workout, Hernandez placed his career in danger by angrily slamming his right hand against

271

a folded up table perched against a cement wall outside the Marlins' clubhouse. He was talking animatedly in Spanish with Julio Sarmiento, the assistant director of publicity, and equipment man Javy Castro, then he started screaming, then he stormed into the clubhouse, closing the door hard behind him, and cursing loudly. Hernandez was angry because Castro hadn't done something he had asked him to do, and there it was: The latest sign that Hernandez had become a star.

Another sign had appeared Wednesday morning on the Marlins' flight home to South Florida, when Hernandez was told he would start Game 1 of the World Series. Although this wasn't unprecedented—nine times previously rookies had started Game One—it was rather remarkable considering that just seven months earlier in spring training, Hernandez had no chance of making the team.

When he got back to his apartment in Miami Beach at 5 Wednesday morning, Hernandez was greeted by a welcome home banner in the lobby and roses on his doormat. That afternoon, he went for lunch at Versailles, the Cuban restaurant on *Calle Ocho*—Eighth Street—in Little Havana. He had eaten there many times before without causing any commotion, but this time, whenever he tried crossing *Calle Ocho,* cars screeched to a halt and people jumped out asking for autographs.

Finally, he made his way across the street to the restaurant, where the owner was waiting to buy him lunch in exchange for taking a picture with the restaurant staff. Until then, Hernandez had always had to pay for his meals. Then Hernandez sat down at his table and needed four hours to eat. Understand that Versailles is not a restaurant that serves lavish meals. It's more like a Cuban version of an American diner, with ostentatious decorations in its gigantic eating areas, an extensive menu, and a waitstaff that doesn't believe in leisurely dining. A person in a hurry could get in and out in less than a half hour. Hernandez needed four hours to eat because hundreds of people wanted to shake his hand and get his autograph. Not that he minded.

"I love that," Hernandez said. "I feel good and they're happy."

After Thursday's workout, Hernandez had more reporters around him than any other Marlin, even though he was answering questions through an interpreter. A reporter pointed out that Orel Hershiser, the Indians' Game One pitcher, was the MVP of the 1988 World Series, and Hernandez pointed out that back then, he was only 13 years old and playing junior baseball in Cuba.

Hernandez didn't seem too impressed by Hershiser's post-season résumé, which included only one loss in sixteen starts, and shrugged his shoulders when asked about the pressure that awaited him Saturday. He didn't seem too impressed by anything, and the reason was simple: World Series pressure was far less meaningful than the pressure he had experienced a few years earlier, when he decided to defect from Cuba and leave behind his family. Back then, he didn't know what awaited him in the United States or whether his family would suffer repercussions from Castro's government.

"It's probably the biggest decision I've ever made in my life," Hernandez said. Far bigger than deciding whether to throw a curveball or fastball to David Justice, the Indians' best hitter.

Before he came to the United States, Hernandez had never seen a World Series game, other than a tape of the 1993 Series between Philadelphia and Toronto. Last fall, his first in the U.S., he had his first chance to watch World Series games live on TV. But instead of doing that, Hernandez went out in Miami with some friends. He didn't tune in until Game Six.

And that, Livan Hernandez could have said, is what the World Series means to me.

◆ ◆ ◆

The Marlins had partied hard on the trip back to South Florida and just about everyone, including the manager, woke up the next morning with a hangover. On Wednesday, Katie Leyland flew home to Pittsburgh to pick up their two children and bring them back to Florida for the World Series, so Leyland dropped by the stadium and sat with equipment manager Mike Wallace and coaches Rich Donnelly and Tommy Sandt. He was in a fog.

"I don't know what I was doing," Leyland said. "I was watching the Cleveland game on TV and I'm not sure I saw one pitch. I talked to Tommy and Rich about Cleveland and Baltimore, then I went out to Pompano Park racetrack, watched some more of the Cleveland game, ran out of money by the third race, and went home."

It would be a hectic week for Leyland. He and Katie would have a houseful of visitors, even though they no longer had much furniture. Just about everything had been moved back to Pittsburgh, so Katie had to rent eight beds.

"To be honest with you," Leyland said, "I don't know who the hell is staying at my house."

Well, it really didn't matter, because Leyland wouldn't be spending much time there. He and his coaching staff were taking a crash course on the Indians.

The Indians, who hadn't won the World Series since 1948 and got ridiculed in the movie *Major League,* were widely considered by the experts to be the weakest of the four teams in the American League playoffs. The Indians won the Central Division with a record of 86-75, then upset the defending champion Yankees in the Division Series and Baltimore in a close, six-game ALCS.

For Leyland, the best part about playing the Indians was that Cleveland was 110 miles from Perrysburg, and he would get to see his family. Although Leyland grew up as a Detroit Tigers fan, he saw his first game at Municipal Stadium in Cleveland. The year was 1954, he was 10 years old, and thirty-three years later, he remembered all of the details, including the lineups for both teams.

"It was a doubleheader between the White Sox and Indians," Leyland recalled. "Garcia and Wynn pitched for the Indians. Larry Doby hit a home run. To say that I saw my first game in Cleveland and to think that I'm going to manage my first World Series game in Cleveland . . . that's unbelievable. I don't know how that works out."

The Indians no longer played their home games at big old Municipal Stadium, the so-called "Mistake By The Lake" which once stood on the shore of Lake Erie, but was ripped down after the Indians and football's Browns packed up and left. Since moving out, the Indians had undergone a resurgence of fan support that the Marlins could envy, and it all had to do with their new ballpark, Jacobs Field. The stadium, like the other new ones in Denver, Baltimore, Atlanta, and Arlington, Texas, had been modeled after old-time ballparks and garnished with modern touches—"gingerbread," as Leyland called it, such as sky boxes, restaurants, and bars—and Clevelanders had been coming out to watch the Indians like never before. In 1985, the Indians drew only 655,181 fans to Municipal Stadium. This season, they sold out every home game: 3,404,750 fans overall.

"I'll tell you this," Leyland promised. "Jacobs Field is gonna make Turner Field and San Francisco sound like a mouse wetting on cotton."

A group of reporters was standing around Leyland when he uttered the "mouse wetting on cotton" line and few of them had any idea what he was talking about. The truth was that Leyland neither sounded nor looked healthy. His eyes were red and his face was more drawn than usual. He sat in his usual corner of the bench, leaning forward with his forearms crossed and rested on a black fungo bat. Two baseballs were tucked between his thighs. His black and white fake stirrup socks were pulled up to his knees from a pair of black spikes, gray bicycle shorts peeked out from underneath black Marlins shorts, and his white Marlins T-shirt had worn through at several spots along the seams. The manufacturer's label on his right sleeve had dog-eared at the corners. A haggard Leyland was visible evidence of how long a baseball season really can be. Between the houseful of company and the World Series, Leyland's physical appearance wasn't going to improve.

◆ ◆ ◆

Leyland announced his pitching rotation for the series. Hernandez in Game One, followed by Brown, Leiter, and Saunders.

Here's an amazing fact: Alex Fernandez, torn rotator cuff and all, tried to talk Leyland into letting him pitch in the World Series. The conversation took place on the afternoon of Game Six of the NLCS, and it wasn't a short conversation, it was a long one. Leyland, who had no interest in causing further damage to Fernandez's recovery prospects, or putting damaged goods on the mound for the World Series, quashed the idea.

As amazing as this revelation was, something far more fascinating attracted a group of twenty TV cameramen, who were circling something, maybe someone, near the home plate backstop during Thursday's workout. It turned out to be someone and something: A grounds crew member applying the World Series logo to the backstop. And, in a truly major event, the World Series logo would soon be unveiled in foul territory near the first- and third-base lines.

Even the grass was a story. It seemed . . . greener. It *was* greener. Unnaturally green. The grounds crew had used green-dyed iron fertilizer to make the grass look bright and vibrant on TV. They might have gotten away with this trick undetected, if the dye hadn't come off on the baseballs during batting practice. When the work-out ended, hitting coach Milt May wheeled a cartful of green baseballs back to the clubhouse.

◆ ◆ ◆

The Indians' manager was Mike Hargrove, who had led the team to three consecutive division championships and two World Series appearances in three years. Donnelly knew him well. Back in 1973, Donnelly was managing Gastonia in the Western Carolinas League and Hargrove was one of his players.

"He was a college kid, but he seemed so much older," Donnelly recalled. "They said to me, 'Can he play in the big leagues?' and I said, 'He can't run, he has no power, but he won't embarrass you.' I never dreamed he'd get into management."

Hargrove played twelve seasons in the big leagues and, since 1991, had been one of the most successful managers in the majors. Not that Donnelly minded being wrong about Hargrove as a player and as a manager, because they had become good friends. Donnelly named his fifth child, Mike, after Hargrove and made him the godfather. Hargrove, in turn, made Donnelly the godfather to Hargrove's oldest daughter, Kim.

Anyway, Donnelly was sitting in the dugout Thursday afternoon during the Marlins' workout telling stories about Hargrove. Hargrove is from Perryton, a small town in the Texas panhandle, and, according to Donnelly, he's a cowboy.

To illustrate his point, Donnelly told about the night Hargrove went dancing at a country-western bar. Hargrove walked into the bathroom and saw a man peeling paint off of the bathroom wall. Hargrove told him to stop. The man told Hargrove to go fuck himself. That turned out to be both a big mistake and a good move.

It was a big mistake because Hargrove grabbed him by the shirt, punched him in the face, and left him a bloody mess. It was a good move because after beating the crap out of this poor paint-peeling slob, Hargrove walked over to the bar and bought him a beer.

"Just like a cowboy," Donnelly said.

◆ ◆ ◆

With hundreds of media members on hand for the World Series, it didn't take long for one of them to commit a breach of clubhouse rules. On Thursday, an out-of-town reporter made himself at home by sitting in one of the cozy leather recliners (Violation No. 1: The furniture is for players only) and making a call on his cellular phone (Violation No. 2: No cell phones in the clubhouse).

Seeing this, Jay Powell walked halfway across the room toward where the reporter was sitting, and called out, "Hey, make yourself comfortable."

Powell made a drinking motion with his right hand. "Want something to drink?"

Well, the reporter had no idea that Powell was talking to him, and just went right on sitting and talking. How was he supposed to know he was violating clubhouse rules? Then Jeff Conine walked over to where Powell was standing, and picked up where Powell had left off. Conine, it should be noted, was by far the most sarcastic player on the team, and sometimes it was impossible to tell whether he was kidding or serious.

"Hey, need any coffee or donuts or something?" Conine inquired. "Go ahead," he said, holding up his hand. "Make yourself comfortable."

Conine paused, walked away, then looked over his shoulder.

"Maybe a greenie to keep yourself alive or something?" he said.

Conine paused again.

"How about some sunflower seeds? We got sunflower seeds coming out of our ears."

The reporter finally got up, but not because of Powell and Conine. He had merely finished making his phone call.

◆ ◆ ◆

On the subject of clubhouse decorum, here's something you might not want to know. John Cangelosi is a nudist. Most ballplayers shower and pull on a pair of shorts before they return to the general clubhouse area, or wrap a towel around their waists and discreetly change into street clothes at their stalls. Not Cangelosi. He'd emerge stark naked from the shower area with only a towel draped over his arm, then walk across the room to his stall as if it were the most natural thing in the world.

Now, Cangelosi had every right to do this. The clubhouse belongs to the players and everyone else is an outsider, invited in to do their jobs. During the regular season, when sometimes no more than five or six reporters were in the room, Cangelosi's nude parades often went unnoticed. But two days before the World Series began, a mixed group of a hundred fully-dressed reporters were standing around the clubhouse, and there came Cangelosi, naked as a jaybird, walking his little walk in full view.

◆ ◆ ◆

The World Series had caught the fancy of fans in Cleveland and South Florida, but to the rest of the country, Indians vs. Marlins was a low-profile World Series without teams most people cared about. No Yankees, no Braves, no Red Sox, no Dodgers. No Griffey, no Bonds, no McGwire, no Walker.

"We're looking for four and out," said Don Ohlmeyer, the president of NBC's west coast division. "The faster it's over with, the better it is."

So much for World Series excitement.

Ohlmeyer was looking ahead. Game Five was scheduled for Thursday, *Seinfeld* and *ER* night on NBC, and he knew if recent history was any indication, ratings for a World Series game would be lower than those for the regularly scheduled shows.

Then, when discussing NBC's rights to the World Series, he said, "I would love it if somebody wanted it right now. If the A&E channel called, I'd take the call."

What, and bump *Biography*?

Ohlmeyer's totally honest statements did not please the people who run Major League Baseball, or the players on both teams. Ohlmeyer issued an apology, which made everybody happy, even though he had already said what he meant. Like *Seinfeld,* his apology was about . . . nothing.

◆ ◆ ◆

Kevin Brown walked through the clubhouse carrying his glove in one hand and his elastic exercise rope in the other, scowled at a group of reporters interviewing Leyland, and said out loud to no one in particular, "Get these fuckers out of here. We can't get any work done."

Having not pitched a no-hitter or clinched the National League championship over the past three days, Brown had no use for the media.

◆ ◆ ◆

Craig Counsell said, "The goal was to win eleven games. We've won seven."

And Leyland added, "We have to win four games. Cleveland has to win four games."

Baseball is a simple game.

◆ ◆ ◆

The three days off before the start of the Series were two days too many. All of the reporters' questions were sounding the same. All of the players' answers were sounding the same. *This is what it's all about. Blah blah blah. This is what you play for all your life. Blah blah blah. They're a great team and we're a great team. Blah blah blah.*

Late Friday afternoon, Conine was standing in front of his locker answering questions he had heard a thousand times since the start of spring training in mid-February. Questions about being an original Marlin and questions about the Marlins spending so much money on free agents and questions about almost getting traded, and Conine couldn't take anymore. The reporters had their heads buried in their notebooks, and never looked up. And if they had, they would have seen Conine making believe he was falling asleep by closing his eyes, dropping his head, and then jerking back to life.

◆ ◆ ◆

The Marlins unleashed a pterodactyl on their fans as part of the festivities before Game One. The gigantic thing was released from the top row of the upper deck in centerfield just as the white Jackson Five finished singing the national anthem, then swooped down ferociously toward the infield. A brown Doberman sitting in the handicapped section barked curiously. He wanted a piece of the pterodactyl.

Bonilla didn't. The Marlins were standing along the first base line after the introductions and Bonilla took a few steps away from where the beast was headed.

"I was taking it in from afar," said Bonilla, who after deciding to play with a bad hamstring didn't want to risk getting attacked by this flying thing.

The pterodactyl—actually an American bald eagle named Challenger—was nearly as big as Bonilla. It looked a little wobbly on descent, but made a perfect landing, right onto the arm of its handler standing on the pitcher's mound. The crowd cheered wildly. The crowd would cheer wildly all night.

The crowd was drunk.

The pre-game festivities started four hours before the first pitch, when hundreds of cars waited outside the stadium for the lots to open, so they could party in the parking lot. The partying was exuberant—a man suffered a heart attack and was taken away in an ambulance—and if anyone ran out of beer, there was plenty of emergency beer available in the party tents. Anybody who didn't know better would have guessed an NFL game was about to be played. Chances are, some of the partiers were so drunk they thought an NFL game *was* about to be played.

Just about every fan was dressed in teal or wearing some kind of Marlins T-shirt. Thousands of cardboard Cuban flags were handed out to fans outside the stadium. Billy the Marlin drove through the parking lot on the back of a truck. Face-painters painted faces in teal. T-shirt and souvenir sales were so brisk that by 7 o'clock, an hour before game time, many of the racks were bare. Young women scantily dressed in skimpy Budweiser dresses posed for photos with drunk, horny young men, as part of a very effective promotion for the beer company.

Inside the stadium, the *Arli$$* guy roamed around the field aimlessly, and looked a little out-of-sorts, maybe because he didn't have a film crew following him. There were hundreds and hundreds of media members on the field. More than twelve hundred had been credentialed for the series. Three planes with advertising trailers circled over the field. The pre-game soundtrack was the sound of two helicopters hovering over the stadium. It sounded like South Central L.A. after midnight.

Finally, the players were introduced. The national anthem was sung. The pterodactyl attacked. Nearly every available seat in the stadium filled up, stretching all around and from foul pole to foul pole, where blue tarps once lay. It was an impressive sight. The crowd of 67,245 would be the largest to watch a World Series game since 1963 at Yankee Stadium.

"I came out early, saw the size of the crowd, and didn't see much orange," Conine said, referring to the colors of the seats. "There were butts in every seat."

Bonilla also looked around, as he always does, before and during games, and decided his first World Series game was everything he had dreamed it would be, only better. "An incredible feeling," Bonilla said. "There's no comparison. I was soaking it all in, honestly."

At 8:10, Hernandez threw the first pitch, a strike, that leadoff hitter Bip Roberts could barely see because thousands of flash bulbs in the crowd went off at the same time. Did these people expect their flashes to have any effect from three hundred feet?

Mercifully, the World Series was underway.

◆ ◆ ◆

As he did in Game Five of the NLCS, Hernandez got off to a slow start in Game One of the World Series. He allowed a run in the first inning, then shut down the Indians for the next three innings. The Marlins tied the game in the third when a groundout by Renteria scored Counsell. Then, in the fourth, with the game still tied, Alou came up with Bonilla on second and Daulton on first.

For the Marlins, there would be five main characters in this series: Bonilla with his bad leg, Hernandez with his young arm, Daulton in possibly the final games of his career, Renteria with his clutch hitting, and Alou with his timely bat. This moment was for Alou. He had only four hits in thirty at-bats during the post-season, but Hershiser threw a split-finger fastball on an 0-2 pitch, and the pitch didn't sink the way it was supposed to.

The pitch crossed the plate up in the strike zone, and Alou made solid contact, sending the ball on a rise, toward leftfield. It kept curving left, hooking and hooking. As he took a few steps away from the plate, Alou didn't think it was going to stay fair. But it did, barely, and struck the inside of the foul pole for a three-run homer. Later on, Alou said, "There's no better feeling than this in the world."

Four pitches later, Charles Johnson hit a prodigious shot into the upper deck and the Marlins led, 5-1.

◆ ◆ ◆

The Fish video was played during the fifth inning, and with 67,245 fans in the ballpark, more people than ever before *didn't* do The Fish. Seemingly, The Fish video had backfired *because* of the wiggling blue-bikini-wearer. Rather than *doing* The Fish, most people were more interested in *watching* the blue-bikini-wearer do The Fish. This was obvious because some of the loudest cheers of the night were reserved for the wiggling blue-bikini-wearer's appearances on the Jumbotron. Yet nobody was doing The Fish.

It was a relatively quiet night for In-Game Entertainment. The Bleacher Brigade had been banished from the World Series and Muscle Boy was history. Muscle Boy was history because Muscle Boy's agent had called the Marlins' marketing department and identified himself as Muscle Boy's Agent. "I represent Muscle Boy," were the words, or something to that effect, although he didn't get to say much more. Mark Geddis, the Marlins' director of communications, was enraged. Muscle Boy's Agent was trying to get something for Muscle Boy and the Marlins didn't plan on giving him anything more than they would give Jackie Gleason's estate.

Jackie Gleason's estate?

You read correctly. One of the pre-game, pump-up-the-crowd videos was a clip from an old *Honeymooners* episode, in which Gleason's character, Ralph Kramden, talks about how much he has always wanted to attend a World Series game. The next day, the Marlins got a call from Gleason's people: If you want to use the clip, pay up.

The Marlins, who were already losing $15 million, or $30 million, or $34 million—depending on who you asked and when you asked them—didn't feel like losing any more, so the clip was edited out of In-Game Entertainment's pre-game presentation.

◆ ◆ ◆

Hernandez supplied the most enjoyable In-Game Entertainment. After allowing a home run by Jim Thome in the sixth, then back-to-back singles, he left the game to a standing ovation and tipped his cap to the crowd. Then he high-fived his teammates. And then he slammed his glove and cap against the dugout wall and kicked over a first aid cart. Hernandez was angry because the Marlins had given him a 7-2 lead, and he couldn't even give them six innings.

"He cooled down quick," said Cangelosi. During the past three days, Hernandez had displayed quite a temper.

Adrenal glands were working on overload all night. Cook did a good job relieving Hernandez and the Marlins took a 7-4 lead into the ninth, when Leyland handed the ball to Robb Nen. All season, Nen had struggled in situations in which a save wasn't at stake, so Nen got his adrenaline flowing by creating a save situation. Justice and Matt Williams singled with one out, bringing up Thome, who had already homered in the game.

The situation was classic: One out, two on, a power hitter at the plate, and Nen throwing fastballs. Baseball science says the faster they come in, the faster they go out, and Thome had the ability to tie the game with one swing. And if he didn't do it, the next hitter, Sandy Alomar Jr., could.

Nen threw a fastball. Thome swung mightily and missed.

"It scared me to death," Nen later said.

But he kept throwing fastballs. The second strike showed on the scoreboard at one hundred one miles per hour and the third showed at one hundred two. Thome went down swinging, hard. Alomar, who had hit twenty-one homers during the season, batted next. Nen threw more fastballs and Alomar struck out swinging, hard. The Marlins had won Game One, 7-4.

◆ ◆ ◆

Darren Daulton said, "You can be either up one or down one. We're up one."

◆ ◆ ◆

Leyland issued an update on his home dormitory. "There's fourteen bunks now and they're all full. My son stayed with me after the game last night. Of course, my wife went to the party in the tent, and I took my son home. And on the way home, he fell asleep chewing Big Red gum, and when I woke up this morning, he had it in his hair and in his neck, and he's in severe pain. His head might be stuck to the pillow. He might be wearing a pillow. But other than that, things are going great."

◆ ◆ ◆

Dick Ebersol, the president of NBC, was on the field prior to Game Two cleaning up the mess Ohlmeyer had created with his "four and out" comment. He was apologetic toward Major League Baseball and the two teams, saying, "We couldn't ask for two more compelling stories in terms of teams. It's like milking a cow, it's so full of stories."

But when the conversation came around to how the speed of games affects TV ratings, Ebersol's apology ended. "I'm sick and tired of people blaming it on the commercials," he said. "Just tell the umpires to move the game along."

The good news for Ebersol was that Game Two moved along: It took only two hours, forty-eight minutes to play.

The bad news for NBC was that the story of Game Two wasn't very compelling.

Chad Ogea, who had gone 8-9 during the regular season, vs. Kevin Brown was supposed to be a mismatch for the Marlins, and the crowd of 67,025 showed up expecting the Marlins to take a two games to none lead. Brown, however, never had his control, and the Marlins' problems started in the bottom of the first, when Sheffield got hit on the left wrist by an Ogea pitch.

"I was holding onto the bat and it hit me pretty solid," Sheffield said. "I thought the worst."

Sheffield dropped to the ground, shook off the hurt, and stayed in the game. But there would be no comeback and no life for the Marlins on this night. Brown left the game in the sixth, after a two-run homer by Alomar gave Cleveland a 6-1 lead. The Marlins never advanced a runner past second after the first inning. By the seventh, the crowd sounded like it was in the middle of a mid-season week-night rain delay. They temporarily entertained themselves by drinking beer and fighting and flinging paper airplanes onto the field, but the stadium was half empty by the eighth inning. The field, however, was half-full with paper airplanes.

Jose Mesa retired the Marlins in the ninth and the Indians won, 6-1.

◆ ◆ ◆

So now it was on to Cleveland, where the Indians and Marlins would experience one of the most drastic temperature changes in World Series history: From seventy-seven degrees, the highest for a World Series game since 1978, for Game Two, to wind chills in the twenties and possible snow for Games Three, Four, and Five. The Marlins hadn't played in such cold weather since early April in Chicago, and equipment manager Mike Wallace prepared by packing an extra twelve hundred pounds worth of clothing: Turtlenecks, long johns, gloves, parkas, ear coverings, and even ski masks.

Leyland wasn't too concerned. "It's going to be cold there," he explained at the press conference before Game Two. "But in the situation we're in, and what the stakes are, the heart stays warm.

"The feet get cold, and the hands get cold, but hopefully the heart stays warm."

Believe it or not, Leyland wasn't reading from a Hallmark card when he said that. Nor was he quoting a character from *Hoosiers*. He sounded dead serious and repeated the final phrase, "the heart stays warm," while placing his hand over his heart.

It was a beautiful performance, although not much different from some of the others Leyland had acted out since the national media arrived at the start of the playoffs. This was another example of Leyland building his reputation with the national media as a sentimental, salt-of-the-earth, down home, good guy. The image failed the test of reality.

Hang around Leyland every day for one hundred sixty-two games and you'll see the real man. There's no way Leyland can maintain this nice guy persona every minute. And Leyland had to know it didn't matter how he acted around the local beat reporters. Unless he went totally nuts—and became, say, Billy Martin or Bobby Knight—there was no way they would reveal what he was really all about. Otherwise they risked reduced access or another form of managerial reprisal, like a cold shoulder.

During the post-season, the national media never heard Leyland berating reporters or cursing a blue streak or speaking negatively—off the record, of course—about his players. They had never heard him dressing down front office workers, nor had they witnessed all of his moods. That's because Leyland had no trouble controlling his behavior for fifteen-minute World Series press conferences, when the national media assessed him for all the world to read and hear. It was over the long haul that the crass, temperamental Leyland came out.

The day before Game One, Leyland was asked what he had brought to the Marlins when he first became their manager. He replied, with all apparent sincerity, "You guys"—meaning the media—"helped me more than anything else, getting quotes from players that gave me decent reviews for whatever reason. So it kind of got my foot in the door with my club right off the bat."

Very nice, right? The thing was, Leyland had never said a word about this all season to any members of the local media, even though he had ample opportunity during spring training and one hundred sixty-two regular season games to thank them for their help. This was all a show, and an effective one at that. Other than in the eyes of the occasional New York reporter—like the one who called him a "raving phony"—Leyland was viewed as "a good man," a sentimental figure, and a decent person who was loved by everyone.

After the Division Series, a San Francisco columnist described Leyland and Giants manager Dusty Baker as "two of the finest men to ever walk this earth."

Forget about the ridiculousness of the statement. It's exactly the image Leyland had successfully conveyed through the national media, and it's the image he nurtured in October. An out-of-town reporter shamelessly asked Mike Hargrove whether it had been a cruel twist of fate when Francisco Cabrera defeated Leyland in the 1992 NLCS.

Cruel? Hardly, and Hargrove said so, but the meaning behind the question was clear: How could the higher powers have done such a thing to such a good man as Leyland. Didn't he *deserve* to win?

And even though Leyland had once told the reporters, "I'll never lie to you," there were times when he wasn't entirely truthful. A few days before Game One, a national reporter asked Leyland whether this might be the Marlins' best chance to win, because the team planned on cutting salaries during the off-season.

Answered Leyland, "I've never heard of anything that we were downsizing."

Jim Leyland flashback, August 20, after Edwin Pope's "see the Marlins while you can" column appeared in The Miami Herald: *"I think this organization will cut back."*

Don Smiley flashback, September 22, discussing the Marlins' 1998 payroll: "It'll be $31 million. North of $31 million."

The Marlins' 1997 payroll had reached $53 million. Smiley and Leyland talked to each other all the time, almost every day. Some of Smiley's quotes about reducing payroll had appeared in the newspapers. The fact that the Marlins planned on "downsizing" was no secret to Leyland.

Leyland could have told the reporter, "I don't care to talk about that right now when my team's in the World Series." Instead, he fudged the truth.

◆ ◆ ◆

The Marlins' traveling party had turned into a caravan. Not just the players' wives, but their children, too, came along to Cleveland and two planes took off from Fort Lauderdale late Sunday night.

The best plane to be on was the one *without* Sheffield. He had brought along his son, Gary Jr., and the little boy was excited, to say the least. His father tried to sleep, but Gary Jr. kept crawling all over him and hitting him in the head. Gary Jr. entertained the other passengers, even if they didn't want to be entertained.

It was not a good trip. Felo Ramirez, one of the Marlins' Spanish play-by-play announcers, tumbled head-first down the stairway while getting off the plane Monday morning and landed on the back of his head. He departed the airport by ambulance. The rest of the traveling party departed for the hotel by bus.

And about that hotel—the Marlins, especially Leyland, were not happy with the accommodations, which were considerably below first class. Cleveland had been overrun by a rubber convention and every hotel room within a fifteen-mile radius of downtown had been booked for months. The Marlins took what they were given, and what they were given was a second-class hotel located five miles from Jacobs Field and in the middle of a bad neighborhood. Players were warned by *hotel employees* not to walk the streets after dark.

"If you cross the street, you die," said one member of the Marlins' traveling party.

Fortunately for the Marlins, the hotel had three restaurants, so they didn't have to worry about venturing outside. Unfortunately for the Marlins, their special requests were not honored. The taller players had asked for longer beds. They didn't get them. Instead of king-sized beds, each room had two double beds, which wouldn't have been so bad if the wives weren't along. The way Leyland saw it, the team was in the World Series and deserved first class treatment.

The situation worsened when the players received their game tickets from the Indians and discovered, again to their dismay, that most of the seats were in the upper deck.

They were understandably angry. The Indians had been given prime accommodations in South Florida: a beautiful hotel on the water and prime seats for their families and friends. And the Indians returned the favor with a bad hotel in a bad area and bad seats. The Marlins were the unhappiest traveling party in World Series history.

◆ ◆ ◆

The treatment of the Marlins improved considerably when they arrived at Jacobs Field Monday afternoon for their off-day workout. The visitor's clubhouse at Jacobs Field is plush and spacious—nicer than many home clubhouses—with plenty of couches and chairs for the players to keep outsiders from sitting on. The stadium, too, is a dream.

Jacobs Field, which opened in 1994, is at the heart of Cleveland's revitalization. The stadium is state-of-the-art in every way and is widely considered the best of the new wave of stadiums. The bottom level consists of a long, gently sloping bank of green field-level seats. Stacked above the field-level seats are three decks of glass-enclosed suites, like boxes in an opera house. The stadium is topped by a steeply banked upper deck that hangs like a balcony high above the field.

A glassed-enclosed, multi-level restaurant is located in the leftfield corner, six sections of steeply banked bleachers rise behind the leftfield fence, and a landscaped picnic area is tucked behind the centerfield fence. The scoreboard rises from the back of the leftfield bleachers and, over the big red script Indians logo perched on top, is a view of Cleveland's modest skyline.

The field is almost symmetrical: three hundred twenty-five feet to left, three hundred seventy to left center, four hundred five to dead center, three hundred seventy-five to right center, and three hundred twenty to right, but what makes it unique is the mini-Green Monster that extends from the leftfield foul pole all the way to centerfield. Although the fence is only half as high as the real Green Monster in Boston, which stands thirty-seven feet, it adds character to the ballpark. The squared-off nature of Jacobs Field, with the rightfield seats extending at nearly a right-angle from the rest of the ballpark, makes it look like an old-time bandbox.

For the past four years, sellout crowds filled Jacobs Field for nearly every Indians home game, and the image of the Indians as baseball's lovable losers had changed. The Indians were winners. Their ballpark was packed.

"The feeling is night and day," Hargrove said. "It's the opposite ends of the spectrum, to where people were at times fearful of letting other people know they liked the Indians, to now where people at times fall over themselves, trying to get the last Indians T-shirt or baseball hat. Our fans are just as loyal and just as loud as ever. We've just got a lot more of them now."

The Indians hadn't won the World Series since 1948, and Cleveland was filled with an air of desperation and hope for this year's team. Seemingly everyone in town was talking about the Indians. Arriving passengers at Cleveland's airport were handed cardboard "Go Tribe!" banners. Nearly every hotel, restaurant, and store had an Indians banner in its window. People on the streets were wearing Indians jackets and caps in far greater numbers than Marlins fans were wearing their team's colors in South Florida.

This much was obvious: A victory would mean more to Cleveland than it would to South Florida. Cleveland had suffered through decades of bad baseball and bad baseball jokes. South Florida had only suffered through rain delays.

Monday night, in the nearly deserted restaurant area surrounding Jacobs Field, a man ran across the street toward the lit-up stadium, leading his wife and two children in a chant of "Kill the Fish! Kill the Fish!" Tuesday morning, a televised Indians rally featured the host smashing a tiny Gary Sheffield figurine with a hammer and screeching, to an audience of teenagers, "I'm Gary Sheffield! My legs have fallen off! Help me! My legs have fallen off!"

He gave the figurine another bash.

"Go see the trainer, Gary," the host bitterly spat at the broken figure.

◆ ◆ ◆

With not much else going on, except for the usual off-day nothingness, the big subject Monday was the weather. It was going to be cold in Cleveland for Games Three, Four, and Five. Very cold.

But Leyland was tired of hearing about the cold, so he decided to have a little fun. When he walked down from the podium after finishing his press conference, he passed Craig Counsell and Edgar Renteria, the next interview subjects.

"Tell them you like playing in cold weather," he whispered to them.

So Counsell, who grew up in Milwaukee and attended college in South Bend, Indiana, called the weather "outstanding," and Renteria, who grew up in Baranquilla, Colombia, where the temperature rarely drops below sixty, said, "I love playing in cold weather." The only reporters in the room not fooled were those who had overheard Leyland's conversation; the rest reported it as fact.

The weather was almost comfortable Monday afternoon, in the high forties, but the cold-loving Marlins weren't taking any chances on freezing. They came out for their workout wearing parkas and wore gloves on both hands for batting practice. Leyland—who, of course, would spend the games sitting in the dugout, sheltered from the cold—decided the weather was nothing to be concerned about. He recalled the two games the Marlins had played in Wrigley Field in April, when the wind chill made the temperature feel like zero. The Marlins won both of those games and Fernandez pitched a one-hitter in the second game.

"I can remember telling my team then, 'Hey, it's going to be cold in October,'" Leyland said, sounding like a prophet because the Marlins didn't have any regular season games scheduled for October. "It's pretty hard to tell your players, like that day in Wrigley Field, that it wasn't cold. I mean, I didn't go out there with short sleeves, myself. It's cold. So what? They know it's cold. I know it's cold. The other dugouts know it's cold. It's no big deal. That's part of the game this time of year."

Besides, the heart stays warm.

The key for both teams would be staying in the dugouts, which had heaters hanging from the roofs. The heaters, gleaming red hot, were turned up so high Monday afternoon that prolonged exposure could have resulted in severe sun poisoning. The temperature could have been fifty below outside, but underneath those heaters, it was nice and warm. Too warm.

"Those heaters are fine," Rich Donnelly said, "but you have to get two inches away from them, and then you burn your face off."

So it was cold in Cleveland and what everybody learned on workout day is that cold weather helps the hitters, because the cold affects the movement on breaking pitches and pitchers can't get a good grip on the ball, and also helps the pitchers, because a ball striking a bat on a cold day produces a numbing sting in the hitter's hand. Taking all this into account, Game Three figured to be either low scoring, high scoring, or somewhere in between. The science on this stuff is pretty exact.

◆ ◆ ◆

Sign in the Tower Center, a few blocks from Jacobs Field, heralding the NFL's return to Cleveland: 609 DAYS TO GO. CLEVELAND BROWNS. NEXT HOME GAME: AUGUST 21, 1999.

Cleveland really did need this worse than South Florida.

◆ ◆ ◆

Sister Mary Assumpta, the nun whose cooking ability has brought good luck to the Indians since 1984, was on the field carrying four trays of her famous cookies. Other than Mother Teresa, there probably isn't a nun in the world who has been interviewed more, and Sister Mary was explaining for about the thousandth time the power of her blessed cookies.

"They have strikeouts in them if the pitchers eat them," she said, "and home runs in them if the hitters eat them. I think I do a good job."

◆ ◆ ◆

It was no weather for an 85-year-old woman who was missing three disks in her back and needed a walker on the rare occasions when she ventured out of her house. But Veronica Leyland, the manager's mother, planned on showing up for Game Three and she wasn't going to sit in one of the warm, comfortable, dry, luxury suites. She was going to sit outside, in Section 255, with the rest of the fans, and watch her son manage a baseball game.

Despite the World Series hype, mothers had become one of the nicest stories of this World Series. Back in Cuba, Miriam Carreras, the mother of Livan Hernandez, had been granted permission by the United States to enter the country, and was awaiting an exit visa from the Cuban government. It seemed unlikely Castro would allow the mother of a famous defector to leave the country, but the Marlins tried everything. The players even sent a letter to the Cuban government which said, in a nutshell, "Please let our teammate see his mother."

Even in her disabled condition, Veronica Leyland would have a much easier time getting to the ballpark than Miriam Carreras. She had her hair done on the morning of Game Three, and at about 3 o'clock in the afternoon, a white stretch limo came to pick her up, along with her four sons and one daughter. A few hours before game time, Leyland kept poking his head out of the dugout to see if his mother had arrived.

Mrs. Leyland was in her seat at game time, in the section behind home plate. Leyland waved to his mother. She waved back. It was cold and windy, so Indians fans kept bringing her blankets. Indians blankets. She lasted the entire game, proving she was tougher than—and at least as stubborn as—anyone at the game, including her son. He was sitting under a heater.

◆ ◆ ◆

Really, it wasn't fair to make an old woman suffer through some of the worst base-ball in World Series history. There might have been worse World Series games than this one, but if there were, they had never been replayed on Classic Sports Network or remembered by anyone with even a passing love for the game.

It was bad, and most of the badness had to do with the miserable weather. There had been plenty of debate over whether cold weather would result in low scoring or high scoring games, but this much became clear from the three games in Cleveland: Cold weather results in high scoring, poorly played games with plenty of bad fielding.

The game time temperature was forty-nine degrees with a wind chill of twenty-nine. Gusts of twenty-five-miles-per-hour winds blew from right to left. The pitch-ing was terrible, so bad that Indians starter Charles Nagy allowed a home run to leftfield in the first inning, even though the wind did everything in its power to keep Sheffield's drive in the ballpark. It was a monumental shot, one of Sheffield's hardest hit balls of the season, yet it cleared the fence by only a few feet.

Nagy was bad. Leiter was worse. Hesitant to throw his curveball in the bad weather, and unable to find his control, he gave himself no chance to win. The Indians scored three runs in the fourth without the benefit of a hard hit ball and because of a throwing error by Bonilla, whose injured hamstring hadn't improved. It was his second error of the game.

In the fifth inning, with one on and Thome up, Leyland decided he had almost seen enough of Leiter. Rothschild called down to the bullpen and had Heredia warm up, but one pitch later, Thome lined a home run into the rightfield seats for a 7-3 Indians lead.

◆ ◆ ◆

How could anyone have suspected the greatest night of Sheffield's baseball life would occur under such unlikely circumstances in such terrible weather? The way Sheffield had dealt with adversity during the season, he was more likely to bail out and coast through this bad game. But if there was one night all season that made Sheffield worth the $61 million contract he signed in April, this was it.

He homered in his first at-bat. He walked, driving home a run, in the third. By the time he came to bat in the seventh, Eisenreich had already closed the gap to 7-5 with a two-run homer, and Renteria had driven home Counsell with the Marlins' sixth run. Renteria was on first when Sheffield doubled off the wall in centerfield to tie the game.

"Stay patient," Bonds had told him. "When they finally challenge you, make them pay."

"I couldn't believe it," said Sheffield, who would walk eight times in the series and once in this game. "I had something to hit every time up."

For all of his offensive contributions—and there would be more—it was a field-ing play, of all things, that made his night stand out. Sheffield, who all season had misjudged fly balls and missed cutoff men, made his career catch in the seventh inning.

Heredia was the pitcher. Thome was the batter. There was one out in the inning and the scored was tied when Thome lifted a fly to right-center that got caught in

287

the wind. Sheffield tracked the ball and raced back. At first, Sheffield looked like he was on another one of his suicide runs, like the one in September when he slammed shoulder-first into the fence.

Sheffield got it right this time. When he reached the warning track, he stopped. Then he took another step backwards, turned sideways, and leaped. Somehow, the ball landed in his glove, right against the yellow stripe at the top of the fence, and stayed there.

The crowd went silent. Sheffield couldn't believe the catch, either. He pumped his fists, then tossed the ball back to the infield. Later, Sheffield would talk about the "bad publicity" he got for his defense, and how this proved otherwise, which it didn't. But he sure had picked the right time to make the catch of his life.

"I've been waiting nine years to get here," Sheffield said with a grin nearly as bright as the $10,000 diamond earring in his right ear. "It finally happened."

◆ ◆ ◆

With the score still tied, 7-7, Bonilla led off the ninth by walking. Daulton singled to right-center and Bonilla, despite his bad hamstring, tried for third. He hesitated rounding second base, and the throw from rightfield had him beat, but it bounced off of his right shoulder and rolled into the third base photo bay. Umpire Ken Kaiser waved him home with the go-ahead run.

"I was excited," Bonilla said later. "I didn't cum or anything like that, but I was excited."

The runs kept coming—six more of them—and the Marlins led, 14-7.

"It kept getting colder," said an Indians fan sitting in the upper deck. "Every run they scored, it got colder."

The temperature had dropped to forty-two degrees and the wind chill had dropped below twenty-five. The time was well after midnight. When the inning ended, Leyland, once again, handed the ball to Nen in a non-save situation.

◆ ◆ ◆

Back in the clubhouse, Leiter was sitting in the trainer's room with Daulton, who had been replaced by Conine after the top of the ninth. Nen was having a rough time out on the mound, and when Bip Roberts doubled home two runs, the Marlins' lead was down to three.

Bad memories started floating through Daulton's mind, memories of Game Four of the 1993 World Series, when the Blue Jays beat the Phillies, 15-14. Leiter was on the winning side that night, Daulton was on the losing side.

"It reminds me of that game," Daulton told Leiter as they sat on the trainer's table. "I don't like to see those fourteen runs on the scoreboard."

"Don't worry about it," Leiter said. "I was on the fifteen-run side."

Leiter had a tough time in the 1993 game, too. He had relieved Todd Stottlemyre in the second inning, and allowed, in order, a bunt single, a home run, a bunt single, and another home run.

Nen wasn't quite that bad, and recovered quickly after working his way into something resembling a save situation: Roberts on second, Vizquel the batter, and Ramirez representing the tying run in the on-deck circle. Finally, Vizquel grounded out to Counsell, and the Marlins had a 14-11 win after four hours, twelve minutes, the second longest nine inning game in World Series history. The time was 12:36 a.m., past a child's bedtime even on the west coast.

"It was such an ugly game," Hargrove said.

"It's uglier to some people," retorted Daulton who, like the other Marlins, didn't care how they won and was happy that this time the winning team had fourteen.

◆ ◆ ◆

At 6:10 p.m. on Wednesday, October 22, while the Indians were taking batting practice for Game Four, snow fell on Jacobs Field. It came down in wet, thick pellets, and for the first time in his life, Marcelino Lugo, the Marlins' Miami-born bullpen catcher, saw snow. He was enthralled.

"Can you eat it?" Lugo asked.

He decided to find out and licked the snow pellets off of his jacket.

"It tastes like water," he said.

A few minutes later, Charles Johnson wandered into the dugout. Word had come down a few hours earlier that Johnson had won his third consecutive Gold Glove Award, so he was surrounded by reporters. One of them asked, "What do you think about this snow?" And Johnson said, "It's cold."

Winter Wonderland and *Let It Snow* blared over the Jacobs Field loudspeakers. The Marlins came out for BP bundled up in heavy teal and black winter coats with black turtlenecks and ski caps pulled tight over their ears. They looked like they were getting ready to rob a 7-Eleven.

◆ ◆ ◆

Tony Saunders had spent the first three World Series games marveling at his position in life. Here he was, a 23-year-old rookie who last season pitched in Double-A, about to start Game Four of the World Series.

"It's hard for me to believe," Saunders said. "When I go inside the clubhouse and watch it on TV and I walk through that tunnel and I'm right in the dugout, I still get chills every time."

When Game Four ended, Saunders was still marveling at his position in his life. His position was in a chair, facing into his stall, with his head buried in his hands. It was the position of a pitcher taking penance and when Carlos Tosca, the Marlins' Triple-A coach, walked over and patted him on the back, Saunders didn't even look up. After ten minutes of staring, he wandered into the trainer's room, and after five minutes of sitting there, he walked back to his stall, where fifteen reporters were waiting.

"I can't look my teammates in the face right now," Saunders said, unable to even look the reporters in the eye. "I feel like I've let everyone down. It's tough to swallow. These guys want to win more than anything, and I feel like I cheated them because I didn't give them an opportunity to do that."

Not even close. In a battle of rookies, Saunders vs. Cleveland's Jaret Wright, the Marlins found themselves on the wrong end of a mismatch. It was a must-win game for the Indians, who would have faced elimination if they didn't win Game Four, and they responded by pounding Saunders from the start. A light snow was falling when Saunders left the game in the third inning, trailing 6-0, and Saunders cursed himself all the way to the clubhouse.

"I came in here and took my uniform off, then I watched the game and rooted for my teammates," Saunders said. "I didn't want to sit in the dugout and piss myself off. I wanted to be out there, not in here after embarrassing myself."

Saunders' post-game self-flagellation sounded like his self-assessment in Los Angeles a month earlier, when he temporarily lost his spot in the starting rotation. *"We're trying to win a pennant and I'm going out there every fifth day and getting my ass kicked,"* Saunders said back then. This time, he decided his butt-kicking was a costly learning experience.

"It's a tough lesson for me to learn," Saunders said. "Maybe it'll make me tougher when I sit down and think about it."

Saunders would try to forget this night. Somebody asked what he would tell his daughter in fifteen years, when she asked him about his first World Series game, and Saunders said, "I'll tell her to change the subject."

Changing the subject, maybe talking about Game Five, was exactly what the Marlins felt like doing in their quiet clubhouse. The final score was 10-3, Indians, tying the series at two games each.

◆ ◆ ◆

The baseball had been awful. The first four games had taken an average of three hours, twenty-five minutes to play. The pitching was inept, the fielding sloppy. There had been forty-three runs, thirty-three walks, nearly nine a game, and seven errors. The average margin of victory was 4.5 runs. A lot of the sloppy play had to do with the cold weather, but that didn't explain the bad TV ratings, which were on track to be the lowest in World Series history.

Sports Illustrated called it the "Faux Classic" and questioned whether the best teams were playing. MLB commissioner Bud Selig—the "acting" commissioner, as Leyland helpfully pointed out—was furious with the pace of Game Three, which started after eight and ended well after midnight.

"I felt the *Unfinished Symphony* had a better chance of being finished," Selig said as he stormed out of the ballpark after the game. "Ball one, ball two, ball three. When you have pitchers who can't throw the ball over the plate, and when they do it hits the wall somewhere, you're going to have long games."

This didn't sound like the kind of thing the commissioner of baseball should be saying during the World Series, but he wasn't alone in his criticism.

"It is as if the Marlins and Indians are using this World Series to officially kill baseball," wrote Dan Shaughnessy in the *Boston Globe*.

On Wednesday, Selig continued his monologue about the slow games. Leyland read Selig's comments in the newspapers the next day and decided to defend his team.

So, late Thursday afternoon before Game Five, during what figured to be another run-of-the-mill press conference, Leyland introduced a new word to baseball's colorful vocabulary. The word was "puke."

His diatribe featured the following points:

1. "I'm sick and tired of hearing about New York and Atlanta and Baltimore. Mike Hargrove said it best. They had the same chance that we did. We won it. It makes me puke when I continue to hear people talking about the Braves and Yankees."

2. "Everybody else is always throwing stones, and I'm trying to take care of my own furniture."

3. "I have to believe that when you're taking batting practice and you feel like you ought to be downtown Christmas shopping, it's not exactly good."

4. "It hurts me, to be honest with you, to think that the Cleveland Indians and the Florida Marlins worked so hard as we did to represent baseball, and I almost have to apologize for being here. I've been in baseball thirty-three years, loading the buses for eighteen years, and I'm not apologizing for anybody being here."

5. "The subject is over and it's making me puke."

Leyland couldn't have been more correct. How could anyone have accused the Marlins and Indians of being unworthy World Series participants when the Marlins had beaten the Braves twelve out of eighteen times, and the Indians had beaten the Orioles and Yankees? In 1997, the Marlins were 17-7 against the three teams that the national media decided should have been in the World Series instead of them.

Leyland was just getting started. After leaving the podium, he walked straight to the dugout, sat down with a group of reporters, and made the following statements:

1. "I get tired of reading that goddamn cheap shot shit all the time about the fucking ratings."

2. "Everybody's saying how much better the ratings would be with Atlanta vs. Baltimore. Fuck 'em! Just cancel the season and let Atlanta and Baltimore go to the goddamn World Series."

3. "That World Series party Wayne Huizenga threw made all other parties look like a bucket of Kentucky Fried Chicken on a blanket held down by a pond somewhere."

4. "I can't help it who watches the game or who likes my team. I'm going to enjoy this. I'm not going to let anybody ruin this for me and my team. It breaks my heart, if you wanna know the truth. I'm pissed off."

With that, Leyland walked away and hit fungoes to his infielders, having given the World Series more life than any of the first four games could muster.

◆ ◆ ◆

At 6:44 p.m., an hour and a half before the start of Game Five, Marlins starter Livan Hernandez walked into the dugout wearing a teal Marlins parka that reached below his knees, long johns, flip flops, and no socks. Compared to the last two days, the weather was almost seasonable: forty-six degrees and not much wind. Hernandez hung around for a few minutes, then walked back inside. It wasn't *that* warm.

◆ ◆ ◆

Puke had become the key word for Game Five, because puking is exactly what Moises Alou felt like doing during the hours before game time. If it wasn't bad enough that his wrist still ached from his attempted catch in the Atlanta series, he was also nursing the flu—the same non-contagious flu that had also affected Bonilla and Brown.

"I caught a cold the first day here during workouts and I haven't been feeling very well," Alou said. "But when the game starts, I don't feel it or think about it. There's a lot of guys on our team that have the flu. A lot of guys play with injuries. When the game begins, nobody worries about that. You just go out and play hard."

The Marlins were in a dire situation when Alou came up in the sixth inning. Hernandez had battled with his control through the first three innings and paid for back-to-back walks in the third when Alomar hit a three-run homer over the mini-monster in left. Hernandez, thanks to a talking-to from Johnson and Fernandez, settled down after that, but Hershiser, who fell behind nearly every hitter in the first two innings—and nearly beaned Alou—rediscovered his control, and retired nine in a row. The Indians had a 4-2 lead.

"There was no reason to believe that he was going to hit the wall and lose his stuff," Mike Hargrove said. "He gave no indication."

Nor was there any indication after Hershiser started the sixth by striking out Renteria. Then Sheffield singled, his second hit of the game, Bonilla walked, Daulton flied out, and Alou came up for the most important at-bat of his career.

"I didn't have very good at-bats, my first or second at-bat," Alou said. "And I didn't make an adjustment. The guys on our bench told me to come in and swing, and I did that."

Alou told himself to be patient. Hershiser's first pitch was a hanging slider that Alou should have been able to drive. He fouled it back. Hershiser threw another slider and a curve for balls. With the count two and one, Hershiser threw one more slider and Alou made contact with the sweet spot of his bat, sending the ball soaring toward centerfield. Grissom headed to the wall, but he didn't have a chance. The ball barely cleared the nineteen-foot-high fence. Alou pumped his fists as he jogged around the bases, and when he touched home plate with the go-ahead run, being sick was the farthest thing from his mind.

◆ ◆ ◆

Baseball lore is full of stories about Game Seven heroics, like Bill Mazeroski's homer in 1960 and Reggie Jackson's grand slam in 1973. It's true that decisive games tend to be the most memorable. Yet, there is something special about the fifth game of a playoff series that no other game can match. It was seen on Leyland's face after Game Five of the NLCS, the anticipation that he was one game away from reaching his life-long goal. When a team wins Game Five and goes up 3-2, its dream is within grasp for the first time, and the expectation of a championship is almost as sweet as the ultimate victory.

So it hardly mattered that Game Five offered only slightly more drama than the previous four. The Marlins scored another run in the sixth, then single runs in the eighth and the ninth, and Hernandez went out for the ninth inning holding a seemingly comfortable 8-4 lead.

A combination of bad calls and bad pitching nearly cost the Marlins the game. Leadoff batter Bip Roberts hit a grounder to first and Conine shoveled to Hernandez for the apparent putout. But Ken Kaiser, the first base umpire, mistakenly ruled Hernandez hadn't touched the bag.

Vizquel, the next batter, singled and Hernandez's post-season run was over. This time, he didn't throw a fit when he got back to the dugout as he had during Game One, because he knew he had done his job. He had battled through the tough early innings, when he felt the home plate umpire hadn't given him a wide enough strike zone.

Nen relieved Hernandez, this time in a save situation, and was no sharper than he had been two nights earlier. Justice singled home two runs, Counsell muffed a potential game-ending double play, and Thome singled home Matt Williams. The Marlins' lead was down to 8-7. The Indians had one on and two out. Alomar, who already had four RBIs in the game, was the batter, and he lifted a 1-2 pitch to right-field. Sheffield settled back shakily, to the edge of the warning track, nearly as far as he could go. The ball landed, precariously, in his glove, and he squeezed it as hard as could. For a split second, it looked like the ball might pop out, but it didn't, and the game was over.

The Marlins were one win away from a world championship. Eisenreich said the team had to "live for the moment," and Leyland muttered the usual cliché about having to win one more game. Sheffield insisted, "We're trying not to think about it," and Bonilla labeled the victory as a big win, but not the ultimate win. Which was true.

But later, after most of the reporters had left the clubhouse and his teammates were boarding the bus, Bonilla allowed himself the pleasure of anticipation. The Marlins had a three games to two lead and were almost there. He admitted what seemed obvious: On Friday, the day off, there was no way he could avoid looking forward to what Game Six might bring.

"Isn't it unbelievable?" he said wistfully. "We're one win away from a dream come true."

◆ ◆ ◆

The dream was in the hands of Game Six starter Kevin Brown, and the feeling in South Florida and around the Marlins' clubhouse was that their ace would deliver the championship. "We have our No. 1 guy pitching," Daulton said. "So looking at the whole picture, I like what I see." Alou spent part of the off day food shopping with his wife and got mobbed by autograph-seekers. Leyland went to the racetrack and won. A T-shirt company readied the presses for a run of Marlins World Series Champions shirts.

TITLE ON DECK blared the headline in the Fort Lauderdale *Sun-Sentinel*, in which a columnist had already declared that the series was over and the Marlins were champions. South Florida was certain Brown couldn't lose to Chad Ogea twice in one week.

Hundreds of fans came out Friday for a rally on Fort Lauderdale Beach. Radio DJs made up silly poems and insipid song lyrics about the Marlins. *"Bad boys, bad boys. Indians. What you gonna do when the Marlins come for you?"*

Muscle Boy had become a cottage industry. On Saturday, three hours before game time, he stood on a street corner outside Pro Player Stadium, shirt off, performing his steroid monster posing routine for passing motorists, while his father and a friend hawked Muscle Boy T-shirts. The shirts featured the words Muscle Boy in writing similar to the Marlins' logo, above a picture of Muscle Boy's bare, nine-year-old chest.

"Are the Marlins involved with this?" one of the Muscle Boy men was asked.

"No," the man said. "But he's not Marlins Muscle Boy. He's Muscle Boy."

"Oh."

"Wanna buy one? Fifteen bucks."

◆ ◆ ◆

On the field and in the dugout at Pro Player Stadium, Biff Henderson, the stage manager from *The Late Show*, with David Letterman, conducted interviews for a comedy bit that would be aired the following week.

"Which Marlin sweats the most?" Biff asked Leyland.

"I think that would be Darren Daulton," Leyland said, breaking into a smile.

"Is it true that the owner of the Marlins is Mrs. Paul?"

"No," Leyland answered, "but I can tell you that the owner of the Florida Marlins is a very big fish."

"Dave has a question for you," Biff asked. "What happens if the series is tied after seven games?"

"I haven't thought about that," Leyland said, laughing. "But if it is, I'll be totally bald instead of balding."

A man standing in the lower level wore a T-shirt that read, "World Series Champion Marlins." Biff walked over to Bonilla and asked, "Any teammates who are *all eyes* in the shower?"

"This is a Letterman question, right?" Bonilla shot back. "Dave just loves doing this shit to me."

"Have you ever pulled your groin?" Biff asked.

His follow-up question was, "Have you ever pulled a teammate's groin?"

The *Arli$$* guy walked past. He would never go away. Biff ignored him.

◆ ◆ ◆

Batting practice seemingly lasted forever. Hundreds of people were milling about. Celebrities. Pseudo-celebrities. Journalists. Pseudo-journalists. Owners. Owner wannabees. Huizenga, wearing green, his favorite color, tossed a commemorative coin to a fan in the stands, then entertained the media with his views about Jacobs Field.

"It shows you what a great facility could do," Huizenga said. "If all of those facilities work in all of those other places, there's no reason they shouldn't work here."

Hmmm . . . It sounded like a hint. Then Huizenga mentioned something about baseball fans coming out "if we solve the weather problems," and since he had no apparent connection with God—except for "In God We Trust"—it was pretty clear that he was talking about getting a stadium built.

HUIZENGA FLASHBACK, June 26, 1997, Sale Announcement:

REPORTER: "Wayne, why should we believe that you're not just bluffing? Is this for real?"

HUIZENGA: "This is for real."

REPORTER: "Cross your heart and hope to die?"

HUIZENGA: "Cross my heart and hope to die."

Whoops. The advantage of being a billionaire businessman is that, like politicians, they're not expected to tell the truth, so nobody blinks an eye when they lie. So who knows what Huizenga was getting at when he mentioned that the Marlins' losses were now up to $34 million. Three months earlier, they were $30 million. When the playoffs started, they were $31 million. Now, somehow, they were $34 million. And, after the Atlanta series, Huizenga had mumbled something about having his $15 million worth of fun. Why not *$34 million* worth of fun? What did he mean by that?

OK, so Huizenga was on a roll. He was opening up to the media, exposing his thoughts, little-by-little, all in the same interview. Then he tossed out his old Panthers' "build me a stadium" line: "People think that stadiums are built for the owner. No. They're built for the community."

With the owner reaping all of the financial benefits, naturally.

Then Huizenga mentioned that he had been getting calls from "elected officials" about building a new stadium for the Marlins. Then he said that if a new stadium was built, he would keep the team. Finally, asked whether the Marlins would cut payroll if a new stadium was, say, three or four years from being completed, he said that they wouldn't.

Now what was that about, "Cross my heart and hope to die?"

◆ ◆ ◆

Far more entertaining than anything taking place on the field was Wayne Huizenga Jr., the owner's son. Not that he meant to be. Wayne Jr. had tried boarding the press elevator, when the elevator operator made the mistake of trying to stop him.

"Hi," Junior said, "I'm Wayne Huizenga Jr." Which, in these parts, was about the same as walking up to the White House doorman and saying, "Hi, I'm Chelsea Clinton."

Fortunately for the elevator operator, Wayne Jr. had a sense of humor and didn't fire the offending worker on the spot. The elevator operator, taking proactive measures, apologized. Then they shook hands and engaged in small talk.

"Think tonight's the night?" the elevator operator daringly asked.

"I sure hope so," Wayne Jr. said. "I can't take this anymore. I can't wait to have a solid bowel movement."

◆ ◆ ◆

Unfortunately for Wayne Jr., his solid bowel movement would have to wait. Brown stunk. Matt Williams led off the top of the second by singling off Bonilla's glove. It should have been an error, but considering how badly Bonilla's hamstring was hurting, maybe the official scorer was being merciful.

As intense and surly as he was, Brown couldn't deal with this latest bit of adversity created by a teammate. All season, his worst problem had been regaining his composure after a teammate made a mistake. This time, in the most important game he ever pitched, Brown responded by walking Thome. With one out, he walked Marquis Grissom to load the bases. Ogea came up, and Brown had a chance to get out of the inning against a pitcher who hadn't had a hit since high school.

Brown threw six consecutive fastballs. Big mistake.

"If he throws a breaking ball," said Indians GM John Hart, "Chad's an easy out. He has no chance."

Ogea knew it. He fouled off four pitches and waited anxiously for Brown's nasty slider. But, on a 2-2 count, Brown threw another fastball, and Ogea reached across the plate and poked a single into right, scoring Williams and Thome.

Right then it was clear. The Marlins had no chance on a night when Brown was too stubborn to throw his slider. Ogea would get not one, but two hits, and account for not two, but three runs, in a 4-1 Indians victory that tied the series. Three hours, fifteen minutes of near-perfect baseball by the Indians included a rally stopping play by shortstop Omar Vizquel and a sensational running catch by centerfielder Marquis Grissom that had Conine muttering, "No fucking way." The crowd of 67,498, the largest in South Florida history, went home wondering if the Marlins had blown their best chance to win the World Series.

When the game ended, riot police lined the field, but they weren't needed. The fans were headed in the other direction after the Marlins' sure thing that wasn't.

◆ ◆ ◆

In a perfect world, here's how the Marlins would have won the World Series. In Game Six, Brown, the surly, rude, inconsiderate pitcher who had never done anything to warrant anyone's sympathy, would fail. Rattled by a fielding play that a teammate failed to make, he would unravel, come apart at the baseball seams, and then later blame the loss on a lack of run support.

Brown after Game Six: "I didn't throw the ball as well as I wanted to, but the nature of the game is if we don't score runs, everything's magnified. If this had been a game where we had scored a bunch of runs, we'd be in here celebrating right now."

But then in Game Seven, Leyland would have no choice but to put the ball in the hands of Al Leiter, the man who had made him break his no-smoking vow and, indirectly at least, caused his first shouting match with Dave Dombrowski. And Leiter, a good man who had never done anything to warrant anyone's derision, would go out and pitch one of the games of his life: Nine innings, no runs, no walks. When he walked off the mound after the ninth inning—to a standing ovation, of course—his entire season would have been redeemed.

The Marlins, however, would have also failed to score, until there were two outs and none on in the bottom of the ninth inning. And then Bonilla, who had played all season in pain and without complaint, and wanted so much to win one for the manager, would hobble to the plate on his bad hamstring and launch a 3-2 pitch into the rightfield seats, sending South Florida into ecstasy and giving Leyland the World Series victory he so much wanted to give him.

Leiter would be the winner, and Bonilla would be the star of the night, and maybe, just for a Hollywood touch, Gregg "Fucking" Zaun—the manager's whipping boy—would have replaced Charles Johnson in the ninth inning, and thrown out Omar Vizquel trying to steal third.

The Marlins would be World Champions and this game would be remembered as one of the greatest ever played.

Of course, that's not the way it happened.

It was even better.

◆ ◆ ◆

After losing Game Six, the Marlins wouldn't have minded going right back out on the field for Game Seven. They would have to wait until Sunday night.

"And that damn clock is going backward," Bonilla said. He was referring to daylight savings time, which clicked in early Sunday morning. The Marlins would have to wait an additional hour.

It was hard to say why they were in such a hurry. Prior to Game Three, pitching coach Larry Rothschild said he thought Leiter was coming up to a good performance, so after Game Six, he was asked whether he still felt that way.

"Any time anyone starts for us, I feel he's capable of a good start," Rothschild said.

That didn't sound like a vote of confidence.

The media wondered whether someone besides Leiter could pitch Game Seven, maybe Hernandez on two days rest, maybe just about anybody.

Responded Leyland: "Who else would you pick?"

That didn't sound like a vote of confidence, either.

When Game Six ended, Bonilla had limped to the trainer's room for ice, then limped back to his locker and sat down. After a while, Bonilla strained to pull over a chair, then strained to prop his injured left leg onto the chair. He grimaced and sighed. Leyland didn't witness this scene, but later, at 3 o'clock in the morning, when he was scribbling possible lineups, he dropped Bonilla to sixth and moved up Daulton to fourth.

Win or lose, only one game remained in the season, and Leyland had no choice but to deal with his situation. Fernandez was injured. Hernandez had thrown one hundred forty-two pitches two days earlier. Brown, the Marlins' ace, had failed. He had to play Bonilla; the alternative was Alex Arias. And he had to pitch Leiter. There were no alternatives.

Leiter had prepared as best he could. Seeking inspiration, he had watched tapes of his no-hitter in 1996 and his four-hitter earlier in the season against the Yankees. On Thursday, he had spoken to his brother Mark and tried to talk through his problems. He planned on being more aggressive in Game Seven and throwing more curveballs. Of course, he had made those plans at other times during the season, and hadn't followed through on them.

"It's all out," Leiter said. "It's all or nothing. I always said I would substitute a bad season for a world championship team." The irony was that if Leiter's season didn't turn around in a hurry, there would be no world championship.

◆ ◆ ◆

Two hours before Game Seven, a man smoking a cheap cigar and wearing a baseball cap stood behind the home plate screen holding a banner that read, "Oh, What A Night!" Who knows what possesses people to do such things, but he stood there all through batting practice, holding up the sign. A few players walked past and gave him sideways glances.

Huizenga stood behind the batting cage and watched the Marlins take BP. Arliss, who just wouldn't go away, talked to anyone who would talk to him. Bruce Springsteen songs played over the stadium speakers. It was inspirational music from one New Jersey boy, Springsteen, for another Jersey boy, Leiter. One of the songs was *Streets of Philadelphia,* from the movie in which the main character dies of AIDS.

Billy the Marlin stuck his fin in everybody's business and did an interview for a TV station. Tommy Lasorda, the former manager known for his colorful language and stories, held court for a few reporters. They seemed enthralled. Then Lasorda went over and talked to Huizenga. He seemed enthralled. They hugged. Marti Huizenga came out wearing a teal dress.

In the clubhouse, Leyland delivered his final inspirational speech of the season to his team and told them, "Next time we're in this room, we'll be world champions."

Sheffield led his teammates in prayer and dedicated the game to Leyland. That morning, he had received a call from his publicist, who told him about this vision of hers, in which he said a prayer and the Marlins won the World Series.

Several Indians also prayed.

So Game Seven would come down to either who prayed more, the Indians or the Marlins, or whether God was a Marlins fan or an Indians fan.

◆ ◆ ◆

At 7:05, fifty minutes before game time, Livan Hernandez walked into Suite 251 at Pro Player Stadium and saw his mother for the first time in more than two years. Surrounded by bodyguards, but oblivious to them, he fell into her arms and cried. Miriam Carreras had been trying for the past two weeks to get permission to visit her son. Carreras finally received a six-month exit visa on Saturday, and Sunday afternoon, she boarded a flight from Havana to Miami. Livan visited with his mother for a half hour, and that's how this remarkable evening began.

Lasorda threw out the first ball. Mary Chapin Carpenter sang the national anthem. At 7:55, with the crowd on its feet and cheering, Leiter threw the first pitch to Omar Vizquel. It was a curveball, and a strike.

Leiter coasted through the first two innings, mixing his curveball and fastball like he hadn't in Game Three, but Jaret Wright, the winning pitcher for the Indians in Game Four, was having no trouble with the Marlins. In the third, Leiter lost his control for the only time all night. He walked Thome leading off, then Grissom singled to left. Wright came up and laid a poor bunt toward first base. Daulton had a play at third, but couldn't get the ball out of his glove and settled for the out at first. With two out, Tony Fernandez singled to center, driving home Thome and Grissom for a 2-0 Indians lead.

At other times this season, that might have spelled the start of Leiter's downfall, and after walking Manny Ramirez, Leiter was one pitch away from being blown out. But he struck out Justice to end the inning.

The Marlins couldn't accomplish anything against Wright. With runners on first and second in the third, Sheffield popped out meekly to third to end the inning. Bonilla flailed miserably in his first two at-bats, grounding weakly to second and striking out. Leiter worked his way out of a first and third, two out jam in the fifth, and received a standing ovation as he left the mound. In the sixth, Williams was on first with one out when Thome came up.

The Marlins were about to get their first emotional lift of the night. Thome grounded the ball directly at Daulton, who threw to Renteria for the force, then rushed back to first to complete the double play. Leiter ran off the field pumping his fist. In six innings, he had allowed only two runs on four hits, and kept the Marlins close, just like they had asked him to do.

◆ ◆ ◆

Leyland put the game in the hands of his bullpen. Dennis Cook pitched a perfect seventh, but the Marlins were nine outs away from losing when Bonilla led off the bottom of the inning. Bonilla had spoken to former Negro League great Joe Black several times during the Series, and before this at-bat, walked over to where Black was sitting behind the backstop screen.

"Stand closer to the plate," urged Black.

Bonilla, hitless in his last six at bats, gave it a try. Wright threw a mistake pitch down the middle of the plate, and Bonilla crushed it, ten rows deep into the rightfield seats, the same seats that had been such a difficult target for him all season. It was the Marlins' second hit of the night and made the score 2-1.

The tension had become unbearable. Wright left the game two batters later after walking Counsell with one out and was replaced by 36-year-old Paul Assenmacher. Abbott pinch-hit for Cook and flied out to right, and White struck out swinging. The Marlins were down to six outs.

Antonio Alfsonseca pitched a one-two-three eighth. Mike Jackson started the bottom of the inning for Cleveland. Renteria tripped and never left the batter's box on a grounder back to the mound. Sheffield struck out on a 1-2 pitch. With Daulton up next, Hargrove went to the bullpen again and brought in lefty Brian Anderson. Leyland went to his bench and sent up Conine, who flied out to left. The Marlins were down to three outs.

Nen worked out of a jam in the ninth, thanks to a smart play by Renteria, who threw home after fielding a grounder, rather than going for a double play, easily retiring Alomar. Hargrove called upon closer Jose Mesa to finish off the Marlins. Alou looped Mesa's first pitch to center for a single, the Marlins' first hit since the seventh inning, but Bonilla, after battling Mesa for seven pitches, struck out.

In the dugout, Daulton was thinking, *We're two outs away from losing.* Over at third base, Rich Donnelly was so tense he felt like he was going to get sick.

Both of them should have realized: They were playing the Indians, who hadn't won the World Series in forty-nine years.

Johnson singled sharply to right. Alou raced around second and easily made it to third. Zaun pinch-ran for Johnson. If the game went into extra innings, the Marlins would be relying on their backup catcher. *If* the game went into extra innings.

"I was thinking about a celebration, the trophy, friends, a lot of things," Vizquel said. "We were two outs away."

And there was Counsell, who three months earlier was playing in Triple-A, standing at the plate, and all he had to do was lift a fly deep enough into the outfield. "I told myself to take a little extra time between pitches," Counsell said. "I had to calm myself down."

Counsell looked at the first pitch, a ball. He fouled off the second pitch, evening the count. Counsell stepped out, then took a deep breath and stepped back into the batter's box. He drove Mesa's next pitch on a line deep to right. At first it looked like an extra base hit, maybe even a game-winner, but Ramirez raced to the front of the warning track, turned, and made the catch.

"I knew I had tied the game," Counsell said later. "I knew I had gotten the job done."

Alou raced home from third with the tying run, Nen, who had been waiting on deck, was the first to meet him, and the crowd let out a collective sigh, which turned into a roar, the loudest ever heard for a baseball game in Florida.

The game went into extra innings. Nen allowed a single, but struck out the side in the tenth. In the bottom of the inning, the Marlins had two on and one out, but Cangelosi pinch-hit and struck out on a 3-2 pitch. Charles Nagy ran in from the bullpen with the season on the line. Alou looked at Nagy's first pitch, then flied out to right, and as he left the batter's box, he spat and cursed himself.

Powell, who nearly seven months earlier had been the Marlins' final cut of training camp, started the eleventh. The Marlins' bullpen had allowed only two hits in four innings, and Powell picked up where Cook, Alfonseca, Heredia, and Nen had left off. Alomar couldn't bunt Williams over to second and Thome grounded into an inning-ending double play.

Nagy stayed in for the eleventh. Bonilla again conferred with Joe Black, then stroked an 0-2 pitch into center for a single. Bonilla hobbled down to first base, looking like he could barely run another step. Zaun tried to bunt, three times, and it was just as well that he failed, because Bonilla was virtually walking down to second on the first two attempts. On the third, Zaun popped out to Nagy, and Bonilla, who had so little left, dove back into first and avoided the double play.

That's when Tony Fernandez made the fatal mistake of the series. The count was two and one on Counsell. The clocks at both ends of the stadium showed 12:01. On the third pitch of the at-bat, Counsell hit a grounder to second, and Fernandez ranged to his left for the start of what might have been a double play.

Bonilla hesitated between first and second and momentarily screened Fernandez. The ball struck the tip of Fernandez's glove and rolled into the outfield. Bonilla looked over his shoulders, saw he had a chance to make it to third, and kept on running. He was limping badly, then he dove the most ungraceful dive imaginable, but he was safe.

Bonilla got up and brushed himself off. Donnelly asked, "Big Boy, you got ninety more feet in you?"

"I will make it, no matter what," Bonilla promised.

He never made it. Eisenreich was intentionally walked, loading the bases. White swung at the first pitch and grounded to second, where this time Fernandez easily fielded the ball and threw home, beating Bonilla by ten feet for the force out. Counsell moved to third.

Now there were two out and the bases remained loaded. Renteria, who had been the Marlins' last inning game winner all season, came up.

"We've been in this situation before," Donnelly thought.

Renteria looked at Nagy's first pitch, a called strike.

The next pitch was a curveball on the outside corner. Renteria swung and sent a soft liner up the middle. Nagy instinctively reached up with his glove, but the ball struck its tip and continued on. Fernandez lunged desperately to his right. Vizquel lunged desperately to his left.

"I was halfway home and hoping the ball got through," Counsell said later.

The ball got through.

◆ ◆ ◆

Counsell raced home—all he could think about was getting there as fast as he could—and when he got there, he leaped as high as his body had ever taken him, bicycling his legs through the air so that he could go higher, and he landed in Zaun's arms. His teammates rushed out of the dugout, toward the area between first and second base where Renteria was now jumping up and down with his arms raised, screaming and pumping his fists. They mobbed Renteria, overwhelmed him with their joy, and the noise coming from the 67,204, the happiness showing on the Marlins' faces, was as heartfelt as it could have been if this team hadn't been bought with a billionaire's money.

Leyland rushed to the screen behind home plate, spotted his wife and son, and pointed at them with both hands, and there wasn't a tear in his eye, just satisfaction. There were two piles of Marlins on the field, one with Renteria at the bottom, one with Counsell at the bottom, and then players started breaking away, going in every direction, and hugging each other. Leyland spotted Bonilla, tugged on his shoulder, then jumped into his arms, and Bonilla—who had so much wanted to win with this manager—lifted him high off the ground. Then Billy the Marlin, looking more than ever like a cartoon character wading through real life, handed a giant teal flag with the Marlins' logo to Devon White, who started a victory lap around the field, with Counsell at his side.

Leyland went on a victory lap of his own, smiling and laughing and pointing to the crowd the whole time, and when he got to the leftfield corner, White handed him the flag. Leyland's face was lit up with a thousand watts of pure ecstasy, and now the manager was the center of attention as he led the parade past the stands, with Billy the Marlin and Rich Donnelly following close behind. The adulation of the crowd swept over Leyland, whose smile somehow grew as he clutched hard onto the flag and wouldn't let it go. It was as if Leyland was by himself at this moment, the joy and glory was his, and that was fine with the crowd, which was dancing and screaming as the Jumbotron lit up with the words proclaiming the Marlins as World Champions.

Tears streamed down Donnelly's face as he followed the manager around the field, just as he had followed him for most of his professional life, just a few steps behind but there all the way, but he wasn't thinking about having won the World Series, he was thinking about his daughter, Amy, who died in 1993, and how much he would have loved for her to be here at this moment. Then Leyland, having completed his lap, stopped behind home plate and waved the flag like a victorious war general, and kept pointing to the crowd. And he was overcome by emotion, utterly caught up in the scene, but he still hadn't cried, he just kept on smiling and laughing.

Then Charles Johnson rushed over and hugged his manager and Livan Hernandez did a victory lap with Alex Fernandez and Dave Dombrowski kissed Leyland on the cheek. Bonilla was embracing everyone he could find—Tony Saunders, who right now was having no trouble looking his teammates in the eye, then Conine. Conine and Bonilla rushed at each other near the pitcher's mound, screaming something totally incomprehensible amid the deafening noise at Pro Player Stadium, and Bonilla grabbed Conine so hard that it looked like he might squeeze the life out of him. And they were both smiling and laughing like winners, and they kept on hugging and pounding each other on the back, squeezing, trying to express what was inexpressible.

Behind a barricade near second base, up on a stage that had been set up for the trophy presentations, Don Smiley and Wayne Huizenga and Dave Dombrowski shook hands and hugged, and shook hands again and hugged again. Who had they already hugged? Who hadn't they already hugged? It didn't matter, they just did it again, over and over, and there was Karie Ross, Dombrowski's pregnant wife, standing next to the stage, just looking up and taking in this crazy scene and not bothering to fight the tears.

Then Leyland got up on stage and the song *We Are The Champions* blared throughout the stadium and Leyland waved his arms to the crowd like a conductor, and it was surely the most joyous singalong anyone there had ever been a part of, and Leyland had his audience, and he sang, too.

And Sheffield hugged Leyland and Huizenga hugged Sheffield, and Huizenga mumbled something to the crowd about all the money he had spent, and Billy the Marlin danced in the background. "I thank Jim Leyland for keeping that fighting attitude in us," Sheffield said, and then one of the NBC guys told Leyland what Sheffield had said, and for the first time, Leyland, hearing such wonderful things said about himself, shed a tear. And Leyland, holding the World Series trophy for the first time in his life, talked about how all of this was a fantasy, and that's exactly what this scene looked like: A wild fantasy, with Billy the Marlin waving the flag in the background and video balloons dancing across the Jumbotron with the words World Series Champions and 67,042 fans screaming as loudly as they could and dancing, too.

The *Arli$$* guy, who would never go away, jumped up on the stage to join the celebration, as if he belonged, then Livan Hernandez came up, joined by his team-mates, and when it was announced that Hernandez was the World Series MVP, the crowd noise actually got louder, and Livan beat his chest like a warrior. The Elton John song *Livon* blared over the stadium sound system for what seemed like the millionth time this season and the real Livan screamed out, "I love you Miami," as he held up his arms in a victory salute. And Huizenga hugged Leyland, and Darren Daulton stood on stage with the first bottle of champagne. He opened it and took a deep swallow while Billy the Marlin danced near the stage and the *Arli$$* guy puffed on a cigar. Then the NBC guy interviewed Renteria, who had just won a game in the Marlins' final at-bat for the ninth time this season, and the crowd let out its loudest cheer of all, and the noise was so loud without the scoreboard operators even once asking for more.

There was this other scene, too, the best of all. It started at a field entrance, where Nicky Daulton was leading a group of players wives past a security guard. The guard didn't stand a chance, there was no way anybody was going to stop this emotion, and Nicky Daulton broke through and ran across the infield as tears streamed down her cheeks. She was looking for her husband, and this was like that final scene in *Rocky,* when Adrian was desperately fighting her way through the crowd, she was so desperate to get to her husband, Rocky Balboa, who had just gone fifteen rounds with the champion. But in this movie, the star was a baseball player, whose career was supposed to be over a year ago, and now, somehow, found himself in this glorious position, at this glorious time, with this happy ending, because this was going to be it, right here: the end of his career. And his wife, who had traveled with him for road games, and walked hand-in-hand with him wherever they went, and on some nights sat in the seats behind home plate with her hands covering her eyes, because she could barely stand to watch, pushed her way between the metal barriers and fell into his arms.

"I love you, I love you," she told him.

"I love you," he told her, and they kissed and they hugged, and she cried. And Billy the Marlin danced and the *Arli$$* guy smoked and Huizenga told South Florida that "this one's for you," when what he really wanted most was for South Florida to say, "Wayne, this stadium's for you." And *We Are The Champions,* which had played at every victory celebration for every champion in every North American city for the past twenty years, blared over the sound system and it was trite and it was meaningless but everyone sang anyway.

And Bobby Bonilla danced and smiled and hugged, because after twelve years, he really did deserve this, and Gary Sheffield thought about the ring he would show off to his friends back home, and Gregg "Fucking" Zaun found himself patting the back of every teammate he could find, and Moises Alou climbed over the bullpen fence and embraced the fans. And Al Leiter thought about the irony of being here after going through what he had gone through all season, and decided that he was a lucky man, because here he was, celebrating his second World Series in five years. So maybe it was true that good things happen to good people. And even Kevin Brown smiled and Jim Leyland kissed his wife, and maybe it was true that good things happen to just about everybody.

And Rich Donnelly's cheeks were red and soaked with tears, and Conine lifted Larry Starr, the trainer, high off the ground, and Darren and Nicky Daulton held on to each other, and they kissed again, and they hugged again, and how could it be that something like baseball can produce such joy?

Epilogue

Well, that didn't last long, did it?

There was a celebration in the clubhouse, with cigars and champagne, wives and the *Arli$$* guy, that ended at 4 o'clock in the morning. On Tuesday, the Marlins held two victory parades—one in Miami and one on the water in Fort Lauderdale —and a victory party at Pro Player Stadium. Nearly seventy thousand people showed up. Gloria Estefan sang. Livan Hernandez, Antonio Alfonseca, and Edgar Renteria danced with showgirls. Jim Leyland smoked.

Right about then, "one heartbeat" slowed down.

A reporter from *Sports Illustrated* requested a phone interview with Gary Sheffield, but Sheffield refused, saying he'd return the reporter's phone call only if they put him on the cover. Sheffield did end up on the cover . . . in the lower right corner, hoisting Edgar Renteria after Game Seven. Moises Alou complained about not being MVP of the World Series.

On October 31, five days after the World Series ended, the Marlins refused the options on the contracts of Jeff Conine and Darren Daulton. Neither move was unexpected.

On November 6, eleven days after the World Series ended, Wayne Huizenga stood behind a podium at Pro Player Stadium and reiterated his decision to sell the Marlins.

He also said, "We do not want to sell the Marlins, but we feel we must in order to improve the chances of a new stadium being built. And unless a new stadium is built, where luxury suite and all other revenue go directly to the team, I do not believe the Marlins will ever be in a World Series again."

The effect was like dumping a huge pail of cold water over South Florida.

So much for celebrations. They ended right there.

A group headed by Don Smiley would buy the team, with Huizenga possibly staying on as a minority owner. The team would have to operate at either break-even or a profit. The Marlins' $49 million payroll would be cut to $25 million or less. The championship team would be dismantled one season after it was formed.

"It's sad," Dombrowski said, almost tearfully. "Unfortunately, it's the reality of the game."

The salary-cutting began immediately. What Dombrowski built he would have to tear apart.

The first to go was Moises Alou, who got traded to the Houston Astros in exchange for three minor leaguers. Alou did not leave quietly. Quoted in a *Miami*

Herald column the next day, Alou whined, "Everybody got used. I feel dirty. I'm angry. Really angry. What bothers me most is that, after everything I did for the club, it means nothing to the organization."

Hmmm. He must have forgotten the $5 million the Marlins paid him for his year's work.

On November 18, Tony Saunders was lost to the Tampa Bay Devil Rays in the expansion draft. Considering that the Marlins planned on trading Kevin Brown and Al Leiter, and Alex Fernandez would miss the entire season, their starting rotation now consisted of Livan Hernandez.

The same day, Devon White was traded to the expansion Arizona Diamondbacks for a minor league pitcher. Robb Nen was dealt to the San Francisco Giants for minor leaguers. So White wouldn't be talking to reporters in a new city and Nen would have a new group of teenagers to tell, "Education? I'm all for it."

On November 20, the Marlins traded Conine to the Kansas City Royals for a minor league pitcher. Conine left gracefully and wrote a public thank-you note to the fans.

Brown went next, to the Padres, for more prospects. He, too, was angry and hurt. Dennis Cook was traded to the Mets for two more prospects. Kurt Abbott was traded for another prospect.

Leiter, Sheffield, Bonilla, Eisenreich, and Cangelosi . . . any player with a large contract was deemed expendable.

By the end of the year, Smiley's group was in danger of falling apart. South Florida's excitement over the Marlins had withered. So had support for building a new stadium.

"Please, don't bury our ballclub just yet," Leyland pleaded to the media. But how could anybody else bury the Marlins when the Marlins were holding the shovel?

As for Leyland, he announced on November 8 that he would remain with the Marlins for at least one more season. The news was surprising, considering a few days earlier he had told front office people he was leaving. At a press conference, Leyland labeled the upcoming season as a critical time for baseball in South Florida and spoke of loyalty to Don Smiley.

But his reasons for staying weren't quite so unselfish. The Marlins had offered to move $500,000 from the final year of his contract to his 1998 salary. Privately, Leyland had spoken of wanting to manage the National League in the All-Star Game, which would be one of his rewards for winning the World Series. And, of course, there was his limited choice of managerial options for the 1998 season.

"I definitely was either going to manage the Florida Marlins in 1998 or my son's Little League team in Mount Lebanon," he said.

Those 6-year-olds never had a chance.

Acknowledgments

About a year ago, the Marlins had finished buying their players for the 1997 season when I suggested the idea for this book to my publisher, Lonnie Herman. His response: "Are you ready to write another book?" Well, Lonnie, that wasn't the point. Somebody else was supposed to write it. But, basically, what he was offering me was the opportunity to spend a year covering a Major League Baseball team that had a decent shot of winning the World Series. How could I resist?

So, thanks, Lonnie, for the suggestion, and thanks, also, for your support, constructive criticism, encouragement, and friendship.

You should know that the author of this book makes his living writing about hockey and had never been around a major league clubhouse. The Marlins had a choice: They could have either granted me press credentials for the 1997 season or refused my request. If they refused, I had no recourse, because I am a freelance writer with no newspaper affiliation.

Well, they granted my request, and they're going to have to live with that for a while.

Grateful thanks to Don Smiley, who made the final decision; Jim Ross, who showed me his David Letterman tape; and Ron Colangelo, who has that baseball information department running like a finely tuned machine. It's a great staff: Julio Sarmiento; Kristin Vandeventer, the super intern; Sandra Van Meek; Margo Malone; and Anamaria Manzano.

Poor Sandra and Margo. You should have seen their faces when a couple of Major League Baseball boot-lickers threw me out of the press box in Cleveland. They were horrified.

Warm thanks to the entire Marlins organization, from top to bottom, in the clubhouse and in the front office. Dave Dombrowski, Alan Brown, Mark Geddis, the players, the coaches. Jim Leyland. You, too. Really.

No doubt, the best part of this project was getting to know the members of the media. Boy, was I lucky! How often does a character like Gregg Doyel come along?

Mid-season book joke: "I'm changing the name of the book to *The Gregg Doyel Story.*"

OK, it's time for some author disclosure. One night I asked the other reporters, "Why doesn't astroturf melt?"

Dan Graziano looked at me and said, in his best Jim Leyland voice, "What is *wrong* with you?"

307

And Cheryl Rosenberg supplied the answer: "Because it's heat resistant."

Of course. It's heat resistant.

Thanks to Gregg, Dan, Cheryl, plus the other beat reporters: Dave O'Brien, Jeff Miller, and Mike Phillips. All part of it. They called me "Book Boy." I liked being "Book Boy."

O'Brien—or O. B., or Obie—also called me "Author," as well as other unmentionables.

Actual conversation:

O'BRIEN: Hey, Jim, have you ever had a book written about one of your teams?

LEYLAND: Yeah, a few.

O'BRIEN: What'd you think about them?

LEYLAND: They're horseshit.

ME: Jim, I guarantee you I will beat horseshit.

So I'll let him be the judge.

Javy Mota of *El Nuevo Herald* picked out great restaurants in Atlanta and San Francisco, supplied party passes in Cleveland, and let me watch his first-year Marlins tapes. Javy, Carl Barger is looking down on you, too.

Jody Jackson, formerly of WQAM: one of the great press box partners. She's now on the verge of fame, and marriage, in Buffalo, New York. Jody, I appreciate you allowing me to watch an inning here and there.

Damian Cristodero edited the final manuscript with care, which is more than any author can hope for.

On the home front—Jacqui, Adam and Elizabeth, Mom and Dad, thanks for your love and support. I know I'm not easy when I'm writing a book. I kind of start resembling . . . a baseball manager?

Dave Rosenbaum
Parkland, Florida
January, 1998

Index